高顿ACCA
助你学习更简单

- 中英双语
- 温馨注解
- 讲解视频
- 三阶段学习
- 机考体验指南
- 在线答疑

Business and Technology
（商业与科技）

下载"高顿网校"APP
微信扫码—点击"点击领取"
在APP"学习/ACCA"频道观看书中全部讲解视频

为中国考生量身定制的
ACCA双语版辅导教材

ACCA PAPER AB

Accountant in Business

会计师与企业课本

■ 高顿财经研究院 编著

图书在版编目(CIP)数据

会计师与企业课本 = ACCA Paper AB Accountant in Business：汉、英 / 高顿财经研究院编著. —上海：立信会计出版社，2020.3(2022.1重印)
 ISBN 978-7-5429-6377-2

Ⅰ. ①会… Ⅱ. ①高… Ⅲ. ①企业管理—会计师—资格考试—教材—汉、英 Ⅳ. ①F23

中国版本图书馆 CIP 数据核字(2020)第 047196 号

策划编辑　　方士华
责任编辑　　方士华

ACCA Paper AB Accountant in Business

出版发行	立信会计出版社			
地　　址	上海市中山西路 2230 号	邮政编码	200235	
电　　话	(021)64411389	传　真	(021)64411325	
网　　址	www.lixinph.com	电子邮箱	lixinaph2019@126.com	
网上书店	http://lixin.jd.com		http://lxkjcbs.tmall.com	
经　　销	各地新华书店			
印　　刷	上海龙腾印务有限公司			
开　　本	889 毫米×1194 毫米	1/16		
印　　张	21.25	插　页	1	
字　　数	653 千字			
版　　次	2020 年 3 月第 1 版			
印　　次	2022 年 1 月第 2 次			
书　　号	ISBN 978-7-5429-6377-2/F			
定　　价	120.00 元			

如有印订差错，请与本社联系调换

致 ACCAers 的一封信

亲爱的 ACCAers：

欢迎开启 ACCA 入门科目 Business and Technology（BT）的学习之旅。

非常荣幸，能将这本凝聚了几十位老师心血的教材呈现在你们的面前。它不仅是一把开启商业之门的钥匙，为你们揭开商业世界的面纱，带你们领略商业世界的独特魅力，也是一份欢迎同学们加入财经行业的礼物，为你们日后学习高阶课程并成为一名优秀的商业精英打下坚实的基础。

在开始之前，请记住这个简单的"123"口诀。
1 For one topic：这门课的主题只有 1 个，即商业。
2 For two components：商业世界是由组织和组织中的人构成的。在学习的过程中，同学们会逐渐体会到这两者是如何密切联系、相辅相成，从而形成一个有机整体的。
3 For three targets：除了上面说到的组织和组织中的人，BT 的研究对象还有一个——环境。通过学习，同学们会掌握纵横商界、管理企业所必备的分析能力，懂得何时顺势而为、何时逆流而上。

本教材分为三大部分：
第一部分为环境篇，通过模型的介绍、案例的解析，帮助同学们认识组织所处的环境，以及常用的分析环境的方法；
第二部分为组织篇，通过层层剖析，引导同学们了解组织架构的方方面面；
第三部分为人员篇，侧重于人力资源管理，助力同学们快速领略身在组织中与人交往的精髓。
希望同学们能"解锁"各个主题，获取必备的专业技能。

值得开始的事情就值得完成。愿同学们一路披荆斩棘，为自己的选择坚持到最后。我们会在"A 考"路上陪伴你们，并为你们倾注自己的热情。真诚地祝福你们！

高顿财经研究院

教材使用指南

科学划分三学习阶段 | 贴合学习与备考路径

知识预习阶段

知识导入
了解章节内容
确定学习方向

单词表
积累重点词汇
学中遇见不陌生

学习指南
明确学习目标
助力高效学习
- Pass level：必学内容
- Distinction level：选学内容

本章考点
提炼核心考点
学中遇见更重视

考点难度划分3级
- 1级：简单，熟记
- 2级：中等，理解
- 3级：较难，运用

★ 温馨建议：按照顺序进行预习，效果更佳。

知识精讲阶段

标签与批注
中文注解
通俗易懂

经典例题
学以致用
吸收运用知识

讲解视频
深入理解
重难点和题目

◆ 微信扫码获取视频

章节总结
归纳梳理
强化知识

章节测评
及时检验
学习成果

- 标签"博学多才"：背景知识延伸
- 标签"精益求精"：理论概念补充
- 批注"基本概念"：概念知识解说
- 批注"核心考点"：考点知识解析
- 批注"专有名词"：专业术语解释
- 批注"知识点解读"：重点难点解读

- Summary：梳理知识框架
- 问法总结：提升应试技巧

★ 温馨建议：可搭配高顿网课，学习效果更佳。

备考复习阶段

机考体验指南
体验Specimen Exam
查漏补缺

线上答疑
三次免费答疑机会
解决疑难

◆ 微信扫码获取指南

◆ 微信扫码提问

★ 温馨建议：优先依循章节顺序学习，训练，再进行样卷（Specimen Exam）测验，最后使用答疑机会。搭配使用高顿ACCA练习册（Golden Pass Kit），备考效果更佳。

考试介绍

考试形式： 机考（当场出成绩）
考试时间： 120 分钟
考试题型： 选择题

Section A（共 76 分）

包含两类题目：
1 分值选择题（难度低），多为判断题（True or False）或二选一。 16 道。
2 分值选择题（难度中等），多为四选一或者五选二。 30 道。

Section B（共 24 分）

4 分值多任务处理题（难度高），实质为选择题，但作答方式可能为连线、匹配、拖拽等形式，偶尔可能会出现填空题（多为填某个关键单词或者计算具体数值）。 6 道。

满分： 100
通过分数： 50

备注： 自 2020 年 9 月，Accountant in Business（AB）科目更名为 Business and Technology（BT，商业与科技）。

温馨小提示

  2020 年 9 月，Accountant in Business（AB）科目名称变更名为 Business and Technology(BT)。 本书围绕科目名称的变化，紧扣大纲，与时俱进地做了内容的修订与更新，还特地为 ACCAers 准备了一个"实时"二维码。 若内容有所优化，将在此发布。 同学们可扫描下方二维码及时获取相关信息。 我们会一直精益求精，不断进步。

  若想对本书提出意见和建议，请发送邮件至下方邮箱；高顿学员也可直接在答疑平台反馈。

  感谢大家对我们的信赖与支持，祝考试顺利！

请联系我们，邮箱：coursenoteacca@gaodun.com

微信扫码
在线查看实时勘误

Contents

Part A Environment ... 1

Chapter 1 Organisations and their stakeholders ... 2
1 The nature of organisation ... 3
2 Stakeholders ... 9
Quick quiz ... 15

Chapter 2 Business environment ... 19
1 PEST/PESTEL analysis ... 20
2 Porter's five forces ... 29
3 Value chain analysis ... 32
4 SWOT analysis ... 33
Quick quiz ... 38

Chapter 3 The micro-economic environment ... 42
1 Defining microeconomics ... 43
2 Basic concepts of microeconomics ... 43
3 Demand and supply ... 44
4 The price mechanism and the equilibrium price ... 50
5 Maximum and minimum price ... 50
6 The economic behaviour of costs ... 52
7 Types of markets ... 53
Quick quiz ... 57

Chapter 4 The macro-economic environment ... 60
1 Definition ... 61
2 Objectives of government macroeconomic policies ... 61
3 Inflation and its consequences ... 62
4 Unemployment ... 63
5 The balance of payment ... 64
6 Economic growth ... 65
7 The circular flow of income and expenditure ... 67
8 Fiscal policy ... 69

9 Monetary policy 70

Quick quiz 73

Part B Organisation 77

Chapter 5 Business structure 78

1 The informal organisation 79

2 Organisation structure 80

3 Centralisation and decentralisation 88

4 Basic organisational structure concepts 89

Quick quiz 93

Chapter 6 Organisational departments and functions 95

1 Organisational departments and functions 96

2 Shared services approach 102

3 Committees 102

4 Levels in the organisation 104

Quick quiz 109

Chapter 7 The role of accounting 111

1 What is accounting? 112

2 The users of accounting information 112

3 Nature, principles and scope of accounting 113

4 Regulatory system 117

5 Manual and computerised accounting systems 119

6 Fintech 120

Quick quiz 125

Chapter 8 Organisational culture 127

1 Culture 128

2 Writers on culture 129

Quick quiz 135

Chapter 9 Corporate governance 137

1 Introduction of corporate governance 138

2 Best practice in corporate governance 146

Quick quiz 153

Chapter 10 Internal control 156

1 Internal check 157

    2 Internal control 158

    3 Internal audit 166

    Quick quiz 172

Chapter 11 Identifying and preventing fraud 175

    1 Definition 176

    2 Types of fraud 176

    3 Implications of fraud for the organisation 178

    4 Three prerequisites for fraud 180

    5 Assessing the risk of fraud 180

    6 Systems for detecting and preventing fraud 181

    7 Responsibility for detecting and preventing fraud 182

    8 Money laundering 184

    Quick quiz 188

Part C Human resource 191

Chapter 12 Individuals, groups and teams 192

    1 Individuals 193

    2 Groups 195

    3 Teams 196

    Quick quiz 205

Chapter 13 Recruitment and selection 207

    1 Introduction to recruitment and selection 208

    2 Recruitment process 210

    3 Selection 212

    4 Evaluating recruitment and selection 217

    5 Responsibility for recruitment and selection 217

    6 Equal opportunity 219

    7 Diversity 221

    Quick quiz 224

Chapter 14 Leading and managing people 227

    1 Related concepts of management 228

    2 Management 231

    3 What is leadership 236

    4 Schools of leadership theory 236

    Quick quiz 245

Chapter 15 Performance appraisal ... 248
1 Performance appraisal ... 249
2 The process of formal performance appraisal ... 250
3 Benefits and barriers of performance appraisal ... 254
Quick quiz ... 258

Chapter 16 Training and development ... 261
1 Learning ... 262
2 Training and development ... 266
3 Training methods ... 271
Quick quiz ... 275

Chapter 17 Motivating individuals and group ... 278
1 Overview of motivation ... 279
2 Theories of motivation ... 280
3 Reward system ... 285
Quick quiz ... 289

Chapter 18 Personal effectiveness and communication ... 291
1 Time management ... 292
2 Ineffectiveness at work ... 294
3 Competence frameworks ... 295
4 Conflicts ... 296
5 Communication in the workplace ... 298
Quick quiz ... 307

Chapter 19 Ethics ... 309
1 Framework of rules ... 310
2 Ethics ... 310
Quick quiz ... 320

Part A
Environment

环境篇

如果我们把周围的商业世界比喻为商海，那么构成商业世界的一个个组织，就类似于商海中航行的一艘艘轮船，组织需要实现其目标，轮船也需要安稳航行到目的地。

而你作为未来的商业领袖，则需要肩负起轮船的掌舵人——船长的职责。在你领导巨轮航行的过程中，首先不能忽略的是外部环境，需要时刻提防外部环境中的"冰山"。

在 Part A 中，总共包含了四章内容，第 1 章介绍了构成商业世界的最小单位——组织，接下来通过 3 章内容的学习，我们将系统地教你如何对组织所处的环境进行分析。知己知彼，方能百战不殆。

欢迎来到 Part A 的学习！

Chapter 1
Organisations and their stakeholders

知识导入

本章主要介绍构成商业世界的最小单位——组织。本章包含了组织的定义、特点、分类以及组织利益相关者等概念,同时引入 Mendelow matrix 这一重要模型,用于分析并处理各个利益相关者之间的关系。这一章为后续章节的学习起到了奠基的重要作用。

单词表

英文	中文
Collective goals	共同目标
Individual limitations	个人局限
Synergy	协同效应
Ownership	所有权
Not-for-profit organisation	非营利组织
Sources of finance	融资来源
Economies of scale	规模效应
Scarce resources	稀缺资源
Private sector	私营部门
Sole trader	个体户
Partnership	合伙制
Non-governmental organisations	非政府组织
Limited companies	有限责任公司
Trade unions	工会
Stakeholders	利益相关者
Pressure groups	施压团体
Secondary stakeholders	次要利益相关者
Accountability	问责制
Value for money	物超所值

学习指南

Learning objectives	Pass level	Distinction level	用时建议
1. Definition of organisation(1.1)	√		5 min
2. Benefits of organisation(1.2)	√		10 min
3. Types of organisation(1.4—1.6)	√		20 min
4. Definition of stakeholders(2)	√		5 min
5. Types of stakeholders(2.1—2.3)	√		15 min
6. Stakeholder conflicts(2.4)		√	10 min
7. Mendelow matrix(2.5)	√		15 min

本章考点

重要考点	难度（1~3）
熟记 organisation 的定义、分类及优缺点	1
熟记 stakeholder 的定义和分类，理解 stakeholder conflict 的各个层面	1~2
理解并运用 Mendelow matrix	3

1 The nature of organisation

1.1 Definition

An organisation is a social arrangement for achieving controlled performance towards collective goals that creates value and which has a boundary separating it from its environment.

The four key words：
- Collective goals
- Social arrangement
- Controlled performance
- Boundary

> **基本概念**
> 在组织的基本概念当中，这4个关键词对于正确理解组织概念非常重要；这4个关键词，有时会以填空题的形式出现，需要同学们熟记。

1.2 Benefits of organisation

众所周知，当今商业世界运作的基本模式是组织而并非个人。 我们有理由相信，商业的发展是一个择优汰劣的过程，那么运作模式的选择也就意味着：组织运作有远优于个人运作的一面，如节省时间（time saving）；克服个人局限性（breakthrough individual limitations）；术业有专攻（specialisation）；促进知识累积与共享（knowledge accumulation and sharing）。 而这些作用，我们可以用一个专有名词来概括——协同作用（synergy）。

（A）Time saving

It is the most direct consequence of forming organisations, which can be achieved through cooperation and brainstorming among individuals.

（B）Breakthrough of individual limitations

It should be admitted that individual's capacity has limitations, no matter in energy or intelligence. The form of organisations can overcome such limitation through pooling different individuals.

（C）Specialisation

With the maturity of organisations, division of labour occurs, which facilitates allocating people to those occupations they are best at. This process can be called as specialisation, which can improve working efficiency and quality to a large extent.

（D）Knowledge accumulation and sharing

It is known that two heads are always better than one. Through knowledge accumulation and sharing, individuals in organisations can learn and adopt the

> **专有名词**
> **Synergy**
> 在一个组织中，大家互相分工与配合，得到的总产出，比每一个人单独完成的工作产出的总和更多。

most suitable methods of working for themselves.

In conclusion, the benefits above can be summarised as one word, **synergy**, which indicates the total output of people working together will exceed the total output of people working separately. Simply speaking, it means 1+1>2.

1.3 Classification of organisations

可以从不同角度对组织进行划分。例如，从主营业务这个角度来看，组织可以分为从事传统生产的制造企业、从事创新研究的高新技术企业；再如，根据组织规模大小，组织可以分为小微企业、大型企业等。在本书中，我们将着重从三个角度进行分析：是否以营利为导向（Profit or non-profit orientation）、所有权（Ownership）以及法律地位（Legal status）。

1.3.1 Profit or non-profit orientation

According to main objectives of organisations, they can be classified into profit orientation and non-profit ones. Profit organisations' main objective is to maximise shareholders' wealth, however, non-profit ones are not (see 1.4).

1.3.2 Ownership

The key characteristic to distinguish different ownership of organisations is whether the organisation is owned by government or not. If the organisation is owned by the government, it is a public sector, otherwise it is a private sector (see 1.5).

1.3.3 Legal status

According to the legal status, organisations can be sole traders, partnership and limited companies. Additionally, in the scope of limited companies, there is another classification due to sources of finance, which is also important (see 1.6).

1.4 Classifying organisations by profit orientation

1.4.1 Profit seeking organisations（Commercial）

Some organisations define their main objectives as maximising the wealth of their owners. Such organisations are often referred to as "profit seeking" organisations.

1.4.2 Not-for-profit organisations

Other organisations do not regard profitability as their main objective and they are called not-for-profit organisations（"NFPs or NPOs"）. Instead, their objectives are usually referred to as **value for money**.

大部分的非营利性组织追求的目标，往往与文化传播、社会福祉提供或者环境保护等有关，它们建立的目的是服务特定需要服务的人群与对象。

NFPs include：
- Museums/galleries
- Public schools
- Medical care

- Charities
- Environmental groups

非营利性组织的目标往往取决于成立时的核心原则，且每个 NFP 的目标差异会很大：医院是为了救治病人、战胜疾病；教育机构为了促进教育资源的交换、支持研究等；不同的慈善机构有着不同的努力方向，可能是跟农业、文化延续、扶持弱势群体与家庭有关；政府相关部门则是为了全民财富的提升，创造一个更好的社会。

以利润为导向可以将组织区分为营利性组织和非营利性组织，此处的利润导向侧重点在于组织的主要目标是营利还是非营利。比如，公立学校，虽然公立学校也会收取学费等费用，但其存在的主要目的是教书育人，而并非以此牟利，因此公立学校就是一种典型的非营利性组织。

根据组织控制权是否归政府所有，组织可以划分为公有组织和私有组织。值得注意的是，1.4 的"利润导向"与 1.5 的"归属导向"是区分组织的两个不同角度，**没有任何包含或者互斥关系**，需要特别留意：并非所有私有组织都是营利性组织。此处的"私有"仅意味着控制权不归政府所有，这个词与营利与否无关。所以，私有组织可以是营利性组织，也可以是社会团体或者慈善机构等非营利组织。

1.5 Classifying organisations by ownership

1.5.1 Public sector

The public sector is concerned with providing basic government services and is thus **owned by government**.

(A) Examples of public sector

(a) Police/Military.

(b) Public transport.

(c) Primary education.

(B) Key characteristics of public sector

(a) Accountability

In the UK, the public sector, especially those authorities, are accountable to their citizens, are answerable for their actions to the parliament.

(b) Funds

The main sources of public sector's funds come from taxes with the rest sometimes from public borrowing.

(c) Demand of service

Public sector organisations are established to provide public goods and services and there are infinite demand for that.

(d) Resource constraint

The scarcity of resources owned by the government leads to a situation that a significant scale of the public demand for goods and services cannot be fulfilled.

公有组织这种形式既有优势也有劣势：

公有组织是提供基本政府服务的组织，为全社会服务，所以强调"公平优先"（**fairness**），能在一定程度上弥补贫富差距造成的鸿沟（可以对比公立医院与私立

核心考点

该考点（1.5）常以判断组织类型的形式出现，混淆点在于考生会将私有组织默认为营利性组织，因此考生应当注意区分标准。

专有名词

Accountability

Accountability 中文译作问责制，英文解释为"be answerable to/for"，指的是负有回答问题的责任，public sector 提供的产品和服务会受到整个公众的监督和监管。在英国，议会代表公众，所以英国的 public sector 对议会承担问责制。

6 ◀ Business and Technology

医院）；同时提供大规模公众服务，公有组织更能实现规模经济（**economy of scale**）；由于是国家信用做担保，相对比其他的组织形式，公有组织的融资成本是最低的（**cheaper finance**）。

但同时，公有组织相对于私有组织，需要承担公众的问责（**accountability**），但是公众往往很难向其问责（如全民医疗的低效率）；大部分公有组织投入的成本都相对较高（**high cost**）(如国防、铁路、大坝等的修建）且容易受到政府政策以及政局动荡的干扰（**interference**）。

专有名词

Economy of scale
规模经济（economy of scale），是指在一定科技水平下，生产规模的扩大，使得长期平均成本呈下降的趋势。

1.5.2 Private sector

Private sectors are **not** owned by government. In paper AB, we focus on two special forms of private sectors, which are called non-government organisations and co-operatives.

(A) Non-governmental organisations

A non-governmental organisation (NGO) is an organisation with social or political aim that is **not owned by any governments** ("NGO", n.d.).

There are some common characteristics of NGO. For example, these organisations are **not commercial** and their funds are mainly raised from social groups, individuals, companies, government grants, etc.

(B) Co-operatives

A cooperative refers to the creation of a non-profit organisation for the benefit of those individuals using its services.

A co-operative is a specific type of mutual organisation, owned by its **members**. They are usually governed on the basis of "one member, one vote", in another word, they are democratically controlled by their members.

Co-operatives are organised to provide and **distribute the surplus profits in proportion to purchases to their members to meet their needs, not to generate a return on investment**.

知识点解读

Co-operatives 成立的初衷即是为了满足其成员（member）的利益，所以这种特殊的组织运营模式，并没有外部投资者（investor）的存在，也没有赚取利益（profit）的目标，仅仅是为服务其成员。

博学多才

追根溯源来看，世界上公认的第一个最成功的合作社，是 1844 年在英国的罗奇代尔镇由 28 个失业纺织工人自发成立的。为了能够继续有工作养家糊口，当时这28 名失业工人每人出资 1 英镑作为 1 股，合计 28 英镑作为驱动资金，建立了"公正先驱者消费合作社"，后来规模逐渐发展壮大，社员增加到近 3 万人，股金增加到 40万英镑。它所建立的罗奇代尔原则后来成为指导国际合作社发展的基本原则。现如今，全球的合作社均遵循以下 7 个基本运营原则。

Cooperatives work under the following 7 principles (What is a cooperative, 2018)：

(a) Anyone can become a member.

(b) Each member has 1 vote.

(c) They divide profits among their members, based on how active each member is within the cooperative.

(d) They are run by and for their members.
(e) They give education and training to members, their representatives, managers and employees.
(f) They maintain local, state, national and international networks for members.
(g) They help to uphold the sustainable development of their communities.

小试牛刀

Example question 1

Which of the following organisation would focus more on performance and profit indicators than on **value for money** indicators?

A. Local public sectors B. A private school
C. A public accountant college D. Environment protection organisations

> 本题为考查组织分类中营利与非营利分类方式中的典型例题。

Example question 2

Which of the following is the feature of a co-operative business?

A. Distribution of surplus in proportion to purchases
B. Staffing by volunteers as well as full time employees
C. Finance from grants or contracts

Example question 3

For cooperatives, which of the following statements are its features?

(1) Its main objective is to maximise profit.
(2) It is owned and controlled by outside investors.

A. Both(1) and (2) B. (2) only
C. (1) only D. Neither (1) nor (2)

1.6 Classifying organisations by legal status

1.6.1 Sole trader

A sole trader, also known as a sole proprietorship, is the simplest business arrangement, in which **one individual runs and owns** the entire business.

1.6.2 Partnership

A partnership is the relationship existing between two or more persons who join to carry on a trade or business. Each person contributes money, property, labour or skill, and expects to **share in the profits and losses of the business**.

1.6.3 Limited liability companies

In a limited liability company, **shareholders' liability is limited to the capital they originally invested**. If such a company becomes insolvent, the shareholders' personal assets remain protected.

有限责任公司，其最大的特征就是具备独立法人地位。所谓"有限责任"，意味着股东的风险仅限于其投资额，对公司的债务不承担无限连带责任（unlimited liability）。与之相对比，sole trader 和 partnership 都是承担无限连带责任的组织类型。

> **专有名词**
>
> **Sole trader**
> 个体户并不是指该组织仅由一人构成，它指的是该组织的所有权和管理权都归属于同一个人，但是完全可以雇佣多名员工为其工作。

博学多才

1599 年秋天，伦敦市场上的胡椒价格突然从每磅 3 先令上涨到每磅 8 先令，这场价格暴涨的幕后推手是垄断香料贸易的葡萄牙和荷兰。伦敦市政厅 80 多名愤怒的英国商人聚集于此商讨应对之策。自从欧洲人发现了到达东方的新航道，浩瀚的大洋就成为追逐财富的赌场，但面对一个空前庞大的蛋糕，精明的英国商人却因为巨大的风险而有些踟蹰不前。原因是，当时筹资组建一支船队到东印度群岛、印度尼西亚香料群岛、印度、美国等地，相当于在今天准备筹措一次到火星或月球的航程。这是一件风险非常大的事。那些船只可能因风暴失事，可能会遭遇海盗。他们会和葡萄牙人作战，荷兰人会和英国人作战，英国人也和荷兰人作战，而且还会受到东南亚商人的袭击。即便没有发生任何意外，商船来回一次至少也要 1 年多的时间，这对商人而言实在是太冒险了。作为新加入远洋贸易的竞争者，英国商人找到了一种汇集资源和资本的新方式。怎么样可以让老百姓、有钱的个人或者家族，愿意把辛辛苦苦挣来的钱拿出来去冒风险，交给别人来运作和管理。所以，16 世纪末 17 世纪初的英国和荷兰就推出了股份有限责任公司。

入股集资的方法古已有之，但有限责任的提出却是开天辟地头一回。自古以来，欠债还钱都是天经地义，而有限责任则创造了一种新的规则，那就是，在某些情况下欠债可以不用还。对投资者而言，有限责任无疑是一种极为有力的保护。这意味着，对个人的信任可以稍微变得不那么重要，因为你不会失去所有的财产。假如你向公司投资了 10 英镑，那么最多也就损失了这 10 英镑。大大降低了投资风险的股份有限公司，使陌生人之间的合作成为可能。

（A）Types of limited companies

（a）**Private limited companies**（e.g. X Ltd）

private limited company 是指股份不能向普通公众出售和交易的有限责任公司，股东承担有限责任。

（b）**Public limited companies**（e.g. X Plc）

public limited company 是指股份面向公众发行和交易的有限责任公司，需要最低 50,000 英镑的股本。

（B）Differences of limited companies

（a）**Number of shareholders**

Numbers of shareholders in public companies are more than private companies due to the restriction on members for private companies.

（b）**Transferability of shares**

Shares of public companies are easily bought, sold or exchanged through the stock exchange market. On the contrary, shares in private companies cannot be transferred without the approval of the major shareholders.

（c）**Control and ownership**

Directors in private limited companies normally own large numbers of shares, while the directors in public companies hold small amount of or even no shares.

在 private limited companies 中，高管往往就是就是持有最多股份的股东，而在 public limited companies 中则不一定，有的时候高管只持有很少一部分股权，甚至没有股权。

(d) Access of finance

A public company can invite the general public to subscribe for shares of the company. As opposed, a private company has no right to invite the public for subscription.

(C) Appraisal of limited companies

Advantages:

(a) Due to the separation of ownership and control, limited companies could enjoy higher level of professional service.

(b) Reduced risk for investors due to the separation of legal personality.

Disadvantages:

(a) Legal compliance costs are increased. Most limited companies' **financial statements should be complied and be audited** before publishing to shareholders. At the same time, most countries have stricter requirement for limited companies, such as corporate governance (see chapter 9).

(b) Agency problem might occur due to the conflict of interests between principals (shareholders) and agents (managers).

2 Stakeholders

Stakeholders are those individuals, groups or entities that have **potential** interest in what the organisation does and **can either affect or be affected** by the activities of organisations.

It is important that an organisation understands the needs of the different stakeholders.

2.1 Typical classification of stakeholders

2.1.1 Internal stakeholders

Internal stakeholders are people whose interest in a company comes through a direct relationship and works **within** the boundary of organisations.

内部利益相关者的关键判断标准为：在组织边界内部（如表 1-1 所示）。

表 1-1　Internal stakeholders

Stakeholder	Need/expectation
Employees	Pay, working conditions and job security
Managers/directors	Pay, bonus, status, job security

2.1.2 Connected stakeholders

Connected stakeholders can be viewed as having a contractual relationship and works **outside** the organisation.

关联利益相关者的关键判断标准为：与组织有合约关系且在组织边界外部（如表 1-2 所示）。

表 1-2 Connected stakeholders

Stakeholder	Need/expectation
Shareholders	Steady flow of income, possible capital growth and the continuation of the business
Debt finance providers	Ability to repay the finance, including interest and principal, and also security of investment
Customers	High quality products and services with competitive prices; design of new product and also follow-up after-sales services
Suppliers	Customers' ability to pay off debts promptly

2.1.3 External stakeholders

External stakeholders are those people who **do not directly** work with a company but are affected in some way by the actions and outcomes of the organisation. This group will have quite diverse objectives and have varying ability to ensure that organisations meet their objectives.

外部利益相关者与组织**没有直接联系**，但是依然会影响组织行为或者被组织行为影响（如表1-3所示）。

表 1-3 External stakeholders

Stakeholder	Need/expectation
Community at large	The general public can be a stakeholder, especially if their lives are affected by an organisation's decisions
Pressure groups	They need to ensure that the organisation does not harm the interest of certain social groups
Government	Company activities are central to the success of the economy (providing jobs and paying taxes). Legislation (e.g. health and safety) must be met by organisations
Trade unions	Taking an active part in the decision-making process, especially the welfare of employees

In addition, **primary stakeholders** are those who **have a contractual relationship** with the organisation, while **secondary stakeholders** are those who **do not have a contractual relationship** with the organisation.

Thus, external stakeholders are **secondary stakeholders.** The internal stakeholders and connected stakeholders are **primary stakeholders.**

小结：利益相关者是指与企业生产经营行为和后果具有利害关系的群体或个人。对企业而言，其利益相关者一般可以分为三类：内部利益相关者、关联利益相关者及外部利益相关者。

> **知识点解读**
>
> 利益相关者有很多不同维度的划分方式，在AB课程中，我们学习两种。一种是"ICE"，可以巧记为"冰块"划分；另一种是将有无合约关系作为判断依据：与公司有合约关系为primary，没有则为secondary stakeholders。

小试牛刀

Example question 4

Which of the following are not considered as connected stakeholders?

A. Loan provider
B. Executive director
C. Shareholders
D. Customer

Example question 5

Rani runs an environmental pressure group against the ABC Co which is not very environmentally friendly because of non-classification of industrial wastes. Her family member Alice is an executive director in the ABC Co.

Are Rani and Alice internal, connected or external stakeholders for the ABC Co?

2.2 Stakeholder conflict

A common problem with numerous stakeholders is that different stakeholders' interests may not all be aligned. In fact, their needs/expectations may conflict.

每个利益相关者群体都希望组织在制定战略决策时能优先考虑他们,以便实现他们的目标,但这些权益主体在相关利益及所关心的焦点问题上存在很大的差别,且往往互有矛盾。

Some of the typical conflicts are shown below.

表 1-4 Typical conflicts between stakeholders

Stakeholders	Conflict
Customers versus shareholders	Product price/quality/service levels versus profits/dividends
General public versus shareholders	Effect on the environment versus profit/dividends
Shareholders versus mangers	Shareholders prefer long-term return while managers usually seek short-term profits and bonus

2.3 Mendelow matrix

It is important that an organisation meets the needs of the most dominant stakeholders, but the needs of the other stakeholders also need to be considered.

图 1-1 Mendelow matrix

核心考点

Mendelow 矩阵的考核方式灵活多样,往往以 case 形式出现,根据描述判断 stakeholder 属于哪个象限,并且应该采用哪种 strategy 进行应对。

2.3 Mendelow matrix

Mendelow 矩阵(如图 1-1 所示)是由 Aubrey Mendelow 于 1991 年提出的一种 power interest matrix(即权力利益矩阵),又叫利益相关者矩阵。该矩阵大致地按照该利益相关者对组织的影响力的高低(power)和对组织感兴趣的程度的高低(interest),将所有利益相关者划分到四个象限中,用来确立公司与利益相关者的关系和策略。

知识点解读

Example question 6 是典型的 Section C 的题目，题干长，同时需要考生在读懂案例的前提下，进行应用。做题的时候切记需要根据题干描述答题，而不是靠自己的主观判断。

Example question 6

小试牛刀

Example question 6

Silver Energy is a listed corporation in clear energy industry and has built nuclear stations worldwide for years. It is one of the very few corporations worldwide that has mature technology in constructing nuclear stations.

The founder of Silver Energy—Mr Silver, who has a significant influence over the decision-making the company, has retired for many years and delegate all the operational and management work to the board of directors.

Nosdia is a country located in North Pole. Due to technology shortage, local government cannot build their own nuclear station and is now cooperating with Silver Energy for the construction: with the local government contributes capital and Sliver Energy contributes technology.

Local government in country Nosdia is actively advancing the process of construction as the new nuclear station will reduce the whole country's electricity cost as well as provide more job opportunities.

The proposal of construction has angered local animal protection group, many of whom noted that the hot air/water polluted by the station will increase local temperature and ice will melt. A local animal called seal lives in iceberg and will be homeless and die finally. Together with local residents, the anti of the proposal has been shown in global news for days and attract the attention of WWF.

(1) **For each of the following, identify whether they are internal, connected or external stakeholders?**

A. Mr. Silver

B. Local government of Nosdia

C. The board of directors

D. Seal

E. Animal protection group

(2) **Which category are these stakeholders? Which Strategy should we use?**

A. The local government

B. Mr. Silver

C. Animal protection group

Answers for example question

1. B
2. A
3. D
4. B
5. Rani：external/Alice：internal

6. (1) Connected/connected/internal/external/external
   (2) Low power and high interest; keep informed
   High power and low interest; keep satisfied
   High power and high interest; key player

Summary

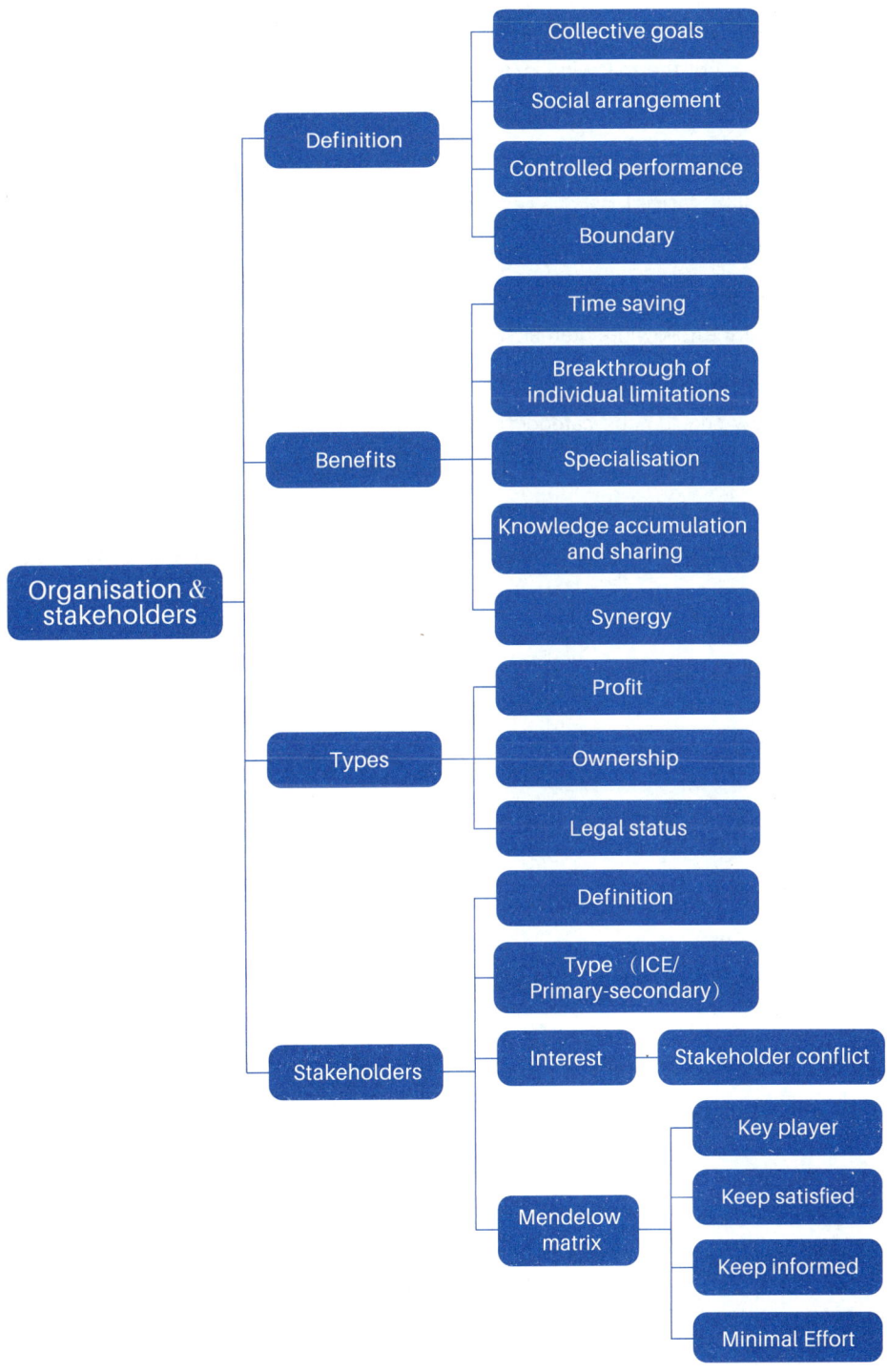

Chapter 1 考试不同问法总结（以"A"公司为例）

1. 针对 organisation 的定义 & 特征
- Which of the following BEST defines the term organisation?
- Which of the following is/is not the feature of organisation?

2. 针对 organisation 的分类
- What type of organisation/business organisation is A Co.?
- Which of the following is normally regarded as business organisation?
- Which of the following is/are not the feature of cooperative/NFP?

3. 针对 stakeholder 的定义
- Which of the following BEST describes the term stakeholder?

4. 针对 ICE model
- Which one/two of the following is/are internal/connected/external stakeholders?
- Are the following internal, connected or external stakeholder?

5. 针对 Mendelow matrix
- How should A be categorized/treated under Mendelow framework?
- Which of the regions in the matrix represents key players to whom strategy must be at least acceptable?
- With reference to Mendelow grid, A exert _____ and should be treated as _____.

Quick quiz

1.1 The purpose of PQR Co is to provide information and advice regarding environmental issues and it pays little attention on profit indicator. PQR Co is an independent association which people voluntarily come and act together.

What type of the organisation is PQR Co?

A. Local retailer

B. Co-operative

C. Non-governmental organisation

D. Public sector

Answer: **C**

Difficulty level: **Easy**

Tag: **Classification of organisation-Non-governmental organisation**

Rationale:

"**NGO**" generally applies to groups whose primary aim is not a commercial one, but within this term is applied to a diverse range of activities, aimed at promoting social, political or environmental change.

在这道题目中,题干提供的信息表明,PQR 公司的目的是提供与环境问题相关的信息与建议,以及它不是以营利为目的,所以排除 A 选项;此外,PQR 公司的成员是自愿组成且共同工作,所以排除 D 选项;并且 NGO 存在的目的就是促进社会、政治或环境的改变,对应的就是提供与环境问题相关的信息与建议,因此答案选 C。

1.2 Which two of the followings are secondary stakeholders?

A. Shareholders

B. Local residents

C. Suppliers

D. Environmental pressure group

Answer: **B, D**

Difficulty level: **Easy**

Tag: **Types of stakeholders-ICE model**

Rationale:

Primary stakeholders are those who have a contractual relationship with the organisation, while secondary stakeholders are those who do not have a contractual relationship with the organisation. Thus, external stakeholders are secondary stakeholders. The internal stakeholders and connected stakeholders are primary stakeholders.

主要利益相关者包括 internal stakeholders 和 connected stakeholders,而次要利益相关者包括且仅限于 external stakeholders。因此,题目问哪些属于次要利益相关者,也就是问哪些属于 external stakeholders,所以答案选 BD。

1.3 Which of the following is the key features of an organisation?

A. Specific goals, hierarchical level, earning profit, providing goods and services

B. Social arrangement, controlled performance, collective goals, separating boundaries from its environment

C. Systems and procedures, operation, a variety of goals, synergy

D. Overcome individual limitation, save time, share knowledge, specialization

Answer: **B**

Difficulty level: **Easy**

Tag: Definition of organisation

Rationale:

Answer B is correct, all of these four features are key elements in an organisation's definition.

Answer A isn't right, as not all the organisations have the hierarchical level, earning profit is also not the objective of all the organisations.

Answer C is the common characteristic of the organisation, not the key features of the organisation.

Answer D is the benefit of the organisation.

Pitfall:

You might have confused of the key features of the organisation with others, such as common characteristic and benefits of the organisation. Thus, keeping firmly in mind of these knowledge is the key to select the right answer.

B 选项正确，选项中的这些是组织的四个关键特征。

A 选项不正确，因为并非所有组织都有层级，赚取利润也并非是所有组织的目标。

C 选项是组织的共同特征，并非关键特征。

D 选项是组织存在的好处。

考生可能会混淆组织的关键特征与组织的其他考点，比如组织的共同特征与好处。因此，牢牢地记住这些知识点是选出正确选项的关键。

1.4 Which of the following organisation would focus on performance and profitability rather than value for money indicators?

    A. Public sector organisation   B. Public limited companies

    C. Local public hospital   D. Non-governmental organisation

    E. Cooperatives

Answer: B

Difficulty level: Normal

Tag: Classification of organisation

Rationale:

Measures such as value for money are often used in not-for-profit organisations, and for-profit organisation would rely heavily on the performance and profitability.

Option B, the pubic limited companies will deliver shareholders returns on investment. Therefore, B is "for-profit" organisation, and will focus on performance and profitability.

"Local public hospital" of option C is one of public sector organisations in option A. Therefore, A and C are both not-for-profit organisations.

Option D and E are both special type of private sector organisation that is unprofitable.

Pitfall:

You might have confused of word "public" in answer A and B. However, they are completely different with its others.

Value for money 业绩衡量方法通常是用在非营利性组织，而营利性组织用的更多的是利润指标，因此，选出哪个是营利性组织是做出这道题的关键。

B 选项中，股份有限公司的成立是为股东提供投资回报的，因此属于营利性的组织。

C 选项中，公立医院是 A 选项公有制组织中的一种，因此，A 和 C 都属于非营利性组织。

D 和 E 选项都是特殊的非营利的私有制组织。

1.5 G Co is a local car company which is operated in an Asian developing country. G Co uses penetration pricing strategy with low price and acquires lots of customers. However, there's a trend that local consumers prefer high quality car and G Co has considered to purchase an oversea car company with high technology. It is predicted that there will be a boom in the sale once the acquisition is completed.

Which of the following best describes the reason for the improved sales in relation to combined entity?

A. Social arrangement　　B. Collective goals　　C. Synergy　　D. High quality

Answer：C

Difficulty level：Easy

Tag：Synergy

Rationale：

This question is asked you to know the meaning of synergy.

这道题考查的是对协同效应的理解。

1.6 H Co is a state-owned company, and it provides LED streetlamps for its local residents. Consider the following lists of statement,

(1) H Co is classified as private sector organisation.

(2) The primary objective of H Co is to earn profit from provides of the LED lamps.

(3) The primary objective of H Co is provision of basic government services.

(4) The funds of H Co is mainly from charitable donation.

Which of the following option is right?

A. (1) and (2)　　B. (1) and (3)　　C. (3) and (4)　　D. Only (3)

Answer：D

Difficulty level：Normal

Tag：Characteristics of public sectors and NFP

Rationale：

This question is set to ask you to understand the characteristic of public sector and not-for-profit organisation. However, you should recognise the type of H Co of being a public sector first. Meanwhile, it is also a not-for-profit organisation and earning money should never be the primary objective. The primary objective of H Co is to provide basic government services. The funds is mainly from government revenue, such as tax.

这道题考查的是对公有制和非营利性组织的概念的理解。然而，你首先应该意识到 H 公司不是私有制企业，因为题中说了，它是被政府所拥有并控制的，因此它属于公有制组织。同时，它也是一个家非营利性组织，因此赚取利润不会是它的首要目标。H 公司的首要目标应该是提供基础的政府服务，如题目中提到的提供路灯。H 公司的主要收入来源是政府的税收。

1.7 Which of the following statements regarding limited companies is true?

A. The number of shareholders in most public limited companies is smaller than those in private limited companies

B. Shareholders cannot easily transfer their shares in public limited companies than those in private limited companies

C. Public limited companies can obtain capital from the public

D. Directors of private limited companies must have high proportion of the company's share than directors in public companies

Answer: C

Difficulty level: Normal

Tag: Limited companies

Rationale:

In most public limited company, the number of shareholders are larger than those in private, thus A is wrong.

Shareholders can easily transfer their share in public limited companies, thus B is wrong.

Directors of private limited companies are more likely to hold a substantial portion of the company's shares, however it will not be necessarily "must".

在大部分股份制有限责任公司，股东人数会比私营公司多，所以 A 选项是错的。

股份制有限责任公司的股东转让股份会比私营公司的股东容易，所以 B 选项是错的。

私营企业很多是家族企业，因此其高层的股份比例一般会比股份制有限责任公司的高层多，但并不是"一定"要比股份制有限责任公司的高层多，所以 D 选项也是错的。

Chapter 2
Business environment

知识导入

上一章介绍了商业世界的最小单位——组织，而组织的平稳运作离不开周围的商业环境，两者紧密相连，互相影响。因此，了解商业环境显得尤为重要。本章将主要介绍商业环境的分析模型。在本章中，我们将从三个不同的角度去分析商业环境：影响整个商业的宏观环境、影响特定行业的微观环境，以及公司的内部环境。

单词表

英文	中文
Capacity expansion	产能扩张
Entry barriers	进入壁垒
Lobbyist	说客
Family life cycle	家庭生命周期
Age structure	年龄结构
Educational attainment	教育背景
Delayering	扁平化
Span of control	控制范围
Decentralise	分权
Outsource	外包
Competitive advantage	竞争优势
Period of notice	提前通知期
Constructive dismissal	推定解雇
Switching cost	转换成本
Substitute	替代
Bargaining power	议价能力
Value chain analysis	价值链分析模型

学习指南

Learning objectives	Pass level	Distinction level	用时建议
1. Components of PEST/PESTEL model（1）	√		5 min
2. How each factor of PEST/PESTEL affects organisations（1.1-1.3）	√		20 min
3. Components of Five forces model（2）	√		5 min
4. The understanding of each force（2）	√		20 min
5. Components of Value chain（3）	√		5 min
6. Classification of primary activities and support activities in value chain（3）	√		10 min

续表

Learning objectives	Pass level	Distinction level	用时建议
7. Understanding the content of each activity in value chain（3）	√		15 min
8. Components of SWOT analysis（4）	√		10 min
9. Porter's three generic strategies（精益求精）		√	10 min

本章考点

重要考点	难度（1~3）
熟记 PEST/PESTEL 的组成要素，理解每个要素如何产生影响	2
熟记 Five forces 的组成，理解每个 force 并能在案例分析中识别运用	3
熟记并理解 Value chain analysis 的组成要素和分类	2
熟记 SWOT 分析的四要素	1

Analysis of environment contains three levels: the whole external environment (PESTEL analysis), the internal industry environment (Porter's five forces), and the organisational environment (value chain). All three levels and models are of importance in the whole ACCA syllables.

核心考点

PESTEL 模型在 FAB/AB 考试中比较简单，但其重要性不能忽视，在今后 p-level 的 SBL 课程学习中难度和深度会加强。在第二章中主要学习 PSTEL，对于 economic factor，会在第四章宏观经济中具体学习。PESTEL 模型主要分析 the situation of external environment，需要同学们理解。

1 PEST/PESTEL analysis

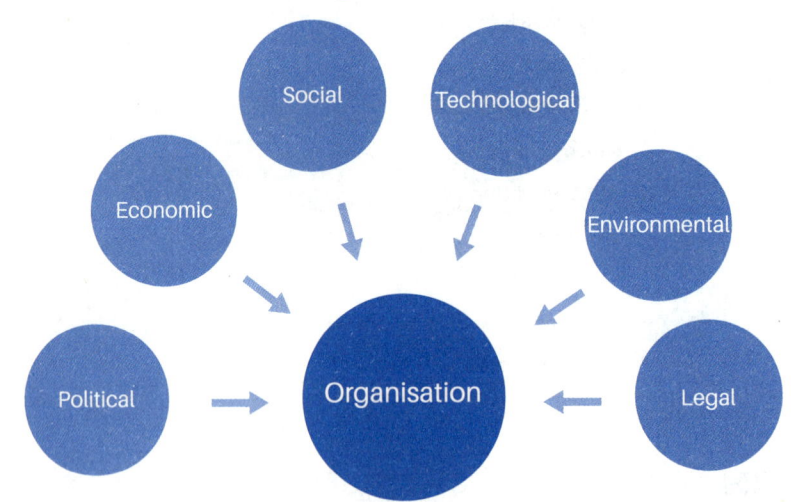

图 2-1　PESTEL analysis

PESTEL 模型（见图 2-1）是一种分析外部宏观环境的工具。该模型中，P 代表政治因素（Political），E 代表经济因素（Economic），S 代表社会文化与人口因素（Social and demographic），T 代表技术因素（Technological），后面的 E 代表环境因素（Environmental）以及 L 代表法律因素（Legal）。在 FAB/AB 这门课程中，我们有的时候可以将环境因素并入社会文化因素，法律因素并入政治因素一起考虑，因此 PESTEL 可被简化为 PEST。这些因素都来源于企业外部环境，很大程度上不受企业掌握，因此这些因素也常被戏称为"pest"（害虫）。

表 2-1　Factors of PESTEL analysis

Factors	Description
Political	**Government⟶Organisation** Government can directly affect organisation through various measures such as political stability, capacity expansion, market competition, entry barriers (tariffs), etc. **Government⟵Organisation** (a) Employ **lobbyists** to influence key individual ministers. (b) Try to influence **public opinion**, and hence the legislative agenda
Economic	As for macro-economic environment, organisations cannot run in a vacuum—they make decisions within a large and complex economic environment. The details will be demonstrated in Chapter 4.
Social	This factor can affect organisations' operation strongly. We will discuss in the following aspects: (a) Demographic trend. (b) Social trend. (c) Cultural trend. The details will be illustrated later in this chapter
Technological	Organisations cannot operate without technical supports in the current society. Technology development has influences on organisations in the following aspects: (a) General effects. (b) Organisational structure. The details will be illustrated later in this chapter
Environmental	**Organisation⟶Environment** Organisations' active activities have significant impacts upon the environment, and we name it as environmental footprint. 生态足迹衡量的是人类和组织行为对生态系统的影响。例如，企业在生产过程中排放的废水、废气，占用的耕地等，都是测量生态足迹的指标。这些指标越高，代表人类对生态环境的破坏程度越高。出于可持续性发展的考虑，很多具有远见卓识的企业已经将尽可能降低生态足迹纳入经营过程，如著名的世界 500 强公司之一的宝洁（P&G），通过新技术优化包装瓶的重量，最大化地节约了需要的瓶装塑料。 **Organisation⟵Environment** Organisations may cost more by environmental factors, such as waste management costs, fines, reporting, employee health and safety and sustainability of raw material inputs
Legal	Legislation can affect whole organisations especially some key laws. For instance: (a) Employment protection law. (b) Health and safety law. (c) Data protection and security law. (d) Consumer protection law. The details will be illustrated later in this chapter

博学多才

英美历史中，Lobbyist（说客）的历史最早可以追溯到 19 世纪。Lobbyist 源自 lobby 一词，意思是走廊，lobbyist 则是指在议会厅外的走廊上苦苦等候议员们散会的那些非公务人员，他们往往都带着各自代表的财阀组织的诉求和愿望而来，试图通过他们的游说来使得这些政客接受他们的提议，为这些财阀组织谋求利益。西方政治中的"说客通道"，可以说是一扇有特色的"政治后门"。

1.1 Social and demographic trends

1.1.1 Demographic trend

人口统计学特征一般包括人口总数、性别、年龄、健康状况、职业、婚姻、教育水平、收入等因素。这些因素对企业战略的制定具有重大影响，尤其在当今大数据得到广泛运用的前提下，很多企业都会利用人口统计数据来对外界环境进行分析，以确定目标客户群体和细分市场。例如，人口总数与市场上的总需求密切相关，而性别与年龄进一步地影响了需求的结构状况。同时，人口的受教育水平又会影响到组织的用工状况等。

（A）Population and the labour market

Labour is the first force of organisation. As a consequence, it is essential for them to put emphasis on the population and labour market. Currently, there are two main demographic trends in the world:

（a）The aging problem

Simply speaking, aging problem means there are more elderly people and less young people in the society, which also means there are less available labour force in the market.

Such problem can be caused by several factors, for example: **low birth rate**, **low death rate**, **low marriage rate**, etc.

小试牛刀

Example question 1

Example question 1

The aging problem is quite common worldwide, which three of the following will be affected by this aging trend?

A. Decrease demand for full-time education

B. Increase demand for health care

C. Conflict in the pension budget

D. Decrease demand for social services

E. Decrease in unemployment

（b）Increasing participation of women in the labour force

Due to the growth of service sector and change of perception in the modern society, there is increasing participation of women in the labour force. This trend can affect many other aspects, for example, the average age at which women have their first children, furthermore, the birth rate.

Therefore, here comes another question, how can organisations cope with these demographic trends? Some general methods are illustrated as following:

- Identify the labour force that organisations want to recruit (e.g. school leavers, part-time workers).
- Familiarise the supply trend of the labour force pool.
- Assess the possibility of using substitute supply to satisfy the demand, for example, artificial intelligence (AI).

(B) Family life cycle

Family life cycle is a "concept that attempts to describe the effect of time on a family through the phases of marriage (and divorce) and births and deaths, reflected in the family's income and consumption". ("family life cycle", n.d.)

在市场中，很多服务与商品的消费对象都是以家庭为基本单位的，如房子、车子和教育资源等，因此在很多人口学学者和企业眼中，家庭是一个重要的研究对象。然而在不同阶段，家庭消费需求的方向和数量都有很大不同，也就是说，家庭的消费行为是一个动态的过程，因此对于企业而言，**特别是企业的市场营销部门**，家庭生命周期是一个重要的研究课题。

1.1.2 Social trend

Social class

Social class means "a status hierarchy in which individuals and groups are classified on the basis of esteem and prestige acquired mainly through economic success and accumulation of wealth. Social class may also refer to any particular level in such a hierarchy". ("Social class", n.d.)

到目前为止，社会阶层依然是一种普遍存在的社会现象。简单来说，同属一个社会阶层的人群具备相同或类似的特征。一般我们可以通过财富（wealth）、教育背景（educational background）、社会地位（status）、收入（income）等方面来划分社会阶层。

企业就是依靠这些特征来划分阶层，并针对不同阶层采取不同的市场营销与销售策略。

1.1.3 Cultural trends

(A) Health and diet issues

Major changes have been taken place in people's attitude toward diet and health. Most notable changes include the surge of vegetarians and increased preference for organic food.

现在市面上以"轻食"为主打的餐饮非常流行，"轻食"是指分量不多、热量不高的简易食品，典型代表为三明治、沙拉以及便利店的小食等。国内"轻食文化"的兴起与人们日益转变的健康与饮食观念紧密相关，尤其是意识更为超前的新一代年轻白领。

The impacts on business

(a) The market for sports-related goods, such as running shoes, tops and leggings, will continue to expand.

(b) New foods such as organic food are springing up.

(c) Employers tend to provide more fitness facilities for employees.

(B) Environmentalism

The development of environmentalism prompts the transformation of consumer concept towards green products. In order to satisfy new trend of customer needs, most businesses devote themselves to reduce pollution and employ renewable materials.

In the long run, these actions can actually benefit the enterprises as they could obtain a competitive advantage through sustainability development.

绿色环保是整个市场的趋势，这个趋势也影响到了公民的消费观念。 越来越多的公司开始使用可再生的原材料以及生产更绿色环保的商品和服务。 最典型的例子就是汽车行业，公民们认为环境损害是由二氧化碳排放造成的，而保护后代的自然资源与环境非常重要，因此公民们开始愿意支付更高的价格去购买低排放的车辆。 同时，绿色产品的可持续性更是逐步成了很多企业的竞争优势。

1.2 The impact of technology on organisations

随着科学技术的迅猛发展，计算机技术也更加广泛地应用到企业的各项经营活动当中。 技术的革新在很多方面为企业的发展添油助力，其中最明显的变化反映在工作效率的提高、成本的普遍降低、信息质量的提升及服务质量的改善等方面。

1.2.1 General effects

随着技术日新月异的发展，组织的方方面面都在受到影响。 近年来，发展势头非常强盛的技术有如下几项：

AI：人工智能；

Blockchain：区块链；

Cloud Computing/Service：云计算；

Big **D**ata：大数据。

1.2.2 Impact on organisation structure

(A) Span of Control

The concept of "span of control", refers to the number of subordinates controlled **directly** by **a** superior. The development of technology makes it possible for managers to have a **wider** span of control ("span of control", n.d.).

(B) Tall and flat organisations

Tall-narrow organisations are characterised by having **many management layers**, with each manager take control of only a few subordinates.

Wide-flat configurations have relatively **few layers**, and each manager take control of more subordinates.

(C) Delayering & Downsizing

The aim of delayering is to **reduce the hierarchy layers** of the organisation, especially the layer of middle management.

基本概念

区分 delayering 和 downsizing：两者都有裁员之意，delayering 主要是针对 middle management level 的裁员，强调中层被裁掉之后公司架构变得更加扁平，故又被称作"机构扁平化"；downsizing 指一般的裁员，各个层级的员工都有可能涉及。

Downsizing is the action to **streamline the organisation**'s number of existing employees.

Although both processes enable the organisation to improve efficiency, only delayering brings about a structural change, that is the move from a tall organisation to a relative flat one.

小试牛刀

Example question 2

Consider the following statement (TRUE OR FALSE):

An aging trend represents a risk to all companies that operate in technologically advanced industries.

1.2.3 Outsourcing and offshoring

(A) Definition

(a) Outsourcing means contracting out tasks, operations, or processes to an external third party.

(b) Offshoring means the practice of outsourcing overseas.

小试牛刀

做这道题可能由于逻辑疏漏而判断出错：因为是高科技行业，老龄化的人口通常不能接受高科技，所以老龄化对所有高科技行业都是风险，这样的想法是错误的。老龄化确实可能对某些高科技企业造成风险，但如果公司能够推出人性化的产品，或者是特别针对老龄化人口使用的产品，就能将风险转变成机遇，从而在行业当中脱颖而出，所以题目中出现"all"的时候都需要特别当心。

核心考点

外包是企业利用外部的资源为企业内部的生产和经营服务。在FAB/AB的学习中，需了解外包的类型及优缺点。P-level 中将继续深化学习。考试中考核外包的优缺点尤为常见，需要记忆。

博学多才

耐克（NIKE）可以算是当今世界上将外包运用得炉火纯青的一家公司了。最初，外包的想法来自其创始人之———奈特。在某个平常的一天，奈特路过养鸡场时看到了正在下蛋的母鸡，突然领悟到了"借鸡生蛋"的道理，即在其他国家或地区设立公司，并且在当地寻找生产商进行生产活动以及销售活动，如此这般，公司可以避免出口他国带来的高关税，也可以避免东道国设置的一系列贸易壁垒，从而顺利进入其他市场。于是在1981年，耐克公司选定日本市场，在日本当地寻找到了合适的生产商帮助其生产商品，并与当地企业设立联营公司进行销售，通过这种方法，耐克公司成功打开了日本市场的大门。在尝到"借鸡生蛋"模式的甜头之后，耐克公司开始步履不停地放眼世界各地寻找合适的合作市场，公司规模也随之日益壮大。

(B) Appraisal of outsourcing

Advantages:

(a) Outsourcing simplifies the operation of businesses, helping to **remove uncertainty of cost** and improve **production efficiency**.

(b) Businesses could enjoy **high-quality service and professionalism** provided by external experts.

(c) Outsourcing helps organisations to be more **flexible** to respond to changes in environment.

Disadvantages:

(a) It is **risky** for businesses to outsource important and/or confidential tasks to external third party.

(b) If outsiders provide unsatisfactory level of service, it is time-consuming and expensive for business to shift to a new outsider or reconstruct their own functions, that is, businesses tend to **lock in contracts** and have no choice but to accept the fact.

(c) Organisations may be lazy to keep up with the new trends/technology once they choose to outsource, thus giving an opportunity to their competitors, which may result in **loss of competitive advantage**.

(d) Outsourcing may be **ineffective** as outsiders have many customers to serve and businesses might **sacrifice control** over operations.

1.3 Legal environment

Key areas of legislation that affect all firms:

(a) Employment protection.

(b) Health and safety.

(c) Data protection and security.

(d) Consumer protection.

1.3.1 Employment protection law

Many countries tend to protect employees from unfair treatment by passing legislations, especially to cover **termination** of the employment. There are usually four common methods of terminating the labor relationship between employees and employers, including retirement, resignation, dismissal and redundancy.

雇主与雇员分道扬镳的场景通常包括四种：退休（retirement）、辞职（resignation）、解雇（dismissal）以及裁员（redundancy）。首先，退休（retirement）往往是因年老、疾病或部分（甚至完全）丧失劳动能力而退出工作岗位；其次，辞职（resignation）是由员工出于主观意愿向雇主提出解除劳动关系的行为，值得注意的是，员工需在正式离职前提前一段时间通知（period of notice）雇主，以便雇主安排合适的人员与其交接有关事项并接替后续工作。退休与辞职相较解雇（dismissal）和裁员（redundancy）而言都是比较平和的离职方式，下面我们着重介绍解雇和裁员。

(A) Dismissal

(a) **Summary dismissal**

Summary dismissal is one kind of actual dismissal, which occurs where the employer dismisses the employee **without notice**. They may do this if the employee has committed a serious breach of contract, therefore the employer incurs no liability.

即时解雇指的是雇主解雇员工的时候没有给任何通知期，而选择立即解雇员工。这种解雇有可能出现在员工严重违反合同的时候，被雇主立即解雇，此时雇主不需要承担任何责任。

(b) **Constructive dismissal**

Constructive dismissal is one kind of deemed dismissal, which occurs where **employer repudiates some essential term of the contract**, for example, by the imposition of a complete change in the employee's duties, and the employee

---

核心考点

最后的法律因素选取了影响所有组织的四项立法，其中劳动者保护法（Employment protection）考试频率最高，需要同学们多理解及运用；健康与安全（Health and safety）、数据保护法（Data protection and security）次之，消费者保护法（consumer protection）考的相对较少，同学们了解即可。

resigns.

推定解雇，属于雇员被迫辞职的情况，常出现于员工劳动合同上的义务被改变的情况。此时，员工必须要证明雇主严重违反劳务合同，他因此而辞职。

(c) **Wrongful dismissal**

Wrongful dismissal occurs when employer breaching the employment contract, relating to the **method** of dismissal. For example, the employer has **dismissed an employee with less than the statutory minimum period of notice**.

(d) **Unfair dismissal**

Unfair dismissal occurs when dismissal **without good reasons**. For example:
- Applying for maternity, paternity and adoption leave.
- Claiming the right of minimum wages.
- Joining a trade union.

(B) **Redundancy**

It should be noted that redundancy is one kind of fair dismissal, and it usually occurs when:
- The employer stops to carry on the business.
- The job requirement of employees to carry out certain work has diminished.

1.3.2 Data protection and security law

In earlier years in the UK, there was no specific law concerning data protection and the law adopted is mainly from the EU. To harmonise and localise the data protection legislation, Data Protection Act was firstly introduced in 1998, which focused on protecting individual privacy. Recently, the third generation of data protection law has commenced in 2018 to modernise relevant regulations, ensuring they are effective in the years to come.

The *Data Protection Act 2018 (UK)* is concerned about how personal information is used by organisations, businesses or the government.

(A) **Rules of data protection act**

The following strict rules, which is called "Data Protection Principles" need to be followed to ensure information is:

(a) Used fairly, lawfully and transparently.
(b) Used for specified, explicit purposes.
(c) Used in a way that is adequate, relevant and limited to only what is necessary.
(d) Accurate and, where necessary, kept up to date.
(e) Kept for no longer than is necessary.
(f) Handled in a way that ensures appropriate security, including protection against unlawful or unauthorised processing, access, loss, destruction or damage.

(B) **The rights of data subjects**

Under the *Data Protection Act 2018 (UK)*, data subjects have the following

---

核心考点

Wrongful dismissal 译为不当解雇，unfair dismissal 译为不公平解雇，两者都是员工向法院提起诉讼的原因，即员工以自己被不当解雇或不公平解雇为由将雇主告上法庭。
具体来说，当出现以下情况，员工可以主张**不当解雇**：
（1）雇主在低于法律规定的最短通知期限将员工解雇（高频考点）；
（2）在定期合同到期前解雇员工；
当出现以下情形（包括但不完全包括），员工可以主张**不公平解雇**：
（1）因为员工怀孕被解雇；
（2）因员工维护"最低工资"权利被解雇；
（3）因加入工会或参与工会活动被解雇。

知识点解读

冗员（遣散）可以分两种情况：
（1）雇主已经停业或者有停业的意图，那么将会出现全体裁员。
（2）雇主根据业务的需求，减少相应的业务或者部门，那么相应部门的员工被裁员属于部分裁员。

知识点解读

Big data，大数据是近年来一直讨论的问题，对于 legal factors 中的数据安全法需要注意这类题目。
需要特别留意，数据保护法是为了保护个人隐私，而不是商业机密。

知识点解读

英国数据保护法案的原则，考纲明确指出不需要记忆，只需要能 identify（指出），即能够识别其是否属于法案当中的一个原则。

rights:

(a) Be informed about how their data is being used.

(b) Access personal data.

(c) Have incorrect data updated.

(d) Have data erased.

(e) Stop or restrict the processing of their data.

(f) Data portability (allowing them to get and reuse their data for different services).

(g) Object to how their data is processed in certain circumstances.

1.3.3 Health and safety law

健康安全保护法（Health and safety law）的主旨在于保护员工在职场中的合法权益。对于公司而言，遵循该项法律是公司的义务所在，同时也能树立公司良好的形象，增强现有员工的忠诚度，并吸引潜在的优质应征者。此外，值得一提的是，该项法律的遵守也可以有效避免员工在工作中受到健康以及安全方面的伤害，从而减少公司可能为此需要付出的代价。

> **核心考点**
>
> 对于健康与安全保护法，考的最多的是雇主与雇员各自的职责，这块很容易出案例分析题，要求同学们理解并应用。

Employer's and employee's duties

(A) Employer's duties

(a) A safe working **environment.**

(b) Safe **equipment and procedures.**

(c) Adequate information, **instruction**, **training and supervision.**

(d) Adequate **investigation** of accidents.

(B) Employee's duties

(a) **Be careful during using equipment.**

(b) **Take reasonable duty of care** to themselves and others.

(c) **Inform** employer of any potentially dangerous situation.

1.3.4 Consumer protection

First of all, some basic concepts about contracts will be introduced, which can help us understand better.

(a) The three elements of contract:

Offer/Acceptance/Consideration.

It should be noted that the contract is between the two parties who offer and accept. Simply speaking, only these two parties are legally bound by the rights and obligation of the contract, which is called as the **privity of contract**.

(b) Sales of goods might meet several items:

- The goods must be delivered for a particular **occasion or date.**
- **The seller must have legal title** or the ownership of the item they are selling.
- The goods must **correspond with this description**.
- The goods sold must be of satisfactory **quality** and fit for their intended purpose.

(c) Provision of service should comply the following requirements:
- Carried out **with reasonable skill and care.**
- Complete within a reasonable length of **time.**
- Completed at a reasonable **price.**

2 Porter's five forces

> **核心考点**
>
> 波特五力模型是 P 阶段 SBL 课程中最重要的商业分析模型之一，是企业制定竞争战略时经常利用的战略分析工具。它有助于解释为什么不同的行业能够维持不同的盈利水平。

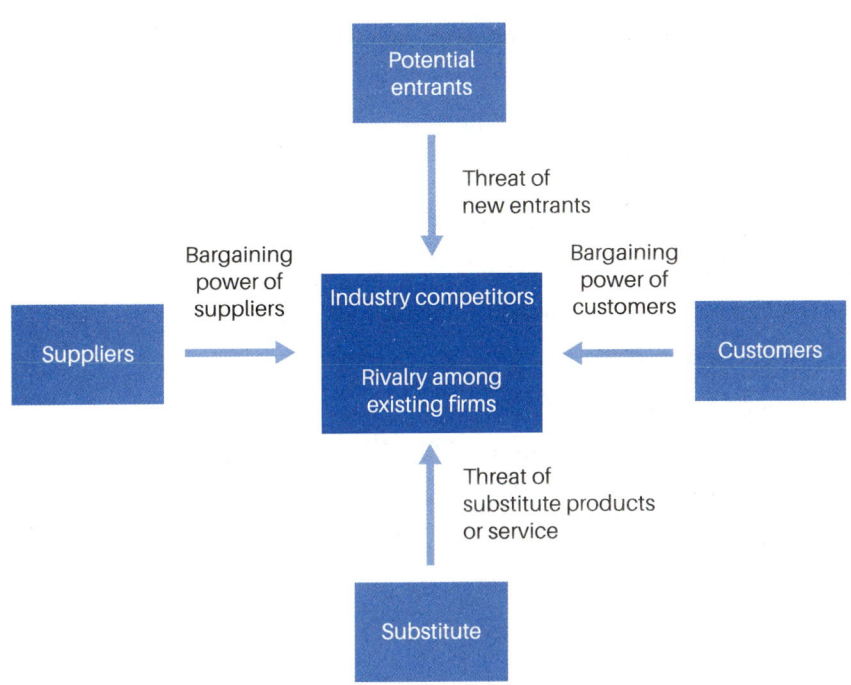

图 2-2　Porter's five forces

Porter's five forces is a business analysis model created by Harvard Business School professor Michael Porter, to analyse an industry's attractiveness and likely profitability. The five forces were well demonstrated (Porter, 1980) in the above graph. It helps to explain why different industries are able to sustain different levels of profitability.

与 PEST 模型用来分析外部宏观环境相比，五力模型（见图 2-2）是用于**具体行业环境**的战略分析工具，可以有效地分析竞争环境。五力分别是：供应商的讨价还价能力、购买者的讨价还价能力、潜在竞争者进入的能力、替代品的替代能力、行业内竞争者现在的竞争能力。

(A) Competitive rivalry

The competitive rivalry describes the level of intensity among the existing competitors in this industry, which as a result impacts the profit they could generate. Generally, the competition behaviour includes price war, sales promotion and product improvement.

Competitive rivalry is likely to be high where:
(a) There are a large number of equally balanced competitors of a similar size.
(b) The rate of market growth is slow.
(c) There is a lack of differentiation between competitor offerings.

(B) The threat of new entrants to the industry

专有名词

Switching cost

Switching cost（转换成本），是指客户从购买 A 产品转向购买 B 产品之后所增加的额外费用。

(C) The threat of substitute products or services

(B) **The threat of new entrants to the industry**

If competitors can easily enter the industry, there will be more opponents to carve up profits. Therefore, the greater the threat, the higher the levels of competition. The ease of the entrance largely determined by the extent of the barriers to entry and the strength of the resistance from existing firms.

The strength of the barriers to entry is determined by **economies of scale**, **switching cost**, **product differentiation**, **capital requirements**, patents, access to distribution channel, etc.

(C) **The threat of substitute products or services**

If there are products from another industry that can be used as substitutes, then the demand for the product will increase or decrease as it moves upwards or downwards in price relative to substitutes.

The threat of substitute is likely to be high where:

(a) The quality of substitute is better and switching cost is negligible.

(b) The loyalty of customer is low.

波特五力模型中的替代威胁指的是行业替代的威胁，具体是指消费者对于某行业的需求，被**另一个行业**的产品或服务所替代，也就是现在媒体上常提到的"跨界竞争"，如外卖行业的崛起替代了泡面。

(D) **The bargaining power of customers**

The bargaining power of customers refers to the degree of power that the customer has to depress the supplier. Powerful customers can force price cuts and/or quality improvements.

The bargaining power of customers is likely to be high where:

(a) The degree of customer concentration is high.

(b) The reliance of buyer on supplier's product is low.

(c) The buyer has a choice of alternative sources of supply and switching cost is low.

(E) **The bargaining power of suppliers**

Similarly, higher supplier bargaining power might also influence the profitability of the whole entity. The power of suppliers to charge higher prices will be high where:

(a) The degree of supplier concentration is high.

(b) The reliance upon one single customer is low.

(c) The impact of brand is powerful.

(d) The switching cost for customer is high.

精益求精

Porter's three generic strategies

波特作为"竞争战略之父"曾于 1980 年在《竞争战略》一书中，从企业层面上提出了三种通用战略，以帮助企业在竞争中长期处于不败之地。这三种通用战略分别为：成本领先战略、差别化战略及集中化战略。这些理论从三个不同角度出发，建议企业根据自身目标确定相应的战略，长此以往，创造出别人难以模仿的竞争优势。

Porter (1985) defines the three generic strategies are as following：

(A) Cost leadership

Set out to be the lowest cost producer in an industry. By producing at the lowest possible cost the manufacturer can compete on price with every other producer in the industry and earn the highest unit profits.

例如，卡西欧电子有限公司通过在劳动力成本低廉的国家建立生产线，大幅度降低生产成本，从而建立成本领先优势。

(B) Differentiation

A firm differentiates itself from its competitors when it provides something unique that is valuable to buyers. Differentiation occurs when the differentiated product is able to obtain a price premium in the market that is above the cost incurred to create the differentiation.

例如，英国航空公司通过提供高质量的旅行服务，以及特色豪华航班，成功地将自己与其他普通航空公司区分开来，并得以设定高昂的机票价格。

(C) Focus

A focus strategy is based on fragmenting the market and focusing on particular market niche. The firm will not market its products industry-wide but will concentrate on a particular type of buyer or geographical area.

例如，服装定制企业针对不同客户的要求定制衣裙鞋履等产品，这种定制服务往往也伴随着不菲的收费。

小试牛刀

Example question 3

XYZ Cooperates in an industry with a high proportion of fixed costs but minimal investment in machinery. The customers have strong loyalty to the existing brand but little switching costs. The market has started to decline in recent years.

Which of the following will result in a greater threat of new entrants to the industry?

   A. The strength of brand loyalty

   B. The declining market

   C. The minimal need for investment in machinery

   D. The high fixed costs

Example question 4

Consider the following statements about Porter's five forces model. (True or False)

   A. The bargaining power of customers may be increased if products can be differentiated effectively

B. A high level of competitive rivalry in an industry is always dependent on the number of producers in the market
C. Threat of new entrant is lower when existing suppliers derive purchasing economies of scale

3 Value chain analysis

Porter's value chain is a collection of activities that are performed by a company to create value for its customers.

波特价值链模型（如图 2-3 所示）认为，组织中的每一个环节都可以为产品或者服务增加价值，它们彼此之间并非是互相独立的；相反，组织不同部门之间是相辅相成的，只有当整个组织的部门之间互相协作，企业才可以创造出更大的价值。

> **核心考点**
>
> 价值链模型是用来分析企业竞争优势的主要来源，波特认为企业竞争优势来源于企业的每一项业务活动，因此他将企业的经营活动分成若干个基础活动，同时他认为活动必然会产生成本，但开展活动却能为顾客创造价值，所以企业的每一项经营活动就是竞争优势的基本单位。活动为客户创造的价值与活动成本之间的差值决定了利润。所以，这就是可以区别于竞争对手的竞争优势来源。

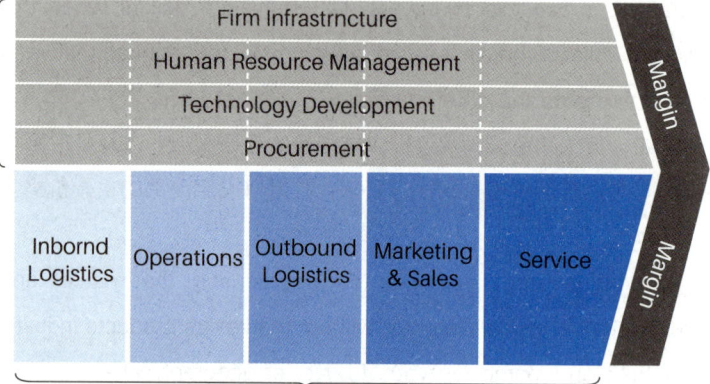

图 2-3　Value chain

3.1 Primary activities

(A) Inbound logistics

(a) Description: inbound logistics are those activities such as receiving, storing and distribution of raw materials for the purpose of inputting to production.

(b) Examples: raw material handling, warehousing, inventory control, vehicle scheduling and returns to suppliers.

(B) Operations

(a) Description: operations are all processes of converting inputs (raw materials) to outputs that are final products which are ready to sell.

(b) Examples: machining, packaging, assembling, equipment maintenance and testing.

(C) Outbound logistics

(a) Description: outbound logistics are those activities involving storing and delivering finished goods and services to customers for outputting of products.

(b) Examples: finished goods warehousing, inventory (finished goods) control, delivery vehicle operations, order processing and scheduling.

> **基本概念**
>
> 区分 inbound logistics, operation, outbound logistics 三个 activities 的最简单方法：在 operation 生产之前都属于 inbound logistics，包括收货（一般是原材料）、储存等活动。Operation 之后，即生产活动结束后，包括产成品的运输、储存都属于 outbound logistics。

(D) Marketing and sales
(a) Description: marketing and sales are activities where introducing products into the market and creating awareness among customers through advertisements and promotions for increasing sales.
(b) Examples: advertising, promotion, channel selection and pricing.

(E) Service
(a) Description: service is such activity that developing good relationships with customers as well as maintaining or enhancing the value of the products to customers.
(b) Examples: installation, repair, training and product adjustment.

3.2 Support activities

(A) Procurement
(a) Description: procurement means supportive activities related to acquisition of inputs such as raw materials.
(b) Examples: purchase of raw materials, other consumable items, machinery, office equipment and buildings.

(B) Technology development
(a) Description: technology development means activities intended to improve the products and processes of the organisation, both internally and externally.
(b) Examples: telecommunication technology, accounting automation software and customer servicing procedures.

(C) Human resource management
(a) Description: human resource management means the support activities where can enhance competitive advantages through developing the workforce within the organisation.
(b) Examples: recruiting, selecting, coaching, training, developing and rewarding staff.

(D) Firm infrastructure
(a) Description: firm infrastructure means all activities which make sure the organisation's daily operations are performed as intended.
(b) Examples: accounting, finance, company structure, system and policies.

4 SWOT analysis

SWOT analysis summarises the key issues from the business environment and the strategic capability of an organisation that are most likely to impact on strategy development.

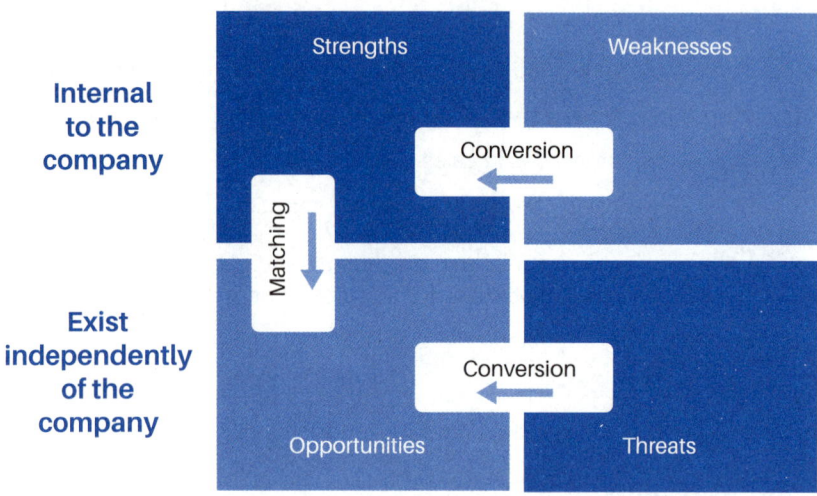

图 2-4 SOWT analysis

不同于专注分析外部环境的 PEST 模型和 Five forces 模型，以及针对自身进行全面分析的 Value chain analysis。 SWOT 模型（如图 2-4 所示）是内外分析兼而有之。 简单来说，它就是将分析对象分为内部因素和外部因素。 内部因素包括自身优势和劣势，外部因素包括机会与威胁。 4 种因素相互匹配会出现 4 个不同场景，即当优势 VS 机会、优势 VS 威胁、劣势 VS 机会和劣势 VS 威胁。 不同场景之下，企业需要对症下药地制定相应决策。 由此可见，SWOT 模型是一个相对全面和动态的分析工具，因此在商业世界中也得到了广泛运用。

4.1 Internal appraisal

Internal appraisal means evaluating strengths and weaknesses of organisations themselves, which usually include those existing resources and experience. For example:

(a) Financial factors
- Strength: The company has sufficient capital;
- Weakness: The company has a poor credit grade in capital markets.

(b) Physical resources
- Strength: The company is possessed with the most developed equipment;
- Weakness: A fast-food restaurant has a poor location which is far away from town.

4.2 External appraisal

External factors include opportunities and threats, which cannot be controlled by organisations. However, organisations are connected with these outside factors closely. For example:

(a) Economic trends (local, national and international financial trends)
- Opportunity: According to economic cycle, it is in the stage of boom;
- Threat: There is financial crisis around the world.

(b) Political, environmental and economic regulations
- Opportunity: The government encourages the development of industry

which the company operates in;
- Threat: The political situation is turbulent of certain country which the company invests in.

博学多才

SWOT 是一个在商业世界中被广泛使用的分析工具，事实上，我们也可以利用这样的模型来对身边的企业做分析，如奶茶界中的低调"黑马"——茶颜悦色。

背景介绍：茶颜悦色于 2014 年成立于湖南省长沙市，是一家以中国风为基调，主打鲜茶饮品，并且只在长沙直营销售的奶茶店。与市面上其他奶茶店不同的是，茶颜悦色的奶茶以特色中国茶为底，加上从新西兰进口的淡奶油调制而成。这家奶茶店通过中西结合的做法，区域性的销售，吸引了大批的年轻顾客，成功地将品牌提高到了与臭豆腐比肩的长沙标志性美食的地位。

1. 优势分析（Strength）

（1）独特的配方，新颖的做法，产品特色鲜明；

（2）与同等定位的产品相比，性价比具有优势；

（3）直营销售的方式使得奶茶质量得到严格把控。

2. 劣势分析（Weakness）

（1）原材料采购成本过高，产品利润被限制；

（2）店面在长沙市区布局过于集中，店铺重叠过大，不利于扩大销售。

3. 机会分析（Opportunity）

现代人的养生观和饮食观逐渐发生变化，越发重视"绿色、天然、健康"，茶颜悦色的原料和制作很好地顺应了这个趋势。

4. 威胁分析（Threat）

奶茶市场进入门槛不高，新旧更迭较快，现代人的品位的风向随时在发生变化，增加了不确定因素。除却主打中国风这个特色，茶颜悦色目前尚未具备得以在市场中长久竞争的其他优势。

Answers for example question:

1. ABC
2. False
3. C
4. False/False/True

Summary

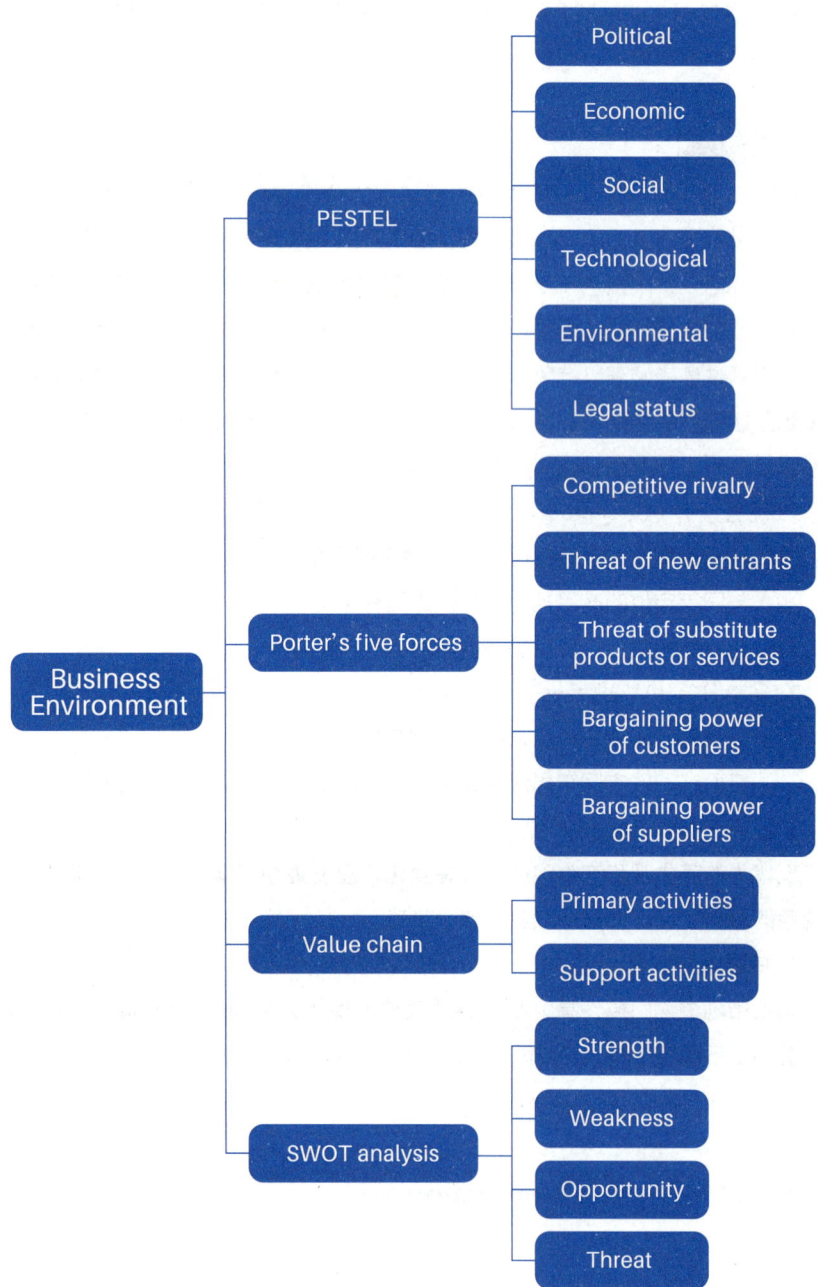

Chapter 2 考试不同问法总结

1. 针对 PEST 中 Technology 相关的问法

- Which of the following is a clear benefit of information technology at work?
- Which of the following BEST describes the concept of delayering?
- Which process would a company follow if they wish to outsource?
- Which two are ADVANTAGES of the effect of technological change on organisation structure?
- Which of the following is a definition of outsourcing?
- What is meant by downsizing in the context of organisational structure?
- Which TWO consequences will the delayer have on the structure of the or-

ganisation?
- Technological change can encourage a reduction in the middle tiers of organisations. This process is known as _____?

2. 针对 PEST 中 Legal 相关的问法
- Which of the following is a basic principle of data protection?
- Which TWO of the following are examples of wrongful dismissal?
- Choose which employee has been terminated in each of the manners listed below? (Constructive or wrongful)

3. 针对 PEST 中 Social 相关的问法
- Which of the following is a social-cultural environmental factor?
- For which TWO types of business or organisations are social or demographic changes especially significant?
- Study of which of the following trends accurately describes "demography"?

4. 针对 PEST 中 Political 相关的问法
- In which parts of a PEST analysis will a "change of government" and "change in lifestyle" be considered?

5. 针对 Five forces model 相关的问法
- Which of the following are components of porter's five forces model?
- Which of the following is a threat that identified in Porter's five forces model?

6. 针对 Generic strategies 相关的问法
- Which of the following is an example of a generic strategy outlined by Porter?

Quick quiz

2.1 Which of the following situation can employee sue the employer for "unfair" dismissal under employment protection law?

A. The employee was pregnant

B. The employee got married with employees of its competitor's company

C. The employee voluntarily applied for resignation

D. The employee disclosed confidential information

Answer: A

Difficulty level: Easy

Tag: Employment protection law-Unfair dismissal

Rationale:

Unfair dismissal emphasize that employee is dismissal without good reasons, such as pregnant, age discrimination etc.

这道题考查的是 unfair dismissal，unfair dismissal 强调的是解雇的原因不合理、不正当。因此，A 选项由于员工怀孕而遭到解雇就构成了 unfair dismissal。B 选项说现在员工由于与竞争对手员工结婚而遭到解雇，在英国，法律上认为这构成了潜在威胁，比如导致企业重要信息泄露，所以认为是潜在的合法解雇，因此不是正确选项。C 选项是员工自愿辞职，故排除。D 选项指的是员工泄露机密信息，这已经构成了合法被解雇，所以员工无法起诉公司。

2.2 Shaw Brothers Co recently outsourced its IT support department to an external supplier, Tang Co for building and maintenance of IT software.

Which TWO of the following are benefits of outsourcing its department for Shaw Co?

A. Relationship with Tang Co will be better

B. The structure of Shaw Brothers Co will become simple

C. The IT services will become more tailored and specific

D. Future uncertainty costs will be reduced

Answer: B, D

Difficulty level: Easy

Tag: PESTEL-Technological factor-Outsource

Rationale:

Outsourcing is the contracting out of specified operations or services to an external vendor. Therefore, it means that uncertainty cost will be removed. However, it also lead to miss competitive advantage and ineffective management.

这道题考查的是 PESTEL 中的技术因素的一个概念，叫作外包。外包强调的是将企业某一个活动或业务交给外部的供应商。外包有其优点和缺陷。其优点是会移除不确定成本，因为企业只会支付外包合同上的金额，对于其他后续费用，企业不需要承担，对应的也就是 D 选项。A 选项为干扰项，外包并无改善关系的作用。C 选项说反了，外包能提供的更多的是普遍的服务，如果需要特殊定制化的服务，更多的还是要依靠自己，而不是借助外部供应商。

2.3 Which model cannot be used for the analysis of external environment?

A. PESTEL   B. PEST   C. SWOT   D. Value chain

Answer: D

Difficulty level: Easy

Tag: Models of external environment

Rationale:

PESTEL model is also called PEST model where PEST stands for Political, Economic, Socio-cultural and Technological. Both are used for describing the key elements of an organisation's external environment.

SWOT stands for Strengths, Weaknesses, Opportunities, and Threats. SW can be used for analysing internal environment, and OT can be used for analysing external environment. As a consequence, SWOT is also a correct answer.

Pitfall:

You might be distracted by D option. You should identify that Porter's value chain model can be only used for describing the internal environment of the organisation.

PESTEL 模型也被称为 PEST 模型，PEST 模型是政治(Political)、经济(Economic)、社会文化(Socio-cultural)和科技(Technological)的首字母缩写。 PESTEL 和 PEST 都是用来分析组织外部宏观环境的关键组成要素。 SWOT 代表了优势(Strength)、劣势(Weaknesses)、机会(Opportunities)和威胁(Threats)。 其中 SW 用于组织内部环境的分析，OT 用于分析外部环境。 因此，SWOT 也是正确的选项。

考生可能会被 D 选项误导，考生一定要清晰地明确波特的价值链模型只能用于内部环境分析。

2.4 Which of the following cannot be regarded as an unfair dismissal under employment protection legislation?

A. The employee was pregnant

B. The employee joined a trade union

C. The employees are threatening to take industrial action in protest at paying conditions

D. The employee concealed his criminal record before engagement

Answer: D

Difficulty level: Easy

Tag: PESTEL's legal element

Rationale:

There are certain situations where employees may claim unfair dismissal:

Where employee is being denied a statutory right, for example, unlawful deduction from wages;

Where the employee is pregnant;

Where the employee is undertaking trade union activities. Thus, under ABC circumstances, employees can claim unfair dismissal.

Pitfall:

You may be confused of D option, as staff has a criminal record, this may prevent him holding a certain job.

当出现以下情形(包括但不完全包括)，员工可以主张不公平解雇：

因为员工怀孕被解雇；

员工遭遇不合法工资扣减后，因维护基本工资权利被解雇；

因加入工会或参与工会活动被解雇。

易错点：D 选项中的员工隐瞒了自己以前的犯罪记录，但是某些工作不能雇佣有犯罪记录的人来做。

2.5 _____ policy influences the economic environment, entry barriers of the industry, industry structure, industry competition.

A. Economic   B. Political   C. Industrial   D. Legal

Answer: B

Difficulty level: Easy

Tag: PESTEL's Political element

Rationale:

The statement defines political policy. Political policy also called government policy, as it can influence firms through legislation and government policy decisions. This question examine the interdependence between government and organisation. You should realise that government could influence organisation though many perspectives.

这句话是政治政策的定义。政治政策也被称为政府政策，因为它能通过立法和政府政策决议来影响企业。这道题考的是政府和组织的相互影响。考生一定要清楚，政府是可以通过很多方面来影响组织的。

2.6 Q Co is one of the best-known internet companies in China, and the CEO of Q Co has announced in the media that "the operation cost of our company is always above budget. I suppose this is because hierarchy level of our company is very high. As our strategic objectives need to be upgraded, the board decides to lay off some middle-line managers because these managers need to make way for young staff."

Which of the following circumstances would happen in this company?

A. Redundancy   B. Downsizing   C. Delayering   D. Outsourcing

Answer: C

Difficulty level: Normal

Tag: PESTEL's Technological element

Rationale:

The CEO of Q Co wants to lower down the hierarchy. In other words, he wants to remove layers of middle management. This should happen in delayering.

Pitfall:

Candidates may hesitate to choose the "downsizing". Downsizing, however, means lay off the staff from the whole levels of the organisation.

考生应当注意那些出现在题目中的关键词，比如，"层级"和"运营成本"。这意味着，Q 公司的 CEO 想降低公司的层级——换句话说，他想移除中间管理层，这就会发生"delayering"。

考生可能会犹豫是否选 downsizing，然后 downsizing 指的是对公司的各个层级进行裁员。

Delayering 强调移除 middle manager，而题干中说"some middle-line manager"。

2.7 Consider the following four statements with respect to outsourcing. **Which of the following statements are correct?**

(1) The dynamics of outsourcing is to remove cost.

(2) The driver of outsourcing comes from the advancement of information technology.

(3) Outsourcing makes operation more and more flexible and complex.

(4) Some operations are too important to outsource, such as accounting and IT services.

A. (1) and (2) only   B. (2) and (3) only   C. (2) and (4) only   D. (2),(3) and (4)

Answer: C

Difficulty level: Normal

Tag: PESTEL's Technological element

Rationale:

Statement (1) is incorrect, as the advantage of outsourcing is removing uncertainty about cost, not removing cost.

Statement (2) is correct, outsourcing is one of the impact of technological factor.

Statement (3) is incorrect, flexibility is one of outsourcing's advantage, and this is correct. However, complex isn't its effect, as outsourcing can make organisation become a simpler organisation.

Statement (4) is correct, it's one of outsourcing's disadvantages.

第一句话是错误的,因为外包的优点是移除了成本的不确定性,而不是移除了成本。

第二句话是正确的,外包是由于技术因素带来的结果和影响,所以推动外包发展的动力是科技。

第三句话是错误的,灵活性是外包的特点,但是外包使得组织变得越来越复杂这是错的,外包会使组织运营变得越来越简单。

第四句话是正确的,这也是外包的缺点。

Chapter 3
The micro-economic environment

知识导入

上一章我们学习了运用 PESTEL 模型分析组织的外部商业环境，接下来我们将把模型中的"E"即 economic factor（经济因素）放大，来了解商业环境中会影响组织的宏微观经济因素。在本章，我们将着重研究 micro-economic environment，欢迎走入微观经济的世界。

单词表

英文	中文
Perfect markets	完全竞争市场
Marginal utility	边际效用
Oligopolies	寡头
Monopolistic competition	垄断竞争
Perfect information	完全信息（信息公开透明）
Complements	互补品
Cross elasticity of demand	需求的交叉弹性
Monopoly	垄断
Barriers to exit	退出壁垒
Perfect complements	完全互补
Equilibrium price	均衡价格
Price mechanism	价格机制
Minimum wages	最低工资
Black market	黑市

学习指南

Learning objectives	Pass level	Distinction level	用时建议
1. Defining microeconomics (1)	√		1 min
2. Basic Concepts of microeconomics (2.1-2.4)	√		10 min
3. Supply and demand (3.1-3.7)	√		25 min
4. The price mechanism and the equilibrium price (4)	√		5 min
5. Maximum and minimum prices (5)	√		10 min
6. Economic behaviour of cost (4)		√	5 min
7. Types of markets (7)	√		10 min

本章考点

重要考点	难度（1~3）
熟记供需之间对价格的影响，理解并能在案例分析中识别运用	3
熟记并理解 PED，IED 和 XED	2
理解最高价格和最低价格的形成原因和运用	2
熟记不同种类市场的特点	3

1 Defining microeconomics

Microeconomics is a branch of economics that studies the behavior of **individuals, firms and industries** in making decisions regarding the **allocation of scarce resources**.

微观经济学（"微观"是希腊文"μικρο"的意译，原意是"小"）又称个体经济学、小经济学，是现代经济学的一个分支，主要以单个经济单位（单个生产者、单个企业、单个市场经济活动）作为研究对象分析的一门学科。

2 Basic concepts of microeconomics

2.1 What is a market?

A market refers to the situation that potential **buyers and sellers** come together for the purpose of **exchanging** with goods or services.

2.2 What is utility?

(a) **Utility**: It describes the **pleasure or satisfaction** as a result of **consumption** of goods or services by a person.

(b) **Marginal utility**: It quantifies the added satisfaction that a consumer gains from consuming additional one unit of goods or services.

(c) **Total utility**: It is the **total** satisfaction that people gain from spending their income.

> **知识点解读**
>
> 这部分会阐述经济学的一些基本概念，在考试中直接考到概率很小，但却是理解微观经济学的重要基础。

> **基本概念**
>
> 效用，是经济学中最常用的概念之一。一般而言，效用是指对于消费者通过消费或者享受闲暇等使自己的需求、欲望等得到的满足的一个度量。

> **基本概念**
>
> 边际效用，是指在一定时间内消费者增加一个单位商品或服务所带来的新增效用，即总效用的增量。也就是说，在其他条件不变的情况下，随着消费者对某种物品消费量的增加，他从该物品连续增加的每一消费单位中所得到的满足程度称为边际效用。

> **基本概念**
>
> 总效用，是指消费一定数量的某种物品得到的总的满足程度。

精益求精

在经济学中，一般情况下**边际效用**是递减的。也就是说，在一定时间内以及其他条件保持不变的条件下，随着消费者对某种商品消费量的增加，消费者从该商品连续增加的每一消费单位中所得到的满意度是逐渐降低的。

比如，大家可以思考这样一个问题：为什么第一口奶茶是最好喝的？对于奶茶爱好者来说，在一天当中，喝第一杯奶茶的时候，这杯奶茶给他带来的效用是很大的。但是随着奶茶摄入量的增加，尽管**总效用**（总满足程度）在持续增加，但此时，每一杯甚至是每一口奶茶所带来的**边际效用**（增加的满足程度）却是递减的，即便对于奶茶深度爱好者来说，也同样如此。并且，当他喝奶茶喝到某个临界值时（比如喝到饱），奶茶的总效用达到最大，但此时如果继续摄入奶茶，大家可以设身处地想一想，会发生什么？ 在这种情况下，边际效用降为零（毫无满足），甚至为负（产生厌恶）。

2.3 Assumptions about consumer rationality

Consumer rationality is the assumption that consumers attempt to obtain the greatest possible satisfaction from limited money they have when making purchases.

> **精益求精**
>
> 消费者在市场上所需要的商品和服务种类繁多并且数量可观。 虽然理想状态是，需要的商品和服务，消费者全都要。 但绝大多数情况下，消费者会遇到一些条件约束，比如有限的收入。 在这种情况下，理性消费者的基本原则就是：在收入的约束下追求效用最大化。 简单来说，即将有限的收入获得最大的满足感。 这也就意味着，消费者应当调整所需要的商品和服务的组合，比如，是买一个包还是出去旅游一次，买一双 AJ 鞋还是入手一台任天堂。
>
> 根据经济学家们的理论，消费者效用最大化可以表现为：消费者最终选择的商品组合，将会使得自己花费在各种商品上的单位货币所带来的边际效用相等（因为如果不相等，作为理性消费者，就会选择能带来更大效用的商品，直到最终不管如何改变选择的商品组合，都只能带来相同的效用为止）。

2.4 What is the Price theory?

The popular viewpoint of price theory examines how **interaction of demand and supply** affects the market prices for goods.

3 Demand and supply

3.1 Introduction

Two important fundamental concepts of microeconomics：

(a) **Individual demand** shows how much of a good or service someone intends to buy at different prices. This demand needs to be **effective**, which means the **consumer should be willing and able to buy**, **rather than just generally desiring them.**

(b) **Individual supply** shows how much of a good or service someone intends to offer at different prices. Similar to demand, supply also need to be effective.

The relationship between supply and demand has a great deal of influence on the price of goods and services. This is normally illustrated by supply and demand curves.

3.2 The demand curve

In economics，the demand curve is the graph depicting the relationship between the price of a certain commodity and the amount of it that consumers are willing and able to purchase at any given price. It is a graphic representation of a market demand schedule.

知识点解读

微观经济学研究的需求，指的是有效的需求，即消费者**有意愿**并且**有能力**购买的需求。
同理，微观经济学研究的供给，也应该是有效的供给，即供应商有意愿并且有能力提供的供给。

核心考点

需求曲线在考试中出现比较频繁。 考核的点集中在以下几点。
（1）需求曲线的形状。
（2）哪些因素引起的需求变化表现为曲线上点的移动；在曲线上上移和下移分别代表什么。
（3）哪些因素会引起的需求变化表现为曲线左右平移；左移和右移分别代表什么。

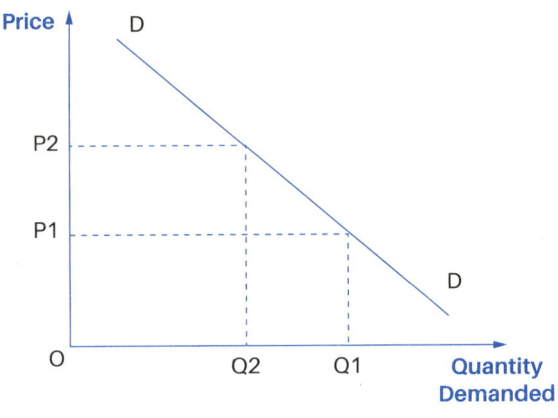

图 3-1 Demand curve

需求曲线是显示价格与需求量关系的曲线,是指其他条件相同时,在每一价格水平上买方愿意购买的商品量的曲线(如图 3-1 所示)。

Demand falls as price increases, demand rises as price falls. This requires the assumption that "all other factors remain constant", which is referred to as *ceteris paribus*.

The diagram above illustrates a normal downward-sloping demand curve. When the demand changes in response to a change in the price of the good, the change is referred to as:

- An **expansion** in demand as demand rises when price falls.
- A **contraction** in demand as demand falls when price rises.

需求曲线通常以价格为纵轴(y 轴),以需求量为横轴(x 轴),对于一般商品来说,其需求曲线呈一条向右下倾斜的直线。 它表示"在其他条件不变"的情况下,商品的**需求量**随该价格上涨而下降。

表 3-1 Point movement along demand curve

Types of effect on demand curve	Factors affecting demand curve	Direction of movement and explanations
Point movement along the demand curve (affecting the **quantity** demanded of a good, which is called **expansion/contraction in demand**)	The **price** of the good, assuming all other factors remain constant	As the price of good increases, the demand quantity for the good decreases, and vice versa

> **核心考点**
> 掌握哪些因素会影响需求量的变化,同时掌握需求曲线的变化(见表 3-1)。

博学多才

英国人吉芬于 19 世纪发现,1845 年爱尔兰发生灾荒,土豆价格上升,但是土豆的需求量却反而增加了。 这一现象在当时被称为"吉芬难题"。 这类需求量与价格成同方向变动的特殊商品以后也因此被称作吉芬物品(Giffen product)。 单就一种现象而言,天底下到处都有吉芬物品或者吉芬现象。 例如,股票、奢侈品等,价格上涨,购买的数量反而会上升。 吉芬物品特殊性在于:它的收入效应超过了它的替代效应。 这也就是吉芬物品的需求曲线呈现出向右上方倾斜的特殊原因。

3.3 Substitutes and complements

A substitute, or substitute good, in economics and consumer theory is a product or service that can be used in place of another.

The demand for substitutes reflects a reverse change which means an increased need of one product will lead to reduced need of another.

Substitution takes place when the price of certain good rises relative to the substitute good.

Examples of substitute goods and services:
- Competitive brands in the same market, like KFC and McDonald.
- Beef and mutton.
- Tea and coffee.

A complement refers to a complementary good or service used in conjunction with another good or service. On the contrary, the demand for two complements reflects a positive change.

Example of complements:
- Vehicles and petrol.
- Toothpaste and toothbrush.

3.4 Factors determining demand for a good

Demand curve only examines the relationship between price of a good and the quantity demanded, assuming other factors remain constant (*ceteris paribus*). Here, these factors, which are called **conditions of demand**, are also considered, **with the price being held constant**.

The effect of changing other factors on demand curve is summarised in the table below (见表 3-2):

表 3-2 Shift of demand curve

Types of effect on demand curve	Factors (conditions of the demand) affecting demand curve	Direction of movement and explanations
Shift of the demand curve (if the shift is to the right, it is called an **increase in demand**; if the shift is to the left, it is called a **decrease in demand**)	**Income** level and **distributable income** level	The demand curve would **shift to the right** if the size/distributable size of income increased, and vice versa
	Price of **substitutes**	The demand curve would **shift to the right** if the price of substitute goods increased, and vice versa
	Price of **complements**	The demand curve would **shift to the left** if the price of complement goods increased, and vice versa
	Tastes and preferences	A change in tastes towards this product would result in the **shift** of demand curve. The demand curve would shift to the right if the product is in line with consumers' taste, and vice versa
	Expectation of future price	The demand curve would **shift to right** if people expect the future price towards this product to increase, and vice versa
	Population	The demand curve would **shift to right** if the population increased, and vice versa

大家一定要区分需求量的变动与需求的变动。

只有本产品价格（price of the good）的变动会导致点的移动，也就是在需求曲线上移动，此时需求量发生变化（point movement-expansion/contraction in demand），而需求曲线不变；而其他因素（conditions of demand）的变化都会导致需求曲线移动（shift-increase/decrease in demand）。

在 3.4 研究了影响商品需求的因素之后，我们开始单独研究某个变量与需求量的关系。在经济学中，我们用弹性来去衡量一个变量相对于另一变量变动的反应度。在 FAB/AB 当中，我们会学习三种弹性。

> **核心考点**
>
> 需求量的变动与需求的变动，这两者的区分在选择题中常常考到，需要大家重视。

> **基本概念**
>
> 需求的价格弹性（Price elasticity of demand，简称 PED），表示的是需求量对价格变动反应程度的指标。PED 有两种计算方式，一种是点弹性（Point elasticity），另一种是弧弹性（Point elasticity），区别主要体现在取值上（如 3.5.1 中的公式所示）。

3.5 Elasticity of demand

Elasticity measures the responsiveness of one variable to a change in another variable.

3.5.1 The price elasticity of demand

表 3-3 PED

PED	Description	Illustration
<1	Relatively inelastic	If the price varies by 10%, then the number of units demanded will vary by **less than** 10%
=1	Unit elastic	If the price varies by 10%, then the number of units demanded will vary by **exactly** 10%
>1	Relative elastic	If the price varies by 10%, then the number of units demanded will vary by **more than** 10%

> **知识点解读**
>
> 对于 PED 计算公式，细心的同学会发现，计算的时候需要加绝对值。这是因为，对于一般商品，我们已经学过，需求曲线为斜向下的曲线，即需求量与价格成反比，所以 PED 算出来即为负数。既然算出来都是负数，就直接加上绝对值，方便研究和比较。

如表 3-3 所示：

当 PED<1 时，也就意味着需求变动的百分比小于价格变动的百分比，此时的需求被称为缺乏弹性，比如刚需品；

当 PED=1 时，也就意味着需求变动的百分比等于价格变动的百分比，此时的需求被称为单位弹性；

当 PED>1 时，也就意味着需求量变动的百分比大于价格变动的百分比，此时的需求被称为富有弹性。

（a）**Arc elasticity** of demand：measure elasticity **between two points on the demand curve**.

PED（arc）——弧弹性测量的是需求曲线上**两点之间**的需求量的变动对于价格的变动的反应程度，也就是需求曲线上两点之间的弹性。

$$PED(arc) = \left| \frac{\frac{Q_2 - Q_1}{(Q_1 + Q_2)/2}}{\frac{P_2 - P_1}{(P_1 + P_2)/2}} \right|$$

（b）**Point elasticity** of demand：measure elasticity at one particular point.

PED（point）——点弹性衡量的是在**某一点**需求量变动率的反应程度（以 Q1/P1 点为例）。

$$PED(point) = \left| \frac{\frac{Q_2 - Q_1}{Q_1}}{\frac{P_2 - P_1}{P_1}} \right|$$

Example question 1

小试牛刀

Example question 1

The price of a good is $2.50 and demand is 900,000 units for one year. If an increase in price of 10 cents per unit will result in a fall in annual demand of 90,000 units.

(1) What is the **arc** price elasticity of demand **over this range**?

(2) What is the **point** elasticity of demand at the current price of $2.50?

3.5.2 The income elasticity of demand

正如之前在学习影响需求的因素时提到的一样，商品的需求不仅会受其本身价格的影响，而且会受到消费者收入的影响，并且不同商品对收入变化的反应是不同的，因此我们会使用需求的收入弹性（income elasticity of demand）来衡量在其他条件不变的时候，消费者对物品需求量相对于收入的敏感程度。

$$\text{Income elasticity of demand (IED)} = \frac{\text{percentage change in demand}}{\text{percentage change in income}}$$

表 3-4 IED

IED	Value	Illustration	Example
Negative	IED<0	Inferior goods	Public transport
Inelastic	0<IED<1	Necessities	Basic food
Elasticity	IED>1	Luxury goods	Yacht

劣质品：指的是 IED 小于 0 的商品，并不代表该商品是质量不好的商品，不要望文生义。

与 PED 不同，IED 是需要关注正负的，不能加绝对值。当 IED 为正时，意味着收入的变化与对该商品的需求量的变化呈同方向波动。同方向波动又可以分成两种情况，一种是处在 0 到 1 之间，此时需求量的变化幅度小于收入的变化幅度，即收入不管变化多少，对该商品的需求量变化幅度很小，对应的是必需品，如五谷杂粮；另一种是大于 1，此时需求量的变化幅度大于收入的变化幅度，即随着收入的变化，对该商品的需求会大幅度变化，对应的是奢侈品，如游艇；当 IED 为负的时候，意味着收入的变化与对该商品的需求量的变化呈反方向波动，如收入增加，对该商品的需求量反而下降，对应的是劣质品，如公共交通、垃圾食品等（如表 3-4 所示）。

3.5.3 Cross elasticity of demand

需求的交叉弹性（cross elasticity of demand）是在其他条件不变的情况下，一种产品的需求对其替代品或互补品价格变动的反应程度的指标。

$$\text{Cross elasticity of demand (XED)} = \frac{\text{percentage change in demand of good A}}{\text{percentage change in price of good B}}$$

表 3-5 XED

Cross elasticity	Comment
XED<0	Complements
XED = 0	Unrelated
XED>0	Substitutes

知识点解读

可以总结出一个简单的结论：
（参见表 3-5）
交叉弹性为负数时，两商品为互补关系；
交叉弹性为正数时，两商品为替代关系。

If cross elasticity equals -1, then the two products are perfect complements;

If cross elasticity equals 1, then the two products are perfect substitutes.

> 博学多才

市场对一种商品的需求受国民收入分配方式的影响。在贫富差距较大，中产阶级占少数的哑铃式社会财富分配结构中，对于优质商品和劣质商品的需求会比较高。相反，在中产阶级占主导的社会财富分配结构中，对生活必需品的需求较大。

3.6 The supply curve

The curve depicts the relationship between two variables: price and quantity supplied. The curve is generally upward-sloping, which illustrates that **supply rises as price increases, supply falls as price falls, if all other factors are assumed constant**.

关于供给曲线的具体描述参见图3-2和表3-6。

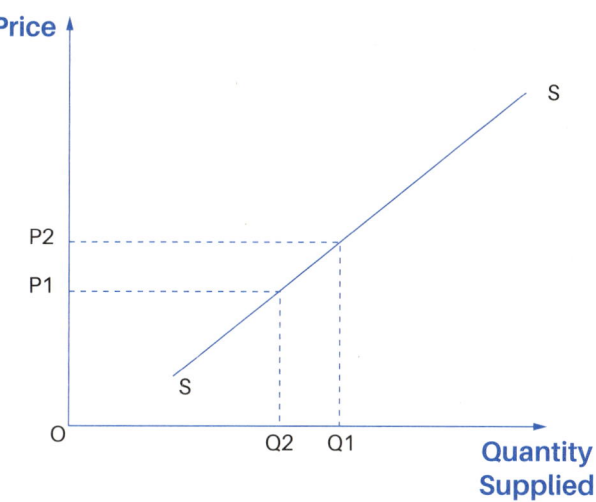

图3-2 Supply curve

表3-6 Point movement of supply curve

Types of effect on supply curve	Factors affecting supply curve	Direction of movement and explanations
Point movement along the supply curve (affecting the **quantity** supplied, which is called expansion/contraction in supply)	The **price** of good	As the price of good increases, the supply quantity for the good increases, and vice versa

知识点解读

对 3.7 这个知识点的理解可以参照 3.4 Factors determine demand for a good。

核心考点

掌握哪些因素会影响供给量以及供给的变化，同时掌握供给曲线的变化（见表3-7）。

Factors that affect the supply quantity

3.7 Factors that affect the supply quantity

表 3-7　Shift of supply curve

Types of effect on supply curve	Factors affecting supply curve (conditions of supply)	Direction of movement and explanations
Shift of the supply curve (if the shift is to the right, it is called an **increase in supply**; if the shift is to the left, it is called a **decrease in supply**)	The costs	The supply curve would **shift to the right** if the costs of making the good decrease, and vice versa
	The prices of other goods	Increase in the price of other goods would lead to decrease in supply of target good whose price no longer seems attractive. The supply curve would **shift to the left**
	Expectations of future price changes	If the expectation of price is to raise, the suppliers would tend to reduce supply (shift to left) while the price is lower and increase supply (shift to right) once the price is higher
	Changes in technology	The supply curve would **shift to the right** supposing the technology improved

4 The price mechanism and the equilibrium price

4.1 The equilibrium price

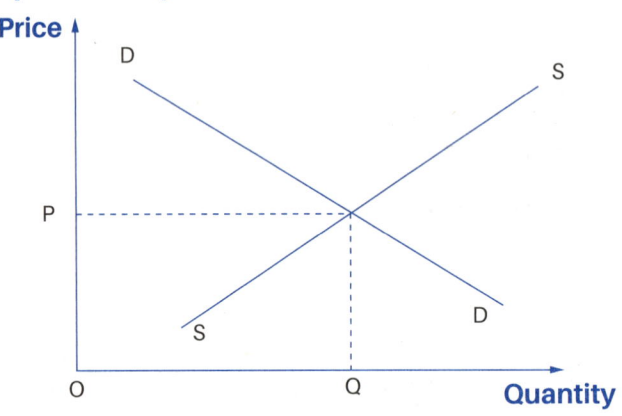

图 3-3　Equilibrium of supply and demand

P is the equilibrium price, and there will only be one equilibrium price（见图3-3）.

4.2 Price mechanism

(a) The supply and demand will push prices towards equilibrium price if the market is in disequilibrium.

(b) The equilibrium price will prevail and remain stable if there is no change.

5 Maximum and minimum price

5.1 Maximum price

A maximum price (**price ceiling**) is sometimes imposed in order to protect

知识点解读

当价格高于P时，供给大于需求，供应商会做出以下调整。
(1) 减少生产: cut down the current level of production。
(2) 降低价格: reduce prices to encourage sales。
相反，当价格低于P时，需求大于供给，供应商则会顺势调高价格，为了逐利，也会生产更多的产品。市场作为一双无形的手就会通过价格机制而达到均衡价格。

consumers. An effective maximum price should be set below the equilibrium price otherwise it would have no effect.

The intent behind implementing such control is usually to maintain affordability of goods even during shortages, and to slow inflation. However, this might result in a situation in which the quantity demanded will exceed the quantity supplied (excess demand-Q1Q2), and an illegal market developing (black market).

> **核心考点**
>
> 最高限价与最低限价造成的后果是考试重点，需要同学们理解。（可参见图 3-4、图 3-5 帮助理解）

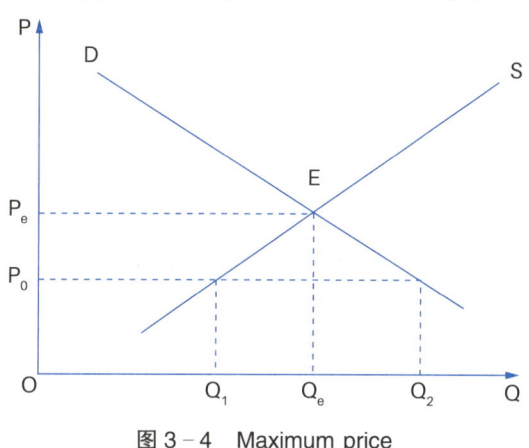

图 3-4　Maximum price

最高价格政策的制定会导致供不应求，为了防止不均等分配商品，政府只能配额供应，如果想要"插队"提前拿到商品，只能借助黑市了。

5.2 Minimum price

A minimum price (**price floor**) is sometimes imposed in order to **protect producers/suppliers**. Here, the quantity supplied will exceed the quantity demanded (excess supply-Q1Q2), provided the minimum price is set above the equilibrium price. As a result, there will be excess supply and waste of resources.

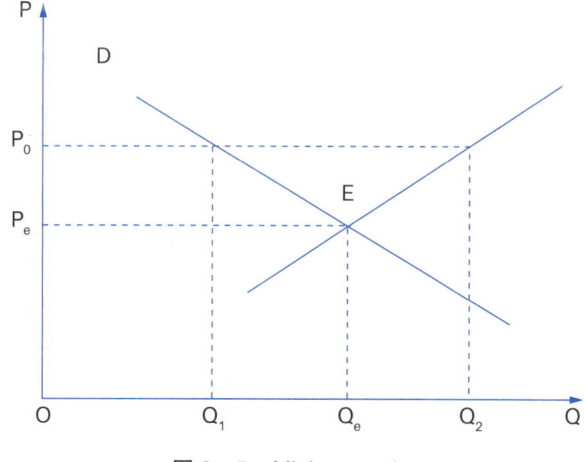

图 3-5　Minimum price

博学多才

20 世纪 50 年代，由于欧洲地区农业生产不足，市场上出现严重的短缺，从而引起了一系列的市场干预。例如，政府通过确保乳制品最低干预价格来补贴牛奶生产，这导致牛奶、黄油和相关产品的供给量激增，直到 20 世纪 70 年代后期产量超过需求，市场上出现严重的供大于求。 仅联邦德国的牛奶产量就从 1960 年的 7500 万吨增加到 1979 年的近 1 亿吨，出售不掉的牛奶堆积成河，卖不掉的黄油堆积成山，这就是我们所说的 "butter mountain"。 无独有偶，在美国经济大萧条时期，发生了类似的事情，政府为了促进生产给予商户补贴，商人的逐利性驱使他们尽可能地扩大生产，从而获得补贴，至于是否能卖得出去，商人们则不会考虑。 在这种情况下，大量的资源被浪费，尤其像牛奶这样的商品，卖不出去就只好倒进河中，甚至传言整条密西西比河都被牛奶染成了银色，被戏称为"银河"。

5.2.1 Minimum wage

The purpose of minimum wage is to ensure that low-paid workers can maintain an acceptable standard of living. Government will set a minimum wage which is usually **above** the current market level.

为什么最低工资会导致失业？ 比如，美国国会规定了最低工资，原意是希望增加贫困工人的收入，在这样一个劳动力价格（工资）水平下，劳动者更愿意提供劳动力，而公司老板们在这个价格水平下就不愿意找人了，需求减少了，愿意提供的岗位就少了，劳动力市场供过于求，这就意味着一部分人失业。 还会出现一些非法劳工，有人为了生存愿意以低于政府规定的工资去工作。

小试牛刀

Example question 2

The government has imposed a maximum price on basic foodstuffs in order to protect consumers.

Which **two** of the following are potential consequences of this measure?

    A. Excess supply   B. Black market

    C. Excess demand   D. Increased tax revenues

6 The economic behaviour of costs

Microeconomics not only study the relationship between prices and supply/demand of goods and services, but also research how costs will vary over time. According to the span of time, it can be divided by short-run and long-run costs.

6.1 Short-term cost behaviour

In the short run, costs can be classified as fixed costs which do not change by other factors and variable costs which vary by quantities.

It is implied that to certain amount of production, average fixed cost per unit will fall with the increase of production, while the variable cost per unit remains constant. As a result, the average cost per unit also falls. However, it should be noted that total fixed cost will increase if the production is beyond certain amount. Under such situation, the total cost per unit will rise due to increase of both fixed and variable cost, following **the law of diminishing returns**.

6.2 Long-term cost behaviour

In the long term, all costs are variable in nature no matter they are variable or fixed before. This is because it is now possible to change the quantities of any factors that were fixed in the short term.

It means that organisations will become inefficient due to some factors like poor management or pressure of supplies when they pursue expansion of businesses. Eventually, the average cost of production will increase. This effect could be referred to **diseconomies of scale**.

7 Types of markets

There are four main assumptions on different types of markets in micro-economic models.

7.1 Perfect markets

完全竞争市场是指一种竞争完全不受任何阻碍和干扰的**理想情况下的市场**，现实中的市场都不具备这些特点，因而都不是完全竞争市场。现实商业世界中，农产品市场是最接近完全竞争市场。例如，农产品市场中，买方卖方数量众多，但没有任何一方能主导市场价格；市场上的商品几乎同质，尤其在当今交通极为便利的状况下，农产品市场上的商品流通毫无障碍。

A perfectly competitive market is one in which:
(a) There are **many** buyers and sellers;
(b) The products/service sold are **homogeneous** (**identical**);
(c) There are **no barriers to enter** into the market **or exit** from the market;
(d) Both producers and consumers have **perfect information** of the market.

Under such conditions, the price and level of output will always tend towards equilibrium as any producer that sets a price above equilibrium will not sell anything at all, and any producer that sets a price below equilibrium will obtain 100% market share. The demand "curve" is perfectly elastic, which means that it will be horizontal.

在完全竞争市场，由于大量买者与卖者的存在，某个卖者抬价，顾客就会去别的卖者那里购买所需的商品；同样，他降低商品的售价，虽然可招来顾客，但因他的供给量微不足道，结果并不会因他的商品已售完而使市场上的总需求受到影响。对于买者方面，个别买者抬高买价，招来卖者向他出售商品，但他的需求影响不了市场总需求与总供给，结果也就对市场价格产生不了影响；他压低物价，卖者就不向他出售商品。这样一来，商品的市场价格既定，任何买者与卖者都只能是价格的接受者（price taker），只能根据价格行事，而无法对市场价格施加任何可以看得见的影响。

7.2 Imperfect markets

Perfect market is seen as the "ideal" market position. If any of the factors above do not realise, the market will be described as the imperfect one.

You need to be aware of three specific forms of imperfect market. Each of these forms depends on **how organisations compete within the market**.

不完全市场包括垄断竞争、寡头垄断和完全垄断。

7.2.1 Monopolistic competition

Monopolistic competition arises in markets where there are **many producers**,

> **核心考点**
>
> 需要根据题目描述的特征辨别是何种 imperfect markets。
> 特别要区别 monopolistic competition 和 oligopoly，前者指的是整个市场有 many producers with fewer barriers，后者是 a few dominant producers with significant barriers。

but they will tend to use **product differentiation** to distinguish themselves from other producers. Therefore, although their products may be very similar, their ability to differentiate means that they can act as monopolies in the short run. There tends to be fewer barriers to entry or exit than in oligopolistic markets.

垄断竞争市场的主要特点在于，这个市场既存在有限度的垄断（特定细分市场），又存在着不完全的竞争。这一特点表现在价格方面，就是价格的差异。

7.2.2 Oligopolies

An oligopoly arises when there **are few producers** who exert considerable influence in a market. As there are few producers, they are likely to have a high level of knowledge about the actions of their competitors and should be able to predict responses to changes in their strategies. The minimum number of firms in an oligopoly is two, and this particular form of oligopoly is called "duopoly".

It is frequently noted that their characteristics include complex use of product differentiation, significant barriers to entry and a high level of influence on prices in the market.

在寡头垄断市场上，每家厂商的产量都占有相当大的份额，从而每一厂商对整个行业的价格都有举足轻重的影响。

7.2.3 Monopoly

Monopoly occurs when **one** company controls all or nearly all of the market for a particular product or service and has no major competitors.

The key features include:

(a) **Only one major supplier** in the market.

(b) **No close substitutes.**

(c) **The supplier has high power to determine prices**.

High barriers to entry and government legislation are main factors that lead to monopoly.

完全垄断市场最大的特征是，在市场上有且只有一家厂商可以提供某商品，并且没有接近的替代品。众所周知，"物以稀为贵"，在这种情况下，这家唯一的厂商对价格就有名正言顺的发言权了。大家可以设身处地思考一下，如果你是这家独一无二的厂商，你会给商品制定怎样的价格？必然是把价格保持在较高水平上，以获取最大利润了。

Example question 3

Which of the following is the characteristic of perfect competition?

  A. Few producers

  B. Horizontal demand curve

  C. Difficult for new firms to enter the market

  D. Significant influence over the prices of the goods and services that they sell

Example question 4

Which of the following is the characteristic of oligopoly?

A. Few producers
B. Many customers and producers
C. Products or service is identical
D. Perfect information

Answers for example question

1. (1) PED = 2.68
   (2) PED = 2.5
2. BC
3. B
4. A

Summary

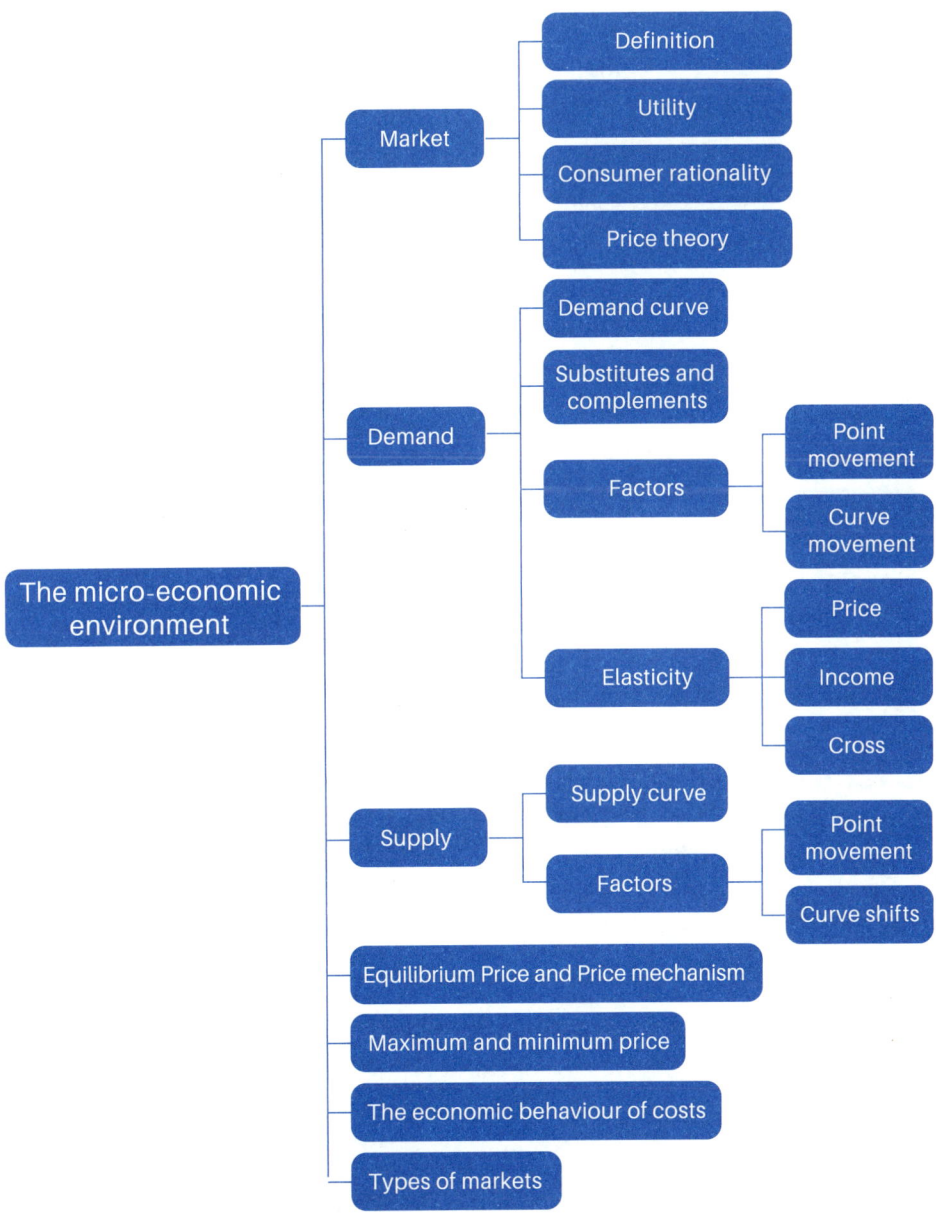

Chapter 3 考试不同问法总结

1. 针对 PED/IED/XED 的计算
- Calculate the price/cross elasticity of demand for the product when the price increases from _____ to _____.
- Which of these items will have a price elasticity of demand of less than one?

2. 针对不同 markets 的定义、分类和特征
- Which of the following is an essential feature of any definition of marketing?
- Which two of the following are characteristics of a perfectly competitive market?
- Select the graphs for the following types of market? (Section B)
- Are the following characteristics of perfect competition or oligopoly?

3. 针对 maximum price 和 minimum price 的意义
- Which two of the following are potential consequences of maximum price?

4. 针对 demand/supply curve
- Select the graph which shows an increase in/on the demand/supply for the product? (Section B)
- Indicate which diagram represents the effect of an increase in personal income/taxation/…?

Quick quiz

3.1 Consider the following statements with respect to demand curve. Which of the following statement is wrong?

   A. Changes in the conditions of demand would create shifts in the demand curve, such as fashion and tastes, etc.

   B. Expansion of demand or contraction of demand for a good are caused solely by changes in its price, rather than variations in the conditions of demand (*ceteris paribus*)

   C. Quantity demanded is affected by price, depicted as a movement along the demand curve

   D. Expansion of demand or contraction of demand for a good are caused by variations in the conditions of demand (*ceteris paribus*)

Answer: D

Difficulty level: Normal

Tag: Demand curve

Rationale:

This question examines the difference between a change in quantity demanded and a shift of the demand curve. That is fundamentally important in this chapter. Candidates should always bear in mind that quantity demanded is only affected by price, and this is depicted as a movement along the demand curve (contractions or expansions) for a good. However, changes in the conditions of demand (*ceteris paribus*) would create shifts in the demand curve.

这道题考查了需求量与需求影响因素的不同，这是本章最基础最重要的知识点。考生应该牢记，需求量只受价格因素影响，在需求曲线上描述为需求数量组合点沿着一条既定的需求曲线的运动。然而，需求会受到其他因素变动的影响，在图形中表现为需求曲线的平行移动。

3.2 Suppose the price of Coca-Cola increases from $1.00 per bottle to $1.30 and the quantity of Pepsi purchased increases from 1000 to 1210 bottles.

   Which of following statements regarding to cross elasticity of demand (XED) is right?

   A. The cross elasticity of demand is 1, they are perfect substitutes

   B. The cross elasticity of demand is 0.7, they are highly substituted

   C. The cross elasticity of demand is −1, they are perfect complements

   D. The cross elasticity of demand is −0.7, they are high complementary

Answer: B

Difficulty level: Normal

Tag: The cross elasticity of demand

Rationale:

 =0.7, therefor, they are highly substituted. 本题考查交叉弹性的计算和理解。

3.3 In a developed country, due to rapidly rising house price, the government has applied price controls over housing price for a number of years.

   Which of the following consequences should now occur?

   (1) Regulated price is below equilibrium price.

   (2) A minimum price for a good has been imposed.

(3) Government might set a price ceiling for the house.

(4) There will be excess supply.

A. Consequences (1) and (3)
B. Consequences (2) and (3)
C. Consequences (2) and (4)
D. Consequences (1) and (4)

Answer: A

Difficulty level: Normal

Tag: Maximum and minimum prices

Rationale:

As the government wants to prevent housing price rising, a maximum price (price ceiling) will be set below equilibrium price. This is because if the maximum price is above the equilibrium price, maximum price will have no effect on controlling inflation at all. When this is the case, there will be an excess of demand over supply.

因为政府想要控制房价，所以会设置最高价格，最高价格也被称为价格上限（price ceiling）。 最高价格会在市场均衡价格以下，因为如果最高价格定在均衡价格以上，最高定价就会变得毫无意义。 如果最高定价低于市场均衡价格的话，那么就会出现供不应求的局面。

3.4 Devil was married and has a half-year-old child. Recently, the prices of all goods have increased by 25% in Devil's city.

Which TWO of below items will have a price elasticity of demand (PED) of less than 1 for Devil?

A. Milk powder B. Limited watch C. Baby diapers D. Luxury cars

Answer: A, C

Difficulty level: Easy

Tag: The price elasticity of demand (PED)

Rationale:

When PED <1, it means that percentage change in demand of those goods is less than percentage change in price, such as necessities. When PED>1, it means percentage change in demand is more than percentage change in price, like luxury goods.

这道题考查的是需求的价格弹性。 PED 小于 1，意味着需求变化的百分比小于价格变化的百分比，比如必需品对于 Devil 而言，包括尿不湿、奶粉。 而 PED 大于 1，意味着需求变化的百分比大于价格变化的百分比，比如奢侈品，也就是选项中的限量手表、高级汽车等。

3.5 Which of the following represents a company's demand curve in a perfect market?

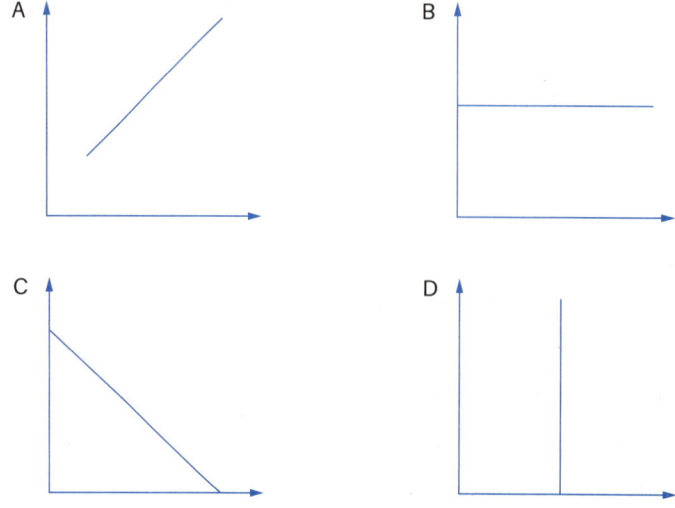

Answer: B

Difficulty level: Normal

Tag: Types of market-perfect market

Rationale:

Perfect market is seen as the "ideal" market position. And it has some main characteristics: none of whom have the power to dominate the market; the products or services sold by all suppliers are same. Therefore, perfect market is showed in the graph is option B.

完全竞争市场中，由于厂商数目很多，资源具有完全的流动性，信息是完全的。每个厂商对产品价格没有影响，即如果厂商单独改变产品价格，那么产品的市场价格不会改变。因此，厂商是既定价格的接受者，在任意产量水平上产品价格都是固定的，即厂商面临的需求曲线是水平的。或者也可以这样理解：由于厂商数目众多且产品完全同质，如果某个厂商单独提高价格，那么消费者肯定会去购买其他厂商的商品。所以，此时厂商的需求曲线呈水平状态。

3.6 Due to rumours of increased prices of necessities, the government of Y Country has issued a maximum price on necessities.

Which Two of the following are potential consequences of this policy?

A. Excess supply
B. Excess demand
C. Black market
D. Wastage of necessities

Answer: B, C

Difficulty level: Easy

Tag: The maximum prices

Rationale:

The maximum prices issued by government will lead to two consequences: excess demand and black market.

这道题考查的是最高价格的设立会导致的潜在结果。政府设立最高价格会导致两个结果：过量的需求，也就是供不应求，以及会导致黑市的出现。因为有过量的需求，所以对于想要获取商品的消费者而言，他们可能会选择非法渠道去获得，也就是黑市。

3.7 The demand of Pepsi coke will fluctuate by lots of factors. Which of the following will lead an increase of demand of Pepsi?

A. The national income decreases
B. The price of coke cola increases
C. Future prices of Pepsi coke are expected to decrease
D. The price of Pepsi coke decreases

Answer: B

Difficulty level: Normal

Tag: The demand curve

Rationale:

Many factors can affect demand for a good. And only changes of the price of the good will lead to **point movement** and other factors change will lead the demand curve **shift.**

这道题考查的是哪些因素会影响需求的变化以及每个因素的变化会如何影响需求曲线。这里同学们只需要记住一个结论：**只有本产品价格的变动会导致点的移动，也就是需求量的变化，最终使得点在需求曲线上移动，而需求曲线不变。**而其他因素的变化都会导致需求曲线移动。D 选项，Pepsi coke 价格下降即为本商品的价格变化，只会引起**需求量**的变化，而题目问的是 increase in demand，即**需求**的变化，所以 D 选项并不正确，AC 选项均导致需求下降，最终答案选 B。

Chapter 4
The macro-economic environment

知识导入

在上一章中，我们研究了 economic factor（经济因素）中的 micro-economic（微观经济），微观经济的相关内容中有个非常重要的单词 individual,，意味着微观经济的研究对象以单个经济体为主。 在这一章中，我们要研究的宏观经济就是这些单个经济体的总和。 欢迎走入宏观经济的世界。

单词表

英文	中文
Full employment	充分就业
Aggregate supply	总供给
Aggregate demand	总需求
Inflation	通货膨胀
Deflation	通货紧缩
Stagflation	滞胀
Business cycle	经济周期
Balance of payments effects	进出口平衡
Consumer Prices Index（CPI）	居民消费品价格指数
Frictional unemployment	摩擦性失业
Structural unemployment	结构性失业
Cyclical unemployment	经济周期型失业
Current account	经常账户
Capital account	资本账户
Fiscal policy	财政政策
Budget deficit	预算赤字
Budget surplus	预算盈余
Monetary policy	货币政策

学习指南

Learning objectives	Pass level	Distinction level	用时建议
1. Defining macroeconomics（1）	√		1 min
2. Objectives of government macroeconomic policies（2）	√		5 min
3. Inflation and its consequences（3）	√		15 min
4. Unemployment(4)	√		10 min
5. The balance of payment(5)	√		10 min

Learning objectives	Pass level	Distinction level	用时建议
6. Economic growth(6)	√		10 min
7. The circular flow of income and expenditure (7)		√	10 min
8. Fiscal policy (8)	√		10 min
9. Monetary policy(9)	√		10 min

本章考点

重要考点	难度（1~3）
熟记 macroeconomics 的定义	1
熟记宏观调控的 4 个目标，理解并能运用	3
熟记并理解宏观调控的两个政策	3
理解 circular flow of income and expenditure	2

1 Definition

Macroeconomics is a branch of economics dealing with the performance, structure, behaviour, and decision-making of an **economy as a whole** rather than individual markets. (O'Sullivan, Arthur; Sheffrin, Steven M., 2003)

宏观经济学（宏观是希腊文"makro"的意译，原意是"大"）是用国民收入、经济整体的投资和消费等总体性的统计概念来分析经济运行规律的一个经济学领域。

2 Objectives of government macroeconomic policies

宏观经济调控指的是，当市场自发调节机制（"看不见的手"）没有带来最大经济效益时，政府会伸出"有形的手"，如通过一系列宏观政策进行干预。最终想实现的目标，即宏观经济调控的目标，包括控制通胀、实现充分就业、实现国际收支平衡以及达到经济增长。

While some economists advocate a free market (one without government interference), in reality most governments intervene through various macroeconomic policies in an attempt to improve the performance of the economy. **Their main objectives are typically**:

(a) To **control price inflation**. This means to achieve stable prices.
(b) To **achieve full employment**. It implies a low unemployment level, other than that everyone has a job.
(c) To **achieve a balance between exports and imports**. The balance refers to the balance of country's payments accounts.
(d) To **achieve economic growth**, and growth in national income per capita of the population. The aim is to achieve a real growth, an increase in national

> **知识点解读**
> 充分就业（full employment），是指在某一工资水平之下，所有愿意接受工作的人，都获得了就业机会，而不是所有人都获得就业。

income, rather than the nominal one which may be caused by inflation.

在学习了宏观经济调控的 4 个目标之后，我们开始逐个仔细学习每个目标的含义及相关理论。

3 Inflation and its consequences

3.1 The definition of inflation

Inflation is the **rise in the prices** of goods and services **within an economy over time**. It reduces the purchasing power of money, meaning that each unit of currency buys fewer goods and services.

3.2 Why is inflation a problem?

（A）**Redistribution of income and wealth**

In respect of transaction by credit, redistribution of wealth might occur among receivable and payable. It means the same amount of receivable is collected, however, the real value (e.g. purchasing power) has been compromised.

（B）**Balance of payments effects**

If the rate of inflation in a country is higher than its major trading country, its export will suffer. In the long term, exchange rate will fluctuate.

（C）**Uncertainty of the value of money and prices**

It is very difficult to determine how inflation will affect the real value of money, thus more labour cost and research cost occur.

（D）**Economic growth and investment**

The existence of inflation may boost the economic growth, which is not real growth. Simply speaking, such economic growth may draw an artificial prosperity.

3.3 How to measure inflation?

(a) Retail Prices Index (RPI).
(b) Consumer Prices Index (CPI).

博学多才

商品零售价格指数（Retail Price Index）是指反映一定时期内商品零售价格变动趋势和变动程度的相对数。零售物价的调整变动直接影响到城乡居民的生活支出和国家的财政收入，居民购买力和市场供需平衡，消费与积累的比例。因此，计算 RPI，可以从一个侧面观察和分析经济活动并判断通货膨胀情况。

消费者物价指数（Consumer Prices Index）反映与居民生活有关的商品及劳务价格统计出来的物价变动指标，通常作为观察通货膨胀水平的重要指标。如果消费者物价指数升幅过大，表明通胀已经成为经济不稳定因素，央行会有紧缩货币政策和财政政策的风险，从而造成经济前景不明朗。因此，该指数过高的升幅往往不被市场欢迎。

核心考点

如果 A 国的通货膨胀率高于 B 国，意味着 A 国出口价相对高，进口价相对低，从而有利于 A 国进口，不利于出口。
久而久之，出口行业和进口商品替代品行业的就业率可能会下降。如果情况加剧，可能导致本国货币相对贬值，汇率下降。

知识点解读

通货膨胀导致货币购买力下降，降低居民实际收入，进而使全社会的储蓄和资金积累下降，这必然会降低对生产经营的投资，导致经济增长率低下。
同时，货币贬值会导致人们蜂拥抢购那些能够保值增值的实物资产如黄金、外汇、珠宝、房产等，势必冲击正常的经济活动。

3.4 Causes of inflation

表 4–1 Causes of inflation

Causes of inflation	Possible solutions
Demand pull—results from an increase in aggregate demand	Reduces aggregate demand (AD)—e.g. tax rises, cut in government spending, increase in interest rates
Cost push—results from an initial increase in costs. Two main increase factors are labour costs and raw materials price.	Get agreement from trade unions not to demand higher wages. Take steps to strengthen domestic currency
Imported—caused by heavy reliance on imports and weak national currency	Encourage firms to use domestic products instead. Strengthen currency
Monetary—over expansion in money supply	Restrict growth in money supply—e.g. issue fewer currency, increase interest rates
Expectation—e.g. anticipation of rising prices leads people to demand higher wages	Prices and income policy

> **核心考点**
> 通胀的形成原因（见表 4–1）是常见考点。考生需要理解并记忆不同的形成原因。

> **知识点解读**
> Prices policy 是指政府为了影响货币收入或物价水平而采取的措施，其目的通常是为了降低物价的上涨速度。
> Income policy 是政府为降低一般价格水平上升的速度而采取的强制性或非强制性的限制工资和价格的政策，其目的在于影响或控制价格、货币工资和其他收入的增长率，是货币政策和财政政策以外的一种政府行为。

4 Unemployment

Unemployment occurs when people are **willing and able** to work but cannot find a job.

$$\text{Unemployment rate} = \frac{\text{Number of unemployed labour}}{\text{Total workforce}}$$

界定失业人员的标准为有意愿工作并且有能力工作但是尚未找到工作的人。例如，被裁员的 A 某，有能力有意愿工作，在尚未找到工作之前，都属于失业人口（unemployment）。但如果 A 某放弃了寻找工作，这就属于失去意愿，此时他就不再被划归为 unemployment。

4.1 Consequences of unemployment

(a) The government will suffer a loss of income from income tax and VAT, as well as increased unemployment benefits payments.

(b) When there is high unemployment, people's basic living standards may be affected, which may lead to social turbulence.

(c) In the long-term, national economy will suffer.

4.2 Categories of unemployment

(a) **Real wage**: **Trade unions** try to keep the wages high to protect employees' benefit, but the high level discourages the employers' demand, and the number of jobs is reduced.

(b) **Frictional**: It is a typical short-term unemployment. It is due to the information asymmetry in the labour market, which results people hard to re-enter the labour force when changing jobs.

(c) **Seasonal**: It is related to predictable cycles in demand of **certain industry**, for example, tourism and agriculture.

> **核心考点**
> 失业的分类在考试中极为常见。但考核方法比较直接，因此考生只需要掌握每种失业类型的含义，理解并记忆，除此之外，能够判断哪些失业类型是长期的，哪些是短期的即可。

(d) **Structural**: Such unemployment is usually caused by the mismatching between skills required by employers and that possessed with employees. And such gap cannot be filled in short term, therefore, the structural unemployment is usually classified as long-term one.

(e) **Technological**: It is a form of structural unemployment. It is long-term unemployment due to occurrence of new technologies.

(f) **Cyclical**: It is related to **business cycle**. That's when demand for goods and services fall dramatically, for example, during economic recession or depression. Businesses are forced to reduce large numbers of workers to cut costs.

4.3 Government employment policies

Government can adopt the following methods to adjust the unemployment rate:

(a) Increasing capital spent on both of creating jobs directly by government itself and encouraging growth of private sector, which can also create job vacancies.

(b) Providing training for people to increase their employability.

(c) Improving information flow to encourage labour mobility.

(d) Lowering minimum wage to encourage employers to expand recruitment.

5 The balance of payment

A country's balance of payments records all financial transactions made between individuals, businesses and its government with foreign consumers and organisations.

5.1 Current account and capital account

The balance of payments is mainly split into three parts:

(a) Current account (import and export of goods and services).

(b) Capital account (net change in ownership of foreign assets, such as **loan between the government and other countries**).

(c) Financial account.

Often when people talk about the balance of payments, they are just referring to the surplus or deficit on imports and exports—the current account.

5.2 The equilibrium in the balance of payment

The equilibrium exists if the annual trade of goods and services is in overall balance over a period of years and the exchange rate is stable.

Generally, governments would like to run an equilibrium balance of payment. However, in the real world, the equilibrium hardly happens.

5.3 Surplus and deficit in the current account

(a) **Deficit** (**export<import**, currency will **depreciate**)

There is a net cash outflow from the country thus the country will drain its

---

知识点解读

Current account（经常账户）和 capital account（资本账户）的区别，可简单记住：capital account 反映的是政府之间的金钱的往来，比如政府之间的贷款，而我们日常所说的国际收支平衡，指的都是 current account 的平衡，也就是对外贸易进出口平衡。对于 financial account（金融账户）了解即可，不是考试重点，该账户是指一国经济体对外资产和负债所有权变更的所有权交易。

reserves.

如果一个国家经常出现贸易赤字现象，为了支付进口的债务，必须要在市场上卖出本币以购买他国的货币来支付出口国的债务，这样，国民收入便会流出国外，使国家经济表现转弱。 政府若要改善这种状况，就必须要把国家的货币贬值，因为币值下降，即变相把出口商品价格降低，可以提高出口产品的竞争能力。 因此，当该国外贸赤字扩大时，就会利淡该国货币，令该国货币下跌。

(b) **Surplus**（**export**>**import**, currency will **appreciate**）

There is a net cash inflow into the country, which could increase aggregate demand, and can lead to problems like inflation.

当出现外贸盈余时，则是利好该种货币的。

知识点解读

可以简单记忆：
当出口小于进口，也就意味着贸易收入小于贸易支出，从而导致逆差，在经常账户上会反映为赤字。 这种情况往往会带来货币贬值这样的连锁反应。
反之，当进口小于出口，也就意味着贸易支出小于贸易收入，因此会导致顺差，在经常账户上会反映为盈余。 这种情况往往会带来货币升值这样的连锁反应。

精益求精

国际贸易状况是影响外汇汇率十分重要的因素。 日美之间的贸易摩擦充分说明了这一点。 美国对日本的贸易连年出现逆差，致使美国贸易收支恶化。 为了限制日本对美贸易的顺差，美国政府对日施加压力，迫使日元升值。 而日本政府则千方百计阻止日元升值过快，以保持较有利的贸易状况。 同样地，关于人民币升值的问题也有这方面的类似情况。

6 Economic growth

6.1 Aggregate supply and aggregate demand

(a) Aggregate supply (AS) refers to the total amount of goods and services (real output) produced and supplied by an economy's firms over a period of time.
(b) Aggregate demand (AD) is the total planned or desired consumption demand in the economy for consumer goods and services and also for capital goods. AD can be calculated as the sum of government spending (G), investment (I), consumption (C) and net export (N_x). That is：

$$AD = G + I + C + N_x$$

6.2 Measurement of economic growth

Economic growth can be measured by two indicators：
(a) **GDP-**Gross domestic product.
(b) **GNP-**Gross national product.

小试牛刀

Example question 1

Which of the following statements not directly increase aggregate demand in the economy?

  A. Investment in capital goods   B. Government spending
  C. Consumption   D. Savings

Additionally, national income can also be used to evaluate economic growth.

基本概念

国内生产总值，是指一定时期内一国境内所有劳务和商品的总和。 它强调地域。
国民生产总值，是指一定时期内一国公民所创造的商品和劳务的总和。 它强调国籍。

核心考点

掌握5种不同状态类型国民收入的成因和影响（见表4-2）。

表 4-2 Different types of national income

National income	AD & AS	Employment of resource	Changes in price
Equilibrium	AD=AS		
Full-employment	AD=AS	Full employment	
Inflationary gap	AD>AS	Full employment	Price increase
Deflationary gap	AS changes as AD varies	Unemployment	Price constant
Stagflation		High unemployment	Price increase

Different types of national income

Inflationary gap（通胀缺口），指的是经济体已经充分就业（full employment），即所有能利用的资源都利用完了，依然 AD 大于 AS，从而形成了需求缺口，供不应求，此时会伴随通货膨胀，AD 增加的越多，通货膨胀越严重。

Deflationary gap（通缩缺口），指的是经济体还没达到充分就业，即还有可投入的资源，这意味着此时 AS 是大于 AD 的，如果 AD 增加，AS 完全可以随着 AD 的增加而变化，大致上 AD 可以等于 AS，那此时价格就会相对平稳。

Stagflation（滞胀现象），在经济学特指经济停滞（Stagnation）与高通货膨胀（Inflation），失业以及不景气同时存在的经济现象。通俗地说，就是指物价上升，但经济停滞不前。它是通货膨胀长期发展的结果。

6.3 Business/trade/economic cycle

在市场经济条件下，关注自身是远远不够的，大环境的重要性不可小觑。前几章我们学习的环境分析模型更多的是应对方法，但倘若能够对大环境进行前瞻性的分析，对企业而言，就可以有足够的时间积极应对外部环境，把握机会，规避风险，增强自身优势，更好地在市场上活动。因此，企业家们越来越多关心"经济大气候"的变化，也就是经济周期的变化。经济周期的各个阶段如图 4-1 所示。

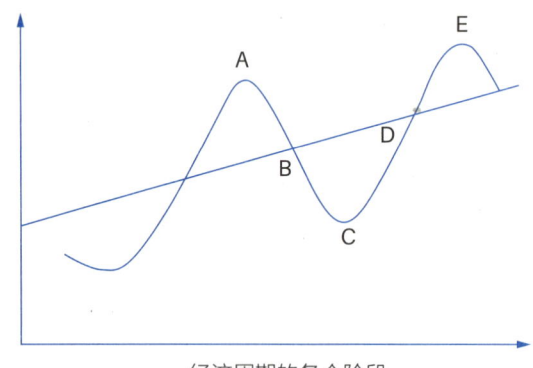

经济周期的各个阶段

图 4-1 Business cycle

(a) Recession (A-B)：
- Decrease：demand；household consumption，companies' output.
- Increase：unemployment.

(b) Depression (B-C)：
- Low：Business confidence；aggregate demand.
- High：Unemployment.

(c) Recovery (C-D):
- Decrease: Unemployment.
- Increase: New technology; demand; firms invest; income level.

(d) Boom (D-E):
- Nearly full capacity in economy.

总的来说，随着时间推进与文明进步，一国产出一定会增加，但并不是直线增加的，而是螺旋循环式增加的，经济周期大致可以分成衰退期、萧条期、复苏期以及繁荣期。

博学多才

乘数效应是一种宏观的经济效应，也是一种宏观经济控制手段，是指经济活动中某一变量的增减所引起的经济总量变化的连锁反应程度。简单来说，乘数效应意味着产出会比投入更多。原理很简单。以生活中很常见的一件事情——政府拨款修路为例。修路带来的一系列后续活动包括：向供应商采购原材料，供应商取得货款后或继续投入运营，或投入消费，无论哪一种都会促进下一步经济活动。除了购买原材料，还需要招募工人提供劳务服务，工人取得劳务费用之后，或投资或消费，都同样促进了经济的发展。公路修好之后能带动当地运输业、农业、旅游业等相继发展。因此，不难发现，一笔修路的投入，带来的后续经济效应远不止初期的投入，这就是典型的乘数效应。

博学多才

经济增长虽然是社会发展的重要基础，但事实上，经济增长尤其是过速的经济增长反而还会带来一些负面效应。比如，曾经一度被称为"雾都"的伦敦，这里的"雾"并不是一个浪漫的字眼，它指的是对人有害的一种烟雾，被称为"伦敦雾"。至于形成原因，除了这个城市本身的天气因素之外，更多的也是由于19世纪末期工业革命的崛起，导致城市的用煤量骤增，城市基建的发电、居民的取暖、工厂的生产等，无一不是依靠煤炭。煤炭燃烧之后，会生成一些有害物质，排放到大气，与空气中的水滴、粉尘、雾气等凝结之后，从而形成了会对人身健康造成严重影响的"伦敦雾"。众所周知，这场工业革命大幅度地促进了经济的发展，但也的确造成了一些非常恶劣的影响。

7 The circular flow of income and expenditure

在学习具体的宏观经济调控的政策之前，我们先学习宏观调控的原理，即如何通过调控经济圈中现金流的多少，来调控总需求，从而调控整个宏观经济。

The circular flow of income and expenditure

If there are **only** firms and households in economy system, then the households will spend the whole of what they have earned on firms' goods and service. This is a circular flow between consumption and income.

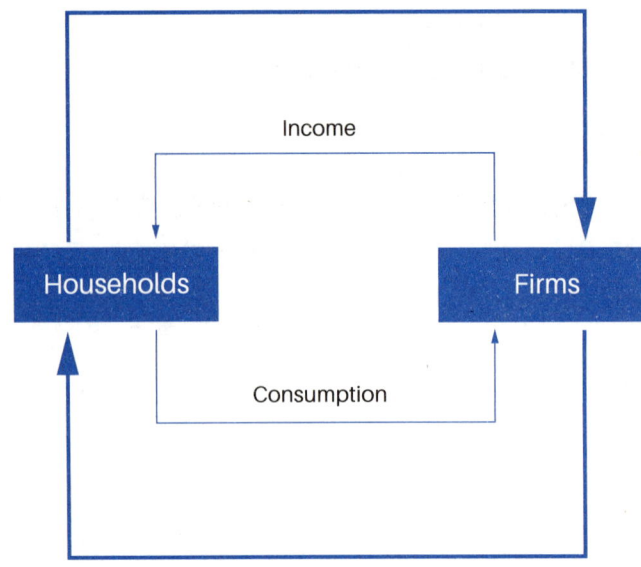

图4-2 Circular of cash flow in economic cycle-1

在整个经济圈只有居民和企业的时候，居民在企业工作，提供生产要素（factors of production），企业则能如期生产产品和服务（goods and service），这是外圈的循环；再看内圈现金流的循环，企业会定期给居民支付工资，收入使得现金从企业流向居民，而居民会将所有赚的钱都用于购买企业的生产的商品和服务（此时假设整个经济体只存在居民与企业），此时现金又从居民手中流向了企业，构成了完整闭合的经济圈循环（见图4-2）。

However, when taking other sectors into account, such as financial sectors, government and foreign sectors, the situation is different.

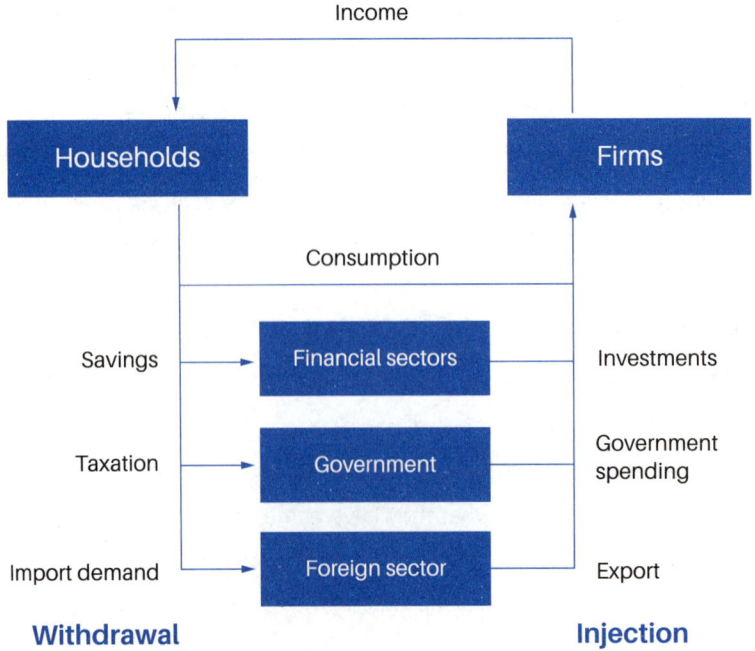

图4-3 Circular of cash flow in economic cycle-2

在实际生活中，经济圈并不是仅仅只有企业和居民两个经济体的存在，还包括了其他经济体（如图4-3所示），例如，金融公司（financial sector）。此时，居民赚的所有的钱，不需要全部用于消费，可以抽出一部分进行储蓄（saving），同样，金融公司手中的钱，又可以通过投资（investment），再一次回到经济圈循环中。又如政府的参与，居民需要将收入的一部分通过税收（tax）的形式缴纳给政府，而税收取之于民，则需要用之于民，所以会通过政府支出（government spending）将钱进一步投放进经济圈中，如修建大型公路铁路、机场、医院、学校等。最后，还有对外贸易的参与，通过进口（import），经济圈的现金流流向别国；而通过出口（export），现金流又再一次回到本国经济圈中。

通过总结规律不难发现，图4-3左边的活动——储蓄、税收和进口，都是对原始经济圈现金流的撤出（withdrawal），而图4-3右边的活动——投资、政府支出和出口，都是对原始经济圈现金流的注入（injection）。循环的现金流增加，则总需求增加，从而刺激经济；反之，循环的现金流减少，则是一种抑制经济的做法。

8 Fiscal policy

Fiscal policy is action by the government **directly** to spend money, or to collect money in taxes, with the purpose of influencing the condition of the national economy.

> **核心考点**
>
> 财政政策的调控工具以及两种政策类型（扩张型和紧缩型）为FAB/AB考试的核心考点。

财政政策是政府**直接**调控一国经济，即通过税收和政府支出的方式，直接影响经济圈中循环的现金流。从中长期来看，政府都希望能够达到收入（税收）等于政府支出的均衡情况（我们称之为预算平衡），但往往市场自发的调节不够有效，此刻便需要通过预算赤字和预算盈余来进行宏观调控。

The two key elements that governments must plan for each year are：

(a) **Income**—this is primarily the money the government raises from **taxes** on individuals and businesses.

(b) **Expenditure**—this is the total amount the government will need **to spend to provide services for the population**, including the costs of the police and army, road and rail building as well as the wages of civil servants, etc.

In the medium-to-long term, most governments would prefer to run a balanced budget. This occurs when government income and expenditure are exactly matched.

8.1 Budget surplus and budget deficit

8.1.1 Budget deficit

(a) To fund a deficit, the government will need to borrow money.

(b) By running a budget deficit, the government is injecting more money into the economy than it is taking out. This will help boost aggregate demand and reduce unemployment.

(c) This is referred to as an "**expansionary policy**".

8.1.2 Budget surplus

(a) This occurs when government spending is lower than government income.

(b) By running a surplus, the government is taking money out of the economy, reducing aggregate demand.

(c) This is referred to as a "**contractionary**" policy.

虽然政府希望达到均衡的情况，但现实中往往事与愿违，那就会出现预算赤字与预算盈余。

预算赤字指的是政府的收入小于支出，即政府缺钱，缺钱则需要借钱，此时会产生正的借款需求。 同时，由于税收小于政府支出，则对经济圈现金流的撤出小于注入，此时经济圈现金流会增加，起到刺激经济的作用，此为"扩张型财政政策"。

预算盈余指的是政府的收入大于支出，即政府不缺钱，所以会有负的借款需求或者是正的偿付债务的需求。 同时，由于税收大于支出，则对经济圈现金流的撤出大于注入，此时经济圈现金流会减少，起到抑制经济的作用，此为"紧缩型财政政策"。

> **核心考点**
>
> （1）掌握货币政策的工具以及扩张型和紧缩型政策对经济的影响。
> （2）区分 monetary policy 和 fiscal policy。

9 Monetary policy

Monetary policy refers to actions that the government undertakes **indirectly** through banks and financial intermediaries.

货币政策是政府**间接**通过央行和其他金融机构对一国经济进行调节，使用的工具为除了政府路径以外其他所有的工具，包括货币供给、利率以及汇率。

9.1 Methods of monetary policy

9.1.1 The money supply

The price and income will increase along with more money supply, leading an increase in demand as a result. Growth in the money supply, however, should therefore be a medium-term target of monetary policy.

9.1.2 Interest rates

Higher interest rate will discourage people to invest and borrow, which leads to reduced demand. Interest rates influence the exchange rates and inflation etc.

9.1.3 Exchange rates

The fall of exchanges rates will stimulate exports and reduce demand for imports. When a country is heavily dependent on overseas trade, it might be appropriate to establish a target exchange rate. However, the exchange rate is dependent on inflation and interest rates.

9.2 Types of Monetary policy

> **知识点解读**
>
> 对货币政策的两种类型（扩张型和紧缩型）的理解，请大家类比财政政策（8.1.1-8.1.2）。

An **expansionary policy** increases the money supply in the economy, decreases interest and exchange rate, helping to increase aggregate demand and boost economy.

A **contractionary policy** decreases the total money supply, increases interest rate and exchange rate, helping to decrease aggregate demand and suppress economy.

Example question 2

Which of the following measures would enable the government of UK to reduce inflationary pressures in the economy?

  A. An increase in welfare benefits paid to the unemployed

  B. A decrease in the level of interested rates

  C. The introduction of export subsidies to key industries

  D. The withdrawal of local authority grants for installation of solar heating

Answers for example question

1. D
2. D

Summary

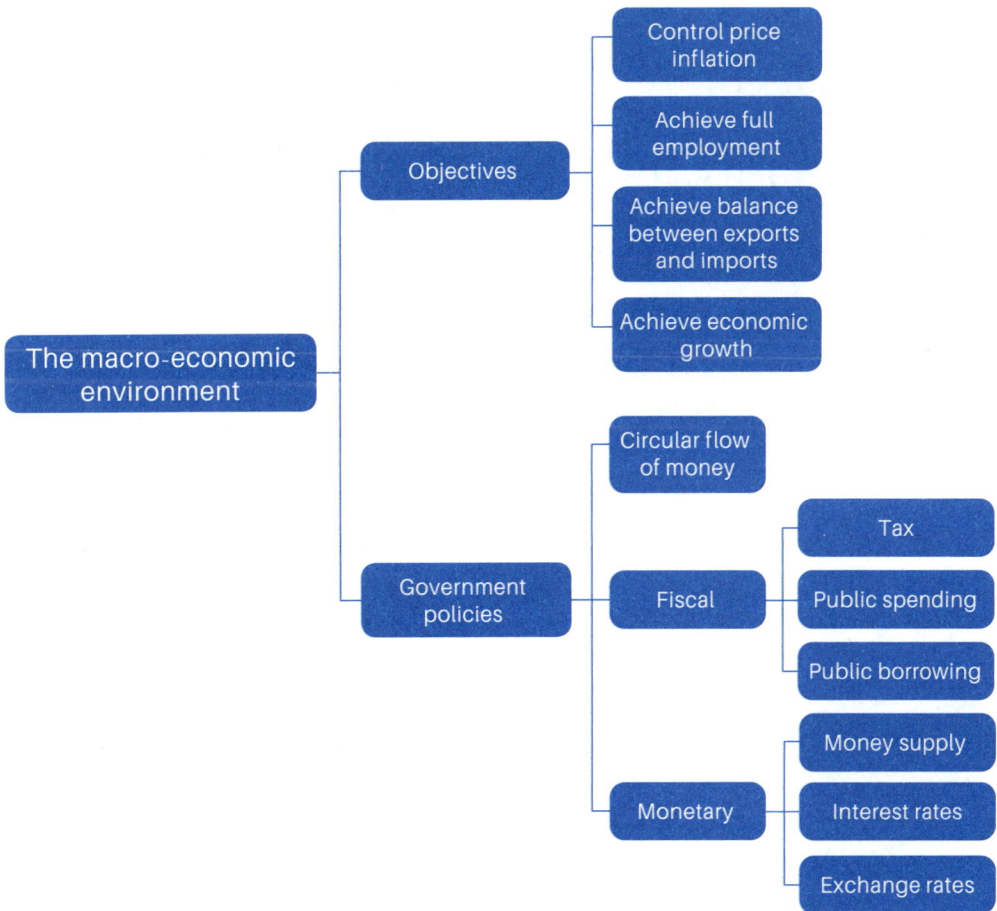

Chapter 4 考试不同问法总结

1. 针对 objectives of macro-economic

- Which of the following is a long-term macro-economic objective of a government?
- Which step could the government take to correct the disequilibrium in the balance of payment in the long run?
- Which type of unemployment is... being affected by?

2. 针对 monetary/fiscal policy 的分类、效果

- Which of the following is an example of a monetary/fiscal policy tool?
- Which of the following would reduce the level of aggregate demand in an economy?
- Does each of the following policies increase aggregate demand in the economy?
- Which TWO of the following measures would enable the government of A to reduce inflationary pressures in the economy?
- Which of the following will be caused by an increase in the interest rates in a country?

Quick quiz

4.1 Which of the following is an element of monetary policy?

(1) Credit control.

(2) Government spending.

(3) Interest rates.

(4) Government borrowing.

(5) Taxation.

(6) Money supply.

(7) Exchange rates.

A. All above

B. (1)(3)(6) and (7)

C. Only (3)(6)

D. (1)(3)(5)(6) and (7)

Answer: B

Difficulty level: Easy

Tag: Monetary policy

Rationale:

Monetary policy refers to the money supply, credit control, interest rates, exchange rates. Government's taxation, borrowing and spending plans is fiscal policy.

本题是典型的财政政策与货币政策的考题。考生需要明确，财政政策是政府直接对宏观经济进行调控，使用的是政府的收入——税收以及政府的费用——公共支出；而货币政策是政府间接通过影响金融市场与国际贸易市场对宏观经济进行调控，使用的是利率、信贷控制、汇率以及货币供给，故本题选 B。

4.2 Consider the following statements with respect to national income. Which of the following statements are right?

(1) Equilibrium national income is always full-employment national income.

(2) Full-employment national income is always equilibrium national income.

(3) Full-employment national income is an ideal equilibrium national income where no inflation gap exists.

(4) When the economy is at the full employment level, a full-employment national income will always exist.

A. Statements(1) and (2)

B. Statements(2) and (3)

C. Statements(3) and (4)

D. Statements(1) and (4)

Answer: B

Difficulty level: Normal

Tag: National income

Rationale:

This question is set to ask you to understand the determination of national income. First, equilibrium national income is not always full-employment national income, there may be a case where unemployment exists. Second, full-employment national income is an ideal equilibrium national income. Third, it doesn't mean that a full-employment national income will always exist at the full employment level of national income, because there may be an inflationary gap. Inflationary gap is the situation where resources(e.g. labour) are already fully employed, but level of demand exceeds the productive capabilities of the economy at full employment.

这道题考查的是考生对国民收入相关概念的理解。考生需要明确以下概念：第一，均衡国民收入指的是总需求等于总供给时的国民收入；第二，充分就业下的国民收入是一种理想情况，指的是经济体中不仅总需求等于总供给，还恰好达到了充分就业。

明确了以上两个概念，本题便好理解了。对于 statement（1），考生一定要清楚，均衡的国民收入不总是充分就业的国民收入，很有可能有不充分就业的情况存在；statement（2）和 statement（3）表述正确，充分就业的国民收入是一个理想的国民收入，此刻已经达到了均衡；对于 statement（4），经济体达到充分就业的状态，并不意味着达到了充分就业的国民收入，毕竟充分就业国民收入为理想情况。

4.3 If the exchange rate of US dollar decreases compared to RMB, which TWO of the following consequence will occur for both countries?

A. An increase of imports in US

B. A reduction in the rate of cost push inflation in China

C. A stimulus to exports in US

D. An increase in the costs of imports in China

Answer: B, C

Difficulty level: Normal

Tag: The macro-economic environment-Inflation

Rationale:

The decreased exchange rate of US dollar means that US dollar is depreciated while RMB is appreciated. Therefore, it will lead imports fall and exports rise in US. And in China, it will reduce imported costs from US due to the appreciation of RMB.

这道题考查的是汇率变化会对两国货币的影响。题干给出的信息说，现在美元对人民币的汇率下降，也就意味着美元贬值，而人民币增值。美元贬值会直接导致美国进口减少，而出口增加，故 C 为正确选项。此外，人民币的增值会导致从美国进口而产生的成本减少，因为购买同样单位产品所花费的钱会减少，故 B 选项正确。美元贬值，则单位美元的购买力会下降，进口减少，A 选项错误；人民币相对升值，单位人民币能够购买更多美元标价的商品，导致使用人民币的进口成本下降，D 选项错误。

4.4 Which of following will lead to a reduction in aggregate demand in the economy?

A. A decrease in savings

B. An increase in public spending

C. Investment in capital goods

D. An increase in tax rates

Answer: D

Difficulty level: Easy

Tag: The macro-economic environment-The circular flow of income and expenditure

Rationale:

Savings, taxation and import demand increase will cause aggregate demand fall, while investment, government spending and exports will lead to increased aggregate demand. Therefore, option D is correct.

这道题考查的是哪些因素会导致总需求波动。储蓄、税收和进口需求的增加会导致总需求下降，而投资、政府花费以及出口的增加会导致总需求上升。反之亦然。故选择 D 选项。

4.5 Cland, Jland, Tlandand, Kland are four countries of Asia. The following economic statistics have been produced for the year 20X9.

Country	Cland	Jland	Tland	Kland
Change in GDP (%)	+0.10	+0.47	+6.26	−2.12
Change in CPI (%)	+31.50	+15.37	+2.25	+2.15
Change unemployed (%)	+19.90	+1.76	−8.76	−4.5%

Which country experienced stagflation for the year 20X9?

A. Cland   B. Jland   C. Tland   D. Kland

Answer: A

Difficulty level: Easy

Tag: Stagflation

Rationale:

This question is set to examine the characteristics of stagflation, candidates must bear in mind that stagflation has a low or negative economic growth, high inflation rate, and high unemployment rate. Thus, Cland is the correct option.

这道题考查的是滞胀的特征，考生一定要牢记滞胀伴随着低或者负的经济增长、高的通货膨胀以及高的失业率。因此，Cland 是正确的选项。

Part B
Organisation

组织篇

恭喜你完成了环境篇的学习,接下来我们开始由外到内,走进组织的内部,来到 Part B 组织篇。

Part B 包含了第 5 章至第 11 章共七个章节,从多个维度帮助你细致地了解组织内部运作的原理与规律。

作为轮船的船长,你需要了解轮船的方方面面,包括了解其架构和每个内部机器设备的功能,如何将轮船情况与内外部利益相关者进行沟通,如何进行内部控制,如何防止船员舞弊,以及如何维持整艘轮船良好的团队文化氛围等等。

通过 Part B 的学习,你将会一一揭开谜底。

Chapter 5
Business structure

知识导入

在前面的章节中,我们系统地了解了组织以及组织外部的"冰山",即商业环境,从这一章开始,我们要去了解这艘行驶在"商海"上叫组织的"商业巨轮"到底是什么样子的。 欢迎来到"巨轮"的内部,我们从它的结构说起。

单词表

英文	中文
Informal organisation	非正式组织(意译为"小团体")
Human relations school	人际关系学派
Rumour	流言蜚语
The Hawthorne Studies	霍桑实验
Strategic apex	战略高层
Middle line	公司中层
Operating core	执行层
Technostructure	技术层
Support staff	支持层
Succession crises	继任危机
Matrix organisation	矩阵式企业结构
Dual authority	双重领导(指令)
Strategic business unit (SBU)	战略业务单元
Virtual organisations	虚拟组织
Standardisation	标准化
Strategic management	战略管理
Tactical management	战术管理
Boundaryless organisations	无边界组织
Crisis decision-making	危机处理决策

学习指南

Learning objectives	Pass level	Distinction level	用时建议
1. The informal organisation (1.1-1.4)	√		15 min
2. Organisation structure (2.1-2.3)	√		25 min
3. Centralisation and decentralisation (3.1-3.2)	√		10 min
4. Basic organisational structure concepts (4.1-4.5)	√		10 min

本章考点

重要考点	难度（1~3）
熟记霍桑实验的实验结果	2
熟记 Mintzberg 的五行理论，理解并运用	3
熟记并理解不同组织类型的区别和特征	3
熟记并理解集权和分权组织的特征	1
熟记并理解组织结构的基本概念	2
理解外包概念与优缺点	1

在学习具体的组织结构之前，我们先学习一种特殊类型的组织——非正式组织，你可以将其理解为"小团体"。每个正式组织中都会自发产生小团体，它们有特殊的结构，很可能绕过正式组织的管理，所以小团体**可能**会对正式组织造成危害，其危害程度取决于管理层是如何进行管理的。

1 The informal organisation

1.1 Definition of informal organisation

Individuals may occupy roles and offices, but they bring to those roles with their own interests, thoughts or assumptions. They develop friendships (or enemies), and preferences for how to accomplish assigned tasks that **may or may not support** the formal organisation. Thus, **informal and formal organisation are born together** and informal organisation involves **flexibility and changes quickly.** ("informal organisation", n.d.)

1.2 Benefits of the informal organisation

(a) **Increased dedication of employees**: It motivates employees and reduces absenteeism and labour turnover.

(b) **Better knowledge sharing among employees**: As the same as formal organisations, informal ones could also help to share knowledge and improve members' performance.

(c) **Better co-ordination between employees**: By providing means of relieving emotional and psychological pressure, it may fill gaps in management ability, and reduce internal politics. Additionally, informal networks and methods are quicker to transmit information, which can facilitate fast communication.

1.3 Problems of the informal organisation

(a) There might be a danger that actions taken by informal organisation members are **averse to the organisational interests**.

(b) The **grapevine** can spread **rumours and may mislead employees.**

(c) Individuals may be expelled or isolated by informal organisations if they do not behave in line with "rules" within such organisations.

(d) There may be a compromise in internal control systems, which could hamper quality of outputs.

1.4 The Hawthorne Studies

> **核心考点**
> 小团体的存在是通过霍桑实验被发现的,同学们需要熟记该实验的名字以及 Mayo 这个人名。

Hawthorne studies are famous experiments contributed by **Elton Mayo, who is the representative figure of human relations school of management theory. In these studies, the concept of "informal organisation" was firstly introduced**, additionally they also showed that **people tend to perform better when they believe they are being valued.**

霍桑实验是心理学史上非常著名的实验,由管理学的重量级人物——哈佛大学的心理学教授梅奥主持。 霍桑工厂是一个制造电话交换机的工厂,具有较完善的娱乐设施、医疗制度和养老金制度,但工人们仍愤愤不平,生产业绩很不理想。 为找出原因,美国国家研究委员会组织研究小组开展实验研究。 从 1924 年开始,美国西方电气公司在芝加哥附近的霍桑工厂进行了一系列实验,包括照明实验以及引入计件工资制度等。 实验结果表明,在工作场合中,确实存在非正式组织(小团体),且人们对人际关系的需求对工作的绩效表现等有一定影响。

小试牛刀

> **典型例题**
> 这道题目是关于 informal organisation 的典型考题,考点在于非正式组织的特点。 除此之外,考试之中也可能经常会出现非正式组织与正式组织的特征对比,因此,需要同学们能够清晰地区分正式组织与非正式组织的特征。

Example question 1

Which of the following is a characteristic of the informal organisation?
  A. Communication flows are mainly upward and downward
  B. It is made up of individuals at the same level in the organisation
  C. It evolves over time and can change rapidly
  D. It exists in certain kind of organisations

2 Organisation structure

2.1 Common structure—Mintzberg's five components

> **核心考点**
> Mintzberg 的 five components 在考试中经常出现。 考核方式比较直接。 一般着重在 five components 的名称以及每个组成部分的含义。
> 因此这个考点需要同学们理解以及记忆。

Mintzberg believes that all organisations can be split into five generic components (见图 5-1)。

(a) Strategic apex
(b) Middle line
(c) Operating core
(d) Technostructure
(e) Support staff

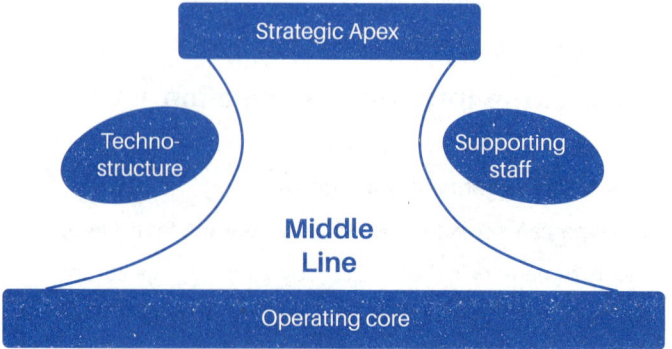

图 5-1　Mintzberg's five components

(A) Strategic apex

This element of the organisation is made up of **directors and senior executives. Their role is to interpret or define the mission** of the organisation and ensure objectives are consistent with missions. The strategic apex is also responsible for managing the organisation's relationship with the **macro-environment**.

(B) Operating core

The operating core carries out the activities directly relating to deliver outputs.

(C) Middle line

This element provides the **link** between the strategic apex and the operating core. The main role is partially one of interpretation, as the work of the operating core has to be consistent with the expectations and plans of the strategic apex.

(D) Technostructure

Mintzberg states that there are several roles here. The technostructure is made up of individuals and teams working in functions such as human resources, training, finance and planning. **Analysers** of technostructure decide on the **best ways to perform jobs** and seek to standardise skills.

(E) Support staff

Support staff work in functions such as public relations and legal services. Their outputs **do not contribute directly** to the core purposes of the organisation, but their activities **contribute to the efficiency and effectiveness** of the whole organisation.

精益求精

The **sixth component** was later added to Mintzberg's model:
Ideology: The organisation's beliefs and values.

博学多才

明茨伯格是在全世界管理学界都享有盛誉的大师，他是经理角色学派的主要代表人物，*Structure in Fives: Designing Effective Organisation* 是其主要代表作之一。非常有趣的是，明茨伯格在这本书中探讨组织结构时"5"这个数字贯穿始终，如我们这个部分需要学习的 Five components。尤其对于明茨伯格这个犹太人而言，"5"这个数字有着不同凡响的含义，"5"代表着宇宙，代表着人，并且他还引用中国文化中的"五彩祥云"和"五行"进一步诠释这个数字的神秘性。因此，明茨伯格的这本著作也被我们翻译为《五行组织学说》。

2.2 How organisations can be differently structured

组织结构的演变与组织所处的发展阶段、规模大小、商业模式等因素密切相关。从组织成立之初的简单型结构，到初具规模的职能型结构，到可以满足多元化的事业部制结构，根据这样的变化过程，我们可以这么认为：组织结构应当根据组织不同时段的需求不断进行优化，以更好地为组织目标服务。

核心考点

组织结构是考试中的一个核心考点。考核方式多变，常见的有以下几种：
（1）给定某个结构名称，让考生选择其对应的特征；
（2）给出组织所在阶段或者环境，让考生分析在这种情况下，组织应当选择哪一种组成结构最为合理；
（3）与后续章节中的"组织文化"这个知识点相关联，根据文化选择匹配的结构，或者根据结构选择匹配的文化。
因此，考生需掌握组织结构的各种类型以及其优缺点，能通过具体情境描述作出判断。

2.2.1 Simple/entrepreneurial structure

The simple structure（见图 5-2）suits small and young organisation as it is often centralised and autocratic. It is informal as the power in this structure is exerted from the strategic apex (often the founder) rather than depending on the formal authority structure. The simplicity gives the organisation flexibility in adapting to the dynamic environment.

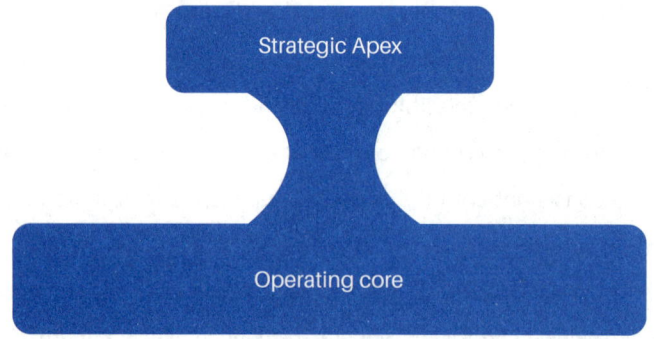

图 5-2　Simple/entrepreneurial structure

Advantages：

(a) **Important decisions are more centralised** in the hand of the chief executive officer thus control is exercised more directly.

(b) **Fast decision making** becomes possible due to the flexibility.

Disadvantages：

(a) It only suits **small** companies.

(b) It is **riskier and more vulnerable** than other types of structure.

(c) The structure is more likely to face **succession crises**.

简单型结构，从其命名可以看出，就是最简单的组织结构，往往出现在组织形成的初期。这种结构的指令由高层管理者从上至下直接传达，不存在所谓的中间层级，很大程度上避免了官僚作风的出现。但该结构对于高层管理者的要求非常高，他们既需要掌握多种技能，还要能随时处理组织面临的各种问题以及下达指令，这对于大多数管理者来说显然是难以胜任的。因此，简单型结构只适合那些规模较小、业务范围较窄的组织。

随着组织规模的日益壮大，简单型结构已然不能负担激增的业务量，在这种情况之下，职能结构应运而生。

2.2.2 Functional structure

The functional structure（见图 5-3）is the most common organisation model. In each function, employees are grouped together to **perform similar tasks**. The duties of individuals are allocated according to the functions they perform such as procurement, accounting and finance, information technology, HR, marketing etc. Each function's manager is responsible for his/her department's staffs and performance.

> **知识点解读**
> 简单型结构更容易面临继承危机，主要原因是简单型结构非常依赖战略顶点，也就是公司高层，而往往简单型的机构都出现在家族式或者初创型的公司，还没有形成聘请职业经理人的文化，一旦找不到合适的继承人，高层位置悬空，整个公司就会陷于混乱。

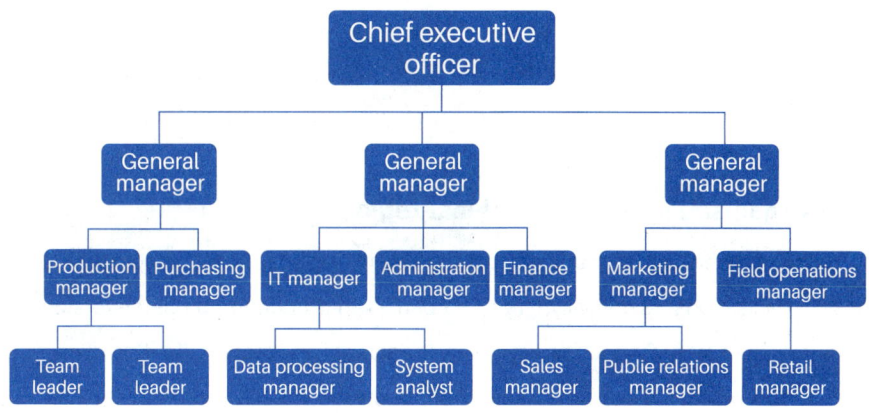

图 5-3 Functional structure

Advantages:

(a) It facilitates **specialisation** by bringing together employees with necessary knowledge and skills, which enables creation of economies of scale.

(b) It enables the organisation to operate through **clear lines of authority** and well-defined responsibilities.

(c) It prevents duplication of effort, thereby **reducing inefficiencies and costs**.

Disadvantages:

(a) **Empire building**: managers of functions may try to make decisions to increase their own power or are just in the best interests of their function, rather than working in the best interest of the company, which leads to conflicts of interest between different functions.

(b) **Poor lateral coordination** and communication problems.

博学多才

何为在组织中建设帝国大厦？为何建设帝国大厦为职能结构的缺点？

同学们最熟悉的是美国的帝国大厦，纽约的地标建筑物之一。而我们这里讲的其实是在组织当中个人或小团体为了自我强化，试图在一个组织内获得更大的权力和权威，通过拥有额外的员工或下属，来建立自己的帝国大厦。

在政治学中，帝国建设是指国家为了扩大其规模、权力和财富而在其边界之外获取资源、土地和经济影响力的趋势，这种扩张可能是以被征服的国家或人民的苦难为代价的。

在商业领域，当个人或小团体试图获得对关键项目和计划的控制权，以最大限度地提高工作安全性和晋升可能性时，就是在建设帝国大厦。由于这种方法阻止组织中的其他人以有意义的方式作出贡献，因此公司整体遭受损失。这种行为本应被上级管理层制止，但在商业环境中却很常见。

职能结构的出现很大程度上减轻了高层管理人员的工作负担，并且职能部门的建立使得组织充分享受到"术业有专攻"所带来的规模经济效应。但在这样的结构之中，同时也出现了不同部门、不同层级。不同部门之间可能会因不同的绩效考核目标导致利益冲突，从而影响协作。而层级的出现则会引发官僚主义等上传下达不通畅的现象。

同时，职能结构虽然给组织带来了高效率，但倘若组织开始扩大业务范围（不管是地区还是商品），职能结构是不足以应付的。因此，根据这样的情况，划分结构的基础逐渐转向地区以及产品。

2.2.3 Organisation by geographical region

Many organisations operate across different regions, so it is appropriate for these organisations, especially large companies that operate across several continents to adopt a functional structure by geographical location. In this way, the organisation maintains separate functional structures in each location（见图 5-4）.

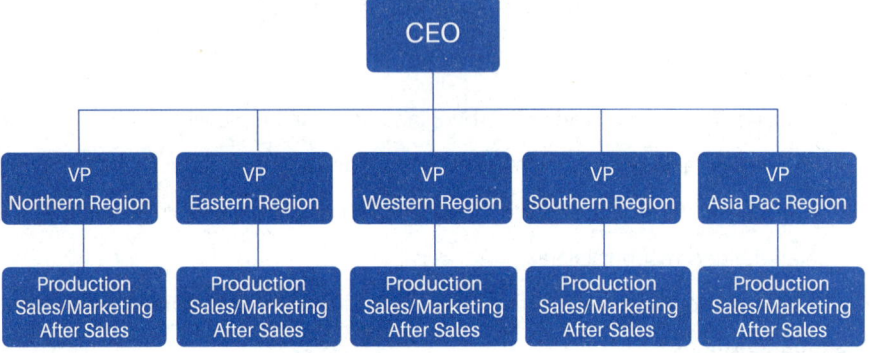

图 5-4　Geographical structure

Advantages：

（a）Better **local decision making** by tailored products and promotion.

（b）Reduced cost of transportation.

Disadvantages：

（a）**Duplication** of functions in different regions, which increases operating costs.

（b）**Inconsistency** of policy/standards might occur across the whole organisation.

2.2.4 Organisation by product

The functional model can be adapted for organisations that offer a range of products. In this way, the manager responsible for each product may have their own production, marketing and finance departments as is shown in the figure below（见图 5-5）.

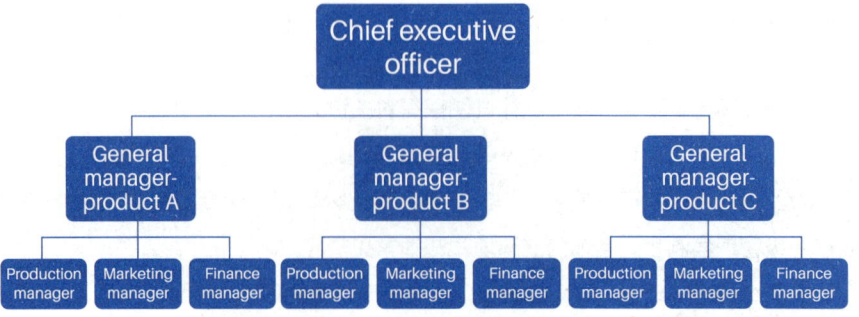

图 5-5　Product structure

Advantages:

(a) **Better decision:** Each manager could make specific, workable decisions rather than obey the arrangement from the headquarter.

(b) **Better accountability:** Each manager should be accountable for the performance and profitability of the product/region he/she operates.

(c) **Better cooperation:** All employees and their efforts are devoted to the product/region they are vested in.

Disadvantages:

(a) **Duplication:** Several functions are duplicated across the organisation.

(b) **Inconsistency:** The autonomy given to regions/products may undermines the consistency of policy across the whole organisation.

(c) **Conflicts:** The scramble for resources might arise between different product/geography divisions.

无论是以地区划分组织结构还是以品牌或商品划分组织结构，这种方式都在最大程度上做到了"因地制宜"，能够帮助组织充分利用相关资源，实现多元化发展或地域扩张。

2.2.5 Matrix organisation

The matrix structure（见图 5-6）is the combination of product/project structure with the functional structure.

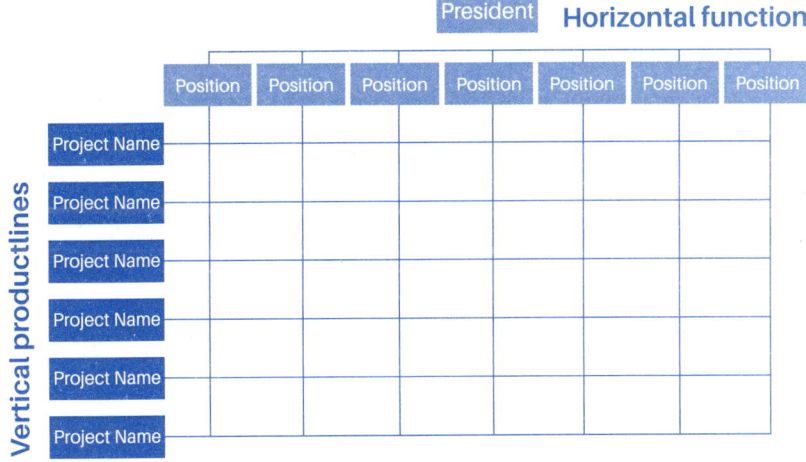

图 5-6　Matrix structure

Advantages:

For organisation:

(a) Bureaucracy is reduced, and communication lines are shortened.

(b) Cooperation between departments can be increased and dependence on rigid chains of command and lines of communication can be reduced.

For employees:

(a) Employees' jobs are enriched, and they could exploit more opportunities for career development, thus their motivation could be enhanced.

(b) The matrix approach may make employees more responsive to change and

> **核 心 考 点**
>
> 双重权限是矩阵型结构最主要的局限性，此时每个下属都会同时有两个上级，很容易产生需求冲突以及造成角色模糊。

more willing to welcome change.

Disadvantages：

(a) **Dual authority.** Employees are likely to be confused by conflicting demands of job arrangement from different managers.

(b) Cost. The matrix structure creates additional time management pressures, which may have an effect on costs.

(c) Inefficiency. If the matrix is not designed or implemented systematically, it can create organisational inefficiencies, such as slower decision taking.

通过图形和以上描述，我们不难看出，矩阵制结构融合了两种结构的特征：职能结构和以产品（项目）划分的结构。在该种结构之下，组织中的团队可以根据不同项目在现有的职能部门中挑选最为合适的人选。这种方式使得项目团队合作能够尽快步入正轨，减少项目初期需要的熟悉和磨合。并且，随着项目的结束，团队解散，成员可以回到原所属部门或者继续投入到下一个项目，无缝衔接。因此，我们通常认为这种结构既灵活又高效。

但对于员工而言，这种结构所带来的工作负担也是很重的，尤其是在同时面临项目任务和原所属部门任务的时候，孰先孰后的问题非常容易引发冲突。

2.2.6 Divisionalisation

2.2.6 Divisionalisation

In a divisionalised structure, the central core would provide guidelines for business units that enjoy a high degree of **autonomy**, and main activities are **decentralised to products/geographical divisions**, which we normally called **strategic business unit（SBU）**. The precondition to establish a division is that it has to undertake **sole responsibility for its own profits or losses**, thus division is a profit centre.

Advantages：

(a) The divisional structure better satisfies the organisation's diversified development/growth.

(b) More attention is paid to the profits, as a result each division would endeavor to improve efficiency and reduce costs.

(c) Divisionalisation encourages delegating authority to junior managers, thus reducing the workload of senior managers. It is also beneficial for future succession planning.

(d) Reduced hierarchy level enables quicker decision making.

Disadvantages：

(a) It is hard for some businesses to identify a totally autonomous division.

(b) There may be more resource scramble problems.

事业部制这种结构可以说是师出有名，它最早是由美国通用汽车的总裁斯隆提出，所以又称为"斯隆模型"。这种结构其实与以地区划分或以商品划分的结构非常相似，但最大的区别就在，**事业部制是独立经营、自负盈亏的一种形式。** 从最初产品的设计、原料采购、成本核算、产品制造一直到产品销售，均由事业部负责。公司总部只保留人事决策、预算控制和监督等间接权力，通过利润等指标对事业部进行控制。

2.3 New organisations
2.3.1 "Jobless" structures

In this structure, the employees are more like the sellers of skills in the open market, and the organisations act as buyers to select what they need and pay for them.

在这种结构之下，员工不再是工作人员，不是工作的拥有者，而是技能的卖家。这是对可雇佣性概念的具体表述，它认为一个人需要拥有一系列在开放市场上有价值的技能。

2.3.2 Boundaryless organisations

Boundaryless organisation is "an organisation breaking down barriers between internal levels, job functions and departments, as well as reducing external barriers between the association and those with whom it does business" ("boundaryless organisation", n.d.).

Essentially, it is an **unstructured design** that is not constrained by having a chain of command or formal departments, with the **focus on flexibility**.

这种组织结构是一种非结构化设计，不受命令链或正式部门的约束，最大的优势是灵活性。它消除了层级、不同职能和不同部门之间的内部障碍，并消除了组织与供应商、客户和竞争对手之间的障碍。为了帮助消除界限，管理者可以使用虚拟的、空心的或模块化的结构，这有助于消除官僚主义，并有助于降低成本。

There are different types of boundaryless organisations:

(a) **Hollow organisations**

Hollow organisation is the one which relies heavily on outsourcing, the majority of the company's **non-core processes and activities are outsourced** to specialist providers so that the company can focus on the most value adding activities.

(b) **Modular organisations**

Modular organisation is the one which firstly divide its production processes into different components and outsource them to different suppliers, and then assemble and/or combine different components into the final products or services.

(c) **Virtual organisations**

A virtual organisation is one which operates primarily through electronic communications, taking advantage of the efficiencies made possible by information technology. People work together remotely, with little or no dependence on physical premises. Instead, communications take place through media such as emails, e-conferencing, extranet and intranet.

> **核心考点**
>
> Centralisation（集权制）和 decentralisation（分权制）是经常出现的考点，需要同学们掌握其特征以及优缺点。

3 Centralisation and decentralisation

3.1 Definition

(A) Centralisation

Centralisation has two meanings：

(a) "The concentration of management and decision-making power at the top of an organisation's hierarchy"；

(b) "The location of all or most main departments and managers at one facility" ("centralisation", n.d.).

(B) Decentralisation

Similarly, decentralisation means：

(a) Empowerment of lower-level subordinates with greater discretion；

(b) The dispersion of all or most main departments in different divisions/places.

3.2 Arguments in favour of centralisation and decentralisation

For centralisation：

(a) Easy to control due to concentration of power.

(b) More thoughtful decisions made on problems.

(c) Coordination of interests between different departments and functions.

(d) Reduction of management costs as a result of less managers.

(e) Fast speed of crisis decision-making (no need to refer back).

(f) Standardisation of organisations' operations.

For decentralisation/delegation：

(a) Reduced workload and stress of senior managers and increased focus on corporate strategy.

(b) Better motivation and development of junior managers through delegation of authority.

(c) Better local decisions and faster routine decisions (no need to refer onwards).

(d) Improved responsibility and accountability.

Example question 2

Which one of the following is an advantage of centralisation?

A. It helps to develop the skills of junior managers

B. It reduces workload of senior managers

C. Accountability is better

D. Senior managers can have a wider view of the company operation

4 Basic organisational structure concepts

4.1 Span of control

It refers to the number of subordinates controlled **directly by a** superior.

没有最好的控制范围的方式,只有最适合的控制范围。 管理者及下属的能力,整个企业本身的企业文化及组织架构,尤其是地理因素,都会影响整个企业的 span of control。

4.2 Scalar chain

Scalar chain refers to a clear line of communication in the organisation where instructions flow down and reports flow back up.

4.3 Tall and flat organisations

The organisation can be tall or flat. Tall organisations have **many levels and long scalar chains**, while flat organisations have **fewer levels and short scalar chains**.

The advantages and disadvantages can be summarised as follows(见表 5-1、表 5-2):

(A) Tall organisation

表 5-1　Appraisal of tall organisation

Advantages	Disadvantages
High participation in decisions-making across the organisation	Limited employees' initiatives due to strict supervision
Better development of employment career planning	Increased management costs and slow decision-making due to too many layers

(B) Flat organisation

表 5-2　Appraisal of flat organisation

Advantages	Disadvantages
Higher motivation for junior managers through delegation	Lower quality of decision-making due to delegation
Reduced overhead costs	Diluted power of control for senior executives
Faster communication between strategic apex and operating core	Less role of interpretation played by middle managers in the organisation

小试牛刀

Example question 3

Which TWO of the following are DISADVANTAGES of a tall organisation?

　　A. Decision making and responses tend to be slow

　　B. Rigid supervision may block employee initiative

　　C. Managers will have a wider view of the operations

基本概念

因为课程安排将两个基本概念——集权（centralisation）分权（decentralisation）与高耸式（tall organisation）扁平式（flat organisation）组织结构放在了一起，很多同学会想当然地认为集权就是 tall organisation，分权就是 flat organisation，这个想法是完全错误的。集权分权是根据权力是否集中进行划分的，tall/flat organisation 是根据组织层级数的多少进行划分的，**两者是从不同维度对于组织架构的剖析，并没有任何交集**，也不应该被联系起来。举一个典型的例子，我们学过的 simple structure，层级数是最少的，是典型的 flat organisation，但是其战略顶点直接控制员工，同时又是典型的集权组织。

知识点解读

结合第二章的知识点理解，掌握导致 delayering 发生的原因。并且能够正确区分 delayering 和 downsizing。

4.4 Delayering

Delayering is the reduction of the number of middle level **management**.

What makes delayering possible?

(a) Some work done by middle managers is replaced by **information technology.**

(b) Many organisations are willing to **delegate** authority to front line of managers which can "touch" customers in order to make better decisions.

(c) Delayering in the organisation can **reduce managerial costs**.

小试牛刀

典型例题

这道题目将 delayering 与 scalar chain 和 span of control 相结合，遇到这种题目，同学们可以先思考 delayering 的定义。Deleyering 指的是组织扁平化，中间层级的员工被移除在组织之外，于是组织结构从高瘦型变成扁平型，自然能够联想到，scalar chain 变短，span of control 变宽。

Example question 4

Delayering can make an organisation more responsive to market needs.

Which **TWO** consequences will the above proposal have on the structure of the organisation?

A. Increased scalar chain B. Reduced span of control

C. Reduced scalar chain D. Increased span of control

Example question 5

Scalar chain is the channel through which instructions flow down and reports flow back up.

True or False?

Answers for example question

1. C
2. D
3. AB
4. CD
5. True

Summary

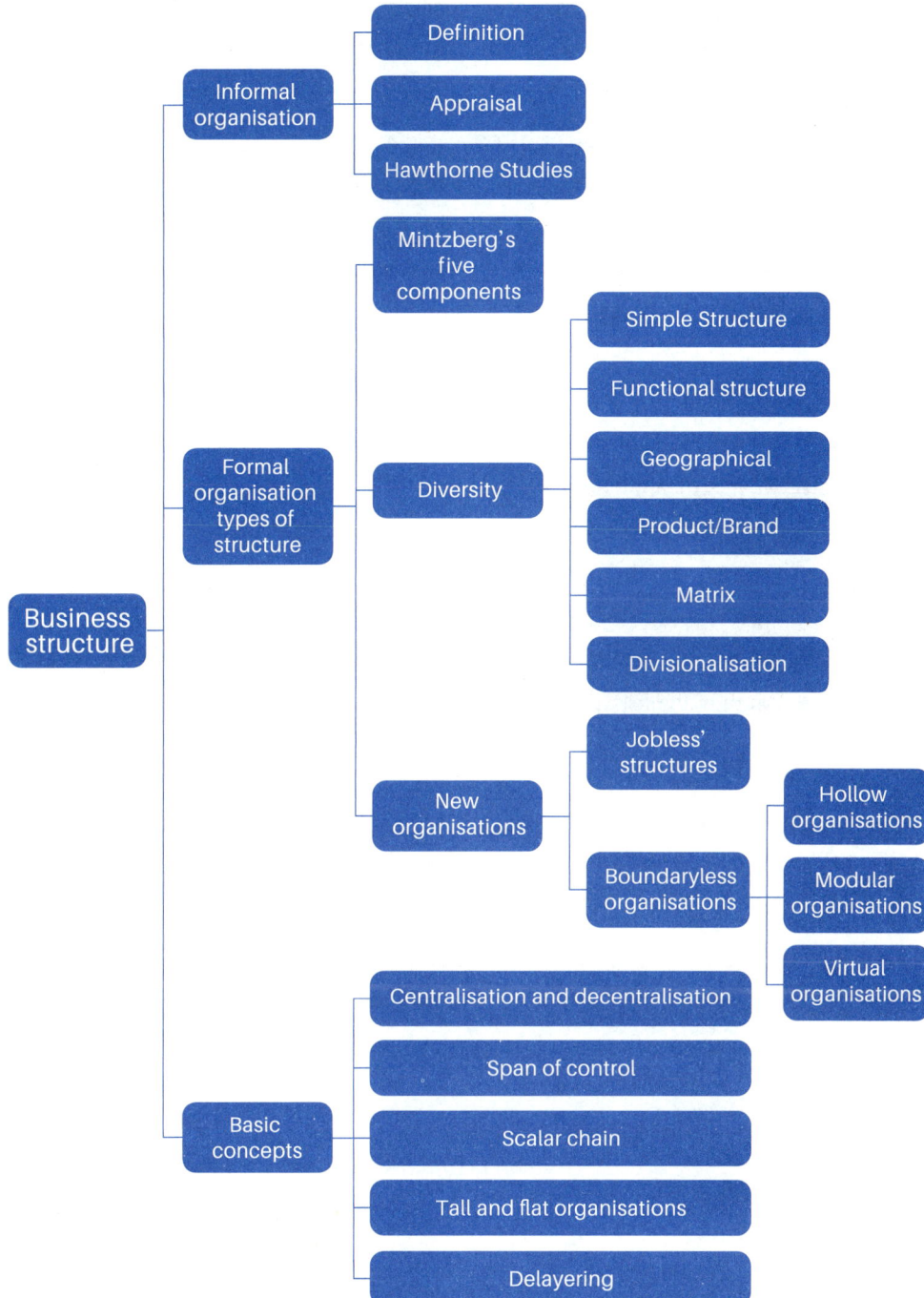

Chapter 5 考试不同问法总结

1. 针对 informal organisation

- Which TWO of the following describe the impact/problem of informal organisation on business?
- Are the activities for each day part of the informal organisation or the formal organisation?
- Which of the following statements about informal structure is correct?

2. 针对 Mintzberg's theory

- Which part of the organisation consists of analysts that design systems and process?
- Are the following components of organisation as suggested by Mintzberg?

3. 针对 organisation structures

- Which of the following is an ADVANTAGE of functional/divisional/... structure?
- What type of organisational structure is described here?
- What type of organisational structure is A Co currently follow?
- Which two of the following are characteristics/features of virtual/modular/... structure?

4. 针对 basic concepts

- What is meant by a manager's span of control?
- Which of the following is described by the scalar chain concept?
- Through which form of communication do instructions flow down and reports flow back up?
- Are the following statements about flat organisation structure true or false?
- Which of the following is an advantage/disadvantage of decentralise/centralise?

Quick quiz

5.1 Which of the following is a disadvantage of a divisionalisation structure?

  A. Speeding up decision-making
  B. Empire building
  C. Authority may be conflicted
  D. It may be hard to identify divisions

Answer: D

Difficulty level: Normal

Tag: Divisionalisation

Rationale:

Candidates should recognise the benefits and drawbacks of divisionalisation structure, as well as other types of structures. Option A is the advantage of divisionalisation structure. Option B is the disadvantage of functional structure. Option C is the disadvantage of matrix structure. Option D is the disadvantage of a divisionalisation structure.

考生应该能够识别出事业部制架构的优缺点,同时也要识别出其他架构的优缺点。 A 选项是事业部制架构的优点; B 选项是职能架构的缺点; C 选项是矩阵式架构的缺点; D 选项是事业部制的缺点。

5.2 In Mintzberg's five components, which component does finance function belong to?

  A. Strategic apex   B. Support base   C. Technostructure   D. Operating core

Answer: C

Difficulty level: Easy

Tag: Mintzberg's five components

Rationale:

The technostructure is made up of key individuals and teams working in functions such as human resources, training, finance and planning.

技术架构是由一些主要员工和团队组成的,他们致力于提升企业流程上的效率,如人力资源、培训、财务以及计划。

5.3 There are four statements regarding the tall/flat organisation:

  (1) Tall organisations have narrow span of control, and long scalar chain.
  (2) Flat organisations have wide span of control, and long scalar chain.
  (3) Tall organisations are usually more centralised, and therefore will inhibits delegation.
  (4) Tall organisations are usually more centralised, and therefore will not enable people to participate in decisions.

  Which of the above statements are correct?

  A. (1) and (2)   B. (1) and (3)   C. (2) and (3)   D. (1) and (4)

Answer: B

Difficulty level: Normal

Tag: Tall/flat organisation

Rationale:

This question is set to examine the benefits and drawbacks of tall/flat organisation, candidates must ensure they understand the meaning of it.

Statement(1) is correct, as it's characteristics of tall organisation.

Statement(2) is false, as flat organisations have short scalar chain.

Statement(3) is correct, because tall organisations are usually centralised, and it will inhibit delegation.

Statement(4) is false. Tall organisations will encourage people to participate in decisions, because they have narrow span of control, meaning fewer subordinates will be supervised and every subordinate may have more chance to participate in decisions.

这道题考查的是高长型组织/扁平化组织的优缺点,考生必须确保能够理解这里的含义。

第一句话是对的,因为这就是高长型组织的特征。

第二句话是错的,因为扁平化组织有更短的层级链。

第三句话是对的,因为高长型组织通常是集权的,它会阻碍向下授权。

第四句话是错的,因为高长型组织会使得人们更多参与决策,高长型组织的控制幅度窄,这意味着上级拥有更少的下级,因此下级就有更多的机会参与决策活动。

5.4 Which type of communication in the organisation do instructions flow down, and reports flow back up?

A. Authority B. Scalar chain C. Empowerment D. Unity of command

Answer: B

Difficulty level: Normal

Tag: The basic concepts of organisational structure

Rationale:

Scalar chain refers to the chain of command from the most senior to the most junior. Therefore, senior managers send instructions to subordinates and subordinates report back to their superiors.

本题直接考查 scalar chain 的定义。

5.5 Which of the following is a characteristic of a modular organisation?

A. The classification standards depend on whether activities are core or non-core

B. All operational activities are offshored

C. Production operations of the organisation are separated and organised independently

D. Core operational activities are identified and then organised sequentially in house

Answer: C

Difficulty level: Normal

Tag: The boundary-less organisation-Modular organisation

Rationale:

For modular organisations, they firstly divide their production processes into different components and outsource them to different suppliers, then assemble and/or combine different components into the final products or services.

本题考查的是模块化组织的特点,考生要注意区分模块化与中空型组织的特点和区别。

Chapter 6
Organisational departments and functions

知识导入

上一章中我们了解了"巨轮"也就是组织的内部结构是什么样子的。 接下来这一章中我们需要了解组织中的各个职能部门到底在发挥什么样的作用。 同学们通过本章的学习，需建立企业运营中的九种重要职能的概念。 在学习过程中，可以将本章内容与前面学习的 Value Chain 结合，帮助记忆。

单词表

英文	中文
Storage space	储存空间
Economic order quantities	经济订货批量
Tied up capital	占用资金
Lead time	订货提前期
Short-term trends	短期趋势
Penetration pricing	渗透定价
Skimming pricing	撇脂定价
Intangibility	无形性
Market segmentation	市场细分
Targeted market	目标市场
Financial accounting	财务会计
Management accounting	管理会计
Raising money	融资
Payables	应付账款
Receivables	应收账款
Standing committee	常设委员会
Treasury	资金管理部门

学习指南

Learning objectives	Pass level	Distinction level	用时建议
1.Organisational departments and functions（1.1-1.9）	√		20 min
2. Levels in the organisation（2.1-2.3）	√		10 min
3. Committees（3）	√		10 min
4. Levels of organisation（4）	√		25 min

本章考点

重要考点	难度（1~3）
熟记每个职能部门的特点	2
着重记忆和理解 marketing 部门	2
熟记并理解安东尼的金字塔模型	2
熟记并理解不同层级需要用到的信息及对应的信息系统	2

1 Organisational departments and functions

1.1 Research and development（R&D）

The main role of R&D department is to improve **product** or **process**. There is a need for sound cooperation between R&D and other departments especially marketing to ensure the outputs meet customers' expectations.

研发部门需要与市场营销部门密切配合，确保研发的产品和服务是市场可接受的。

> **知识点解读**
> 对于制造型企业来说，产品就是产成品，如苹果手机。
> 对于服务型企业来说，企业的产成品则是服务。

1.2 Purchasing

The main function of purchasing department is to acquire all necessary inputs（materials）for business operations. In order to make the best purchasing decisions, the purchasing manager need to weigh factors involved in purchasing mix.

The purchasing mix is quantity, quality, price and delivery（见表 6-1）。

> **知识点解读**
> 掌握 purchasing mix 包含的 4 个因素。考生在理解记忆时，可联系实际生活案例，如你在淘宝上购买产品会考虑哪些因素。

表 6-1　Illustration of purchasing mix

Quantity	When and how much quantity of the purchasing are determined by the following two factors： （a）Stockout risk. （b）Holding costs arising from storage, insurance and etc. In order to improve the efficiency of the purchasing activities, it is sensible to develop a sound inventory management system and determine the optimum reorder level and economic order quantities（EOQ）
Quality	The purchasing department need to communicate with production and marketing department first to ensure the quality of the final products could meet the customers' requirement
Price	Ensure goods are purchased at **competitive prices** with reasonable quality
Delivery	An appropriate leading time should be fixed to reduce additional costs（arising from stockout or over-storage）

1.3 Production

Production is a value-added process to transfer inputs (e.g. raw materials) into outputs (e.g. finished goods). It is essential for us to note that production is an important function in the network of the whole organisation, which should cooperate with other functions closely. For example:

(a) The quantities of production should be discussed with sale department, which is the front line of the market.
(b) The requirement of property, plant and equipment should be communicated with finance department, which is responsible for the use of organisation's funds.
(c) The design of products need to cooperate with R&D department.
(d) Training and career development of personnel needs the help of human resource department.

1.4 Marketing

The UK's Chartered Institute of Marketing states the definition of marketing is "the management process responsible for identifying, anticipating and satisfying customer needs profitably" ("Marketing", n.d.).

1.4.1 The basic marketing mix (4Ps):

The marketing mix is a model used when considering the range of activities necessary to construct and implement a comprehensive marketing strategy.

The marketing mix is product, price, place and promotion.

市场营销组合（Marketing Mix）是企业市场营销战略的一个重要组成部分，是指将企业可控的基本营销措施组成一个整体性活动。市场营销的主要目的是满足消费者的需要。在20世纪60年代初，根据需求中心论的营销观念，麦卡锡教授把企业开展营销活动的可控因素归纳为四类，即产品、价格、销售渠道和促销，因此，提出了市场营销的4P组合。

(A) Product issues

(a) Size/brand name/package.
(b) Core product & augments (installation/warranties/after-sales service).
(c) Product life cycle: a product may be expected to go through the stages of introduction, growth, maturity, decline and senility, this is product life cycle. Product might show different profitability in different life cycle.

(B) Price issues

There are different pricing tactics that companies could make a choice and they should take costs, customer acceptance, competition and company's strategy into consideration before implementation.

Common pricing tactics including:

(a) **Penetration pricing**: setting a low price when a new product is introduced to the public in order to capture substantial customers quickly.

> **核心考点**
>
> Marketing 是整个职能部分最重要的考点，marketing orientation 及 the marketing mix 考试频率很高，同时也为 p-level 的学习奠定基础。

> **核心考点**
>
> 区别前两种定价方式：
> Penetration pricing 一般是在产品进入市场初期时将其价格定在较低水平，以吸引更多的消费者。前期会牺牲部分毛利，在短期内迅速扩大市场占有率，进而达到规模经济（economic of scale）来获取利益。
> Skimming 是相对 penetration pricing 的一个概念。当生产厂家把新产品推向市场时，利用消费者的求新心理，定一个高价，先从这一部分特定消费者那里取得高额利润，然后再逐渐把价格降下来，以适应大众的需求水平。

(b) **Skimming pricing**: setting a high price oppositely with the aim to skimming high profits of the market from customers who are insensitive of prices.

(c) **Cost plus pricing**: setting the price after adding a certain percentage mark-up on the costs.

(d) **Perceived quality pricing**: setting a high price to form a perception of quality product of customers.

(e) **Price discrimination**: setting different prices for different customer groups.

(f) **Going rate pricing**: setting a same price of the prevailing price of the market.

(g) **Loss leaders**: setting an unprofitable price with the aim to attract and stimulate customers to buy more products and the previous loss could be covered finally.

(h) **Captive product pricing**: setting a low price with the core product but a high price of the captive (complementary) product.

(C) **Place**

This refers to all activities related to moving the product from the producer to the consumer. It is concerned with distribution through the producer's channels to market. In brief, they are issues about where and how the products are sold.

(D) **Promotion**

Promotion refers to all activities that are intended to inform the customer and influence the purchasing decision (e.g. advertising, sales promotion, public relations).

Promotion activities are usually carried out follows the sequence of raising awareness, arousing interest, stimulating desire and promoting actions of customers (AIDA).

在这里，产品是指考虑为目标市场开发适当的产品，选择产品线、品牌和包装等；价格是指考虑制订适当的价格；渠道是指要通过适当的渠道安排运输储藏等把产品送到目标市场；促销是指考虑如何将适当的产品，按适当的价格，在适当的地点通知目标市场，包括销售推广、广告、培养推销员等。

> **知识点解读**
> 后续几种定价方式考生了解即可，考试概率很低。

精益求精

The additional marketing mix (3Ps):

(E) **People**

It matters on how to improve employees' services to meet customers' expectations.

(F) **Processes**

It considerations about how to improve effectiveness of delivering benefits to the customers.

(G) **Physical evidence**

It matters on how to design and implement physical cues to which the customer may respond positively.

1.4.2 Marketing orientation

(a) Market orientation means a business philosophy that focuses on identifying customer wants or needs and then meeting them ("What Is Market Orientation", n.d.).

(b) Product orientation approach lays emphasis on a totally different direction compared to the market orientation approach. Companies with product orientation put more efforts on exploring their own advantages in product design rather than responding to customer needs to improve products.

The difference between these two orientations are briefly summarised in the picture below (见图 6 - 1).

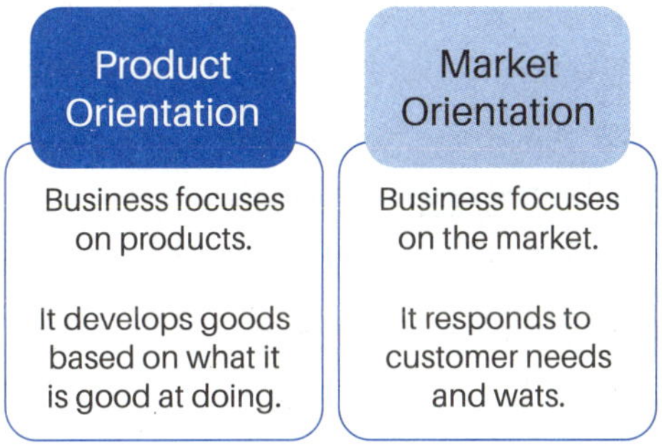

Product Orientation
Business focuses on products.
It develops goods based on what it is good at doing.

Market Orientation
Business focuses on the market.
It responds to customer needs and wats.

图 6 - 1 Different types of orientation

> **核心考点**
>
> 这 4 种不同的营销导向方式，在考试中可以通过抓关键词迅速作出判断。分别为注重产量(production)、注重产品特征(product feature)、说服顾客(persuade)以及注重市场需求(market needs)。Production orientation 是指由于商品供不应求，市场经济呈卖方市场状态；在 Product orientation 的营销理念下，生产者认为消费者愿意付出更高的价格以购买到更好质量、性能的产品，如"酒香不怕巷子深"；不同于前两种的是消费者主动来消费，sales orientation 生产观念、产品观念由 pull 变为 push，通过不同定价模式以及市场方案销售产品，赚取利润；Marketing orientation 认为实现企业目标的关键是满足目标顾客的需求和期望，企业在生产中以消费者的需求为主要向导。

精益求精

在实际商业运作中，一般存在 4 种不同的营销导向方式，分别为注重产量(production)、注重产品特征(product feature)、注重销售(sales orientation)以及注重市场需求(market needs)。Production orientation 指由于商品供不应求，市场经济呈现卖方市场状态；在 Product orientation 的营销理念下，生产者认为消费者愿意付出更高的价格以购买到更好质量、性能的产品，如"酒香不怕巷子深"；不同于前两种是消费者主动来消费，sales orientation 生产观念、产品观念由 pull 变为 push，通过不同定价模式以及市场方案销售产品，企图说服(persuade)顾客，赚取利益；Marketing orientation 认为实现企业目标的关键是满足目标顾客的需求和期望，企业在生产中以消费者的需求为主要向导。

小试牛刀

Example question 1

ABC Ltd is a car-manufacturing company. In order to increase its profitability level, it focuses largely on doing market research about customers' preferences and begin to provide customer-tailored cars.

This is an example of which type of "orientation"?

  A. Production   B. Sales   C. Marketing   D. Purchasing

1.4.3 Market segmentation

  Market segmentation involves analysis of the market which enables companies to divide the market into sub-sets according to different characteristics of different customer groups.

Commonly used segments include:
- Age.
- Gender.
- Geographical location.
- Socio-economic groups.
- Psychological factors, such as risk appetite, desire to conform or be different, and so on.

市场细分(market segmentation)就是指企业按照某种标准将市场上的顾客划分成若干个顾客群,每一个顾客群构成一个子市场,不同子市场之间,需求存在着明显差别。 市场细分是选择目标市场的基础。 市场营销在企业的活动包括细分一个市场并把它作为公司的目标市场,设计正确的产品、服务、价格、促销和分销系统"组合",以满足细分市场内顾客的需要和欲望。

对于这个知识点的理解,可以结合第二章讲到的 PESTEL 模型,特别是 social 的部分,商家可以根据不同消费者的消费模式(buying pattern)、家庭生命周期(family life cycle)和社会阶层(social class)等,进行市场细分。

Segmentation provides insights into strategic opportunities and options.

(a) Mass (undifferentiated) marketing: the most convenient strategy as there would be only one product applies in all sub-markets.

(b) Targeted marketing: a highly focused approach by targeted marketing aimed at very specific market segments.

(c) Differentiated marketing: address several segments deploying different marketing mixes.

小试牛刀

Example question 2

Analysis of costs and revenues of different products would assist the marketing department in respect of which activity?

A. Differentiating the technical features of products from those of competitors

B. Calculating the maximum discounts that sales personnel are permitted to offer

C. Determining production bonuses to be paid

D. Targeting sales efforts towards the most appropriate socio-economic groups

知识点解读

服务具备 4 个特征:无形性(**Intangibility**)、不可分离性(**Inseparability**)、差异性(**Variability**),以及不转移所有权(**Ownership**)。

1.5 Service

1.5 Service

Services are rather different from goods, the most obvious difference is that services are intangible, while goods are possessed with physical existence. This is called as **intangibility**. In addition, there are three other features of services due to intangibility:

(a) **Inseparability**. The inseparability means the provision and consumption of service cannot be separated. Simply speaking, service is consumed when it is provided, and it cannot be stored.

(b) **Variability**. Due to lack of physical existence, it is difficult to exert clear standards on services. which is dependent on variety of factors, for example, the person who delivers it, the place where it is provided, and so on.

(c) **Ownership**. Provision of services does not result the transfer of ownership, and customers just pay for the process of consumption, which also distinguishes services from goods.

1.6 Administration

Administration includes the range of activities concerned with organising and supervising methods that organisations operate with. In this chapter, we focus on the function of monitoring, controlling and updating office documents, to ensure the availability of them when there is the need of presentation, reporting in organisations.

Administration function is often centralised to enjoy better control and consistency, and also economies of scale.

1.7 Finance

(a) **Transaction recording**: accounts should be recorded according to daily operation;

(b) **Money controlling**: finance department should keep close eye on movement of money;

(c) **Fund raising**: a company might raise new funds from the following sources (using the expertise in its treasury department if it has one): capital markets, money markets, retained earnings, bank borrowings, government sources and the international markets.

(d) **Information provision**: information should be prepared to both internal and external users.

> **知识点解读**
>
> 财务部门的职能以及会计体系的学习，是 AB 的重点，我们会在第 7 章具体学习，在这里大家先对财务职能作初步了解。

博学多才

Capital market 被称为资本市场，又叫作长期金融市场；Money markets 被称为货币市场，又叫作短期金融市场，两者共同构成了金融市场。顾名思义，这两种金融市场最大的区别在于该市场上交易的金融工具到期日不同。

资本市场中，涉及的融资活动期限较长，金融工具到期日一般都在 1 年以上，其对应的风险也较大，证券市场就是一个典型的资本市场。

相对的，货币市场中融资活动的期限通常在 1 年以内，由于期限短，该市场具备了流动性强以及风险相对较小的特点。票据贴现市场是货币市场的典型代表。

1.8 Human resources

Human resources or HR is the company department charged with finding, screening, recruiting, and training job applicants, and administering employee-benefit programs. As companies reorganize to gain a competitive edge, HR plays a

> **知识点解读**
>
> 整个 ACCA 体系中，只有 AB 课程涉及了人力资源的部分，我们会在本书的 Part C 中详细解读，包含了 HR 的方方面面。

key role in helping companies deal with a fast-changing environment and the greater demand for quality employees.

小试牛刀

Example question 3

F Technology Group is an offshoring company that manufactures mobile phones. Recently it has built a new production line that can reduce product defects. Therefore, raw materials which are bought in from suppliers, has been reduced by advanced manufacturing processes.

Which of the following organisational activities have directly contributed to the increased competitiveness of F Co?

A. Production only
B. Service and marketing
C. Purchasing and production
D. Purchasing and service

2 Shared services approach

The shared services approach is a medium through which defined services can be provided **across the organisation** by a dedicated unit. This differs from outsourcing, in that the shared services provider **is a part of** the organisation.

(a) Shared services organisations reduce the level of duplication of tasks. For example, instead of each part of the organisation employing human resources or information technology specialists, these services can be provided centrally through a single team.

(b) In this way, they can reduce costs significantly and standardise the policies and processes across the business.

(c) While the use of shared services organisations is increasing, the model is not suitable for all. For example, if the business units are very diverse, a centralised model may not be appropriate.

3 Committees

3.1 Types of committee

表6-2 **Types of committee**

Types	Function of committee
Executive committee	This type of committee is made up of people occupying top positions in an organisation who have the powers to administer the day to day affairs of the organisation
Standing committee	Refers to any committee that is a permanent feature within the management structure of an organisation
Ad hoc committee	An ad hoc committee is set up for the main purpose of performing a specific task. Once the task is completed, the ad hoc committee is then dissolved

---

核心考点

Committee（委员会）是一个核心考点，考试中出现频率非常高。其主要考核内容集中在：

（1）不同类型的committee，题目可能会给出背景描述，让同学们识别这是哪一种committee（见表6-2）；

（2）Committee的意义，也就是committee的优点，一般这个考点涉及的题目比较直接，同学们直接判断即可（见表6-3）；

（3）Committee chair（委员会主席）and committee secretary（委员会秘书）的不同职责。这个考点虽然简单，但出现非常频繁，请同学们务必记忆。

Types	Function of committee
Sub-committee	A sub-committee is connected with a larger committee that is more powerful and important than it. A large committee can appoint one or more of its members to form another committee under it in the name of a sub-committee
Joint committee	This committee acts as a link between two committees and coordinates their actions or activities together

这里不同委员会可以分成三大类，第一类根据委员会所执行的事务进行划分，可以划分为 executive committee（执行委员会）；第二类根据委员会存在的时间长短划分，可以分为 standing committee（常务委员会）和 ad hoc committee（临时委员会）；第三类根据形成过程是合并还是拆分，可以划分为 sub-committee（下设委员会）以及 joint committee（联合委员会）。分成这三类进行记忆对同学们来说会方便快捷许多。

3.2 Purposes of committees

(a) **Facilitating ideas generation** through brainstorming.
(b) Ability of **problem solving** can be improved by combining abilities and skills of various members.
(c) **Coordination.** All relevant interests will be taken into consideration and coordinated by committees.
(d) **Making recommendations** to relevant parties for the purpose of improving organisations' operations.

3.3 The roles of Chair and secretary of committee

(A) **The committee chair**

(a) To ensure that the committee operates efficiently and effectively.
(b) To promote regular attendance and full involvement in discussions.
(c) To decide the scope of each meeting.
(d) To be responsible for time management of committee meetings.

(B) **The secretary of committee**

(a) To prepare agendas in liaison with the chair, monitor the progress and schedule of the committee's business.
(b) To ensure that the committee operates in accordance with these guidelines.
(c) To advise the chair on issues relating to the committee and to ensure that the chair is well informed.
(d) To take the minutes of the meeting according to agreed conventions and ensure that the necessary follow up action is taken.

> **核心考点**
> 再次提醒大家，3.3 这个考点虽然简单，但是非常容易考到，务必记忆背诵。

3.4 Appraisal of committees

表6-3 Appraisal of committees

Advantages	Disadvantages
Combination of authority and skills	Slower decision-making and high management costs
Motivating lower level managers by delegation of authority	Managers cannot fully concentrate on operations due to interference of meetings hold
Encourage open discussion and brainstorming due to blurring responsibility	Quality of decisions may be compromised due to blurring responsibility
Delay. A committee is used to gain time and reduce conflicts	Delay. Efficiency of operations may be compromised due to frequent conferences and discussions among committees.

4 Levels in the organisation

4.1 Levels of strategy

4.1.1 Corporate strategies

The **most general** strategy, **long-term**, relatively complex, focuses on the activities of the **whole** company, the threats and opportunities in the **environment**, the value systems of people, obtaining and allocating **corporate resources**.

公司总体战略主要考虑的问题是公司应当做什么，是否需要拓展新的业务或者市场等。

4.1.2 Business strategies

Business strategy is more detailed than corporate ones, which focuses on **specific divisions and specifies how to use resources.** For example, some large companies are divided into different SBUs (strategic business units) which have different products or different locations. In brief, business strategies are those aiming to achieving goals of each SBUs.

业务单元战略关注的是，在公司总体战略选定的市场或行业中，应当如何经营才能取得竞争优势；以及如何调配资源给公司不同的业务单位才能最大程度地满足公司整体的利益。

4.1.3 Operational/functional strategies

Functional/operational strategies put emphasis on certain functions such as marketing, production, finance, human resources management, information system, R&D, IT etc.

4.2 Levels of management-The Anthony hierarchy/triangle

Robert Anthony classified managerial activity as three levels（见表6-4）.

表 6-4　Levels of management-Anthony hierarchy

Levels	Who	What	Time frame of decisions
Strategic management	Senior level managers, e.g. chief executives	Macro matters, for example: • General direction for the whole organisation. • Standard policy for the whole system. • Handling crisis on behalf of whole organisation	Long term, usually 3~5 years
Tactical management	Middle level managers, e.g. head of departments	Translating strategic management requirements, and adopting appropriate methods to achieve them, for example: • Utilising resources among organisations. • Arranging coordination between functions. • Identify available and profitable markets	Medium term, usually 1~3 years
Operational management	Operational level managers, e.g. supervisors	Dealing with day-to-day activities of each department	Short term. Usually less than 1 year

Note：The time frame of three levels above is a quite flexible estimation, which should be considered with different organisations' conditions.

4.3 Levels of information

在了解跟层级相关的信息之前，我们应当先了解两个基本概念：data（数据）与 information（信息）。

- Data consists of numbers, letters, symbols, raw facts, events and transactions, which have been recorded but not yet processed into a form that is suitable for making decisions.
- Information is data that has been processed in such a way that it has meaning to the person that receives it, who may then use it to improve the quality of their decision-making.

在组织中，信息存在的意义之一就是辅助管理层作出正确的决策。通过前面的学习我们已经知道，不同管理层级的技能背景、关注层面以及战略制定的目光长短都不一样，因此，不同的管理层级需要不同的信息来帮助他们进行决策制定。根据管理层级，信息同样可以被分成三个层级（见表 6-5）。

> **核心考点**
>
> 组织中的层级是考试中的核心和高频考点，考生需要准确区分每个层级的特征，并着重记忆描述特征的关键词。例如，monitor and control 通常是针对 tactical level 的。

> **核心考点**
>
> 将管理层级与信息的层级匹配进行考核是一个常见的考点，考生需要理解和记忆不同层级需要什么样的信息。如果考题复杂一些，可能不会直接告诉考生这是什么层级，而是通过背景描述进行暗示，在这情况之下，同学们需要先行判断层级，再匹配其相应的所需信息。

表 6-5　Levels of information

System level	System purpose	Information required
Strategic	Top level information aims to help **senior managers** to set **long-term** strategies, which can match organisations' strengths and capabilities with external environment	The information should be core and connected with environment, for example: (a) Overall market analysis. (b) Key industry ratios. (c) Government policies

System level	System purpose	Information required
Tactical	**Middle level** information aims to help **middle managers** to **monitor and control** operations.	The information would be in a summarised form, but detailed enough to allow tactical planning of resources and manpower, for example: (a) Budgets. (b) Variance reports. (c) Exception reports
Operational	Lowest level information aims to help **operational managers** to **supervise** the organisation's **daily** operational activities	The information is detailed and precise, for example: (a) Customer orders. (b) Invoices. (c) Shift pattern of employees

小试牛刀

Example question 4

ABC Co. is one of the best restaurants in the town. Andy as a manager for the ABC Co. He tries to analyse how many customers will have dinner in their restaurant every day. Which type of information should Andy use to help him analyse the situation?

A. Tactical   B. Operational   C. Strategic

4.4 Information system to support decision making

As each level of managers need different type of information, we need different information system to support them.

表6-6 Levels of information system

Levels of information	Information system used to support
Operational	Transaction processing system (TPS)
Tactical	Management information system (MIS)
Strategic	Executive information system (EIS)

4.4.1 Transaction processing system (TPS)

A TPS records all the **daily** transactions of the organisation and summarises them so they can be reported on a routine basis. TPS is used mainly by operational managers to make basic decisions.

4.4.2 Management information system (MIS)

MIS **convert data from TPS into information** for tactical mangers to help them **monitor and control** performance.

4.4.3 Executive information system (EIS)

It provides **strategic** managers with flexible access to information from the **entire business** as well as the external environment.

核心考点

这个知识点经常会与 level of information（见表6-6）结合起来出现，考生需要掌握不同层级需要的信息类型，以及在该层级需要什么样的信息系统来支持信息的采集和获取。

4.4 Information system to support decision making

Answers for example question

1. C   2. B   3. A   4. B

Summary

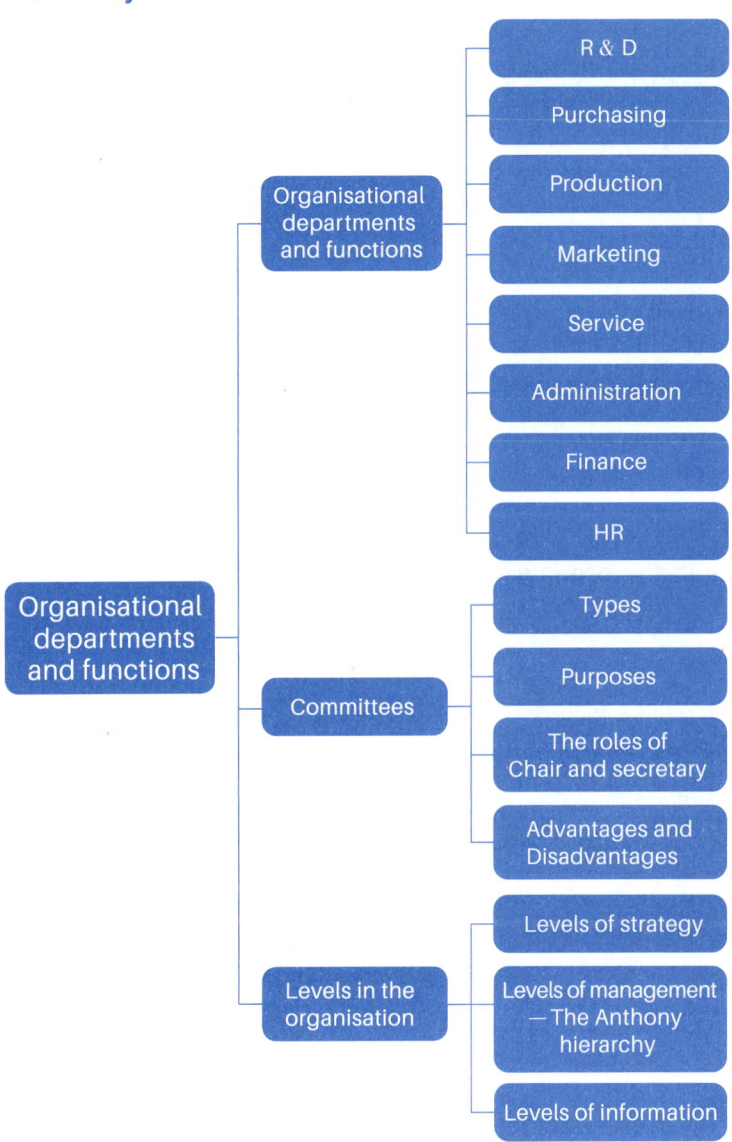

Chapter 6 考试不同问法总结

1. 针对 departments

- In which of the following business functions is A working?
- Which TWO of the following departments are involved in devising ways to reduce product costs?
- Which of the following is a financial consideration of a marketing manager in a business that follows a marketing orientation?
- Which of the following is an Advantage of a just-in-time purchasing strategy?
- Which of the following is an essential feature of any definition of marketing?
- Which of the strategies should A recommend if the company want to per-

suade as many people as possible to buy the product in its early stages?
- Which of the following pairs of components of the marketing mix is the work of the procurement department MOST relevant?

2. 针对 committee
- What is the purpose of a committee?
- Which TWO of the following are Advantages/Disadvantages of committee (as opposed to individual decision-making)?
- Which TWO of the following statements regarding committees/about management by committee are correct?
- Which of the following are important consideration when deciding the size of a committee?
- Which TWO of the following are responsibilities of a committee secretary?
- Which member should sign the minutes of a committee meeting to confirm they are true and accurate record of meeting?
- In which of the following types of committee is each individual active?
- Should each activity below be undertaken by chair or secretary?

3. 针对 Levels in the organisation
- Which of the following describes/would be classified as the tactical level of Anthony's hierarchy?
- At which level of the organisation would this information be required?
- Indicate the level within an organisation to which the following types of information are relevant.
- Which TWO of the following are most relevant when taking strategic level decisions?
- Annual budgets and reports on how employees and machinery will be deployed for the year ahead are examples of which type of information?

Quick quiz

6.1 Which of the following is/are not objectives of human resource management?

(1) To develop an effective human component for the organisation which will respond effectively to change.

(2) To obtain and develop HR required by the organisation and to use and motivate them effectively.

(3) To meet the organisation's social and legal responsibilities relating to the human resource.

(4) To administer payroll.

 A. (1) and (2)   B. (2) and (3)   C. (3) and (4)   D. Only (4)

Answer: D

Difficulty level: Easy

Tag: Human resource management

Rationale:

 This question is set to examine the objectives of human resource management. Statements (1)(2)(3) are all objectives of human resource management. Statements (4) is the finance function which administer payroll, not HRM.

 这道题考查的是人力资源管理的目标，前三个陈述都是人力资源管理的目标，第四个陈述管理薪酬是财务部门的职能，而不是人力资源管理职能。

6.2 Which of the following would usually not be included in the role of the committee secretary?

 A. Fixing date, time and location

 B. Preparing and issuing documents

 C. Assisting Chair

 D. Give immediate ruling on points of dispute or doubt

Answer: D

Difficulty level: Easy

Tag: Role of the committee secretary

Rationale:

 This question examines the role of the committee secretary. Option D is the role of the committee chair.

 这道题考查的是委员会秘书的角色，D 选项是委员会主席的角色。

6.3 F Ltd is an automobile producer in the A island. It produces a new model car recently, and the cars are so popular that its supply drop far behind its demand. And the cars can only be available in black. The CEO of F Ltd insisted arrogantly, "We never care about customers' favourite colours, because customers will buy whatever we produce". **This is an example of which type of "orientation"?**

 A. Production   B. Sales   C. Marketing   D. Product

Answer: A

Difficulty level: Easy

Tag: Marketing orientation

Rationale:

 A production orientation assumes that customer will buy whatever is produced. In this case, it's also said car's supply cannot meet customer's demand, so if customers want to buy this car, they have no other choices. The CEO's words about car's colour has also proved this.

A product orientation assumes that producer will add more features to the product no matter whether customer actually want it or not.

A sales orientation occurs when customers are persuaded to buy the products.

A marketing orientation focus on customer's needs to design products and to produce what customers want to buy.

产量导向意味着厂家生产什么客户就会买什么，在这个案例中，厂家的汽车产量无法满足客户的需求，因此客户如果想买这个型号的汽车，就没有别的选择。 CEO 关于汽车颜色的言论也证实了这一点。

产品导向意味着厂家会在产品中加入一些新功能，无论客户是否想要这些功能。

销售导向阶段，客户通常被劝去买产品。

营销导向阶段，厂家会关注客户的需求，然后去生产客户想要买的产品。

6.4 **Which TWO of the following activities are performed by the accounting function in a multinational company?**

A. Obtaining price quotations

B. Preparation of financial reports

C. Acquiring raw materials

D. Producing invoices to clients

Answer: B, D

Difficulty level: Easy

Tag: The accounting/financing department

Rationale:

Financial accountant is responsible for producing financial reports and producing sales invoices to clients. Therefore, option B and D are correct answers. However, option B and D are the purchasing department's duties.

这道题考查的是会计/财务部门的职责工作。 A 选项，获取供应商报价单，这是采购部门负责的工作，所以排除 A 选项。 B 选项，准备财务报告，这是会计部门的工作，所以 B 选项正确。 C 选项，采购原材料，这同样是采购部门的工作，因此排除 C 选项。 最后，D 选项，发销售发票给顾客，这也是会计部门的工作。 所以，最终答案为 BD。

6.5 **Which of the following correctly describes the purpose of a committee?**

A. To promote fast decision-making

B. To reduce power of a manager

C. To facilitate rounded decisions through brainstorming

Answer: C

Difficulty level: Easy

Tag: The purposes of a committee

Rationale:

The purposes of a committee contain creating new ideas, excellent means of communication, problem-solving, combing abilities, coordination, etc. In a committee, all members are specialists in their fields and can make contributions to the final decision. Therefore, in theory, a committee can make better decisions.

这道题考查的是成立委员会的目的。 委员会成立有很多目的，其中就包括促进问题的解决，作出一个高质量的决策。 因为委员会中的成员都是某一个专业领域的专家，所以可以作出各自的贡献，因此最后委员会作出的决策，在理论上，一定是高质量且全面的决策，也就是选项 C。

Chapter 7
The role of accounting

知识导入

上一章中我们考察了公司内部的各个部门，了解了它们是什么，以及它们在公司中起到什么样的作用，而其中有个部门与会计师有千丝万缕的联系，那就是财务部门，有时又称为会计部门。那么，会计到底是什么？会计部门又有什么样的划分？让我们一起走进会计部门。

单词表

英文	中文
Statement of financial position	资产负债表
Statement of profit or loss	利润表
Statement of cash flows	现金流量表
Variance reports	差异报告
Exception reports	特例报告
Credit control	信贷管控
Invoices	发票
Bias	偏见
Discretion	自由裁量权
Alter	修改
Inventory	存货
Working capital	营运资本
Liability	负债
Equity	所有者权益
Receivable ledger	应收账款分类账
Payable ledger	应付账款分类账
Database	数据库

学习指南

Learning objectives	Pass level	Distinction level	用时建议
1. What is accounting	√		2 mins
2. Users of accounting information (2.1-2.2)	√		5 mins
3. Nature, principles and scope of accounting (3.1-3.2)	√		10 mins
4. External and internal reports (3.2.1-3.2.2)	√		20 mins
5. Regulatory system (4)	√		10 mins
6. Common software applications (5)	√		10 mins
7. Fintech (6)	√		10 mins

本章考点

重要考点	难度（1~3）
熟记并理解会计的定义	1
着重记忆和理解会计信息的使用者的侧重点	1
熟记并理解会计部门的构成以及 FA 和 MA 的区别	2
熟记并理解内外部报告的含义与区别	3
理解 Regulatory system	2
理解常用电算化系统的运作方式及优缺点	2
理解 Fintech 大致特点	3

1 What is accounting?

Accounting is a systematic process of **recording**, **analysing** and **summarising** transactions of a business.

The person in charge of accounting is called accountant, and this individual is typically required to follow a set of rules and regulations.

博学多才

会计历史悠久，在远古时期就是人类文明的一部分。从严格意义上讲，自旧石器时代到奴隶社会繁盛时期（距今约四五千年）为止，这一时期被称为会计的萌芽阶段，或者称为原始计量与记录时代。随着社会的发展，劳动生产力的不断提高，会计逐渐从生产职能中分离出来，要委托专门的人，采用较先进、科学的计量与记录方法。

1494 年，意大利数学家卢卡·帕乔利的著作《算术、几何、比及比例概要》问世，创建了复式簿记方式（double entry），这是会计发展史上非常重要的里程碑，标志着近代会计的开端。一直延续到现在，我们仍然采用复式簿记的方法（具体记账方法会在 FA 财务会计科目中学习）。与此同时，会计从特殊的、专门委托当事人的独立职能发展成为一种职业。

既然会计是记录并总结交易信息的，我们接下来就看看，会计提供的信息都有哪些常见的使用者（见表 7-1）。

知识点解读

会计信息的使用者不仅仅是管理层或股东，企业的各类 stakeholders（利益相关者）也会关注会计信息中的方方面面，并且每一个 stakeholder 都有各自的要求和需要。
作为公司，重要的是知道每一个 stakeholder 的需要，这样能够更加准确地了解并且满足他们的需求。

2 The users of accounting information

表 7-1　Users of accounting information

WHO (stakeholder)	WHAT (information)	WHY
Managers	All information	Effective control and decision making
Employees	Financial situation	Career development/Pay
Shareholders	Profitability	Management's performance Change of shareholder wealth

知识点解读

在所有的利益相关者中，管理者是需要最多信息的人，他们不仅需要财务信息，还需要非财务信息；不仅需要了解过去业绩表现，也需要了解现在以及未来的业绩预测。

续表

WHO (stakeholder)	WHAT (information)	WHY
Trade contacts: supplier/customers	Creditability/supply	Risk
The creditors	Creditability/liquidity	Risk
Tax authority (Her Majesty's Revenue and Customs)	Profit	Tax assessment
Financial analysts and advisers	Information (depend on their clients)	For client
Government	Financial situation	Resource allocation; National statistics
The public	Relevant information	Local economy; Employment position; Environment (pollution)

会计信息是由财务部门提供的，接下来我们系统地学习财务部门的架构。 总体来说，财务部门的架构可以分成三条线，分别为财务会计线、管理会计线，以及资金管理线。 其实这几条线的学习，也刚好对应了ACCA的课程设置。 财务会计线主要是FA/FR/SBR三个科目，管理会计线主要是MA/PM/APM三个科目，而资金管理线则对应了FM/AFM这两个科目。 具体每条线的细节与核心内容，同学们可以在接下来的ACCA课程中感受。

3 Nature, principles and scope of accounting

3.1 The structure of accounting function

The structure of accounting function is as follows（见图7－1）.

In many larger companies, the finance director has one or more deputies below him/her.

核心考点

关于3种职位各自职责的内容是非常重要的考点，同学们要学会进行区分辨析，通过不同职责的具体工作内容来确定职位。

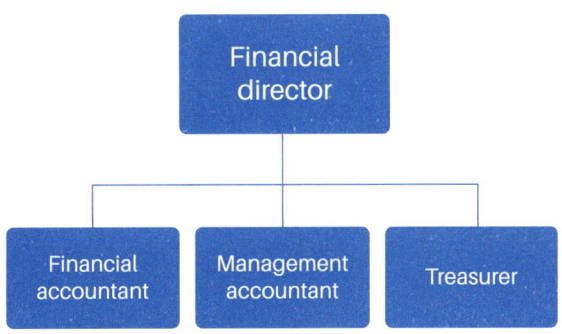

图7－1 Structure of accounting function

3.1.1 Financial accountant

(a) Routine accounting, for example, recording of daily transactions.

(b) **Providing accounting reports** about **historical performance.**

3.1.2 Management accounting

(a) **Cost** analysis.

(b) **Budgets** and control.

3.1.3 Treasurer

Treasury management is the acquisition and deployment of financial resources, mainly focusing on **investment and financing** decisions.

(a) Raising funds by borrowing.

(b) Investing surplus funds.

(c) Cash management (preparation of cash budgets and arrangement of overdraft).

(d) Working capital management (working capital represents the net current assets available for day-to-day operating activities. It is calculated as current assets minus current liabilities. The components are usually inventory, trade receivables, trade payables and cash).

(e) Foreign currency risk management.

(f) Tax management (such as tax mitigation, not tax evasion).

These three functions performing on different tasks, however, **they also need cooperation and may rely on another role's works.**

> **知识点解读**
> 营运资本是指可供日常经营活动使用的流动资产净额。它的计算方法是流动资产减去流动负债。净营运资本的多少可以反映偿还短期债务的能力。

小试牛刀

Example question 1

With which **TWO** of the following is cash and working capital management concerned?

A. Controlling the level of receivables

B. Monitoring the level of long-term liabilities

C. Verifying the existence and condition of non-current assets

D. Managing quantities of inventories and work-in-progress

在学习了财务部门的职能划分之后，接下来我们细致地区分管理会计与财务会计，这部分内容是考试重点，需要同学们多理解。

3.2 Financial accounting and management accounting

(A) Financial accounting

It is mainly focused on recording, processing financial information and preparing financial statements **mainly to the external** users.

(B) Management accounting

It is mainly focused on analysing data to provide information as a basis **for managerial action** to act as assistance for managers to plan, direct and control organisation's operations.

The main differences between financial accounting and management accounting are summarised below:

> **基本概念**
> 学会区分财务会计和管理会计。财务会计专注于对外的信息披露，披露的信息格式较为固定。管理会计专注于对内提供有用的信息以供决策者进行计划决策，信息没有固定的格式（见表7-2）。

表 7-2 Differences between financial accounting and management accounting

Classification	Targets	Forms	Types of data	Apply standards?
Financial accounting	External shareholders and other stakeholders	Financial statements	Mainly financial focus	Yes
Management accounting	Internal management	Internal reports	Both financial and non-financial	No

通过前面的学习，我们了解到财务会计提供的更多的是服务外部利益相关者的报告，我们统称之为外部报告（external report）；而管理会计使用的更多的是服务内部利益相关者的报告，我们称之为内部报告（internal report）。接下来，我们就系统地学习每个报告的组成部分和主要内容。

3.2.1 External reports

（A）The statement of profit or loss（SOPL）

The statement of profit or loss, also called income statement, reports a company's profitability **during** a specified period of time.

The income statement is a company's financial statement that indicates how the revenue is transformed into profits by deducting expenditures. The purpose of the income statement is to show managers and investors whether the company made profit or loss during the period being reported.

（B）The statement of financial position（SOFP）

The statement of financial position, also known as a balance sheet, is a financial document which provides a financial overview by listing all the assets owned, all the liabilities owed and the residual equity of a business **at** a particular date.

The statement of financial position is demonstrated according to the accounting equation：

$$Assets = Liabilities + Equity$$

Asset is any resource controlled by an entity and from which future economic benefits are expected to **flow into** the entity. Assets listed in a balance sheet can be divided into current assets (e.g. cash, inventory, receivables) and non-current assets (e.g. property, plant, equipment).

Liability represents a present obligation an entity owes to other entities and the settlement of which would result in future economic benefits to **flow out** of the entity. Liabilities listed in a balance sheet can also be divided into current liabilities (e.g. trade payables) and non-current liabilities (e.g. loan note).

Equity refers to the owners' interests in the business, which is the **residual claim** of all assets after deducting all liabilities. The most common components of equity are retained earnings and share capital.

（C）The statement of cash flows

Most companies prepare their financial statements based on accrual basis, rather than cash basis, which means profit or loss is merely a reflection of financial

---

核心考点

对于内部报告和外部报告内容以及理解的考查，是这一章最高频的考点，同时也是 AB 与 FA 重合的考点，需要同学们特别留意。

知识点解读

利润表反映的是企业在一定会计期间内的经营成果，它又被称为损益表、收益表。

知识点解读

资产负债表呈现的是公司在某一个时间节点的财务状况，而并非每一个时间段内的经营表现。

知识点解读

现金流量表是反映一定时期内（如月度、季度或年度）企业经营活动、投资活动和筹资活动对其现金及现金等价物所产生影响的财务报表。

position in accounting. Thus, a cash flow statement could help the company to understand the **real cash movements** of it during a specified period of time.

The cash flow statement shows the cash receipts and payments in operating, financing and investing activities during the past accounting period. It could assist analysing and identifying problems such as whether the company is solvent or has liquidity trouble (liquidity reflects the ability to pay short term liabilities).

小试牛刀

Example question 2

Example question 2

Jack is carrying out an analysis of Thor Co., and has obtained its published statement of financial position and statement of profit and loss.

In which financial statement will Jack find the following information?

	A Statement of financial position	B Statement of profit or loss
Non-current assets		
Turnover		
Gross profit		
Shareholders' funds		
Firm's liquidity		
Intrinsic value of a business at a point in time		

Example question 3

Example question 3

Which **TWO** of the following activities could not affect a company's cash flow?

A. Repayment of bonds
B. Accruals
C. Interest expense paid
D. Depreciation of non-current assets

Example question 4

Anna is carrying out an analysis of Avengers Co and has obtained its published statement of financial position and statement of profit and loss.

Which **TWO** information can be found in statement of financial position?

A. Non-current assets
B. Gross profit
C. Shareholders' funds
D. Turnover

3.2.2 Internal reports

(A) Cost schedule

It is an analysis of the expenses spent by organisations and can be produced for any expenses such as costs of sales, administration costs, departmental costs, etc. Cost schedule can support managers in making pricing decision, break-even analysis and investment appraisal etc.

(B) Budgets

Budgets are prepared to show **projected** sales, costs, overheads and profits.

Budgets enable managers to identify potential cash shortage and arrange overdraft facilities with the bank **in advance**. At the same time, budgets could also help managers identify potential cash surplus and search for investment opportunities.

(C) Variance reports

The variance reports detail the **differences between the actual performance and budgets** and explain the reasons behind any material variances. Variance reports could assist the management in controlling the procedures and performance of the business.

(D) Exception reports

Exception reporting is one special form of variance reports which focuses attention on those items where performance differs **significantly** from standard or budget.

> **知识点解读**
>
> 当实际成本与预算成本存在差异，相应的层级需要对这个差异的来源进行调查和分析，以优化生产过程，充分利用资源。这就是差异报告。
>
> 当差异重大时，差异报告已经不足以引起重视，此时需要例外报告来对该重大差异进行解释。
>
> 两者还有其他的区别：差异报告属于日常经营活动中的一部分，而例外报告只在重大差异发生时才需要撰写，并对上级报告。

精益求精

3.3 Integrated reporting

Integrated reporting is a different way of presenting business's information to its stakeholders, trying to make financial reporting more complete, transparent, coherent and relevant.

It combines the financial and any other relevant information into one single document. The main purpose is to provide an illustration on how the organisation creates value over time.

3.3.1 The core content elements of IR are as follows:

(a) Organisational overview.

(b) Governance.

(c) Opportunities and risks.

(d) Strategy and resource allocation.

(e) Business model.

(f) Performance.

(g) Future outlook.

> **精益求精**
>
> 在现有的外部报告形式下，公司的年报和可持续发展报告是各自独立的，无法给报表使用者一个更加全局的角度。而综合报告简单来讲是把公司的财务信息和一些重要的非财务信息（如环境、公司治理等）整合在一份报告当中，可以更全面地帮助相关方了解企业的发展状况和运营情况。

4 Regulatory system

企业内外部报告都必须遵循相应法规的规定，我们接下来会学习约束会计处理的法规以及制定法规的相关机构。在考试中大多考概念题，难度不高，但是需要同学们能熟记，这是作为会计人的基本常识。约束的法规大致可以分为两类，一类是法律规定，一类是会计准则的规定（现在大部分会计准则的规定都有法律效力）。

4.1 Company law

Limited companies are required by company law to prepare and publish accounts **annually.** The form, content of accounts as well as the accounting standards used are regulated.

A company can be **fined** and also face the **suspense** by the stock exchange if both requirements were violated.

(a) Failing to keep proper accounting records.

(b) Failing to file financial statements after the year end.

会计师在实际操作准备财务报表的过程中，往往会基于一些约定俗成的会计理念。每个人对于理念的理解不同，判断标准不同，可能就会造成差异。为了更好地提升会计信息的一致性，会计准则就产生了。我们主要学习全球较为通用的两类会计准则，一类是 U.S. GAAP，一类是大家在之后 ACCA 学习过程中一直会学到的 IFRS。

4.2 U.S. Generally Accepted Accounting Principles (U.S. GAAP)

U.S. GAAP is a set of **rules** governing accounting which may derive from company law, accounting standards, statutory requirements in other countries, stock exchange requirements.

4.3 International Financial Reporting Standards (IFRS)

To harmonise and bring about convergence of accounting standards in different countries, the International Financial Reporting standards (IFRS) Foundation has set up an offshoot called **International Accounting Standards Board to develop and approve IFRS.**

The Financial Statements are required to show a true and fair view. **Company directors (board of directors) are responsible** for it although the finance director is always delegated to make preparation for the Financial Statements. External auditing is required in listed companies each year to reasonably verify the 'true and fair view' of the Financial Statements.

> **知识点解读**
> 公司的董事（或者董事会）对公司的财务报表是否真实公允负责，尽管在实务中，财务报表的编制通常是委派财务总监来做。

小试牛刀

Example question 5

The government of Tayo carries some legal requirements which local companies must meet. Which of the following requires local companies to keep financial records and prepare accounts?

A. GAAP　　　　B. IFRS　　　　C. National legislation

Example question 6

Is each of the following statements true or false in relation to the purpose of International Financial Reporting Standards (IFRS)?

　　　　　　　　　　　　　　　　　　　　　　　　　　　　　True　False

(1) IFRS are used as national requirements in some countries.

(2) IFRS are required for a stock exchange listing in some countries.

(3) International reporting standards always intended to override local accounting regulations.

Example question 6

Example question 7

Which of the following is responsible if the financial statement of a company does not show a true and fair view of the financial performance of a company?

- A. The finance director
- B. The board of directors
- C. The external auditor
- D. The company chairman

5 Manual and computerised accounting systems

随着最近几年 IT 技术的迅猛发展，大部分企业的会计处理都过渡到了会计电算化(computerised accounting system)。

诚然，传统手工会计处理系统存在着很多问题，如效率低下（lower productivity），人工操作犯错误风险更高（higher risk of error）导致产出结果质量偏低（lower of quality of output），且传统手工账需要大量空间进行储存（bulky to handle and store），不易处理。但传统手工会计处理系统也有相对的优势，如不用承担 IT 系统崩溃导致的风险，也不需要电算化系统那么大的资本投资。

但不管是手工处理系统（manual accounting system），还是电算化系统，其背后遵循的原则都是一致的。接下来，我们就来学习电算化系统组成部分的一些基本概念。

5.1 Common software applications

(a) **Code**: Computers need to handle and process information in the forms of **codes**.

(b) **Module**: It is a program in an accounting system which focuses on one particular part of accounting function.

A simple accounting system might consist of only one module while more likely to consist of several modules (which constitutes to a suite) such as inventory, receivable ledger, payable ledger etc.

5.2 Integrated software

Integrated software is a software that **connects the most commonly used functions into one application. Each module is internally connected with the others**, so that any data entered in one module will be **linked automatically** (or by simple operator request) **to any other module where the data is of some relevance**.

整合系统，指的是把有相关性的模块融合在一个模块，当其中任何一个模块变动的时候，其他模块也能自动更新。譬如，当系统完成发货，更新了给顾客的发票信息的时候，应收账款、销售额和库存会进行自动调整。

整合系统的存在，极大地优化了工作流程。员工输入信息的时候，可以仅输入一次（**only need to make one entry**），其他信息自动更新；反之，提取信息也变得简单，任何有相关性的信息，都能快速查找到（**easy to extract required data from relevant**），从而极大地减少了系统使用者的工作量（**reduce the workload** of the user）。但是，整合系统也存在一定的缺点，因为它是为大部分公司日常运营服务的，提供的功能较为单一（**fewer facilities** of the program），很难提供定制化系统服务（**less specific/less tailored**）。

5.3 Database

Database aims to pool data, which can support a variety of applications among the whole organisations.

5.3.1 Objectives of database

(a) Sharing data and information between different departments and users.
(b) Preserving integrity of data.
(c) Updating timely to fulfill future requirements.

5.3.2 Appraisal of database

表 7-3　Appraisal of database

Advantages	Disadvantages
Avoiding duplication	Great initial investment
Better security than traditional manual system by restricting authority of users to update and change data	Time needed to integrate data into new system

> **知识点解读**
>
> 在日常工作中，接触更多的 spreadsheet 是 Excel。工作者可以通过 Excel 完成更多的操作，例如计算、分析数据、整理数据等。它可以实现无纸化办公，进而减少对环境的污染。

5.4 Spreadsheet

A **spreadsheet** is kind of electronic paper, which can be used conveniently for recording, calculating and generating statements. It is quite useful in accounting.

博学多才

大家可能对这些 IT 类的名词依然有些许的陌生，我们以饭店为例帮助大家理解。一个软件就好比一个饭店，饭店主要由餐厅、仓库和厨师三者组成。

（1）在餐厅中，有各式各样的菜。这个集各式各样的菜于一身的餐厅就是整合系统（integrated software），其中的各种菜就是这个系统中的不同模块（modular）。

（2）做菜的素材都存放在仓库里，所以仓库好比软件里的数据库（database）。

（3）仓库里的菜不可能直接拿到客人面前，需要厨师进行加工，对应到软件中就是 coding 的过程，需要靠程序代码对数据库里的数据进行调取，然后再通过 coding 加工转译成我们人类能看懂的软件界面。而 spreadsheet（电子表格）就是一个典型的加工转译的工具。

其实准确来说，spreadsheet 是一个编程软件，它**能进行逻辑运算**，比如我们熟悉的加减乘除，复杂一点的电子表格中甚至还包括函数运算（if etc.），再复杂一点的 Excel 甚至还能连接数据库进行数据处理与分析。

除此之外，同学们还需要了解一个常识，即数据库本身不具备编程能力，它能做的只有四件事，即增、删、改、查内部的数据。

6 Fintech

6.1 What is Fintech

In its broadest sense, the term "fintech" generally refers to technology-driven innovation occurring in the financial services industry. For the purposes of this reading, fintech refers to technological innovation in the design and delivery of financial services and products. Many of these innovations are challenging the traditional business models of incumbent financial services providers.

6.2 Artificial intelligence (AI)

It is a computer system which can perform tasks better than human intelligence. The system may be better to identify complex, non-linear relationships between data than traditional quantitative and statistical methods.

For example, when business analysts want to generate insights relating to sentiment and behaviour of potential consumers, they could find this trends by using AI to do data mining, by sorting through enormous amounts of data (company filings, annual reports, and earnings calls).

6.3 Blockchain

Blockchain has been a popular topic recently. Barbara and Robert (2018) points out that:

*Blockchain is a type of **digital distributed ledger** in which information, such as changes in ownership, is recorded sequentially within blocks that are then linked or "chained" together and secured using cryptographic methods. Each block contains a grouping of transactions (or entries) and a secure link (known as a hash) to the previous block. New transactions are inserted into the chain only after validation via a consensus mechanism in which authorised members agree on the transaction and the preceding order, or history, in which previous transactions have occurred.*

6.4 Cyber security

Cyber security refers to the body of technologies, processes, and practices designed to protect networks, devices, programs, and data from attack, damage, or unauthorised access. Cyber security may also be referred to as information technology security.

Cyber security is extremely important to financial sector because of sensitive information. Organisations transmit sensitive financial data across networks and to other devices while doing businesses. Cyber security can help protect financial information systems that process or store financial data.

6.5 Big data

Big data is the extremely large collections of data (data sets) that may be analysed to reveal patterns, trends, and associations, especially relating to human behaviour and interactions.

In 2001 Doug Laney, an analyst with Gartner (a large US IT consultancy company) stated that big data has the following characteristics, known as the 3Vs.
(a) Volume (a very large amount of data, more than can be easily handled by a single computer, spreadsheet or conventional computer system).
(b) Variety (disparate, non-uniform data of different sizes, sources, arriving irregularly).

(c) Velocity (data arrives continually and often has to be processed very quickly to yield useful results).

Answers for example question:

1. AD
2. ABBAAA
3. BD
4. AC
5. C
6. TTF
7. B

Summary

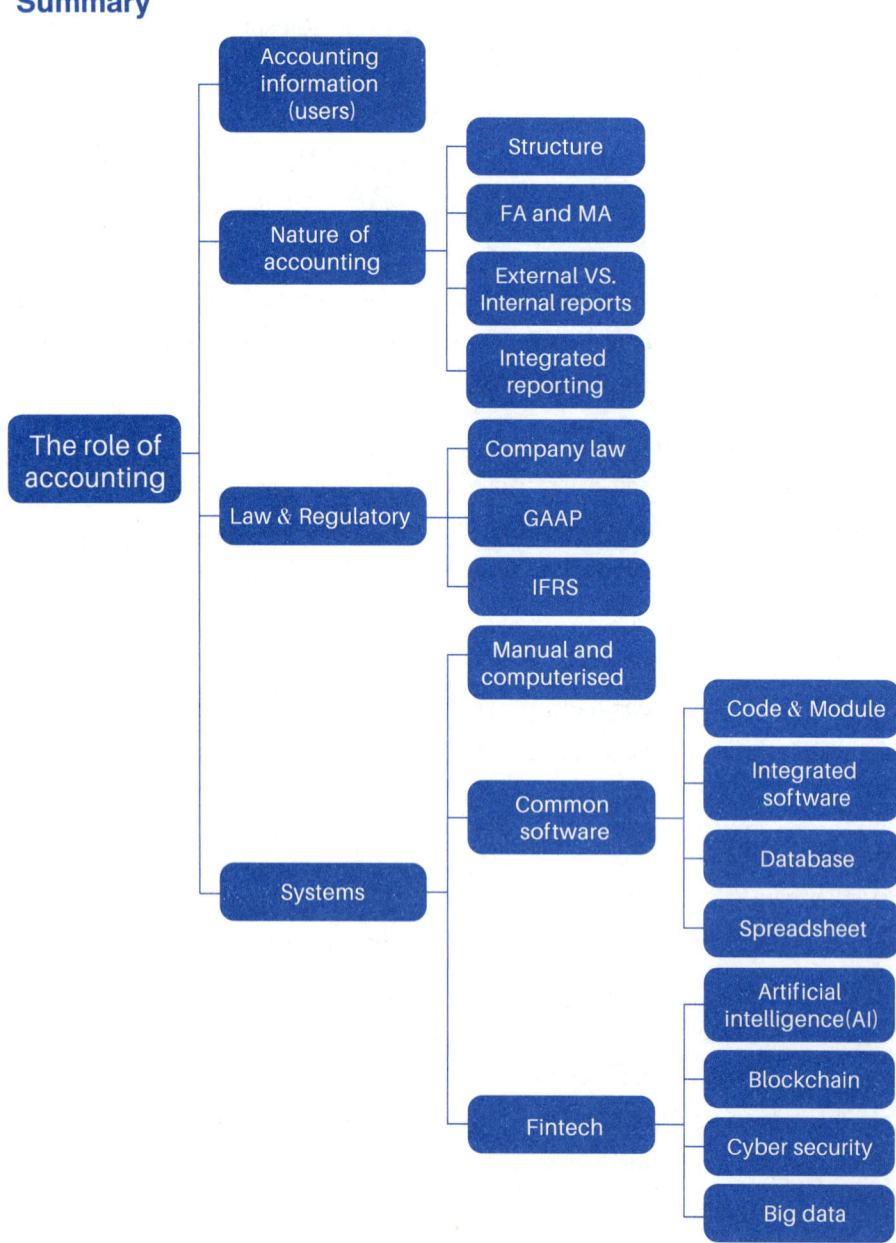

Chapter 7 考试不同问法总结

Section A

1. 针对 Regulatory system

- Which of the following requires companies to keep financial records and prepare accounts?
- Which of the following is not a potential consequence of a listed company failing to file its accounts?
- Which of the following does GAAP stand for?
- Is each of the following statements true or false in relation to the purpose of IFRS?
- Is IFRSs always intended to override local accounting regulations?

2. 针对 three main functions in Accounting department

- Which TWO of the following are responsibilities/the role of the management accounting/financial accounting/treasury in an organisation?
- Which TWO of the following responsibilities/activities will be assigned to the management accountant/financial accountant/treasurer?
- A cost accountant is responsible for which of the following?
- With which TWO of the following are cash and working capital management concerned?
- On which matters will the purchasing department need to consult with the accounting department?
- Which accounting technique or function is MOST useful to a purchasing department when making decisions about capital equipment purchase?
- Which TWO of the following marketing-related functions require input from the accounting department?

3. 针对 External reports

- Are the following statements about Financial Statements true or false?
- Are the following items included in the profit or loss account or the statement of financial position account?
- For which TWO of the following purpose would A refer to the Statement of Cash Flow?
- Which TWO of the following items could appear in a company's Statement of Cash Flow?

4. 针对 Internal reports

- Which of the following can those cost schedules be used for?
- Which TWO of the following does variance reports help in determining?

5. 针对 Integrated report

- Which of the following explains the overall purpose of an integrated report?

6. 针对 Responsibilities over accounting system

- Who, in companies, is usually ultimately responsible for determining broad

- financial policy matters?
- Which of the following is responsible if the Financial Statements of a company do not show a true and fair view?

7. 针对 Computerised accounting system

- Which TWO of the following statements will apply if A choose to switch to a computer-base system?
- Are the following Disadvantages of using a computerised accounting system?
- Which TWO of the following IT application would enhance numerical analysis at work?
- Which of the following statements is correct in relation to a database system?

Section B

Complete the following to show whether each task is the responsibility of the treasurer, the financial controller or the management accountant.

Quick quiz

7.1 Which of the following correctly describes GAAP?

A. Generally Accepted Accounting Practice
B. Generally Accepted Accounting Principles
C. Globally Accepted Accounting Practice
D. Globally Accepted Accounting Principles

Answer: B

Difficulty level: Easy

Tag: Regulatory system-GAAP

Rationale:

The full name of GAAP is Generally Accepted Accounting Principles. Therefore, option A is correct answer.

这道题考查的是 GAAP 一般公认会计原则的全称，记住每个字母的全称即可，因此正确答案为 B 选项。

7.2 Which of the following can be the MOST appropriate technique for a purchasing manager regarding acquisition of material equipment?

A. Supplier price quotations
B. Ratio analysis
C. Treasury management
D. Investment appraisal

Answer: D

Difficulty level: Normal

Tag: The role of accounting

Rationale:

Investment appraisal is a collection of techniques used to identify the attractiveness of an investment. The aim of investment appraisal is to assess the feasibility of project, programme or portfolio decisions and the value they generate. Therefore, purchasing material equipment also includes investment decision.

投资评估是一组用来识别投资吸引力的技术。投资评估的目的是评估项目、方案或投资组合决策的可行性及其产生的价值。因此，采购物资设备也包括投资决策，所以 D 选项正确。

7.3 Accounting is a way of recording, _____ and reporting the performance and position of an organisation. **Which of the following best fits in the blanks?**

A. Auditing
B. Summarising
C. Interpreting
D. Processing

Answer: D

Difficulty level: Normal

Tag: The definition of accounting

Rationale:

Accounting is a way of recording, analysing and summarising transactions of a business, and above three key words can be expressed in other forms, for example, analysing means processing information and summarising can be equal to reporting. So option D is correct.

这道题考查的是会计的定义。定义题可能不会直接以原句的形式考查，而是要求考生掌握真正的含义。会计是记录、分析和总结企业交易的一种方式，这是会计的定义，但上述定义中的三个关键词可以用其他形式表达。例如，分析意味着处理信息，总结可以等同于报告。所以，D 选项正确。

7.4 There is a need for coordination between sections in accounting management. **Which following section should give inventory records to financial accounting staff?**

A. Cost accounting staff
B. The receivable ledger section
C. The credit control staff
D. The payables ledger section

Answer: A

Difficulty level: Easy

Tag: Role of accounting

Rationale:

This question is set to examine the role of accounting, and coordination between different section within accounting department. The financial accounting staff responsible for preparing inventory accounts might rely on the cost accounting staff for data about inventory records so as to place a value on closing inventory.

这道题考查的是会计角色,以及会计部门内不同职能部分的配合。 负责编制存货账簿的财务员工可能会依赖成本会计编制的存货数据,从而确定存货的期末价值。

7.5 All the following, with one exception, are examples of advantages of a manual system over a computerised accounting system. **Which statement is the exception**?

A. A manual system will be more stable than a computerised system

B. Low capital cost will be needed

C. A manual system will have a lower risk of error

D. People without computer experience can also use manual system easily

Answer: C

Difficulty level: Easy

Tag: Appraisals of manual accounting system

Rationale:

Candidates should identify the advantages and disadvantages of manual and computerised system.

Computer data are more vulnerable than manual ones, such as accidental damage, disaster, and hacking. Low capital cost is also the advantage of manual system. A manual system will have a higher risk of error, thus option C is incorrect. There're no needs of computer experience if using a manual system.

考生应当识别出电算化和计算机系统的优缺点,计算机数据相比手工数据更易受到伤害,如遭遇意外毁坏、灾难和黑客破坏。 低资本投入也是手工系统的优点。 手工系统有更高的错误风险,因此 C 选项是错误的。 使用手工系统不需要有电脑经验。

Chapter 8
Organisational culture

知识导入

上两章中我们了解了关于各个职能部门的故事，并且详细地去会计部"走了一趟"，而这些职能部门也构成了一个完整的公司组织。 而每个组织都会有它自己的"脾气性格"，这些"脾气性格"被我们称为"组织文化"，那文化到底是怎么产生的？ 它又会被什么所影响？ 在本章中我们将具体了解这块内容。

单词表

英文	中文
Artefacts	人工制品
Uncertainty avoidance	不确定性规避
Individualism	个人主义
Masculinity	男子气概
Femininity	女性气质（阴柔）

学习指南

Learning objectives	Pass level	Distinction level	用时建议
1.Culture（1.1-1.2）	√		10 min
2. Writers on culture（2.1-2.2）	√		15 min

本章考点

重要考点	难度（1~3）
熟记每位作者的名字以及他们的论点是什么	3
着重记忆和理解 Schein 的理论	1
熟记并理解 Handy 的文化模型以及对应的 structure	2
熟记并理解 Hofstede 指出的不同国家文化会对企业文化会带来什么不同	3

组织"类"人，如果说组织的结构可以类比成骨骼，职能类比成器官，那么组织文化对应的就是人的灵魂和性格。 世界上没有两片完全相同的树叶，人与人之间千差万别，组织文化同样各有千秋。 在本章中，我们将依次探讨以下问题：什么是文化？ 什么是组织文化？ 什么影响了组织文化？ 如何分析不同的组织文化？

1 Culture

1.1 Definition

Hofstede: Culture is the collective programming of the mind which distinguishes the members of one category of people from another.

Edgar Schein: Organisational culture is the set of shared, taken for granted assumptions that a group holds and that determines how it perceives, thinks about and reacts to the environment.

Schein (2004) suggests that there are three levels concerning culture (见图 8-1):

> **核心考点**
>
> 在 Three Level of Culture 这个理论中，第一层是常考点，一般会以该层级的特征为背景，让考生进行判断。

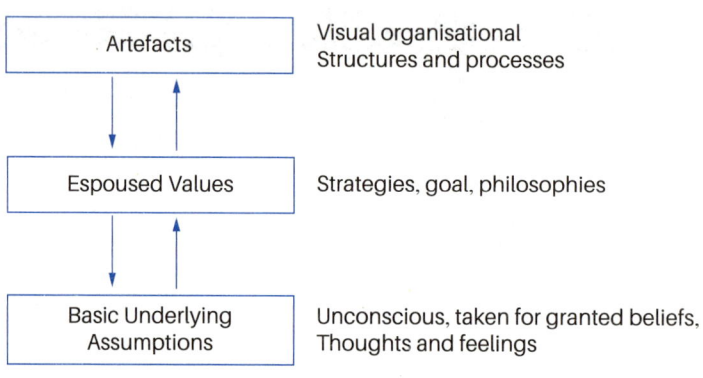

图 8-1 Levels of Culture

(a) Artefacts. These are the influences on culture that can be seen. For example, how employees dress, the layout of the office, the way in which people behave and their attitude.

(b) Espoused values. These are the strategies, goals and objectives of the organisation. For example, an emphasis on low cost or an emphasis on excellent service.

(c) Basic underlying assumptions. These are the taken-for granted beliefs. They can be called a "paradigm", which is a set of assumptions held in common.

Handy: It shows **the way we do things around here**.

事实上，到目前为止，业内对文化这个概念并没有统一的定义。但是通过以上三位理论家的陈述，我们可以感受到，文化是人以类聚物以群分的体现，是区别不同组织的存在，更是组织中行为处事的反映。

1.2 Factors shapes organisational culture

(a) **Founder**. The founder's own values and beliefs set the tone of the organisational culture.

In other words, the founder basically determines the company's culture.

每当我们说起苹果公司的形象代言人，第一个浮现在我们眼前的就是它的创始人——乔布斯。原因很简单，乔布斯的性格与苹果公司文化的高度契合是这家公司的传奇制胜点。众所周知，苹果公司创立初期，办公场所是在一间小小的车库中。随着不断发展，公司逐步走上正轨，规模日益壮大。但乔布斯并不满足于此，他认为虽然公司团队越来越像正规的海军，但还是要保持最初的叛逆精神。在这位创始人眼中，"海盗精神"就是叛逆的完美诠释，这种精神代表着果敢决断，勇往直前，打破传统，以异类的思维方式来思考问题。也正是在这种"海盗精神"的指引下，才有了后来的苹果帝国。有趣的是，在苹果公司创立40周年那一天，公司总部门前升起了一面海盗旗，以此表达对这种文化的敬仰和传承。

(b) **History**. Culture reflects what past experiences organisations have experienced.

虽然现在苹果公司是一个非常成功的商业帝国，但纵观它的发展历史，其实并非是一帆风顺。苹果公司在创立初期推出的数项产品，可以说是反响平平，甚至有些遇冷。但这家公司并没有就此放弃，而是以iPod系列产品重振旗鼓，打了一个漂亮的翻身仗。

(c) **Leadership and management style**. Different leadership and management style could have a direct impact on employees as well as culture of organisations.

领导与管理风格会非常直接地反映在公司文化之中。最典型的就是乔布斯与库克分别担任苹果公司的CEO期间公司文化不同。即便是作为消费者的我们，也能直观地感受到两个时期的差别。在乔布斯时代，苹果公司的创新意识深入骨髓，新旧产品更迭时间短，新变革大，总是能走在同类产品的最前沿。反观当下，在库克带领下的苹果公司逐渐褪去了激进的创新势头，逐渐迎合消费者市场，更多的是维持稳定的增长。

(d) **External environment**. The differences between various countries, regions, industries and businesses could all contribute to the formation and transformation of an organisation's culture.

即便都是苹果公司，处于不同国家的分公司，文化也会有差异，这是由于不同地区的不同情况所导致的。

> **知识点解读**
>
> 地域以及行业的差异，会造成组织文化的不同。例如，同一个集团中，地处德国的公司相比位于美国的公司而言，会更加严谨；高新科技产业会比传统制造业更加灵活。

2 Writers on culture

2.1 Harrison and Handy（culture and structure）

Harrison classified four types of culture, to which Handy gave the names of Greek deities.

(A) Power culture（Zeus）

In this culture, **power is concentrated** in the hands of one person, "the boss". This culture is often found in small, family businesses. Fast—but perhaps arbitrary—decisions can be made. As businesses grow, it becomes more difficult for one person to wield absolute power. However, it is sometimes seen in large organisations, but then it is usually taken as a danger sign.

在古希腊神话中，宙斯是众神之神，象征着至高无上的权力，因此Handy用宙斯来形容组织创立初期的权力文化，即由创立者拥有最高权力，一人统筹决策组织的所有事务。**往往权力文化会伴随着简单结构出现。**

(B) Role culture（Apollo）

This is characterised by a **traditional** organisational structure in which jobs are

> **核心考点**
>
> 需要理解并记忆每种文化的特征，考试经常以情境描述的方式来考查考生对此知识点的理解。建议同学们熟悉关键词，同时这几个希腊神话的人名也要记忆，有时题目的选项会用神话人物去代替这4种文化特征。并且同学们需要将这些文化的分类与组织结构相匹配，能够判断在不同结构中会出现什么样的文化。

arranged by function and seniority, and each employee has a distinct role and job specification. This culture can be efficient in a stable environment in which employees are expected to do the same tasks repeatedly but can lead to inflexibility and can slow down response to change as employees defend their roles and rewards.

阿波罗是太阳神，掌管着太阳的东升西落，即人间的秩序。 因此，Handy 选择他作为职能角色文化的代表，即在组织中，人们根据不同的分工应当各司其职，不存在僭越和职能的交叉。 **职能文化往往会伴随着职能结构出现。**

(C) Task culture (Athena)

Here, the emphasis is on **getting the job done** by teams with expertise. Flexibility is encouraged, and it is more important to serve customers and clients well than to defend one's role. This culture is much more responsive to environmental and competitive developments.

雅典娜是战神，在古希腊神话中也象征着智慧女神，不管是多复杂艰难的战事，雅典娜都会妥当解决。 因为她代表的就是以任务和工作为导向的文化，拥有这种文化的组织往往着力点都是放在完成不同的项目上的。 **任务文化往往会伴随着矩阵结构出现。**

(D) Person culture/Existential (Dionysus)

In this culture the **individual is the central point**. The organisation is seen as serving the individuals within it. Barristers' chambers, architects' partnerships and small consultancy firms often have this person orientation. The organisation structure is as minimal as possible.

狄奥尼索斯是古希腊神话中的酒神，他的职位跟这里的组织文化貌似并不相关，Handy 之所以用这位酒神的名字来命名，是因为他的性格。 狄奥尼索斯是一位沉醉于酿制葡萄酒的神祇，以自我为导向。 他代表的文化是个人文化，拥有这种文化的组织内往往有着高度自由，组织架构的存在也是为了服务特定个人，实现特定个人目标，可以说是颠覆了传统的组织文化的一种存在。 个人文化往往会伴随着某些特殊类型组织的产生，如经纪公司，是专门为旗下艺人服务的。

小试牛刀

Example question 1

An organisation is controlled by a key central figure, owner or founder. It is a small organisation where people all know each other and get on well.

Which of the following is the culture of the above organisation as recognized by Handy?

    A. Authority   B. Dominance   C. Power

Example question 2

Which kind of culture is typically found in a matrix organisation?

    A. Task culture   B. Person culture

    C. Power culture   D. Role culture

精益求精

Handy also matched appropriate cultural models to Robert Anthony's classification of managerial activity—**Anthony hierarchy**.

(a) **Strategic management** (performed by senior managers) deals with setting direction & policies and managing crisis for the whole organisation. Therefore, the **power culture** is more suitable because it enables the organisation to take mighty and decisive measures as a response to environment changes.

(b) **Tactical management** (performed by middle managers) deals with establishing methods to accomplish corporate objectives, allocate resources and innovate. It focuses on how to compete successfully in particular market, which align with the core concept of the **task culture.**

(c) **Operational management** (performed by supervisors and operatives) deals with implementing everyday activities to achieve tactical objectives. It refers to how functions of organisation such as marketing, finance and IT support overall strategy. Therefore a **role culture** is more suitable as employees under this culture would perform their duties conscientious.

> **知识点解读**
>
> Anthony hierarchy 这个知识点是一个高频考点，经常会与安东尼的 three levels of organisation 结合起来考，同学们需要掌握在不同的层级当中需要有什么样的文化来与之进行匹配。

2.2 Hofstede（culture and national environment）

Hofstede recognised that people in different countries often hold different values and that these will influence organisational culture. His research mainly focuses on the impact of national culture on organisational culture. The influences are:

霍夫斯泰德文化维度理论（Hofstede's cultural dimensions theory）是荷兰心理学家吉尔特·霍夫斯泰德提出的用来衡量不同国家文化差异的一个框架。

1967—1973年,霍夫斯泰德在著名的跨国公司IBM（国际商业机器公司）进行了一项大规模的文化价值观调查。 他的团队对IBM公司的各国员工先后进行了两轮问卷调查,用二十几种不同语言在72个国家里发放了116 000多份调查问卷并回收了答案。 调查和分析的重点是各国员工在价值观上表现出来的国别差异。 他认为,文化是在一个环境下人们共同拥有的心理程序,能将一群人与其他人区分开来。 通过研究,他将不同文化间的差异归纳为六个基本的文化价值观维度。

> **核心考点**
>
> 文化维度理论前4个维度为考试重点，需要同学们能够结合案例描述应用。 它也是最早期被提出的理论，后面两个维度是后来补充的，同学们对后两个维度了解即可。

(a) **Power distance**

Power Distance is the extent to which the less powerful members of organisations and institutions (like the family) accept and expect that **power is distributed unequally.**

Cultures that favour low power distance expect power relations to be relatively consultative or democratic. In high power distance countries, the less powerful accept power relations that are more autocratic.

各个国家由于对权力的理解不同,在这个维度上存在着很大的差异。 欧美人不是很看重权力,他们更注重个人能力。 而亚洲国家由于体制的关系,注重权力的约束力。

(b) **Uncertainty avoidance**

Uncertainty avoidance deals with a society's **tolerance for uncertainty and ambiguity**.

> **核心考点**
>
> Uncertainty avoidance 表示人们对未来不确定性的态度。 对不确定性规避程度较强的文化（high UA）往往有明确的社会规范和原则来指导几乎所有情况下发生的行为，而规避不确定性程度较弱的文化（low UA）的社会规范和原则就不那么明确和严格。

> **知识点解读**
>
> 个人主义、集体主义表示个人与群体间的关联程度。个人主义文化（individualism）注重个体目标。相反，集体主义文化则更强调集体目标。个人主义文化中，人们应当自己照顾自己和直系家庭，而在集体主义文化（collectivism）中，人们期望他们的内群体或集体来照顾他们，作为这种照顾的交换条件，他们对内群体拥有绝对的忠诚。个人主义没有圈内（in-group）和圈外（out-group）的明显差别，而集体主义却有明显的圈内和圈外的差别。

> **知识点解读**
>
> 男子气概、女性气质这一维度主要看某一社会代表男性的品质（如竞争性、独断性）更多，还是代表女性的品质（如谦虚、关爱他人）更多，以及对男性和女性职能的界定。

> **知识点解读**
>
> 长期导向性、短期导向性表明一个民族对长远利益和近期利益的价值观。
> 具有长期导向的文化和社会（long-term orientation）主要面向未来，较注重对未来的考虑，对待事物以动态的观点去考察；注重节约、节俭和储备；做任何事均留有余地。
> 短期导向性的文化与社会（short-term orientation）则面向过去与现在，着重眼前的利益，注重对传统的尊重，注重负担社会的责任；在管理上最重要的是此时的利润，上级对下级的考绩周期较短，要求立见功效，急功近利，不容拖延。

> **知识点解读**
>
> Indulgence（自身放纵）的数值越大，说明该社会整体对自身约束力不大，社会对任自放纵的允许度越大，人们越不约束自身。

People in cultures with high uncertainty avoidance tend to be more cautious and proceed by careful planning. Low uncertainty avoidance cultures feel relatively comfortable making unstructured situations and dealing with changing and novel environments.

回避程度高的文化比较重视权威、地位、资历等，并试图建立更正式的规则，不容忍偏激观点和行为，相信绝对知识和专家评定等手段来避免这些情景。回避程度低的文化对于反常的行为和意见比较宽容，规章制度少，在哲学、宗教方面他们容许各种不同的主张同时存在。

(c) Individualism (vs. Collectivism)

Individualism is the extent to which people feel **independent**, as opposed to being **interdependent** as members of larger wholes.

Individualistic societies place stress on personal achievements. In collectivist societies, individuals act predominantly as members of a group or team.

个人主义倾向的社会中人与人之间的关系是松散的，人们倾向于关心自己及小家庭；而集体主义倾向的社会则注重族群内关系，关心大家庭，牢固的族群关系可以给人们持续的保护，而个人则必须对族群绝对忠诚。

(d) Masculinity (vs. Femininity)

Masculinity is the extent to which the use of force in endorsed socially.

Masculine cultures include **competitiveness and assertiveness**; feminine cultures place greater emphasis on relationships, life quality and tenderness.

这一维度表示人们对男性和女性社会角色如何分配的认识。阳刚型社会性别角色有明确的划分。阴柔型社会性别角色有所重叠。阳刚型社会的文化成员赞扬成就、雄心、物质、权力和决断性，而阴柔型社会的文化成员则强调生活的质量、服务、关心他人和养育后代。

> **精益求精**

(e) Long-term orientation (vs. Short-term orientation)

Long-term orientation deals with change.

Long-term oriented cultures attach importance to the future and place emphasis on persistence, flexibility and a willingness to change. Short-term oriented cultures emphasise tradition and meeting social expectations.

这一维度指的是某一文化中的成员对延迟其物质、情感、社会需求的满足所能接受的程度。研究表明，长期取向的强弱与各国经济增长有着很强的关系。20世纪后期东亚经济突飞猛进，学者们认为长期取向是促进发展的主要原因之一。

> **精益求精**

(f) Indulgence (vs. Restraint)

Indulgence means the extent of control over desires and pleasure.

In an indulgent culture it is good to be free, doing what your impulses want you to do is good. In a restrained culture, the feeling is that life is hard, and duty, not freedom, is the normal state of being.

自身放纵指的是某一社会对人基本需求与享受生活享乐欲望的允许程度。

Example question 3

Which writer is MOST closely associated with differing national perspectives on culture?

A. Handy　　　　　　B. Hofstede　　　　　　C. Schein

Answers for example question

1. C
2. A
3. B

Summary

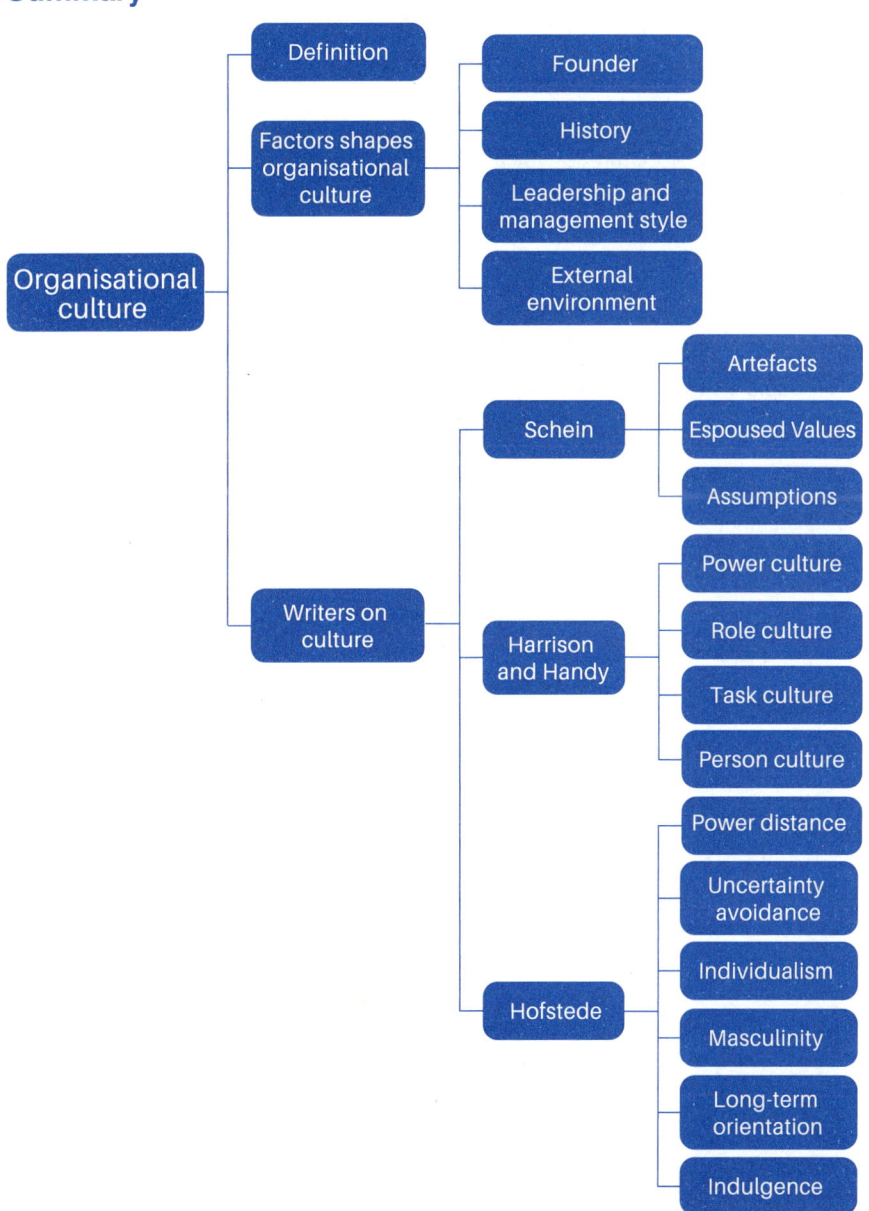

Chapter 8 考试不同问法总结

Section A

1. 针对 basic concepts
- Do the following influence the organisation's culture?
- Which of the following is a definition of organisational culture?
- Which writer proposed this definition of culture?
- Which of the following form part of an organisation's culture?

2. 针对 Schein's model
- Which TWO of the following are identified by Schein as distinct levels of organisational culture?

3. 针对 Handy's organisational culture
- What of the Handy's culture stereotypes is MOST appropriate within the organisation stated above?
- Which cultural type of organisation is described in the above statement?
- Which writer proposed the model that defines four basic types of organisational culture?
- Which kind of culture is typically found in a matrix organisation?

4. 针对 Hofstede's national culture
- Which writer is MOST closely associated with differing national perspectives on culture?
- Which cultural dimension is described as 'the degree of inequality among people which the population of a country considers normal'?
- Which of the following is related to the uncertainty avoidance dimension?
- Which of the following would you find in a country with strong uncertainty avoidance?
- Does these observations relate to which of Hofstede's cultural dimension?
- Which of the following is not a key dimension in Hofstede's model of national cultures?

Section B
- Which dimension of Hofstede's model is being discussed by each individual?

Quick quiz

8.1 Who defined culture as "the collective programming of the mind which distinguishes the members of one category of people from another"?

  A. Hofstede   B. Schein   C. Mullins   D. Handy

Answer: A

Difficulty level: Easy

Tag: Definition of culture

Rationale:

  This definition is proposed by Hofstede, and there's many definitions about culture in the FAB exam. Candidates should remember these theorists and theorists' name.

  这是由 Hofstede 提出的文化概念。在 AB 这门课里，有很多关于文化的概念，考生应该记住这些理论和理论提出者的名字。

8.2 Which kind of culture is typically found in a simple structure organisation?

  A. Task culture B. Person culture C. Power culture D. Role culture

Answer: C

Difficulty level: Easy

Tag: Handy and Harrison's theory

Rationale:

  This question examines Handy and Harrison's theory. In power culture, the organisation is controlled by a key owner or founder and it suits small organisation and simple structure.

  这道题考查的是 Hand 和 Harrison 的理论。在 power culture 下，组织被一个关键的创始人或者股东所控制，它适合小型企业和 simple 架构的组织。

8.3 Under Handy's cultural theory, which type of culture is found in a matrix organisation?

  A. Power culture B. Role culture C. Task culture D. Person culture

Answer: C

Difficulty level: Easy

Tag: Harrison and Handy's cultural theory

Rationale:

  In task culture, organisations focus on outputs and results, problems solved, projects completed and matrix organisations is coordinated by crossing functional with project/product structure. Therefore, employees in a matrix organisation will concern about project completing.

  矩阵型组织结构包含了两种组织结构：职能部门型组织和产品/项目型组织。因此，处于矩阵型组织结构内部的员工会看重任务的完成情况，而任务型文化的特征是关注最终的结果和输出，所以答案选 C。

8.4 Hofstede stated that national culture may affect organisational culture in six dimensions: power distance, uncertainty avoidance, individualism, masculinity, long-term orientation and indulgence.

  Which TWO of the following would you find in a country with strong uncertainty avoidance?

  (1) Prefer formal structures and written rules.

  (2) Expect centralised organisations.

  (3) Low tolerance for deviance and changes.

(4) High involvement and participation in decision making from subordinates.

A. (1) and (2)　　　　B. (1) and (3)　　　　C. (2) and (3)　　　　D. (2) and (4)

Answer: **B**

Difficulty level: **Easy**

Tag: **Hofstede theory-national culture**

Rationale:

People in a strong uncertainty avoidance country respect certainty, value written rules and regulations, prefer standardisation, strong need for consensus and no tolerance for deviance. Therefore, the correct answer is option B.

高度不确定性规避的国家有以下特征：尊重确定性，重视明文条例、规章制度，偏好标准化工作流程，强烈需要达成共识，不能接受差异。因此，说法（1）和（3）是高度不确定性规避的特征，故选 B。

8.5 Which of the following correctly describes a definition of organisational culture?

A. Corporate logos, interior design and internal symbols of power and influence

B. Structure of communication type and leadership style

C. Shared beliefs and expectations determining norms and behaviour

Answer: **C**

Difficulty level: **Normal**

Tag: **Definition of organisational culture**

Rationale:

Edgar Schein stated that organisational culture is the set of shared, taken for granted assumptions that a group holds and that determines how it perceives, thinks and reacts to the environment. Therefore, option C matched above sentences.

这道题考查的是沙因对于组织文化定义，根据沙因的定义，他认为组织文化是一套被一群人所共享，且认为是理所当然的假设，并且这些假设会决定这群人对于外界的感知、思考和行为。所以答案选 C。

Chapter 9
Corporate governance

知识导入

我们已经学习了将近一半的内容，也是时候回顾下之前我们学了什么。第一章中我们了解过两个群体，即公司的所有者（shareholders）和公司的经营者（directors）。通过学习，我们也知道了他们之间很可能因为利益（interest）不一致而会发生冲突（conflict），那么公司到底有没有有效的方法来解决这些冲突呢？解决这一冲突是公司唯一要考虑的问题吗？带着这些问题，我们来了解下一个重要的概念——公司治理。

单词表

英文	中文
Agency theory	代理理论
Corporate governance	公司治理
Corporate social responsibility	企业社会责任
Sustainable development	可持续发展
Company secretary	董事会秘书
Non-executive directors	非执行董事
Remuneration committee	薪酬委员会
Nomination committee	提名委员会
Audit committee	审计委员会
Risk committee	风控委员会
AGM（annual general meeting）	年度股东大会

学习指南

Learning objectives	Pass level	Distinction level	用时建议
1.Corporate governance（1.1-1.2）	√		10 min
2.Corporate social responsibility（1.3 definition）	√		10 min
3.Importance of CSR（1.3.2）		√	5 min
4. Four strategies of implementing CSR（1.3.3）		√	5 min
5. Approaches to corporate governance（1.4）	√		10 min
6. Main principles of corporate governance（1.5）		√	15 min
7. Contents of corporate governance report（1.6）		√	10 min
8. Best practice in corporate governance（2）	√		15 min

本章考点

重要考点	难度（1~3）
理解狭义的公司治理和广义的公司治理	3
着重记忆和理解不同公司治理理论之间的区别（agency theory/stakeholder theory/stewardship theory）	2
熟记并理解企业社会责任	2
熟记并理解原则导向和规则导向的区别	1
着重记忆董事会的构成以及其成员责任	3
熟练掌握薪酬委员会和审计委员会的职责与成员构成	2
熟记并理解外部审计的职责	2

基本概念

细心的同学可能已经发现了，在1.1当中有两段对公司治理的定义，之所以出现这种情况，同学们可以结合1.2来理解。早期的（狭义的）公司治理基于代理理论，更注重对公司内部的监督，这便是1992年的定义；而随着时间推移，公司开始逐渐意识到利益相关者对其的影响，于是公司治理开始逐渐将目光从公司内部，转移到了外部，从而引出了更广义的公司治理，这便是2004年的定义。迄今为止，学术界对于公司治理还没有一个统一的定义，因此同学们对于定义的掌握，更多在于理解其精髓，不需要背诵。

知识点解读

公司治理的定义有时会和其他重要概念，如内部控制、内部牵制、企业道德放在一起让同学们区别，所以对于其概念，虽然不需要背诵，但需要同学们能熟记加粗的关键词，这有助于快速做题，选出正确答案。

1 Introduction of corporate governance

1.1 Definition

"Corporate governance is the **system** by which organisations are **directed and controlled** by **senior officers**"（Cadbury，1992，p. 14）.

The Organisation for Economic Co-operation and Development（2004）defines Corporate governance as：

Corporate governance involves a set of ***relationships between a company's management, its boards, its shareholders and other stakeholders***. *Corporate governance also provides the structure through which the objectives of the company are set, and the means of attaining those objectives and monitoring performance are determined*（p. 11）.

It should be noted that in the UK, **listed companies must conduct in accordance with corporate governance**.

1.2 Perspectives on corporate governance

关于公司治理，我们可以从狭义和广义两个角度来分析。

狭义的公司治理秉持较为传统的观念，认为公司治理的最终目标就是确保股东财富最大化。基于这样的目标，公司以及公司的所有者（股东）需要对经营者实施严格的监督，以避免经营者为了实现自身利益而损害所有者利益。这是一种典型的"股东至上主义"。这种观点的逻辑源自"代理理论"（Agency theory），在接下来的部分我们会着重讲解代理理论。

广义的公司治理突破了传统观念的束缚，它不再将目光锁定在公司内部以及股东身上，它放眼于更广阔的"森林"——所有与公司息息相关的方面，即利益相关者。根据这种理论来看，公司并不仅仅属于股东，确切地说，公司象征着利益各方的集合体。因此，它的治理目标不仅包括股东利益最大化，也包括考虑各方利益相关者的需求，这是另一种典型的"利益相关者理论"（Stakeholder theory）。

1.2.1 Agency theory

Agency theory describes the relationship between agents and principals, in which agents act on the behalf of principals. In modern companies, the relationship exists between those executives, who are involved in the day-to-day operations, and shareholders, who are the owners of the company.

Agency theory recognises that the interests of principal and agent are not always in alignment. In brief, if the executives sacrifice shareholders' interest to benefit themselves, then conflict of interest occurs, which is called as agency problem.

> **基本概念**
>
> 在公司中，所有权属于股东，经营权被委托给管理者，此时，股东属于委托人，管理者就属于代理人。简单来说，代理理论指出，代理人有可能通过牺牲委托人的利益，来满足代理人自己的利益，这被称作为代理问题。

根据代理理论，公司的所有者（即股东）是委托人，真正负责管理和使用这些资源的是代理人（管理者）。代理理论认为，当代理人本身就是股东的时候，代理人会努力地为自己而工作，这种情况下就不存在代理问题。但是，当代理人开始使用外部投资者投入的资金，即没有在真正为自己奋斗的时候，代理人员就会有动机将自己的利益放在首位，如在职期间进行奢侈的消费，玩忽职守等。如果企业的管理者是一个理性经济人，他的行为将会与当自己同时作为拥有者和控制者时有显著的差别，这就形成了代理问题。

通过上述内容我们已经了解，作为代理人，管理者有可能在经营过程中面临代理问题，因此，需要更加强调管理者对股东委托授予的经营权承担责任，那么这种责任就被称为 **fiduciary duty**。

Managers **owe** a fiduciary duty to shareholders. They should always put shareholders' interest in the first place and be responsible for their actions.

Fiduciary duty，信托责任。根据定义，信托是指委托人基于对受托人的信任，将其财产权委托给受托人，由受托人按委托人的意愿以自己的名义，为受益人的利益或者特定目的，进行管理的行为。那么在公司中，股东将公司的经营托付给管理者，管理者同样拥有了这样一种信托责任。

> **精益求精**
>
> 针对代理理论提出的观点，理论界存在一种从其对立角度出发的理论。这种理论被称为管家理论（Stewardship theory）。概括来说，该理论认为经理人和委托人之间存在另外一种关系，即经理人是值得信任的管家。这种看法可以说是为公司治理开启了新世界的大门。
>
> 现代管家理论认为，代理理论对经营者内在机会主义和偷懒的假定是不合适的，而且经营者对自身尊严、信仰以及内在工作满足的追求，会使他们努力工作，做好"管家"。现代管家理论认为，在经营者的自律基础上，经营者与股东以及其他利益相关者之间的利益是一致的。

1.2.2 Stakeholder theory

Stakeholder theory can be regarded as a more developed theory from agency theory. It describes organisations as collections of various individual groups with different interests, which means decision-making should take all voices into consideration. That is, stakeholder theory focuses on the **claims of all stakeholders**.

> **基本概念**
>
> 利益相关者理论（stakeholder theory）的治理目标不仅包括股东利益最大化，也包括考虑各方利益相关者的需求。

The concept of stakeholder theory is closely connected with **corporate social responsibility.**

小试牛刀

Example question 1

Example question 2

Example question 1

Jim, Mike and Dime are managers for ABC Co. All their salary and their bonus will be based on company performance. Which of the following best describes the approach to governance in ABC Co?

A. Stewardship theory
B. Agency theory
C. Stakeholder theory
D. None of the above

Example question 2

Governments in many countries are encouraging improved standards of corporate governance, focusing mainly on public companies whose securities are listed on recognised capital markets. Why the best practices of corporate governance are important to these companies?

A. Public companies are subject to a greater degree of separation between those who manage the company and those who own it
B. Public companies are subject to less stringent regulation than other types of commercial organisation
C. Public companies have institutional investors and have greater responsibilities to these investors than to personal investors
D. All other types of business organisations are already subject to and fully implement high standards of corporate governance

1.3 Corporate social responsibility

> **基本概念**
> CSR 的定义不需要背诵，理解即可。

Corporate social responsibility (CSR) is a self-regulating business concept that emphasise accountability of companies to not only shareholders, but also stakeholders. By practicing CSR, companies could be conscious of their impacts on all aspects of the society (for example, economic, social, and environmental). The goal of CSR is to encourage a **positive** impact on the stakeholders generally.

The application of CSR is highly connected to the concept of **sustainable development** which suggests the organisations should **use resources in such a way that they do not compromise the needs of future generations**.

> **知识点解读**
> 可持续发展（sustainable development），是既能满足当代人的需要，又不对后代人满足其需要的能力构成威胁的发展。

我们可以这么来看，营利性企业存在的主要目的是确保股东财富最大化，这是对股东的责任；企业经营的基本门槛是遵纪守法，这是对政府的责任；企业应当对员工一视同仁，这是对员工的责任。 总的来看，股东、政府和员工，这些都是与公司存在商业关系或是其他经济关系的主要利益相关者。 根据利益相关者理论来看，仅仅考虑这三种利益相关者是远远不够的，企业应当能够承担起对其他利益相关者（如消费者、供应商以及环境等）的相应责任，这种责任就被我们称为企业的社会责任（corporate social responsibility）。

那么，对于企业而言，利益相关者无处不在，我们应当如何有条不紊地应对企业社会责任呢？简单来说就是两步，首先我们应当识别利益相关者并分析其需求；其次就是考虑如何应对。

1.3.1 Stakeholder identification and analysis

In order to execute CSR better, organisations must first identify their stakeholders and what they need.

对于利益相关者的识别与分析，我们在第一章当中通过 Mendelow matrix 已经学习过，但是，这仅仅是对于利益相关者的整体分析；1.3.1 这里指的是每个公司需要找到利益相关者的特定需求。

接下来，我们就通过具体的案例，来了解公司是如何更好地履行企业社会责任的。

星巴克作为一家享誉全球的咖啡品牌，其**可持续咖啡目标**包括：

（1）采购承诺：100%的咖啡都以合乎道德的方式采购；

（2）种植咖啡树：到 2025 年为农民提供 1 亿棵咖啡树；

（3）开源农艺：到 2020 年培训 200,000 位咖啡农。

从这些可持续目标当中，我们可以发现这家公司在不同方面履行着相应的社会责任。例如，采购渠道，公司致力于"道德采购"，即选择与富有道德的供应商合作；为了确保不会过度消耗资源，公司消费咖啡豆的同时也在持续地种植咖啡树；更有意义的是，"授人以鱼，不如授人以渔"，星巴克通过提供培训的方式，培养咖啡农，一方面满足了自己公司的用人需求，另一方面也提高了这些咖啡农的可雇佣性，促进了一方就业。

星巴克的社会责任宣言并非只是口号。例如，早在 2015 年 9 月，星巴克就曾推出过一项活动，承诺"每售完一袋咖啡，就捐赠一棵树"，这项活动的目标就是为了确保咖啡的长期供应和咖啡农的经济前途。这项活动大获成功，星巴克向咖啡农捐赠了超过 2,500 万棵咖啡树。在此基础上，星巴克乘胜追击，承诺在 2025 年前为农民提供 1 亿棵咖啡树。

星巴克公司董事长、创始人霍华德舒尔茨（Howard Schultz）曾在一次演讲中很好地概括了星巴克这家公司的社会观，他说："星巴克不是一个完美的公司，我们每天都在犯错误，我们的商业模式可能不比人家好，但从公司创建的第一天开始，我们的商业模式就是要在赚钱和社会责任之间取得平衡，我们既要赚钱也要回馈。"

1.3.2 Importance of CSR

There are many reasons why a company might engage in social responsibility as it can：

(a) Enhance brand reputation：the public perception of a company is critical to customers and shareholders' confidence；

(b) Attract and retain customers and employees by enhancing good reputation；

(c) Help companies stand out from the competition.

However, it is noted that fulfilling social responsibility **may** also have an adverse effect on business：

知识点解读

虽然有句话叫"君子喻于义，小人喻于利"，但对企业而言，重利又重义的双保险才是稳步制胜的不二法宝。在当代，重利的同时又能承担起社会责任的企业越发受到市场以及消费者的追捧。然而，天下并没有免费的午餐，承担社会责任，满足不同利益相关者的需求往往是需要花费成本的。例如，通过安装净化系统达到减排的效果。因此，社会责任到底应该承担到一个什么样的程度，甚至是否需要承担，都是要经过深思熟虑的。简言之，就是成本与利益的权衡。

(a) Increased management time of CSR planning and implementation;

(b) Reduced revenue from declining unethical contractors and extra expenses of implanting CSR activities.

> 精益求精

1.3.3 Strategies of implementing CSR

根据 stakeholder theory 来看，企业适当地承担社会责任是非常重要的，不仅可以提高声誉，在长远来看，还有机会减少成本，提高利润。 但不可否认的事实是，很多情况下，承担社会责任的当下会给企业增加一定成本。 那么逐利性质的企业，就会在是否需要承担社会责任以及承担社会责任的程度等方面作出抉择。 不同企业会选择不一样的策略，大致可以分成以下 4 种：

(a) **Proactive** strategy: under this strategy, companies would take **full** responsibility of CSR.

(b) **Reactive** strategy: under this strategy, companies do nothing and remain unsolved until found out by third party.

(c) **Defence** strategy: under this strategy, companies take actions to **minimise or to avoid** social obligations.

(d) **Accommodation** strategy: under this strategy, companies take their obligations under **encouragement of interest parties** or because of **government intervention**.

到这里，我们已经学习了关于公司治理的两种观念——agency theory 和 stakeholder theory。 不管是哪一种观念，其根本都在于倡导公司治理。 事出皆有因，我们接下来就来探讨是什么促进了公司治理这一概念的提出和发展，即公司治理的驱动因素。 首先，随着全球化的进一步推进，为了吸引更多全球的投资者，公司迫切需要引入更高标准的公司治理；其次，美国和英国等国家都在带头积极推进公司治理，为其余国家提供了借鉴的模版；最后，全球太多公司严重的财务造假与丑闻，导致公司一夜之间倒闭破产，对投资者造成了不可挽回的损失，也加速了政府将更严苛的公司治理提上日程。

> 博学多才

安然事件

安然公司曾是美国一家叱咤风云的能源公司。 该公司因规模之大、盈利之丰厚，曾连续 6 年被《财富》杂志评选为"美国最具创新精神公司"。 然而真正使它在全世界名声大噪的，却是使这个拥有上千亿资产的公司在几周内破产的财务造假丑闻。

2001 年年初，一家投资机构老板切欧斯公开对安然的盈利模式表示了怀疑。 他认为，虽然安然的业务看起来很辉煌，但实际上赚不到什么钱，也没有人能够说清它是怎么赚钱的。 切欧斯还注意到有些文件涉及了安然背后的合伙公司，这些公司和安然有着说不清的幕后交易，作为安然的首席执行官，斯基林一直在抛出手中的安然股票———而他不断宣称安然的股票会从当时的 70 美元左右升至 126 美元。而且按照美国法律规定，公司董事会成员如果没有离开董事会，就不能抛出手中持有的公司股票。

也许正是这一点引发了人们对安然的怀疑，并开始真正追究安然的盈利情况和现金流向。到了 2001 年 8 月中旬，人们对于安然的疑问越来越多，并最终导致了股价下跌。2001 年 8 月 9 日，安然股价已经从年初的 80 美元左右跌到了 42 美元。紧接着，安然的状况便一发不可收拾。

2001 年 10 月 16 日，安然发表 2001 年第二季度财报（是第三季财务报表），宣布公司亏损总计达到 6.18 亿美元，即每股亏损 1.11 美元。同时首次透露因首席财务官安德鲁·法斯托与合伙公司经营不当，公司股东资产缩水 12 亿美元。

2001 年 10 月 22 日，美国证券交易委员会瞄上安然，要求公司自动提交某些交易的细节内容。并最终于 10 月 31 日开始对安然及其合伙公司进行正式调查。

2001 年 11 月 8 日，安然被迫承认做了假账，虚报数字让人瞠目结舌：自 1997 年以来，安然虚报盈利共计近 6 亿美元。

2001 年 11 月 28 日，标准普尔将安然债务评级调低至"垃圾债券"级。

2001 年 11 月 30 日，安然股价跌至 0.26 美元，市值由峰值时的 800 亿美元跌至 2 亿美元。

2001 年 12 月 2 日，安然正式向破产法院申请破产保护，破产清单中所列资产高达 498 亿美元，成为美国历史上最大的破产企业。

前后仅仅几周时间，一家如此"成功"的公司轰然倒塌。无独有偶，2002 年，同样是在美国，发生了一起美国有史以来规模最大的破产案，其涉事金额甚至是安然公司的两倍之多，这就是有名的"世通案件"。接二连三发生的丑闻引起了美国当局的高度警惕，强调改进公司治理、强化内部控制的"萨班斯法案"就是在这样的情况下应运而生的（财务欺诈之安然事件，2016）。

非常有意思的是，英美两国对公司治理的概念是稍微有些不同的。总的来说，英国遵循的是以原则为导向的公司治理，而"一朝被蛇咬"的美国遵循的是更为严格的以规则为导向的公司治理。这是我们接下来 1.4 要学到的内容，需要同学们对这两大派别有基本的认知。

1.4 Approaches to corporate governance（Principle-based VS Rule-based）

表 9-1　Two types of approaches to corporate governance

UK	USA
Principle-based	Rule-based
Guidelines（best practice）	Rules
Comply or explain（not compulsory）	Must comply（compulsory）

公司治理一般有两种类型（如表 9-1 所示），ACCA 课程更注重学习英国的公司治理，即以原则为导向的公司治理。接下来，我们来看看英国提倡的公司治理的一些最有代表性的原则。

> **知识点解读**
>
> 很多同学对于在英国，公司治理的要求并非强制，不是很能理解，尤其是针对 comply or explain（遵循或解释）尤为困惑。其实并不难理解，在英国，市场以及政府鼓励遵循公司治理的准则，这是最佳行为规范（best practice），但如果公司选择不遵守，那么它应当给予合理的解释，倘若该公司既不遵守也不能给出解释，那么市场以及投资者会对该公司的治理产生疑问，进而影响市场上投资者的选择。

1.5 Main principle of UK corporate governance code

According to the UK corporate governance code (2014), the following are main principles that organisations need to comply with.

(A) Leadership

Every company should be headed by an effective board which is collectively responsible for the long-term success of the company to ensure no one individual should have unfettered powers of decision.

(a) The chairman is responsible for leadership of the board and ensuring its effectiveness on all aspects of its role.

(b) Non-executive directors should constructively challenge and help develop proposals on strategy.

(B) Effectiveness

The board and its committees should have the appropriate balance of skills, experience, independence and knowledge of the company to enable them to discharge their respective duties and responsibilities effectively.

(C) Accountability

The board should establish arrangements to ensure that the information presented is fair, balanced and understandable, internal control and risk management system is sound and relationship with auditors is appropriate.

(D) Remuneration

Executive directors' remuneration should be designed to promote the long-term success of the company. Performance-related elements should be transparent and ensure no director involved in deciding his or her own remuneration.

(E) Relations with shareholders

There should be a dialogue with shareholders based on the mutual understanding of objectives. The board should use general meetings to communicate with investors and to encourage their participation.

> **精益求精**

There may be some problems of CG when the followings occur in a company:

（1）公司中存在一家独大的现象(domination of one single person);

（2）董事会缺乏参与（lack of participation of the board）;

（3）缺乏足够的内部控制（lack of sufficient internal control）;

（4）缺乏独立监督（lack of independent scrutiny）;

（5）缺乏与股东的沟通（lack of dialogue with shareholders）;

（6）过分注重短期利益（excessive attention on short-term interest）;

（7）提供误导性的会计信息（provision of misleading accounting information）。

通过以上的学习，我们可以看到，安然的崩溃并不是一个偶然，究其原因就是公司治理存在缺陷。

> **知识点解读**
> 关于董事会、内部控制、独立监督等内容，我们会在 AB 后续课程中，逐一学习。

安然的核心文化就是盈利。在安然，经营者追求的目标就是"高获利、高股价、高成长"。《财富》杂志撰文指出：正是由于安然公司的主管们建立了以盈利增长为核心的文化，经理们才有了很大的动力去涉险，安然追求的目标最后也只剩下一个，那就是盈利。安然的公司精神就是冒险。安然鼓励的是不惜一切代价追求利润的冒险精神，用高盈利换取高报酬、高奖金、高回扣、高期权。安然甚至把坚持传统做法的人视为保守，很快将其"清理"出去。同时安然内部不断地进行着"大换血"，新人一进门就会立即获得 500 万元的炒作能源期货大权。

本应该独立公正的外部审计安达信，却和被审计客户安然坐在了同一条船上。安达信自安然公司 1985 年开始就为它做审计，做了整整 16 年。除了单纯的审计外，安达信还提供内部审计和咨询服务。20 世纪 90 年代中期，安达信与安然签署了一项补充协议，安达信包揽安然的外部审计工作。不仅如此，安然公司的咨询业务也全部由安达信负责。2001 年，安然公司付给它的 5200 万美元的报酬中一半以上的收入（2700 万美元）是用来支付咨询服务的。安然从 1997 年到 2001 年间虚构利润 5.86 亿美元，并隐藏了数亿美元的债务。美国监管部门的调查发现，安然公司的雇员中居然有 100 多位来自安达信，包括首席会计师和财务总监等高级职员，而在董事会中，有一半的董事与安达信有着直接或间接的联系。这不仅意味着，安然公司十几年来的账务都缺乏独立的监督，还侧面预示着，安然公司的董事会存在一家独大的现象。

以上种种迹象都说明了安然公司存在严重的公司治理缺陷，它的陨落并不是一场意外。在漫长的公司以及公司治理发展历程中，安然事件成为一个敲响世人的警钟。

1.6 Corporate governance report

根据伦敦证券交易所的要求，上市公司的公司治理报告应当反映其是否遵循公司治理的准则，以及是如何遵循的。除此之外，公司治理报告应当包含以下内容（Cadbury，1992）：

(a) Review of structure and responsibilities of the board of directors.
(b) Role of auditors and recommendations to the accountancy profession.
(c) Rights and responsibilities of shareholders.
(d) Director's responsibility for preparing accounts.
(e) The operating and financial review (**OFR**)：It provides stakeholders a thorough analysis of the company from the perspective of the management.

> **知识点解读**
>
> Operating and financial review（运营财务检查），顾名思义，这部分内容主要是站在管理层的角度，针对公司的运营效率以及财务效果进行分析，以提供给投资者一个既包含历史信息也囊括未来展望的报告。

通过上述内容的学习，我们了解了与公司治理相关的一些基本内容，到目前为止，同学们心里应该都还存有一个疑问：公司治理到底是通过什么样的方式来完成其目标？其实这个问题并不难，倘若站在"代理理论"的角度上看，股东担心的无非就是作为代理人的这些管理者是否真的在为公司以及股东利益尽心尽力。既然找到问题的核心，那治理方式就可以对症下药，对管理层及其所作所为加以独立的监督。**在本章，我们主要介绍四种可以达成目标的方式，即在公司设立董事会、建立专门的委员会、引入公众的监督（public oversight），以及聘请外部审计。**

2 Best practice in corporate governance

我们接下来学习公司治理当中具体的举措：股东通过年度股东大会（Annual general meeting，AGM）选出董事（Directors），同时股东任命非执行董事（Non-executive directors，NED）。董事会（Board of directors，BOD）由非执行董事和股东大会选出的董事构成。董事会任命董事会主席（Chairman）和首席执行官（Chief executive directors，CEO）并负责日常公司的管理和运行，并且代理行使决策权和管理权。

2.1 Board of directors

2.1.1 Role of the board

> **知识点解读**
>
> 董事会大多数职能都跟"重大"一词相关，其实这并不难理解，董事会并不会实际参与到日常运营中去，它处理的事项主要是监督。

Every company should be headed by an effective board which is collectively responsible for the **long-term success** of the company, the main role of the board is to:

(a) Set out the company's strategic aims.

(b) Ensure necessary financial and human resources are in place.

(c) Set the company's values and standards.

(d) Establish effective controls and risk management practices.

All directors need to act and make decisions in the best interest of the company.

2.1.2 Required qualities of board of directors

> **知识点解读**
>
> 董事会成员需要具备该公司所处行业的相关知识、技能，除此之外，同学们需要尤为注意，董事会中执行董事与非执行董事的数量应当取得平衡，以避免执行董事在董事会中有一手遮天的嫌疑。

(a) The board should have appropriate **balance of skills, experience, independence and knowledge** of the company to enable them to discharge their respective duties on responsibilities effectively.

(b) **Appropriate combination of executives and non-executive directors** (and in particular independent non-executive directors) such that no individual (or small group of individuals) can dominate the board's decisions.

(c) All directors need to allocate **sufficient time** to the company.

2.1.3 Structure of the board

The board needs to be organised in appropriate size and structure in order to make itself more effective.

(A) Executive directors (EDs)

Executive directors (EDs) are full-time employees of the company and they work for the company in a senior position. The chief executive officer (CEO) and the finance director (in the US, chief financial officer) are nearly always executive directors. Executive directors are usually recruited by the board of directors.

(B) Non-executive directors (NEDs)

Non-executive directors (NEDs) are **not employees** of the company so they do not participate in the day-to-day operation. The main aim of involving NEDs is to provide a **balancing influence** and help to minimise conflicts of interest. The

Higgs Report (2003), summarised their roles as:

(a) **Strategy**: to propose or challenge strategies.
(b) **Performance**: to scrutinise the performance of the executive directors.
(c) **Risk**: to provide an external perspective on risk management.
(d) **People**: to deal with people issues, such as remuneration and nomination decisions.

In general, NEDs are beneficial in **providing external knowledge and independent judgment** on important matters, which is called **dual nature**. Thus, NEDs could act as **comfort factors** for stakeholders. However, the quality of the NEDs should be evaluated prudently before being appointed. Lacking inside consideration of the operation or independence would diminish its effectiveness.

公司董事会之所以引入非执行董事，就是因为他们的独立性可以对公司的"代理人"起到监督作用，因此确保这种独立性尤为重要，我们可以从以下几个方面来保证这种独立性（Safeguards of the independence of NEDs）：

（1）非执行董事不得与公司有商贸以及经济交易往来（NEDs should have no business, financial or other connection with the company）;

（2）非执行董事只能从公司领取固定的薪资以及拥有一定限额的少量股份，并且不能参与公司的股权激励计划（NEDs should not take part in share option schemes apart from fixed fees and shareholdings）;

（3）非执行董事的任期应当限于一定期间，并且任期结束若还需要继续聘用，应当经过正式流程批准（NED's appointment should be limited for a specified period and approval is needed for reappointment）;

（4）公司应当建立流程确保非执行董事能不受阻挠地发表独立意见和拥有独立汇报路径（NEDs could take independent advice and have independent reporting access）。

It is highly recommended as best practice that a public company should have more non-executive directors than executive directors.

> 核心考点
>
> Non-executive director（非执行董事），是考试中的常见考点，主要考核非执行董事的4种职能，出题方式一般比较平铺直叙，因此同学们需要理解记忆。NED 的主要特征包括：
> - Engaged in the business operations but not executive;
> - Challenging the decision made by directors but supportive;
> - Independent but involved.

> 知识点解读
>
> 非执行董事的四大角色：
> **战略**：非执行董事应当为公司的战略制定添砖加瓦，不仅仅是提出建议，更应当在认为有问题时提出质疑;
> **绩效**：非执行董事应当对执行董事的业绩起到监督、检查的作用;
> **风险**：非执行董事应当运用自身的专业技能和远见卓识为公司的风险管理体系做出贡献;
> **董事与管理层**：非执行董事不仅对执行董事以及管理层的日常工作进行独立监督，还应当对执行董事及管理层的薪酬、提名、任命等做出监督。

小试牛刀

Example question 3

To encourage executive directors to operate in the best interests of the shareholders, they could:

A. Be given a high basic salary
B. Receive share options based on both individual and company's performance
C. Be entitled to large payment upon resignation or termination
D. Be asked to attend AGMs

2.1.4 Responsibilities of main roles in board of directors

There should be a clearly accepted **division of responsibilities** at the head of a company, which will **ensure a balance of power and authority**, such that "**no one individual has unfettered power of decision making**". (Higgs,

> 知识点解读
>
> 董事会各个成员的职责，特别是董事会主席和董事会秘书各自的职责，是考试的重点。

2003, p. 23)

(A) Role of Chairman

The chairman is the leader of the board of directors. Chairman is responsible for:

(a) Setting agenda of the board and ensure its effectiveness in all aspects.

(b) Deciding the scope of each board meeting and ensure all matters have been fully discussed.

(c) Ensuring effective communication with shareholders.

(d) Facilitating contribution of NEDs and constructive relations between EDs and NEDs.

(B) Role of CEO

CEO is the leader of the executives and is responsible for the **day-to-day** management of the organisation.

(C) Role of Company secretary (Chief administrative officer, CAO)

(a) Filing the following documents (financial statements, director's reports, auditor's report).

(b) Organising board meetings of shareholders and taking formal minutes.

(c) Establishing and maintaining a registered office for **official communication**.

知识点解读

董事会秘书，俗称董秘，属于上市公司的高管人员。上市公司与证券交易所之间的沟通联络都是通过董秘进行的。现今，投资人（股民）在很多炒股软件中，也可以直接通过留言向董秘询问有关公司的信息。

Example question 4

Example question 5

小试牛刀

Example question 4

Who should sign the minutes of a committee meeting to confirm they are a true and accurate record of meeting?

A. Chief executive　　　　B. Any two members

C. Secretary　　　　　　D. Chairman

Example question 5

It is important to promote proper and complete dialogue between the company registration body and a company. It is also important to ensure that essential administrative requirements laid down by the company registration body come to the attention of the board.

Which TWO positions should be responsible for the above events?

A. Director　　　　　　B. Chairman

C. Chief executive officer　　D. Company secretary

精益求精

关于董事会，你还需要知道的二三事

（1）虽然在英国并没有明文规定要求董事会主席与CEO这两个职能进行分离，但鉴于希望董事会主席的职能能够充分发挥，英国2003发布的《希格斯报告》(*Higgs report*)中强烈建议由两个人分别担任董事会主席与CEO这两个职能，并且董事会主席最好由非执行董事担任，以加强其独立的监督性。

（2）董事会在公司架构中虽然起着一定的监督作用，但其自身也需要被监督，一般每年会对董事会进行一次评估。

（3）有效的董事会运作依赖于 chairman/NED/ED 三者间的动态制衡，才能使得公司治理真正发挥有效性。

2.2 Committee

根据委员会的职能作用，我们可以将委员会划分为以下几种类型。

2.2.1 Remuneration committee

（a）Composition of members：entirely constituted by **non-executive directors.**

（b）Functions：take responsibility for setting the organisation's policy regarding executive directors' remunerations and specific pay structures for each director.

2.2.2 Audit committee

（a）Composition of members：
- Entirely constituted by **INDEPENDENT non-executive directors.**
- At least one member to have significant, recent and relevant financial experience.

（b）Functions：
- To monitor the integrity of the financial statements of the company, reviewing significant financial reporting judgments.
- To review the company's internal financial control system and, unless expressly addressed by a separate risk committee or by the board itself, risk management systems.
- To monitor and review the effectiveness of the company's internal audit function.
- To make recommendations to the board in relation to the appointment of the external auditor and to approve the remuneration and terms of engagement of the external auditor.
- To monitor and review the external auditor's independence, objectivity and effectiveness, taking into consideration relevant UK professional and regulatory requirements.
- To develop and implement policy on the engagement of the external auditor to supply non-audit services, taking into account relevant ethical guidance regarding the provision of non-audit services by the external audit firm.

> **薪酬委员会（Remuneration committee）：**
> 薪酬委员会存在的目的是为执行董事设置合理的薪酬水平，而并非为全体员工；正是因为该委员会是为执行董事设置薪酬，为了确保独立性，薪酬委员会的成员必须全部由非执行董事构成。

> **审计委员会（Audit committee）：**
> 审计委员会要求全部由独立的非执行董事构成并且至少有一个成员具有最近和相关的财务经验；此委员会主要负责：
> - 监控公司财务报表的完整性，审查重大财务报告错报；
> - 审查公司的内部财务控制制度，除非另有风险委员会或董事会明确规定，否则还应审查风险管理制度；
> - 监督和审查公司内部审计部门的有效性；
> - 就外部审计师的任命向董事会提出建议，并批准外部审计师的薪酬和任命；
> - 根据英国相关专业和监管要求，监督和审查外部审计师的独立性、客观性和有效性；
> - 制定并实施聘用外部审计师提供非审计服务的政策，同时考虑到有关外部审计师提供非审计服务的道德指引。

博学多才

除了以上两种委员会以外，有的公司的董事会，还会设立提名委员会（Nomination committee）。此委员会的主要职责是为董事会筛选并推荐合适的董事会成员，因此建议提名委员会由大部分非执行董事组成，而并非全部非执行董事，因为董事会中的执行董事对企业更为了解，所以能更明确地知晓企业实际所需要的成员要求。

2.3 Public oversight

As referred above, public oversight is also one kind of measures to facilitate corporate governance. In retrospect, the establishment of public oversight can be traced to the Sarbanes-Oxley Act 2002 in the US. In this Act, the Public Company Accounting Oversight Board (PCAOB) was firstly introduced.

It is found later that the principle of public oversight is vital and applicable to other countries, e.g. the UK, both in **improving audit quality** and emphasising the importance of **compliance with standards** in a company's control environment.

小试牛刀

Example question 6

Which two of the followings are principles of a public oversight board?

A. To review internal controls

B. To improve audit quality

C. To approve the appointment of board members

D. To emphasize the importance of compliance with standards in a company's control environment

核心考点

外部审计职责以及审计报告的两种分类是 AB 高频考点，需要熟记。

知识点解读

Unqualified report（无保留意见审计报告），是指审计人员对被审计单位的会计报表，依照独立审计准则的要求进行审查后，确认被审计单位采用的会计处理方法遵循了会计准则及有关规定。会计报表反映的内容符合被审计单位的实际情况；会计报表内容完整，表达清楚，无重要遗漏；报表项目的分类和编制方法符合规定要求，因而对被审计单位的会计报表无保留地表示满意。

Qualified report（保留意见审计报告），是指审计人员对被审计单位的会计报表的某些方面存在不一致的意见，但整体而言是公允的，从而发表保留性的意见。

2.4 External auditor

审计是从公司外部聘请专业的第三方，运用专门的方法，对公司财务报告的真实性、正确性、合规性等进行审查和监督的鉴证业务，这是一种历史悠久的监督活动。

2.4.1 External audit

External auditors are those qualified accountants from auditing firms which are **independent** from client companies. As independent third parties, they have a **periodic** purpose to **express an opinion** on clients' financial statements. Such opinion is up to whether the accounting records and financial statements are prepared, in all material aspects, in accordance with applicable accounting standards.

After the examination, if the accounts and financial statements are prepared in accordance with applicable accounting standards, auditors will issue an **unqualified audit report**. If the auditor disagrees with the preparation of accounts which are important and cannot persuade the management to change the accounts, then a **qualified report** will be issued. In brief, external audits provide **assurance** to shareholders about the reliability of the financial statements prepared by company's management.

Additionally, **for the listed companies, the external audit is compulsory and must be conducted annually**. However, for some companies which are not on the list, they may conduct the external audit if the shareholders and other stakeholders requires.

Answers for example question

1. B
2. A
3. B
4. D
5. BD
6. BD

Summary

Chapter 9 考试不同问法总结

Section A

1. 针对 basic concept

- Which of the following corporate governance theories describes the situation above?
- In this relationship, which party is the principal and which is the agent?
- Which of the following statements reflects the stakeholder approach to decision-making?
- In relation to corporate governance, with which of the following is a public oversight body MOST concerned?
- Which of the following is a feature of good corporate governance?

2. 针对 CSR & Sustainability

- Is this policy above reflective of SCR or ethics?
- Which of the following is a definition of CSR?
- Which of the following is a benefit of sustainability?

3. 针对 board

- In relation to non-executive directors, which TWO of the following are recommendations of best practice in effective corporate governance?

4. 针对 committee

- Which TWO of the following are recommended as best practice with regard to remuneration committee?
- Which TWO of the following have their reward packages determined by the remuneration committee?
- Which of the following statements reflects the responsibility of an audit committee?

Quick quiz

9.1 Which of the following have their reward determined by remuneration committee?

A. Shareholders   B. Executive directors

C. External auditors   D. All employees

Answer: B

Difficulty level: Easy

Tag: Remuneration committee

Rationale:

Remuneration committee determines the organisation's general policy on the remuneration of executive directors and specific remuneration packages for each director.

薪酬委员会主要负责对公司的高管人员的薪酬政策提出建议,以及制定每个特定人员的薪酬结构与水平。

9.2 Which of the following about audit committee is true?

A. The audit committee determines who could join the board

B. The audit committee sets the company's policy

C. The audit committee should be entirely staffed by independent non-executive directors

D. The audit committee appoints the external auditors

Answer: C

Difficulty level: Easy

Tag: Audit committee

Rationale:

The nomination committee is responsible for selecting and recommending members who constituting the company's board. The board of directors is responsible for setting the company's general policy. The audit committee is responsible for appointing company's internal auditors who review the operation and control of the company. The audit committee should be entirely composed of independent non-executive directors.

提名委员会主要负责对董事会成员和经理人员的标准提出建议并选出合适的候选人名单。董事会负责制定公司的政策及制定重大决策。审计委员负责任命公司的内审人员,而外审是由股东投票选出。审计委员会全部成员需由独立的非执行董事组成。

9.3 _____ means that directors must be accountable to shareholders regarding of company's performance. Fill the correct answer in the blank.

A. Fiduciary duty   B. Corporate governance

C. Ethical behaviour   D. Financial duty

Answer: A

Difficulty level: Easy

Tag: Fiduciary duty

Rationale:

Fiduciary responsibility means that managers owe a fiduciary duty (duty of faithful service) to shareholders and managers should avoid conflicts of interests and be responsible for their actions.

受托责任指的是管理者受到来自股东托付的委托,要求其尽心尽责地管理企业,帮助股东、企业实现自身的目标,并且要避免任何会损害企业目标的行为。故答案选 A。

9.4 Richard and Morgan are executive directors of Delya Co. Recently, they are considering a proposal of take-over which is favourable to their own performance rather than company's further prospects.

Which of the following correctly describes the above situation?

A. Stewardship theory

B. Stakeholder theory

C. Corporate governance

D. Agency theory

Answer: D

Difficulty level: Normal

Tag: Perspective on governance-Agency theory

Rationale:

In agency theory, the key point is the owners are the principal and the managers are the agent, and the agents are empowered to act in principals' interest and should avoid any conflict of interest. Therefore, the answer is option D.

代理理论的核心是管理者应该为股东/企业的利益着想，而不能为自己谋取私利，并且要避免任何的利益冲突。所以在这种观点下，它认为一个好的公司治理应该避免任何的代理问题出现。故答案选 D。

9.5 External audits provide assurance to shareholders that the financial statements are prepared, in all material aspects, in accordance with the applicable financial reporting framework. **Which of the following is not correct?**

A. Examination of the books of account and records of an entity all the time

B. Independent third party

C. Comply with established concepts, principles, accounting standards, legal requirements

D. Give a true and fair view of the financial statement

Answer: A

Difficulty level: Normal

Tag: External audit

Rationale:

External audits provide assurance to shareholders during periodic examination of the books of account and records of an entity not at all the time. Therefore, A is the answer.

这道题考查的是审计是从公司外部聘请专业的第三方，运用专门的方法，对公司财务报告的真实性、正确性、合规性等进行审查和监督的鉴证业务，而外审在提供鉴证业务的时候是对一定时期之内的财务状况进行鉴证，而不是无时无刻。所以这道题答案选择 A。

9.6 Non-executive directors play very important role in the board of directors. Which of the following is not correct?

A. NEDs are employees of the company

B. Exist to reduce conflicts of interest

C. Contribute to the strategy and challenge the strategy if necessary

D. Scrutinize the performance of management

Answer: A

Difficulty level: Normal

Tag: NED

Rationale:

Non-executive directors are not employees of the company, but they do take part in decision making at board meetings. They do not take part in the day-to-day running of the company. Therefore, A is the answer.

这道题考查的是非执行董事的特点。非执行董事是整个公司治理里非常重要的一个角色，他们参与到整个公司的战略决策、风险管理等，但是他们并不是公司内部的员工。所以这道题答案选择 A。

Chapter 10
Internal control

知识导入

上一章我们了解了一个非常重要的概念——公司治理。 而有效的公司治理，其中非常重要的环节就是内部牵制。 随着时间的推移，内部牵制慢慢演化成一个内控系统，那么如何才能做好内控系统，这个系统有谁来做，又由谁来检查它是否有效？ 让我们通过学习这一章来了解内部控制的奥秘。

单词表

英文	中文
Discretionary	自由裁量权
Interpretation	说明，解读
Disaster recovery	灾难复原（应对计算机中大量数据遗失等重大事故的程序）
Segregation of duty	职责分离
Non-current assets	非流动资产
Pay slips	工资单
Deductions	扣减项
Statutory	法定的
Distribution	分配
Custody	保管
Bank reconciliation	银行对账
Balances outstanding	余额
Prenumbered	预先编号的
Internal check	内部牵制
Substantive test	实质性测试

学习指南

Learning objectives	Pass level	Distinction level	用时建议
1. Internal check（1）	√		5 min
2. Internal control（2.1-2.2）	√		10 min
3. Components of internal control（2.3）	√		15 min
4. Control over main transactions（2.4）	√		20min
5. Limitations on the effectiveness of internal controls（2.5）		√	5min
6. Responsibility for internal control（2.6）	√		5 min
7. Internal audit（3）	√		25 min

本章考点

重要考点	难度（1~3）
熟记并理解内控的三个目的	2
熟记和理解内控五要素中的控制环境与控制活动	3
理解 SPAMSOAP	3
理解三个系统的流程和控制方法	2
熟记并理解内审	2
着重记忆审计的方法	2
熟练掌握内审和外审的联系和区别	2

"在早期的企业中，由于群体劳动和分工的结果，为了保证财物的安全，在企业内部实行了互相牵制，从而形成了内部牵制的实践。 在15世纪，随着资本主义企业的发展和复式记账法的出现，以账目间的相互核对为主要内容，实行职能分离的内部牵制开始得到广泛应用，内部牵制不仅保证财物的安全，也保证会计信息的真实性。 由于早期的内部牵制主要是指企业的业务活动必须经过两个或以上的部门分工，以形成相互制衡。此时的内部牵制的内涵和外延相对狭小。"（谢志华，2007）

1 Internal check

Internal check is a system through which the accounting procedures of an organisation are allocated in the way that any procedures are **not under the absolute and independent control of a single person**. The work of one employee is **complementary of that of another**, enabling a **continuous audit of the business to be made** and no one person has exclusive control over transactions.

1.1 Essential elements of an internal check

(a) Checks are implemented on day-to-day transactions.

(b) Checks operate continuously as a part of the system.

于玉林（2010）认为，简单来说："内部牵制的核心在于制衡，即经济业务的处理均由两个或两个以上的人员负责，以达到互相制约，防止舞弊的目的。 这种方法的实施基于两种基本假设：

（1）两个或以上的人或部门无意识地犯同样错误的机会是很小的；

（2）两个或以上的人或部门有意识地合伙舞弊的可能性大大低于单独一个人或部门舞弊的可能性。"

1.2 Examples of internal check

(a) **Arithmetical** internal check：**pre-list/post-list/control total**.

(b) Bank reconciliation.

内部牵制的出现较早，但随着企业规模、架构及多元化的不断发展，内部牵制并不足以帮助公司建立完善的治理模式，因此，内部控制出现的意义极为重要。 杨胜雄（2005）认为："没有系统而有效的内部控制，公司治理将成为一纸空文，而内部控制是实现公司治理的基础设施建设。"同时，王蕾（2001）认为："内部

> **基本概念**
>
> 内部牵制是确保公司有效管理的非常重要的理念，需要考生多理解，同时这个基本概念也会和别的概念，如内部控制、公司治理、企业社会责任等混在一起出题，需要进行区分。

> **知识点解读**
>
> Arithmetical internal check（核算牵制），规定对经济业务的核算记录要有对照平衡关系，如采用复式记账法，总账与明细账的平行登记等。
> 例如，我们在去超市之前，会列出一张 pre-list（预编清单），列明自己要购买的物什，在逛完超市之后，我们会得到超市小票，这就是一种 post-list（事后清单）。 通过两者的核对，我们可以查漏补缺，发现自己是否少买东西，这个过程就是 control total（检查统计）。

控制与公司治理具有高度的相关性，一个健全的内部控制机制实际上是完善的公司治理结构的体现，反过来也成立，内部控制的创新和神话也将促进公司治理的完善和现代企业制度的建立。"

接下来，我们就开始学习什么是内部控制。

2 Internal control

2.1 Definition

Internal control describes the process designed, implemented and maintained by those charged with governance, management and other personnel to provide them with **reasonable assurance** that an entity will achieve its objectives. Simply, internal control is **any action taken by management to enhance the likelihood of achievement of organisations'** objectives.

> **知识点解读**
>
> 针对 internal control 的定义，不同的版本有不同的解释。我们采用了最全面，也相对比较好理解的定义。刚接触这个概念时可能会不好理解，大家可以在 AB 阶段暂时简单地将内部控制理解为：企业采取的一些措施，目的是为了提高企业运营，达到企业设定目标。这些措施所形成的流程和系统，称为内部控制。

2.2 The purposes of internal control

(a) Facilitating effective and efficient **operation** to achieve corporate objectives, including **safeguarding of assets**, identifying and managing liabilities.

(b) Ensuring the quality of internal and external **reporting**. This requires the maintenance of proper records and processes that generate a flow of timely, relevant and reliable information.

(c) Helping ensure **compliance** with applicable laws and regulations, and also with internal policies with respect to the conduct of business.

内部控制的目标可以归纳为以下三点：

（1）经营目标：促进企业的有效经营，以完成目标；

（2）报告目标：确保对内对外报告的可靠性；

（3）合规目标：合理保证企业的行为合乎法律、政策的要求。

> **知识点解读**
>
> Those charged with governance：治理层。治理层是指对被审计单位战略方向以及管理层履行经营管理责任负有监督责任的人员或组织，治理层的责任还包括对财务报告过程的监督。一般认为，董事会属于治理层。

2.3 Components of internal control

接下来，我们需要深入了解内部控制的要素。总的来说，内部控制总共包括五要素：控制环境（control environment）、风险评估（risk assessment process）、信息系统（information system）、控制活动（control activity）以及内部监督（monitoring of controls）。在 AB 课程学习中，我们将重心放在控制环境以及控制活动这两个要素上，剩余的内容会在 AA（审计与鉴证）以及 AAA（高级审计与鉴证）课程中进行深入学习。

2.3.1 Control environment

Control environment is the foundation of the whole internal control system as it "**set the tone**" by creating a culture, attitudes, awareness and actions of **management**.

"内部控制环境是整个内部控制的基础，是推动企业发展的引擎，也是其他一切核心要素的核心，决定了其他控制要素是否能发挥作用，是内部控制其他要素作用的基础。"（范月光，2013）控制环境主要由组织的**管理层**对待内部控制的态度，对于内部控制的意识与采取的行动，以及最终形成的组织文化所决定。

企业中好的控制环境对内控系统的运行发挥着十分重要的作用，其中包括企业应对风险的完善战略、支持风险管理的文化、企业内部对待内控的氛围、清晰的责任权限的划分和有效的沟通等。

2.3.2 Control Activity

Control activities are the policies and **detailed procedures** that help ensure the effectiveness of internal control.

（A）Classification of control activities

表 10-1　Classification of control activities-1

Classification	Comment
Prevent	Avoiding errors before they occur
Detect	Identifying errors once they have occurred (e.g. intruder detection/bank reconciliation/inventory control)
Correct	Minimising and addressing the consequences of errors (e.g. back-up procedure/data restore)

表 10-2　Classification of control activities-2

Classification	Comment
Discretionary	These are controls which managers may be permitted discretion according to their interpretation or judgement of risks in given circumstances. For example, authorisation of a payment
Non-discretionary	These are controls which must be applied. For example, entering a password at the ATM before taking out money

表 10-3　Classification of control activities-3

Classification	Comment
Voluntary	These are controls applied according to the judgement of the organisation and its managers
Mandated	These are controls which **must** be applied, irrespective of circumstances. These are widely used to prevent breached of laws or policy, as well as to minimise risks relating to health and safety

表 10-4　Classification of control activities-4

Classification	Comment
Manual	These controls are applied by participation of individuals
Automated	These controls are programmed into the systems of the organisation

The following classification of controls applies **specifically to information systems**.

> **核心考点**
> 控制活动分类（见表 10-1 至表 10-5）是最容易出现在考试里的分类形式，建议考生两两对应去对比记忆。

> **核心考点**
> 关于 correct control 纠正性控制的理解，重点把握关键词 minimize the effect 减少错误带来的影响，考官经常会考察对 back-up 备份的分类辨析，它属于 correct control 的范围，因为它的存在只能减轻不良结果的影响，而不能预防和防止错误的发生，所以不属于 prevent control，这是最常见的易错点。

The classification of control procedures

核心考点

关于 General & Application control 的辨析，是考试的常见考点，考生重点需要把握各自的主要特征：这两者都是用来降低和电脑相关的风险的，其中，Application control 是具体的用来预防探测纠正错误的一些控制，比如数据及交易的完整性测试，保证数据从录入到处理过程中都是完成的没有丢失的；而 General control 是指对大范围的运行环境的控制。

表 10-5 Classification of control activities-5

Classification	Comment
General	General controls help to ensure the reliability of data generated by systems, helping to ascertain whether **systems** operate as intended and output is reliable. Examples： (a) Physical controls. (b) Hardware and software configuration. (c) Logical access. (d) IT technical support. (e) Disaster recovery
Application	Application controls are automated and designed to ensure the complete and accurate recording of data from input to output. Examples： (a) Sequence checks. (b) Range checks (example of input control). (c) Authorisation of transaction entries. (d) Audit trail

小试牛刀

Example question 1

Which of the following is a non-discretionary control?

　　A. Staff must be checked against national criminal records prior to employment

　　B. Orders must be signed by a manager before processing

　　C. Access to a database is password protected

　　D. Authorisation of purchase orders

Example question 2

Which of the following are application controls?

　　A. Passwords to login to the system

　　B. Sequence checks

　　C. Standby staff of IT system

　　D. Hardware and software configuration

(B) Types and features of effective internal control procedure ('SPAMSOAP')

(a) **S**egregation of duty

　　To minimise the risk of errors and fraud, duties associated with cash handling are often segregated. For example, the separation of role between cashier and bookkeeper is required so that no one will have unfettered power.

　　职责分工控制，要求根据企业目标和职能任务，按照科学、精简、高效的原则，合理设置职能部门和工作岗位，明确各部门、各岗位的职责权限，形成各司其职、各负其责、便于考核、相互制约的工作机制。

(b) **P**hysical control

　　These controls include restrictions on access to essential sites by using locks or passwords.

知识点解读

对于财务控制程序的种类，可记住"SPAMSOAP"字母的简写。同时，需要同学们能理解每一个字母代表的含义，此块内容在考试中不会直接考，但对于理解内部控制活动非常关键。

财产保护控制，要求企业限制未经授权的人员对财产的直接接触和处置，确保财产的安全完整。

(c) **A**uthorisation and approval

Personnel at all levels must undertake responsibilities within the scope of authorisation to avoid unauthorised transactions.

授权控制，要求企业根据职责分工，明确各部门、各岗位办理经济业务与事项的权限范围、审批程序和相应责任等内容。企业内部各级管理人员必须在授权范围内行使职权和承担责任，业务经办人员必须在授权范围内办理业务。

(d) **M**anagement

Controls carried out by managers are part of their essential duties. Typical examples are performance management of subordinates and variance analysis.

管理控制，要求公司建立和完善内部报告制度，全面反映经济活动情况，及时提供业务活动中的重要信息，增强内部管理的时效性和针对性。

(e) **S**upervision

Supervision controls are exercised following down the chain of command, in respect of day-to-day transaction to ensure that all employees are aware that their work will be checked, reducing the risk of errors.

监督控制，要求公司加强针对日常交易的运行以及记录的监督，如预算控制、执行、分析、考核等环节的管理，明确预算项目，建立预算标准，规范预算的编制、审定、下达和执行程序，及时分析和控制预算差异，采取改进措施，确保预算的执行。

(f) **O**rganisation

Organisation controls are implemented according to the disposition of the organisation structure, reporting line and staff responsibilities.

组织机构控制，包括组织机构的设置、分工的科学性、部门岗位责任制、人员素质的控制。在设置内部机构时，企业管理者既要考虑工作的需要，也应兼顾内部控制的需要，使机构设置既精炼又合理。

(g) **A**rithmetical and accounting

Establish proper procedures to ensure the accurate recording and processing of transactions in time, e.g. reconciliations, trial balances.

核算控制，要求通过建立适当的程序，及时、准确、完整地记录交易的发生，并且能够进行比对以确认数据的质量。

(h) **P**ersonnel

Controls are implemented for all aspects of human resources management, especially perform a thorough background check when recruiting new staffs.

人员控制，公司应当从招聘活动开始着重注意人员的个人诚实守信的特质。

2.4 Control over main transactions

接下来，我们将通过介绍公司日常运营中的薪酬系统、采购流程、销售流程以及现金保管这最常见的四个方面，让同学们进一步了解控制活动是如何进行的。

在正式了解之前，同学们可以先行奠定这样一个观念：控制活动的存在是为了防止负面情况的发生，简而言之，控制活动的制定过程就是，担心哪里出问题，就在哪里打补丁。所以，控制活动的制定流程就应当是：首先，找出该项活动中有哪些因素；其次，这些因素可能会出现怎样的偏差，这也是我们要防范的，也就是控制目标；最后，找出合适的办法避免这些偏差。

2.4.1 Payroll system

(A) Process of payroll system

(a) Inputs: employee attendance record;

(b) Process: calculation of net pay after various deductions and make payments to appropriate employees;

(c) Outputs: pay slips or payroll analysis.

In payroll system, standing data (sometimes called reference data) is data which doesn't change very much but is used or referred to many times. For example, rate of pay, employee names and address, tax codes, employee bank account details, etc.

> **知识点解读**
>
> Standing data（常规数据/信息），即工资单上常载的信息，一般不会更改。例如，姓名、地址、税号等。

小试牛刀

Example question 3

Which of the following would not be classified as standing data in the payroll system?

A. Rate of pay

B. Gross pay to date

C. Name and address

Example question 4

Which of the following is an example of standing data recorded in a payroll system?

A. Pension contributions deducted from salary

B. Total deductions from gross income each month

C. Tax reference number issued by the tax authority

D. Total salary received in the year to date

(B) Control aims and corresponding activities of payroll system

薪酬系统的目标是，只有真实存在的员工、真正工作的时间，才能用作支付薪酬的基准。我们可以将这个目标拆分成三个小目标，即**薪酬计算正确、发放准确、记载无误**。通过这些目标，我们就可以对症下药地建立控制活动（如表10-6所示）。

> **知识点解读**
>
> 真实存在的员工这个词汇对应着另外一个专有词汇，叫做"ghost employee"，即公司中并不存在，但的确出现在工资单上领取薪酬的"幽灵员工"。这是一种典型的薪酬舞弊。

表10-6 Control over payroll

Control Aims	Control Activities
The amounts of wages and salaries have been **authorised** and are **calculated correctly**	(a) Verify authorisation regarding wages and salaries, such as overtime, performance-related pay. (b) Segregation of duties between calculation and review of payroll

Control Aims	Control Activities
The **correct amounts** of wages and salaries **are paid** to related parties in appropriate means	(a) Segregation of duties between payment and management of wages and salaries. (b) Custody of unbanked cash. 　• Verification of identity. 　• Comparison of bank transfer lists to payrollrecords. (c) Reconciliation of payroll ledger and bank
Wages and salaries of employees are **correctly recorded** in the general ledger	Recording all relevant data and information for the purpose of review, such as: • Basis for compilation of payroll. • Preparation, checking and approval of payroll. • Handling with non-routine matters

小试牛刀

Example question 5

The payroll function for an organisation is often high risk for fraud.

Which of the following can be defined as effective payroll control activity?

A. Poor wage distribution procedures

B. Segregation of duties between those responsible for preparation, checking and approval of payroll

C. Maintenance of personnel records and checking of wages to details in personnel records once a year

2.4.2 Purchases system

(A) **Process of purchase system**

(a) Inputs: invoices from suppliers, returns and payment slip;

(b) Process: constant update balances outstanding to suppliers;

(c) Outputs: summary of payable balances of each supplier.

　　The purchasing cycle is connected to the account payable, inventory account, cash account and purchase account in the statement of financial position.

(B) **Control aims and corresponding activities of purchase system**

　　采购流程的控制目标是，向**指定的供应商**采购**所需数量**的货物，并**及时支付**与之**对等的款项**（如表 10-7 所示）。

表 10-7　Control over purchase

Control Aims	Control Activities
Ordering: (a) Obtaining proper authorisation of purchase. (b) Only authorised suppliers are being considered and selected during purchase	(a) Purchases are only processed after approval. (b) Select and use appropriate suppliers in the supplier list. (c) Use pre-numbered forms

> **知识点解读**
>
> Sales 和 purchase 两个循环对于刚学 AB 的同学来说不太容易理解，其实这些循环指的就是一系列的流程——采购和销售的流程，在这些流程中都有 input（输入）、processing（处理）和 output（输出）的环节。我们要学习的就是怎样在这些环节中加入控制，来确保它们都正确地被执行，所以这里说的控制的具体目标和方法都是围绕这一点来阐述的。

Control Aims	Control Activities
Receipt: (a) Only ordered goods are accepted. (b) Once received, all liabilities of goods and services are recognised and recorded accurately and correctly	(a) Check qualities of goods delivered from suppliers and return all defective goods. (b) Compare and match goods received note (GRN), supplier invoice to purchase order
Accounting: All purchases and returns occurred are correctly accounted in the general and payables ledger	(a) Segregation of duties between accounting and checking of purchases. (b) Purchases (invoices) and returns (credit notes) occurred are accounted promptly. (c) Review and reconcile supplier statements received from suppliers and payable ledger

2.4.3 Sales system

(A) Process of sales system

Inputs: sales order, credit note and receipt.

Process: constant update of balances of each customer.

Outputs: Summary of receivables balances of each customer.

(B) Control aims and corresponding activities of sales cycle

销售流程的控制目标是，将商品销售给**真实存在且信用良好的客户**，并能够**及时且正确地进行会计记录**，以便之后能够**及时发现潜在的呆账或坏账**（如表10－8所示）。

表10－8 Control over sales

Control Aims	Control Activities
Selling: (a) Sales are only made with customers who have good credit ratings (b) Sales orders are all dealt with and recorded correctly	(a) Customer credit assessment should be conducted and approved before making sales (b) Use prenumbered orders so that any missing forms will be identified timely
Delivery: (a) All goods delivered are accompanied by sales invoices, sales orders and goods delivered notes. (b) Credit notes are only issued with appropriate reasons	(a) Obtain authorisation before despatch of goods. (b) Verify sales invoices and delivery notes before despatch of goods. (c) Compare and match sales invoices, goods delivered notes (GDN) and sales orders. (d) Check goods returned from customers and only accept goods in perfect conditions
Accounting and receivables control: (a) All sales and returns occurred are correctly accounted in the general and receivables ledger. (b) Effective management of potential doubtful debts (the risk of irrecoverable debts)	(a) Segregation of duties between accounting and checking of sales. (b) Sales (invoices) and returns (credit notes) occurred are accounted promptly. (c) Compare cash receipts with invoices. (d) Update and review receivable statements on a regular basis and follow up overdue accounts

小试牛刀

Example question 6

Which **Two** of the following would help to prevent potential bad debts?

A. Obtain authorisation for credit limit

B. Segregation of duties between banking and receiving cash

C. Obtaining references for new customers before offering them credit terms

D. Reasons and amount of the payment must be obtained

Example question 6

2.4.4 Controlling cash

任何一家公司日常运营都离不开现金，我们从收到现金和支付现金两方面来学习对于现金的控制活动（如表10-9所示）。

表10-9 Control over cash

	Control Activities
Controls over receipts	(a) Cash received must be banked immediately, or otherwise deposit in a safe place. (b) Segregation of duties between receiving cash and recording. (c) All received cash must be completely recorded. (d) Measures must be taken to prevent cash theft or accident events
Controls over payments	(a) Reasons and amount of the payment must be obtained. (b) Payment must be authorised and it should be evidenced by a signature. (c) Only special individuals will have the authority

Note: The most important controls to detect fraud and error is **reconciliation**. Bank reconciliation should be performed on a weekly/monthly basis and should be reviewed by a supervisor/manager

内部控制活动的存在虽然是为了促进公司目标的实现，但是其本身运行是否有效，也是存在一些影响因素的。

2.5 Limitations on the effectiveness of internal controls

(a) Collusion between employees cannot be eliminated.

(b) Even though authorisation system can be applied strictly, however, it cannot be guaranteed that authorities under certain person will not be misused.

(c) There does exist override risk, which means management can place themselves over the controls set up by themselves.

(d) The costs of control may exceed the benefit from control.

(e) The control procedures may not catch up with the development of transaction.

2.6 Responsibility for internal control

(a) According to the UK Corporate Governance Code, the **board of directors** is responsible for maintaining a sound internal control system.

(b) Furthermore, the management take the role in implementing board policies to

知识点解读

在内控这一事项中，公司人员各司其职：
（1）董事会负责维持良好的内控系统；
（2）管理层负责执行董事会的政策以建立完善的内部控制活动；
（3）内部审计负责评估内部控制系统的有效性，并且当发现不足时，应当能够及时提出建议。

establish control activities.

(c) Internal auditors are responsible to evaluate the effectiveness of internal control system and make recommendations.

根据2.6，董事会负责维持健康完善的内控系统，而内审（internal audit）则需要评估内控系统有效性以及提出改进意见。 接下来，我们就来详细学习内审的知识点。

3 Internal audit

"内部审计是'外部审计'的对称。 由部门、单位内部专职审计人员进行的审计。 目的在于帮助部门、单位的管理人员实行最有效的管理。 内部审计与外部审计相配合并互为补充，是现代审计的一大特色。 健全的内部审计制度，可为外部审计提供可信赖的资料，减少外部审计的工作量。 在中国，内部审计不仅是部门、单位内部经济管理的重要组成部分，而且作为国家审计的基础，被纳入审计监督体系。"（邹瑜，1999）

Internal audit is an independent appraisal activity established within an organisation to examine and evaluate the activities of organisations. Internal audit can be described as "the control of controls", which facilitates management through verifying other controls and propose viable suggestions to improve the effectiveness of the internal control system.

3.1 The features of internal audit

It should be known that there are two main features of internal audit, that is independence and appraisal. Here, the independence means an important quality of them, and appraisal means the function.

(a) **Independence**

To ensure quality of internal audit service, the occupation should be independent of other departments, especially those they would audit. Furthermore, the existence of audit committee is also an assurance for the degree of independence.

(b) **Appraisal**

There are two points should be noted with this function. Firstly, the internal audit function does not have managerial or operational duties that are outside of the internal audit function. Secondly, internal auditors should not review any work done by themselves, in order to avoid self-review threat.

3.2 The objectives of internal audit

同学们需要对内部审计的职责和存在目标有这样一个印象：**相对于我们本章后面要讲的外部审计，内部审计几乎负责公司运营的每个方面，其职责范围远大于外部审计。** 内部审计的主要职责范围包括：

(a) Review the compliance with laws, regulation.

(b) Review the implementation of corporate objectives.

(c) Review the accounting and internal control system.

(d) Examination of financial and operating information.

知识点解读

内部审计的核心在于两点：第一是**独立**，内部审计虽然是公司内部设立的一个部门，但是独立性是其执行本部门职责的基础所在。 第二是**评估**，正因为内部审计具有独立性，它才可以对公司其他部门的工作进行有效评估。 为了规避自我审核的威胁（我们会在第19章学习），内部审计并不会亲自承担管理或者运营的职责以及审核自己完成的工作，仅仅是对他人的工作进行评估。

(e) Identification of significant business and financial risks, monitoring the organisation's overall risk management strategies.

(f) Special investigation into particular areas, for example suspected fraud.

(g) Review the "3E" (economy/efficiency/effectiveness) of operations.

3.3 Types of audit

In the course of their duties, internal auditors may carry out various types of audit. These include the following:

(a) **Operational audit** may be concerned with the efficiency of the organisation's activities. They consider performance relative to pre-determined criteria.

(b) **System audit** are used to test and evaluate whether internal controls are implemented as described. Meanwhile, they also test whether the information provided by the organisation's systems is accurate. Two tests would be conducted:

- **Compliance tests** verify that whether **internal controls** are being applied as prescribed.
- **Substantive tests** verify the figures entered in accounts to **discover errors and omissions**.

If the compliance tests reveal that internal controls are working satisfactorily, then the amount of substantive testing can be reduced.

(c) **Transactions audit** (Probity audit) is concerned with detecting fraud and other types of criminal or unlawful behaviour.

(d) **Social audit** may be concerned any matters relating to governance such as matters relating to fairness of dealings, impartiality, accountability and transparency.

小试牛刀

Example question 7

Which of the following are substantive tests rather than compliance test?

A. Checking a sample of invoices for authorisation

B. Checking the addition of the purchased daybook

C. Checking the signature in the sales daybook

D. Checking the prenumbered forms is follow the sequence

Example question 8

A systems audit involves tests to check that the figures entered in the accounts are correct.

What sort of tests will be used for this purpose?

A. Compliance tests   B. Substantive tests

C. Tests of control   D. Analytical procedure

知识点解读

3E 是指：Economic（经济）、Efficiency（效率）以及Effectiveness（效果）。3E 评估往往是在非营利组织或企业管理部门中使用。

Economic（经济）：是指用尽可能少的成本去购买规定的质和量的输入物品；

Efficiency（效率）：是指运用尽可能少的资源来提供规定的质和量的服务。

Effectiveness（效果）：效果关心的是"目标或结果"，往往以是否完成目标为衡量标准。

知识点解读

系统审计可以分为控制测试和实质性测试。

控制测试（compliance test）： 控制测试又叫合规性测试，是指用于评价内部控制运行有效性的审计程序。控制运行有效性强调的是控制能够在各个不同时点按照既定设计得以一贯执行。

实质性测试（substantive test）： 实质性测试是指在控制测试的基础上，为取得直接证据而运用其他具体方法对会计报表的真实性和财务收支的合法性进行审查，以得出审计结论的过程。

这两者的关系需要着重注意：控制测试在先，通过这种测试我们可以知晓整个内部控制系统的运行状况。如果内部控制运行健康，这意味着出差错的可能性会相对减少，那么实质性测试的工作量也就可以相应减少。反之，则情况相反。

Example question 7

> **核心考点**
>
> 内部审计和外部审计的区别（见表10-10）是核心考点，请同学们特别留意。通常情况下，我们所说的审计一般是指由外部的第三方进行的审计（external audit），审计是商业活动中非常重要的一个环节，ACCA 的 AA 和 AAA 就是专门介绍审计的课程。外部审计存在的意义是为了证明一个企业的财务报表是否给出了 true and fair 的财务信息，确认了这一点后，各种 stakeholders 才能放心地使用相关的信息进行决策。

3.4 Relationship with external audit

"审计"这个词大家并不陌生，在上一章"公司治理"中，我们曾学习过 external auditor（外部审计），那么外审、内审同为审计工作，到底有何联系，这是我们接下来要学习的内容。

3.4.1 Difference between internal audit and external audit

表 10-10 Differences between internal audit and external audit

	Internal audit	External audit
Reason	Add value and improve **organisations'** operations	Express an opinion on the financial statements
Reporting to	**Board of directors** or the audit committee	**Shareholders** or other external stakeholders
Focus	Operations of the organisation	The **financial statement** and the financial records
Done by whom	**Internal employees of the organisation**, although sometimes the internal audit function is outsourced to reinforce independence	**Independent third party** appointed by the shareholders
Legal basis	Depend on company needs	Legal requirement for large companies, especially public ones.

虽然外部审计与内部审计在上述几个方面存在较大的区别，但值得一提的是，内审计结果对于外部审计来说，的确有借鉴意义。同学们通过常识的判断，也不难推测，如果当我们想要通过借鉴他人成果来减轻自己的工作负担时，我们首先应当考虑的就是该对象到底是否足够可靠，是否能够让我们借鉴。同样的，当外部审计决定借鉴内部审计成果之前，也应当做这种评估。

> **知识点解读**
>
> 外部审计师应当通过评价下列事项，确定是否能够利用内部审计的工作以实现审计目的：
> （1）内部审计在被审计单位中的地位，以及相关政策和程序支持内部审计人员客观性的程度；
> （2）内部审计人员的胜任能力；
> （3）内部审计是否采用系统化、规范化的方法进行。

3.4.2 Assessment by external auditors

Much of the work performed by a company's internal audit function can **overlap** with the work conducted by the external auditor. As such, **co-ordination** between the external and internal auditors of an organisation will minimise duplication of work and encourage a wide coverage of audit issues and areas.

However, when external auditors wish to rely on the work of internal auditors, they first should consider the following things:

(A) Organisational status

External auditors should seek evidence shows that the internal audit function's organisational status supports the objectivity of the internal auditors.

Favourable situations include:

(a) The internal audit function reports to those charged with governance (e.g. the audit committee) rather than solely to management (e.g. the chief finance officer);

(b) The internal audit function does not have managerial or operational duties that are outside of the internal audit function.

(B) Scope of function

External auditors should also evaluate the **nature and extent of the assignments** which internal audit performs and whether management and the directors **act on internal audit recommendations** and how this is evidenced.

(C) Technical competence

External auditors should assess whether the internal auditors possess the required knowledge and skills and whether have adequate technical training and proficiency in auditing

(D) Due professional care

External auditors should verify whether internal audit work is **properly planned, implemented and documented**.

Example question 9

True or False

(1) External auditors are appointed by the shareholders of a company.

(2) The primary responsibility of external auditors is to investigate financial irregularities and report them to shareholders.

(3) External auditors may rely on the work of internal auditors, if they first assess its worth.

Example question 10

Which of the following statements concerning external audit is CORRECT?

    A. External auditors are often employees of the company

    B. External audit is designed to add value and improve an organisation's operations

    C. External auditors report to shareholders on the reliability of financial statements provided by directors

    D. External auditors are appointed by board of directors

Answers of example question

1. C
2. B
3. B
4. C
5. B
6. AC
7. B
8. B
9. T/F/T
10. C

Summary

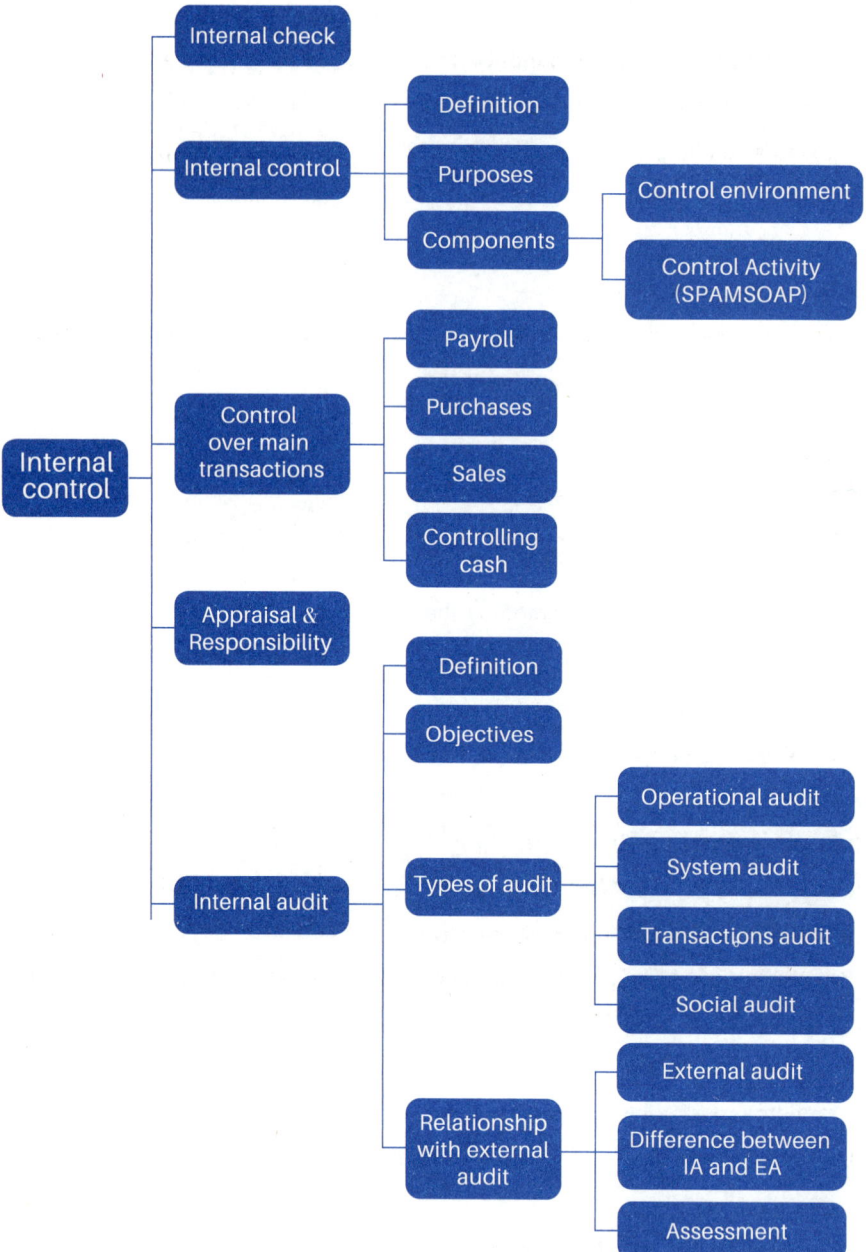

Chapter 10 考试不同问法总结

Section A

1. 针对 Control

- Which TWO of the following are control objectives for cash?
- Which of the following is general controls in relation to IT systems?
- Which of the following is physical control?
- Indicate which TWO of the following will be inputted to the system as standing data?
- Which of the following are standard controls over sales at A Co?

- Are the following control procedures concerned with the prevention or the detection of errors?

2. 针对 Audit
- What is a primary purpose of an internal audit?
- Which of the following are responsibilities of the external/internal audit function?
- Which of the following is typically performed by internal auditors?
- A systems audit involves tests to check that the figures entered in the accounts are correct. What sort of tests will be used for this purpose?
- Is each of the following tests carried out by a substantive or compliance?
- To which of the following does the external auditor of a company report?

Section B
For each of the following security risks, identify the most appropriate control.

Quick quiz

10.1 Which one of the following option is not control objectives for cash?

    A. To obtain evidence for authorisation of payments

    B. To restrict personnel for approval of authorisation

    C. To prepare and manage cash flow forecasts

    D. To ensure that all receipts are banked promptly

Answer：C

Difficulty level：Normal

Tag：Controlling cash

Rationale：

Organisations can control cash in two aspects. One is controls over receipts, and another is controls over payments. Regarding objectives of receipts, they contains banking cash, safeguards of cash, complete recording and prevention of theft or accident. For cash payments, there are three main objectives: obtaining proper reasons of payments, obtaining authorisation of payments and managing individuals for approving authorisation. Therefore, option C is answer.

关于现金管理，主要从两个方面着手，一方面是现金的流入，另一方面是现金的流出。 对于收到的现金，有三个主要目标：要立刻存入或者放置在安全的地方；要完整地记录收到的现金；要采取措施预防因意外情况或偷窃而造成的现金遗失。 而关于支付现金，也同样有3个主要目的：支付应有恰当的理由；支付应获得授权且有相关证据来证明；只有特定人员能进行授权。 根据以上目的，只有选项C不是现金控制的目标，故选C。

10.2 Which TWO of the following are physical controls?

    A. Password and logical access system   B. Archiving

    C. Swipe cards before entering equipment   D. Back-up controls

Answer：A，C

Difficulty level：Easy

Tag：Physical controls

Rationale：

Physical controls rely on the proper application of physical barriers and deterrents to control behaviour. It's through the use of physical controls that an organisation controls physical access to facilities and systems.

物理（实体）控制指的是通过一系列措施保护控制大环境，比如，防止未经授权人员接近系统设备，使人员权责分离，配置安保人员等。 因此，这些措施都没有真正进入系统内部，所以答案选AC。

10.3 Which of the following regarding internal audit is true?

    A. The management designs the scope of work of internal audit

    B. The internal auditors should report their outcomes to external auditors

    C. Reviewing the internal control system is one main function of internal audit

    D. The purpose of internal audit is to protect the company's assets

Answer：C

Difficulty level：Normal

Tag：Internal audit

Rationale:

One main purpose of internal control is to recommend on the internal control and corporate governance, thus reviewing the company's internal control is one of its main task. However, internal auditors should be independent of management and other staff who are involved in complementing internal controls. They should be appointed by audit committee and have an independent report line to the audit committee/board. Safeguarding company's assets can be achieved by control procedures such as locking important assets.

内审的一个主要目的就是对公司的内控系统和公司治理提出改进意见来帮助公司更好地发展，所以内审的一个主要职责就是检查内控的有效性。 为了保证内审人员的独立性，他们需由审计委员会任命，并将检查结果直接报告给审计委员会或者董事会，以确保其不受其检查对象（管理人员）的干扰。 保护公司重要资产是内控的目标之一，可以通过设置门锁、安全柜等内控活动来完成。 因此 ABD 都错误，C 正确。

10.4 Which of the following is an effective control procedure over sales?

  A. Credit given to customers authorised by superiors

  B. Sequentially numbered goods received notes

  C. Security locks at machine room

  D. Regularly review payable and reconciliations with suppliers

Answer: A

Difficulty level: Normal

Tag: Internal control

Rationale:

Authorisation on setting credit to customers could ensure the company only sell goods to customers with good credit rating, it is an effective control over sales. Using sequentially numbered goods received notes and reviewing supplier's reconciliation are controls over purchases. The purpose of security locks at machine rooms is to safeguarding the factory or warehouse rather than facilitating selling.

授权可以确保公司只跟信用良好的顾客进行交易，可以提高公司销售环节的有效性，因此 A 正确。 B 选项（检查收货单）及 D 选项（与供应商核对应付账款数额）都是采购环节常见的内控活动。 C 选项（在厂房和机房上锁）的主要目的是保护资产而不是确保销售的有效性，不直接相关。

10.5 The types of common control activity can define as "SPAMSOAP". **What does "M" stand for?**

  A. Monitor   B. Management   C. Manual

Answer: B

Difficulty level: Easy

Tag: SPAMSOAP

Rationale:

The "SPAMSOAP" is used to remember the types of common control activity. They included Segregation of duty, Physical, Authorization and approval, Management, Supervision, Organisation, Arithmetical and accounting, Personnel.

这道题直接考查的是对 SPAMSOAP 的记忆，考生需要了解每个字母分别对应什么。 M 对应的是 Management，所以答案选 B。

10.6 Authorisation of the payroll is a very important part of any business.

  Which of the following does not control relate to inputs of payroll system?

  A. Clock cards B. Time sheets C. Pay slips D. overtime worked

Answer: C

Difficulty level: Easy

Tag: payroll system

Rationale:

The purpose of a payroll system is to compute the gross wages and salaries of employees and produce pay slips and/or listings sent to banks instructing them to make payments correctly. There are three stages of payroll systems: input, process and output. Pay slips is belonging to outputs. Therefore, C is the answer.

这道题意在区分工资系统的流程。时钟卡、考勤表和加班时间都属于 Input 这个环节，而工资单属于 output 这个环节，所以这道题答案选择 C。

Chapter 11 Identifying and preventing fraud

知识导入

上一章我们了解了内控系统以及内控的重要性。如果内控系统不完善，就会导致组织中有空可钻。近年来，舞弊的问题越来越严重，尤其是上市公司的舞弊，无论是性质还是数量方面都非常令人担忧。英国的南海公司，美国的安然、世通事件，中国的银广厦、蓝田股份等典型舞弊案例，都对广大投资者造成了不可估计的损失和难以磨灭的阴影，严重地破坏了经济的健康发展和市场信心。在这一章中，我们就来深入了解舞弊这个重要的知识点。

单词表

英文	中文
Fraud	舞弊
Manipulating prices	操纵价格
Collusion	合谋
Bank reconciliation	银行对账单
Disposal of assets	处置资产
Depreciation	折旧
Working capital	营运资金
Business risks	商业风险
Computer hackers	电脑黑客
Whistleblowing	告密，揭发
Grievance	申诉
Signature	签字
Money laundering	洗钱
Insider trading	内幕交易

学习指南

Learning objectives	Pass level	Distinction level	用时建议
1. Definition (1)	√		2 min
2. Types of fraud (2.1-2.2)	√		15 min
3. Implication of fraud for the organisation (3.1-3.2)	√		10 min
4. Assessing the risk of fraud (4)	√		10 min
5. Prerequisites for fraud (5)	√		8 min
6. Systems for detecting and preventing fraud (6)	√		10 min
7. Responsibility for detecting and preventing fraud (7)	√		10 min
8. Money laundering (8)	√		15 min

本章考点

重要考点	难度（1~3）
熟记并理解舞弊的两种主要分类	2
理解两种舞弊对企业造成的影响	2
熟记并理解舞弊三要素	2
熟记并理解各方对于欺诈有什么样的责任	2
熟记并理解洗钱相关的法律法规	2

> **知识点解读**
> 舞弊是指使用欺骗手段获取不当或非法利益的故意行为；舞弊与错误不同，舞弊是蓄意为之，错误是无意造成的。

1 Definition

Fraud is an intentional action involving the use of deception to obtain an illegal advantage.

Fraud should be distinguished from error. While **fraud is an intentional action, error is unintentional**. For example, if an accountant deliberately overstates the revenue, this is fraud. However, if an accountant miscalculates the revenue amount, this is an error.

2 Types of fraud

舞弊的两种主要分类见表11-1和表11-2。

> **知识点解读**
> Theft of inventory，那些低值易耗的存货更容易成为目标，因为很难被发现。例如，厂房里的螺丝或螺丝刀的丢失，很难引起注意。

2.1 Removal of funds or assets

表11-1 Fraud-removal of funds or asset

Types	Explanation
(a) Theft of cash	Employees may steal company's cash and keep the proceeds as his or her own money
(b) Theft of inventory	Employees may also steal inventories especially low-value consumption inventories
(c) Payroll fraud	Payroll fraud can occur within or outside the payroll department
(d) Teeming and lading	It involves deliberate allocation of one customer's payment to another customer's account with the aim to hide a shortfall or theft
(e) Fake clients	It takes place where the company does a business with fake clients and ends with bad debts
(f) Collusion with clients	Employees may collude with some clients in order to obtain illegal benefits
(g) Fake provision of goods or services	Employees may gain illegal rewards for claiming supply of goods or services while not providing in fact
(h) Deliberately setting inappropriate budgets/ performance targets	Setting excessively high budgets or low performance targets for departments/employees may result in huge losses for companies

> **知识点解读**
> Payroll fraud，工资舞弊极可能发生在薪酬部门内部，也会发生在其他部门。
> （1）虚报加班时间已获得报酬（其他部门）；
> （2）故意错误计算工资条（薪酬部门）；
> （3）添加虚假员工到工资列表中获得额外薪酬（薪酬部门）。

> **核心考点**
> Teeming and lading，挪用资金，俗称"拆东墙补西墙"，指的是员工私自挪用某笔资金，一般指先挪用从客户那里收到的应收账款，再用随后收到的资金来填补上一笔资金的空缺，循环往复下去，直至找到另外的资金填补漏洞或者事迹败露。

续表

Types	Explanation
(i) Manipulation of cash books	Fraudulent activities may be covered up through manipulating cash books with wrong description or figures to match bank reconciliations
(j) Intentional misallocation of pension funds or other assets	Companies may use unauthorised pension funds or other assets to achieve their own purposes
(k) Improper disposal of assets for own purpose	Special employees can deliberately manipulate book value for purpose of obtaining disposable assets

知识点解读

Fake clients，员工可以通过自导自演虚构客户这样一出戏，获取不正当报酬。比如，虚构一个并不存在的客户 A，并宣称向 A 进行了销售并计入应收账款，因此可以获得相关销售报酬，最后计入的应收账款会以坏账的形式收尾，从而掩盖自身舞弊行为的事实。

知识点解读

Fake provision of goods or services，抓住服务的无形性这个特质，从而实现舞弊。比如，咨询师可以声称给客户提供了诸多实际并未发生的服务，从而获得相应的奖金。

知识点解读

Intentional misallocation of pension funds or others assets，对于员工养老金和相关的资产，在英国，公司只是帮员工保管但无权使用这些资产，因而一旦公司滥用这些资产来达成自身的目的，就构成了舞弊。

知识点解读

Improper disposal of assets for own purpose，这里指的是员工不正当处置企业资产以供私用。假如员工看中了公司的车，想要挪作私用，可以通过加速折旧的会计处理让车的账面价值迅速降低，从而以远低于市场的价格获得。

小试牛刀

Example question 1

In the context of fraud, teeming and lading is MOST likely to occur in which of these combinations of duties?

A. Payable ledger and goods inwards

B. Payroll and cash handling

C. Inventory and goods outward

D. receivable ledger and cash receipts

2.2 Intentional misrepresentation of the financial position of the business

表 11-2 Fraud-intentional misrepresentation of the financial position

Type	Description
Over-valuation of inventory	It should be noted that the inventory here means the year-end figure which could affect the financial statements. Usually, there are several methods to overstate inventory: (a) Miscounting the inventory on purpose; (b) Deliberately omitting records, e.g. deliveries to customers and returns from customers; (c) Recording obsolete inventory with full value in the financial statement
Irrecoverable debt policy may not be enforced	Receivable forms part of asset in the statement of financial position. To dress up the statement of financial position, those obviously aged receivable (that is, bad debts) will not be recognised. Therefore, assets can be overstated
Overstating revenues	Revenues can be overstated through fictitious sales, and there are several methods relating to fictitious sales: (a) Deliberately generating invoices with wrong content (e.g. prices or numbers); (b) Overcharging customers with those discounted goods; (c) Selling goods and promising to buy back in the future

知识点解读

公司之所以要高估库存，一方面是为了增加资产负债表上显示的资产，另一方面也使得利润表中的利润虚高。

高估库存导致利润虚高的原理很简单，假设当年并没有任何库存的增加，那么期初库存与期末库存之间的差就是当年销售产品的成本。如果高估期末库存，那么也就意味着当年用于销售的产品成本会被低估。不考虑其他费用的情况下，利润等于收入减去成本，如果成本被低估，利润自然就会被高估。

知识点解读

应收账款(receivable)初次确认的入账金额并不意味着都能收回，由于客户破产等种种原因，其中有一部分可能无法收回，这对公司而言是种损失。因此要将之前确认的应收账款进行冲销，并确认坏账损失。

知识点解读

Manipulation of depreciation figures，影响固定资产折旧的计算主要有几个因素，如固定资产成本、预计净残值、使用寿命等。其中，固定资产的使用寿命很大程度上依赖于会计师的专业判断，会计师可以通过延长或减少使用寿命，来影响折旧的金额，从而影响年末的资产的价值以及利润的计算。

续表

Type	Description
Manipulation of years end events	To boost the sales, the year-end sales may be deliberately over-invoiced. And the related credit notes will be issued at the start of next year
Understating expenses	Manipulation of expenses can affect profits directly. Over-statement of expenses can result in understatement of profits, while understatement of expenses can lead to over-statement of profits
Manipulation of depreciation figures	Firstly, it should be known that the figure of depreciation will affect both of profit in the statement of profit or loss and value of assets in statement of financial position. Secondly, the calculation of depreciation relies on several factors which are mainly based on accountants' judgment, for example, useful life. As a result, it is convenient for accountants to take advantage of the discretion on depreciation policy to affect financial statements

综上所述，虚假陈述的常用手段包括：

(1) 编制虚假的会计分录，特别是在临近会计期末时；
(2) 滥用或随意变更会计政策；
(3) 不恰当地调整会计估计所依据的假设及改变原先作出的判断；
(4) 故意漏记、提前确认或推迟确认报告期内发生的交易或事项；
(5) 隐瞒可能影响财务报表金额的事实；
(6) 构造复杂的交易以歪曲财务状况或经营成果；
(7) 篡改与重大或异常交易相关的会计记录和交易条款。

值得注意的是，在现实中虚假报告的源头可能是掩盖侵占资产的事实。实际上，侵占资产通常伴随着虚假或误导性的文件记录，其目的是隐瞒资产缺失或未经适当授权使用资产的事实。

3 Implications of fraud for the organisation

我们依然通过舞弊的两种主要形式来分析舞弊对公司的不利影响。

3.1 Removal of funds or assets from a business

挪用资产对公司造成的影响，可以分成即期影响（immediate implications）与长期影响（long-term effects）两类(如图11-1所示)。

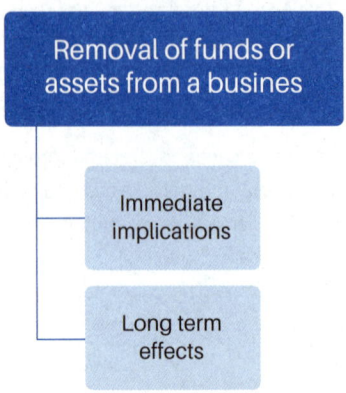

图11-1 Implication of removal of funds or assets

(A) **Immediate financial implications**

(a) The working capital and the net asset are impaired.

(b) Profits are diluted and return for shareholders is lower.

(B) **Long-term effects on company performance**

(a) Fraud makes it difficult for company to operate effectively.

(b) Fraud can even result in collapses of a successful business.

总的来说，侵占公司资产这种舞弊行为，短期来看，造成的影响是资产减少，收入降低。但长远来看，影响更为恶劣，这种舞弊现象可能会影响到公司在市场舆论中的形象，打击投资者、消费者等利益相关者的信心，造成资金短缺，经营逐步恶化等后果，最终导致破产。

3.2 Intentional misrepresentation of the financial position of the business

故意做假账对公司造成的影响，可以分为高估结果（overstated results）和低估结果（understated results）两类（如图11–2所示）。

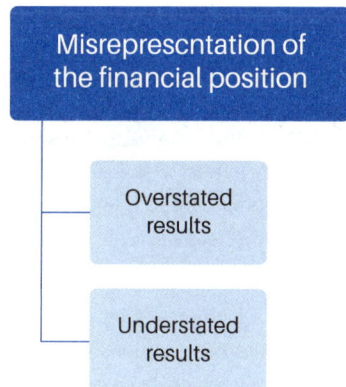

图11–2　Implication of misrepresentation of the financial position

(A) **Overstated results**

Overstated results, especially overstated profits, will lead to excessive distribution given to shareholders, which may arise two negative effects. The first is that external stakeholders would receive misleading signals, the second is that companies may face a shortage of working capital during operation.

博学多才

根据国家有关规定和企业章程、投资者协议等，企业需对当年的利润进行分配。分配给所有者（shareholders）的那部分叫做股息（dividends），而留存收益（retained earnings）是企业出于对未来经营发展的需要或法定的原因等，没有分配给所有者而留存在企业的那部分利润。

(B) **Understated results**

Understated results inversely bring about reduced investor return, which sends out false signal to stakeholders. Thus, the company may face the risk of restriction on loan and slump of share price. And even worse, there might be fines from tax authorities.

综上所述，蓄意虚假陈述的目的往往有两种，一是高估利润，二是低估利润。但不管是基于何种目的，虚假陈述都会影响财报使用者的判断，导致投资者做出错误的决策。

> **小试牛刀**

Example question 2

In a recent audit, it was discovered that ABC Co deliberately overstated its receivables. Because aged receivables which are obviously not going to be paid have not been written off. Which of the following is a possible implication of this type of fraud?

A. Receivables will be undervalued
B. Capital will be understated
C. Reported profit will be higher than it should be

4 Three prerequisites for fraud

业界认为人员风险的舞弊存在三个先决条件（如表 11-3 所示）。

表 11-3 Three prerequisite of fraud

Prerequisite	Description
Dishonesty	It is a subjective quality and is a tendency to act in ways that contravene accepted norms. Dishonesty can be prevented by careful screening and references checking (see chapter 13)
Motivation	This is likely to involve a consideration whether a given action is worthwhile, which means balancing the potential rewards in relation to the potential sanctions. Motivation for fraud could be prevented by provision of good working conditions and effective grievance procedures
Opportunity	This can be a "loophole" in the regulation and control system that allows the fraudulent activities to occur undetectably. Opportunity can be prevented in a number of ways, for example: (a) Effective internal control. (b) Continuous monitoring and review of all controls

5 Assessing the risk of fraud

Under the following circumstances（见表 11-4、表 11-5、表 11-6），fraud is most likely to happen:

表 11-4 Potential of fraud-1

Potentials of fraud		Specific indicators
Potentials from sources	External factors	It comes from the **general environment** in which the business operates, for example: (a) The industry (luxury/auction/building industry). (b) The degree of competition. (c) The economic cycle (recession or depression stage)

核心考点

对于舞弊三要素，需要掌握三要素的定义、典型的例子以及预防方式。

知识点解读

评估 fraud 发生的风险，需要同学们分别掌握从外部因素、内部因素、商业风险和个人风险 4 个不同的角度对 fraud 发生可能性大小作出正确的判断，理解记忆每一大类相关的 indicators，是此考点的关键。

知识点解读

外部迹象（External factors）：企业所处的外部大环境的确可能是舞弊发生的温床，以下是一些可能存在舞弊的外部迹象。
（1）特定的行业。如建筑行业，由于建造周期相对其他行业较长，因此为了粉饰报表，可能在收入的确认以及费用的分摊上存在舞弊的现象。
（2）竞争程度。一般来说，市场上的竞争程度越是激烈，企业越是可能存在为了营造出强势的市场地位而弄虚作假的行为。
（3）经济周期。我们在前面的章节中已经学习过关于经济周期的内容，我们知道在经济周期处于衰退或萧条阶段时，企业的经营会由于整个经济环境的不景气而下滑，在这种情况下，企业可能存在为了掩饰这种经营不善而粉饰报表的行为。

续表

Potentials of fraud		Specific indicators
Potentials from sources	Internal factors	(a) Changing operating structures. (b) Rapid expansion. (c) Introduction of new personnel/products/information system

表 11-5　Potential of fraud-2

Potentials of fraud		Specific indicators
Potentials from sources	Business risks	(a) Profitability diverges obviously from the industry level. (b) Poor reputation. (c) Complex structure of business units
	Personnel risks	(a) Sneak behaviour. (b) Luxurious lifestyle. (c) Lack of rest for employees. (d) Authoritarian management approach. (e) Poor staff morale

表 11-6　Potential of fraud-3

Potentials of fraud		Specific indicators
Potentials from Technology	Computer fraud	There are some problems particularly associated with computers. (a) Computer hackers. (b) Insufficient skills of management. (c) Technology limitation on detecting risk. (d) Preference for handy process than tight control

小试牛刀

Example question 3

Fraud is an intentional act involving the use of deception to obtain an illegal advantage. Which of the following is not a prerequisite for fraud?

　　A. Motivation　　B. Opportunity　　C. Dishonesty　　D. Authority

6 Systems for detecting and preventing fraud

6.1 General prevention policies

(a) **Emphasising ethics** can reduce fraud risk, which could be done in corporate code of ethics (see chapter 19 later).

(b) **Personnel controls**. Careful review should be conducted during employee recruitment and selection stages, especially reference checking (see chapter 13 later), so that dishonest candidates could be refused.

(c) Ongoing **training** (see chapter 16 later) should be conducted to **raise anti-fraud awareness among employees**.

6.2 Specific prevention policies

(a) **Dates**

Writing down occurred dates on forms and orders to facilitate cut-off testing.

(b) **Standard procedures**

Standard procedures should be set up and implemented across the whole organisation and related responsibilities should be taken by staffs.

(c) **Holidays**

All employees in the organisation should be required to take a leave in order to increase employees' satisfaction and reduce possibility of fraud.

(d) **Responsibilities of employees**

All related responsibilities should be identified and allocated to employees with aims of identifying and detecting fraud. Ensuring there is a fraud officer, who takes responsibility of initiating and overseeing fraud investigations, implementing the fraud response plan and any follow-up actions.

(e) **Whistleblowing**

It is essential to establish a system among employees to facilitate fraud detection, which can involve all employees into detecting and preventing frauds. A whistleblowing system encourages employees to report any suspicion and fact of fraud. In addition, there should be protections for whistle-blowers to ensure the effectiveness of this system.

(f) **Evolving control systems**

It is quite necessary to update control system after a certain period, which can defence attacks from external environment.

(g) **Recruitment policies**

It is essential to exert control over staffs from the recruitment stage. It has been referred above that there are three prerequisites for fraud, in which dishonesty is included. Therefore, there should be careful reviews on applicants' backgrounds and resumes.

7 Responsibility for detecting and preventing fraud

表 11 - 7　Responsibility for detecting and preventing fraud

Directors	The management and those charged with governance take the **primary responsibility** for fraud and error. They should: (a) Ensure an integrity atmosphere within the business. (b) Set up procedures(controls) to prevent and detect fraud. (c) Ensure the quality of financial information
Audit committee	It is recommended by the UK corporate governance code that the audit committee should **review** the company's internal control and risk management systems

Internal audit	The internal auditors should have sufficient knowledge to evaluate the risk of fraud and **make recommendations** to improve controls with the purpose of detecting fraud in the future
External auditor	The secondary responsibility of detecting frauds lies with external auditors. The auditors are required to plan and perform auditing effectively with professional scepticism to verify the "true and fair" view of the company's financial statements. Step1: The auditor should strive to identify potential misstatements to confirm whether the misstatement is due to fraud or error. Step2: Any identified misstatement should be recorded and notified to the company's management. Step3: If the misstatement arises from fraud, the auditor should request the directors to make a report. Step4: If the directors refuse then the auditor should be alert to the integrity of the director, as a result auditors report the findings themselves. Step5: If the fraud causes material misstatements of the financial statements, the auditor should modify the audit report

续表

> **知识点解读**
>
> 外部审计师的职责只是对公司的财务报表是否真实公允发表意见。但是，由于舞弊欺诈行为通常会带来一些财务后果，会反映在财报当中，所以，外审可以通过核查报表是否有重大错报的方式帮助企业发现舞弊现象。

小试牛刀

Example question 4

Consider the following two statements：

（1）The management and those charged with governance take the primary responsibility for fraud and error.

（2）The internal auditors should have sufficient knowledge to evaluate the risk of fraud and design the control system with the purpose of detecting fraud in the future.

Which of these options is/are correct?

  A.（1）only   B.（2）only   C. Both   D. Neither

Example question 5

In relation to fraud prevention, which of the following statements is correct in respect of the role of the external auditor?

  A. The external auditor has primary responsibility for preventing and detecting fraud and is accountable to the shareholders for this

  B. The external auditor must ensure that all internal systems are capable of detecting every type of fraud

  C. The work of the external auditor has nothing to do with fraud prevention, so the external auditor has no responsibility in this aspect

  D. The external auditor's procedures should provide reasonable assurance that misstatements arising from fraud will be identified

知识点解读

洗钱的实质即把非法所得的资金通过一定的方式合法化。

8 Money laundering

Money laundering means transferring the "dirty" money and assets that have been criminally obtained into "clean" money and assets that have no clear link to criminal activity to conceal the origins of the proceeds.

"Dirty money" refers to the proceeds obtained from certain crimes, such as extortion, insider trading, drug trafficking and illegal gambling. It needs to be "cleaned" to appear to have been derived from legal activities so that banks and other financial institutions will deal with it without suspicion.

博学多才

"洗钱"这一名词的来历非常形象,据说在20世纪20年代,美国芝加哥黑手党一个金融专家购买了一台投币洗衣机,开了一家洗衣店。每天晚上结算当天洗衣收入时,他将非法所得的赃款加入其中,再向税务局申报纳税,税后钱款就全部成了他的合法收入,之后这种将非法所得变为合法的活动就被人们口口相传为"洗钱"。

知识点解读

英国法律中涉及洗钱的罪名有三个:
(1)洗钱,即实际参与了洗钱的过程,这种情况下最高刑罚为14年有期徒刑,并可以同时判处罚款。
(2)知情不报,即有理由怀疑或明确知晓洗钱行为,但没有尽到通报义务,那么这种纵容行为将被最高处以5年有期徒刑以及相应的罚金。
(3)通风报信,即向参与洗钱的各方走漏搜捕的消息,并且妨碍到了调查,这种行为最高面临2年有期徒刑。

8.1 UK relevant laws and regulations

There are three categories of criminal offence(见表11-8)。

表11-8 Offences of money laundering

Laundering	Involved in disguising the original and illegal source of money and proceeds into legitimate source
Failure to report	Failure to report under the consciousness and suspect
Tipping off	Disclose relevant information to the laundering party which prejudices the investigation

In many countries, relevant companies are required by law to put controls in place to identify money laundering transactions. These companies are usually those deal with large volumes of cash or high value item, such as banks.

8.2 Methods of detecting and preventing money laundering

(a) Ongoing monitor and risk assessment of unusual transactions.

Attention should be paid on the following types of customers:

- New customers (with large, one-off transactions, especially cash transactions);
- Customers introduced to you by a third party;
- Customers who come from other places other than your business base city.

(b) Ensuring all customers are identified by appropriate customer **due diligence**. This is to check background information of your customers by asking for official identification such as an identification card, passport or driving license, together with bank statements.

(c) **Set a special role which is named as Money Laundering Reporting**

Officer (**MLRO**). This role will be in charge of overseeing organisation's activities and receiving whistleblowing from employees about suspicions of money laundering (see 8.3).

(d) Ensure that managers and employees are trained properly and regularly and fully understand their responsibilities in anti-fraud, especially in money laundering.

(e) Maintaining full and up to date records.

8.3 Reporting procedures of suspicions of money laundering

(a) Employees report illegal activities or suspicions to the MLRO;

(b) The MLRO needs to conduct investigations further;

(c) If there is sufficient evidence for reasonable suspicion, the MLRO should report to the relevant authorities.

小试牛刀

Example question 6

Which of the following is **NOT** a method of detecting and preventing money laundering?

A. Ongoing monitor and risk assessment system of unusual transactions

B. Ensuring all customers are identified by appropriate customer due diligence

C. Creating a Money Laundering Reporting Officer who is the only person responsible for money laundering matters

D. Maintaining full and up to date records

博学多才

除了公司自身应当建立适当的程序以及部门来落实反洗钱活动，国际上也有两个组织同样致力于反洗钱，它们分别是：

（1）金融行动特别小组（Financial Action Task Force/FATF）。反洗钱金融行动特别工作组，是西方七国为专门研究洗钱的危害、预防洗钱并协调反洗钱国际行动，而于1989年在巴黎成立的政府间国际组织，是目前世界上最具影响力的国际反洗钱和反恐融资领域最具权威性的国际组织之一，其成员国遍布各大洲主要金融中心。

（2）国际货币基金组织（International Monetary Fund IMF）。国际货币基金组织是根据1944年7月在布雷顿森林会议签订的《国际货币基金组织协定》，于1945年12月27日在华盛顿成立，与世界银行同时成立，并列为世界两大金融机构，其职责是监察货币汇率和各国贸易情况，提供技术和资金协助，确保全球金融制度运作正常。

Answers for example question

1. D
2. C

3. D
4. A
5. D
6. C

Summary

Chapter 11 考试不同问法总结

Section A

1. 针对 fraud

- Which of the following is an implication of understating/overstating expenses/this type of fraud?
- Which of the following is one of the prerequisites in order to make fraud?
- Which TWO of the following are relevant to the internal factors that may increase the company's risk exposure to fraud?
- Is the external auditor responsible for preventing and detecting fraud?
- To which TWO of the following should an auditor report the fraud discovered at the client's business?

- Which of the following would assist management in preventing and detecting fraud?

2. 针对 money laundering

- Have A and B committed offence under money laundering legislation?
- Who in this scenario is guilty of a money laundering offence?
- Do the following involve disguising the source of illegally obtained funds?

Section B

Which type of frauds has been carried out by each of the following staff at A Co?

Quick quiz

11.1 Jack is a senior auditor. He discovered that one of his clients, Aquaman Co deliberately overstated its inventory.

Which of the following is a possible implication of this type of fraud?

A. Payable will be undervalued

B. Capital will be understated

C. Reported profit will be higher than it should be

Answer: **C**

Difficulty level: **Normal**

Tag: **Implication of the fraud for the organisation**

Rationale:

Over-valuation of inventory may be caused by several reasons, such as deliberate miscounting the inventory, dealing deliveries to customers or returns to suppliers with no records, and not writing off of obsolete inventory. These will lead to overstated profit and asset. Over-valuation of inventory has nothing to do with payable and capital. Thus, Option A and B are incorrect.

高估存货可能由很多原因导致，比如故意算错存货数字，发货给客户或者退回给供应商的存货没有记录，没有核销掉过期的存货等。这些都会导致高估利润和资产。高估存货与应付账款和股本都没关系，因此，A 和 B 选项都是错的。

11.2 Which TWO of the following are responsibilities of the external auditor?

A. Preventing fraud

B. Identifying material fraud

C. Reporting to shareholders on the stewardship of directors

Answer: **BC**

Difficulty level: **Easy**

Tag: **Responsibility for preventing and detecting fraud**

Rationale:

Candidates should clearly tell the differences between directors and external auditors regarding fraud. It's directors' responsibilities to prevent and detect fraud. Directors should take all reasonable steps necessary to prevent and detect fraud. External auditor should make efficient audit plan and procedures to identify potential misstatements of fraud or error and provide reasonable assurance to shareholders that the financial statements are prepared, in all material aspects, in accordance with the applicable financial reporting framework.

考生应该清晰地区分董事和外部审计师关于欺诈的责任。董事的责任是预防和检查欺诈，而外部审计师应当执行充分的审计计划和程序来识别潜在的由欺诈和错误引起的财务错报，然后要给股东提供合理的鉴证业务，说明财报在所有的重大方面都符合财务报告框架的要求。

11.3 Alan is an auditor who has discovered a suspected serious fraud at a client's business.

To which TWO of the following should Alan report the fraud?

A. The shareholders

B. The audit committee

C. The management

D. The government

Answer: **B, C**

Difficulty level: Normal

Tag: Role of the external auditor

Rationale:

According to ISA 240, if external auditor identifies potential misstatements of fraud or error, the findings should be documented and reported to management and audit committee. Thus, option B and C are correct.

根据国际审计准则 240 号，如果外审识别到了潜在的由欺诈或者错误而引起的财务错报，发现应当被记录并报告给管理层和审计委员会。因此，B 和 C 选项是正确的。

11.4 Management is primarily responsible for the prevention and the detection of fraud.

Which of the following would assist them in the discharge of this duty?

(1) Whistle-blower schemes.

(2) Monitoring of the risk environment.

(3) Culture of openness and transparency.

(4) Promotion of accountability.

A. (2)(3) and (4)
B. (1)(2)(3) and (4)
C. (1)(3) and (4)
D. (1)(2) and (4)

Answer: B

Difficulty level: Easy

Tag: Responsibility for preventing and detecting fraud

Rationale:

It's directors' responsibilities to prevent and detect fraud. Directors should take all reasonable steps necessary to prevent and detect fraud. These include building a culture of openness and transparency, whistle-blower schemes, promotion of accountability and monitoring of risk environment.

董事的责任是预防和检查欺诈，他们应该采取所有合理的措施预防和检查欺诈。这包括营造一种开放透明的文化氛围，建立揭发检举的渠道和监控风险环境。

11.5 Jack is an external auditor of a public limited company and he identified a deliberately understated expense.

Which of the following is an implication of this fraud?

A. Net asset position will be weaker
B. Working capital will decline
C. Net profit will be overstated
D. Cash balances will be increased

Answer: C

Difficulty level: Easy

Tag: Implication of the fraud for the organisation

Rationale:

Understating expenses will lead to overstated profit. Thus, option C is correct.

低估费用会导致高估利润，因此，C 选项是对的。

Part C
Human resource

人力资源篇

恭喜你来到了本书最后的篇章!

作为船长,你还有一个重任——领导整个船队,这不是一件易事。

每个船员有自己的脾性,从单个个体发展为高效率的团队,需要人力资源管理的各个环节密切配合。 从最初的招聘与筛选,到后续对船员们进行管理与领导,定期对船员绩效评估、培训与激励,培养船员职业价值观与道德等方面,事无巨细,都需要作为船长的你,密切关注。

Part C 正是包含了现实工作中,人力资源管理的大部分基本内容,从第 12 章到第 19 章共 8 章内容,帮助你快速掌握与人打交道的秘诀。 合理用人,才能为轮船安稳驶向目的地保驾护航。

Chapter 12
Individuals, groups and teams

知识导入

我们已经把 AB 里很重要的一大块内容学习完毕，它叫作 organisation（组织），之前我们从组织的外部一层一层地剖析直到组织的内部。从这一章开始，我们要学习的是 FAB 的另一大块的内容，它叫作"人"。大家试想一下，一个组织最重要的组成部分是什么？是人。就好比如果一艘巨轮失去了船长，那么船员也无法正常地航行在大海之上。那么，我们要怎样把合适的人放在合适的位置上呢？让我们先来了解每个人、每个团体到底有什么不能说的秘密。

单词表

英文	中文
Personality	性格
Perception	感知、看法
Team identity	团队身份感
Complementary	互补的
Attributes	特性、属性
Temperamental	脾性的、性情的
Compromise	妥协
Restore	恢复、修复

学习指南

Learning objectives	Pass level	Distinction level	用时建议
1.Individuals(1.1-1.2)		√	10 mins
2.Groups (2)	√		10 mins
3.Teams(3)	√		25 mins

本章考点

重要考点	难度（1~3）
理解并区分个性、认知和态度的区别	1
熟记并理解角色理论	2
着重记忆团体（Group）的贡献有正向也有负向	1
着重记忆团队（Team）的概念和不同团队的区分	1
熟记并理解 Belbin's "nine team roles"	3
熟记并理解 Tuckman 团队的形成步骤	2

1 Individuals

1.1 Characteristics of individual behaviour

1.1.1 Personality

It is the complex of all the attributes—**behavioral**, **temperamental**, **emotional** and **mental**—that characterise a unique individual.

> **知识点解读**
>
> 在 individuals 这一部分，我们会学习影响个人行为的一些共同因素，包括个性、认知、态度和智能等，考试难度不大，概率也不高，考生能了解基本概念即可。通过这部分的学习，我们能更好地认知自己以及周围的其他人。

精益求精

世界上没有两片完全相同的树叶，人的性格存在差异是司空见惯的现象，那么在团队中应当如何去处理这些差异可能带来的碰撞与冲突，于管理者而言就是一门重要的学问了。

Individual's potential is mostly used when their personality matches the jobs they perform.

Different individuals are possessed with different personalities, and it is essential to handle them to be compatible with the requirements of tasks. In respect of compatibility, there are three aspects should be taken into consideration（见表 12-1）.

表 12-1 Three aspects of compatibility

Compatibility	Comments
With the task	For example, sociable employees are suitable for sales-related jobs while prudent employees are more suitable for accounting-related jobs
With the systems and management style of the organisation	Centralisation is acceptable for some people while others do not like to be controlled
With other personalities in the team	Personality clashes is detrimental to cooperation and synergy generated of the team

当团队中发生矛盾时，有以下几种方式可以用来解决问题。

1. 重新分配（Restore compatibility）

可以根据团队中成员的不同性格安排与之相匹配的工作。例如，可以将沟通类的工作交由性格外向健谈的成员处理，计划类工作可以由性格内向、思维缜密的成员经手。

2. 求同存异（Achieve a compromise）

应当鼓励团队中的成员们互相理解，在团队目标大同的前提下，互相包容小的差异。

3. 排除异己（Remove the incompatible personality）

当以上方法均无效时，最后的处理方法就是将与团队不合的成员剔除，以确保团队目标顺利达成。

1.1.2 Perception

Perception is the process of dealing with outside incoming data, including identification organisation and interpretation of them. Through the process, people can produce their own knowledge and understanding. It is worth noting that people will behave according to what they perceive—not according to what really is.

非常有意思的是，即便人们面对相同的信息，得到的认知也是不一样的，这就是所谓的"仁者见仁，智者见智"。那么到底是什么导致了这种感知上的差异呢？

简单来说，认知是人们对信息的处理过程，这个过程会受到不同因素的影响，比如：

（1）受背景以及所处情形的影响，同样一件事情，人们往往只愿意见到他们想看到的一面。例如，同样是红色和绿色，股民看见的是涨跌，司机看见的却是"红灯停，绿灯行"。

（2）受刺激物本身性质的影响，人们产生的认知过程也会随之产生变化。典型的例子之一就是脑白金的广告，它通过不断重复、魔性的旋律以及明亮的色彩，深深印刻在观众心里，达到了家喻户晓，逢年过节送礼就会想到脑白金的效果。

（3）人们的认知过程同样会受到自身的一些内部因素的影响，如性格、需求、利益等。

（4）过去经受过的创伤和恐惧会在很大程度上影响人们的认知过程，如 PSTD（创伤后应激障碍）。

1.1.3 Attitudes

Attitude indicates an evaluation of favor or disfavor towards objects, such as persons, places, events, or general environments.

1.1.4 Intelligence

Intelligence, the way it has traditionally been understood (logically, as with I. Q. tests), does not explain the wide variety of human abilities.

博学多才

20 世纪 80 年代，美国著名发展心理学家、哈佛大学教授霍华德·加德纳博士提出多元智能理论，30 多年来，该理论已经广泛应用于欧美和亚洲许多国家的幼儿教育上，并且获得了极大的成功。霍华德·加德纳博士指出，人类的智能是多元化而非单一的，主要是由语言智能、数学逻辑智能、空间智能、身体运动智能、音乐智能、人际智能、自我认知智能、自然认知智能八项组成，每个人都拥有不同的智能优势组合。

1.2 Role theory

1.2 Role theory

Each person is an actor representing a typical individual in a real-life scenario performing within a specific context. This theory suggests that individuals' behaviour depend upon other people's expectations of them and how they should behave in that situation (Bruce, 1979).

(a) A **role set** is a group of people who respond to you in a given role.
(b) **Role behavior**: Certain types of behaviour can be associated with a particular role in an organisation.

(c) **Role signs** are visible indications of a role.
(d) **Role ambiguity** is a situation where individuals are unsure of what role they are to play.
(e) **Role conflict** is where you would perform in two or more roles at one time and you find conflicts between different roles.

> 知识点解读
>
> Role conflict（角色冲突），这个知识点可以跟组织结构中的 matrix structure 相联系。

博学多才

角色理论是由布鲁默（Bulmer）、莫雷诺（J.L. Moreno, 1934）、林顿（R. Linton, 1936）等理论学家先后研究的成果，该理论认为人既是社会的产物，又能对社会作出贡献。它是一种试图从人的社会角色属性解释社会心理和行为的产生、变化的社会心理学理论取向。

2 Groups

A group is a collection of individuals who relate to each other in one place at one time. The most obvious difference between group and random crowd is that people of group usually have the same interests or purposes, and they will organise themselves to work together towards the collective goals.

> 虽然在很多场合下，group 和 team 两个单词会互相替代使用，但在专业术语当中，两者是有明显区别的。

2.1 Characteristics of groups

(a) Identity：A group has defined boundaries and it is clear who is within the group and who is not.
(b) Loyalty：Group members have certain standard behaviours that they follow. This binds the group together and excludes others.
(c) Goals：Most groups have their specific goals.
(d) Leadership：Leadership may occur formally at the same time when goals are set.

团体区别于随机人群的最明显的3个特征就是：身份认同感、对团体的忠诚度以及团体的组成具有目的性。非常直观的一个例子就是流量明星们的粉丝应援团。这个团体存在的目标非常明确，就是为了自己喜爱的偶像应援。在这个团体中，粉丝们对身份的认同感非常强烈，并且以这个身份为傲，会自发地积极捍卫这个团体的利益和荣誉，并且在这个团体中，也会有一些领导性的人物存在，负责组织相关的应援活动。

There are mainly two types of groups：

(a) **Formal groups** are task-oriented and become teams (see later).
(b) **Informal groups** are similar to informal organisations which we have learnt before. They have fluctuating membership and structure and are a group of individuals who voluntarily join together to meet their social or security needs.

小试牛刀

Example question 1

Which of the following is an example of an informal group?

A. Board of directors   B. Committees

C. Trade union   D. Interest groups

2.2 Group norms

According to business dictionary, group norms are unspoken and often unwritten set of informal rules that govern individual behaviours in a group. Group norms vary based on the group and issues important to the group. Without group norms, individuals would have no understanding of how to act in social situations.

2.3 Groups' contribution

Group-working has many benefits:

(a) The pooling of people will provide the mixture of skills, experience and expertise and better communication.

(b) Greater flexibility as different people can do different works at the same time.

(c) The form of groups may create **synergy**.

However, it should be admitted that group-working is not always efficient due to the following factors:

(a) Group decision making tends to be slow.

(b) There may be too many social interactions among the group, which may hamper the implementation of group work.

(c) Group thinking may exist as decision is shared and agreed between all members, which may lead to higher risks of decisions made than individuals due to consistency of opinion.

In conclusion, group's contribution can be either positive or negative.

> **知识点解读**
> Group 的 contribution 与 organisation 的优点有共通之处，比如技能的集中以及协同效应，因此在学习这块内容的时候，同学们可以做一下对比，简化记忆。

小试牛刀

Example question 2

With respect to the relationship between group size and group performance, which of the following is correct?

A. Performance will increase up when group enlarges to an ideal size, then performance declines quickly

B. Performance increase up to an ideal group size, then levels off or declines slightly

C. Performance will always increase when group size increases

D. Performance will decline as group size increases

3 Teams

In contrast with group, there are two main characters of a team:

> **核心考点**
> Team 与 group 的区别，是本章的高频考点，需要考生多熟悉。

(a) The members of team should have **complementary skills**, thus they are **mutually accountable**;

(b) The members should be task-orientated.

In addition, we should pay attention to that teams are usually a form of group. Conversely, groups do not always constitute teams.

相比团体而言，团队的目标性会更强，而且人员配备会更注重在技能上的互补，以确保团队目标能顺利完成。

小试牛刀

Example question 3

Which **TWO** following ways does a team distinguish itself from a group?

A. Teams help to generate creative ideas

B. Teams contain people who possess a range of complementary skills

C. Team members hold themselves mutually accountable

D. Team members have a common interest

3.1 Appraisals of team working

(A) Strengths

(a) Expertise pooling: team working can facilitate the efficiency of task;

(b) Commitment to the team: the sense of identity can be a motivator for members to keep line with high standard;

(c) Synergy: Team members can work better through brainstorming, and experience sharing.

(B) Weakness

(a) Team-working is not suitable for some people with certain personality;

(b) The process of discussion and achieving consensus may delay decision-making;

(c) Group norms may be a factor which blocks the development and initiative of members;

(d) It is possible that different personalities in the team will hamper the coordination;

(e) "**Group thinking**": team consensus and cohesion may lead the team to make risky, ill-consideration decisions.

3.2 Types of teams

(a) **Multi-disciplinary teams**

Multi-disciplinary teams involve and pool several professionals who have different skills from different functions, focusing on the issues in which they specialise.

(b) **Multi-skilled teams**

A multi-skilled team is formed of individuals who are possessed with a variety of skills. It means that members of the teams can perform any part of group's

---

核心考点

团队合作的评价是经常考核的一个知识点，但考核方式比较直接，会开门见山地考核团队的优缺点，因此这个知识点考生理解记忆即可。此外，这个知识点可以与organisation及group的优缺点结合起来记忆。

知识点解读

Group thinking（群体思维），往往发生在凝聚力非常强的团队中，在这种高凝聚力的情况下，团队成员会惯性地认为团队决策一定没有错误，会无条件支持，在这种情况下，成员们会忽视团队中出现的不同声音，很可能会错失更好的想法或决策。

知识点解读

Multi-disciplinary teams：团队中每个人只会一项或者几项的技能，成员相互补充技能。
Multi-skilled teams：团队中每个人掌握了完成团队任务的几乎所有技能，都是全面能手。这两个团队非常容易混淆，在考试过程当中需要同学们加以区分。

tasks.

3.3 Theories of teams

3.3.1 Belbin's "nine team roles" model

> **核心考点**
> 贝尔宾团队角色理论是高频考点，通常会有案例描述这个团队成员的特点、个性，以及在团队中的贡献和缺点，要求判断属于哪一种角色，需记忆。

贝尔宾团队角色理论认为，团队工作的成效取决于成员之间的团结协作。在一个完整的团队当中，不同性格的成员们会有自己的角色，每个人都应当明确自己所扮演的角色需要对团队做出怎样的贡献，并且必须了解其他成员的角色，从而清晰认识到如何相互弥补团队不足，发挥协同效应的最大优势（"Belbin's role"，n.d.）。

Role 1：Plant（智多星）

(a) Characteristics：Creative, imaginative, unorthodox.

(b) Contribution：Tend to be highly creative and good at solving problems in unconventional way.

(c) Weakness：Ignore details.

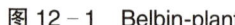

图 12-1　Belbin-plant

智多星在团队中往往充当创新与发明的角色，他们主要只能是站在整个团队的角度，为团队的发展和完善进行谋划。他们往往标新立异，不走寻常路，但也存在着忽略可行性的缺陷。

Role 2：Resource investigator（外交家）

(a) Characteristics：Extrovert, enthusiastic, communicative.

(b) Contribution：Uses their inquisitive nature to find ideas to bring back to the team.

(c) Weakness：Lose interest.

图 12-2　Belbin-resource investigator

外交家在团队中充当着打交道的角色，他们性格外向，行动力强，是谈判的一把好手，善于为团队寻找新的机遇，挖掘好的资源。但他们需要来自外界的激励与鼓舞，否则热情极易退却。

Role 3：Coordinator（协调者）

(a) Characteristics：Mature, confident, a good chairperson.

(b) Contribution：Need to focus on the team's objectives, draw out team members and delegate work appropriately.

(c) Weakness：Manipulative.

图 12-3　Belbin-coordinator

协调者成熟稳重，在团队中颇受成员信赖。他们能够快速发现成员们的优势所在，并因人而异地分派工作，以最有效的方式达成团队目标。但鉴于协调者承担着分派工作这一职能，因此他们可能会存在对团队成员颐指气使这一弊端。

Role 4：Shaper（鞭策者）

(a) Characteristics：Challenging, dynamic, thrives on pressure, highly-strung.

(b) Contribution：Provides the necessary drive to ensure that team keeps moving.

(c) Weakness：Hurt people's feeling.

图 12-4　Belbin-shaper

鞭策者正如他们的名字一般，精力充沛，渴望成功，热衷于取得团队的胜利，即便在面对挫折与失败时，也能以强烈的意志克服困难，找出解决办法。但由于他们过强的胜负心，可能缺乏人际沟通相关的技巧，在团队中容易伤害到团员的情绪。

Role 5：Monitor/evaluator（审议员）

(a) Characteristics：Sober, strategic and discerning.

(b) Contribution：Provides a logical eye, making impartial judgements.

(c) Weakness：Over critical.

图 12-5　Belbin-monitor/evaluator

审议员态度严肃，谨慎理智，他们虽然做决定较慢，但却能够思虑周全。通常他们非常具有批判性思维，尝试从不同角度看待问题，寻找可能出现的差错。但他们有时候可能过于批判性的眼光，会使得团队成员们压力倍增。

Role 6：Team worker（凝聚者）

(a) Characteristics：Cooperative, mild, perceptive and diplomatic.

(b) Contribution：Uses their versatility to identify the work required and complete it on behalf of the team.

(c) Weakness：Easily influenced.

图 12-6　Belbin-team worker

凝聚者是在团队中起着凝固剂一般的作用，他们在很大程度上影响着团队成员们的向心力。凝聚者往往性格温和，有很强的共情能力，善于关怀他人。因此，他们也是团队中的最佳倾听者。但较强的共情能力也是一把双刃剑，这使得凝聚者们在面对危机时，往往优柔寡断。

Role 7：Implementor（执行者）

(a) Characteristics：Reliable, disciplined, conservative and efficient.

(b) Contribution：Needed to plan a workable strategy and carry it out as efficiently as possible.

(c) Weakness：Inflexible.

图 12-7　Belbin-implementor

执行者，顾名思义，是团队中系统化地解决问题，推动工作的角色。他们有强烈的自制力和自律精神。但他们或许会因过于严苛而显得工作过于死板。

Role 8：Completer/finisher（完成者）

(a) Characteristics：Painstaking, conscientious, anxious.

(b) Contribution：Most effectively used at the end of tasks to polish and scrutinize the work for errors.

(c) Weakness：Nit-picker.

图 12-8　Belbin-completer/finisher

完成者承担着坚持不懈地完成工作的角色，他们往往非常注重细枝末节，竭力避免差错，从而影响团队工作的完成。因此通常情况下，大多数完成者都不喜欢委派他人，而是更偏好自己来完成所有的任务。但他们对于避免差错的敏感程度过高，显得有些吹毛求疵。

Role 9：Specialist（专家）

（a）Characteristics：Single-minded, dedicated and self-starting.

（b）Contribution：Brings in-depth knowledge of a key area to the team.

（c）Weakness：Overlook "big picture".

图 12－9　Belbin-specialist

专家主要为团队提供专业技能和知识。然而由于专业师们将绝大多数注意力都集中在自己的领域，因此他们对其他领域所知甚少，可能会忽略团队工作的整体蓝图。

Conclusions：

（a）The nine team roles are complementary.

（b）Team members can occupy more than one role.

（c）An ideal team should represent all of these roles.

小试牛刀

Example question 4

Chanel is a member of a project team. His team member describes him as："Chanel is awesome! He has the drive and courage to overcome obstacles, but sometime will upsetting them". According to Belbin's role theory, Chanel is an example of which of the following?

　　A. Coordinator　　　B. Shaper　　　C. Plant　　　D. Specialist

3.3.2 Tuckman：Stages of group development

塔克曼的团队发展阶段模型如图 12－10 所示。

> **核心考点**
>
> 团队每个阶段的特点是考点，需要掌握关键词，比如看到题目当中有关键词"争论、冲突"，那么就是属于第二阶段 storming。

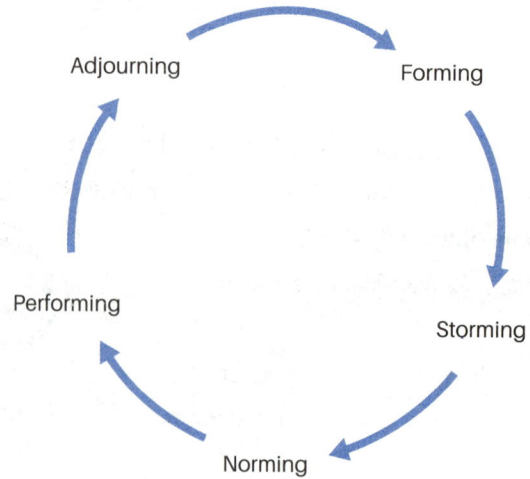

图 12－10　Tuckman-stages of group development

Step 1: Forming(组建期)

At this stage, the team is just a collection of individuals, finding out about one another and discussing unclear tasks and objectives. Although the stage may be time-consuming, it is essential to build trust between team members.

组建期,顾名思义,这个期间以建立起团队成员的相互关系、形成团队标准等为主要目的。

但在这个期间,团队缺乏明确统一的目标,可能导致整体可能不稳定。

Step 2: Storming(激荡期)

The phase involves conflict, ideas generation, ideas and behavior being challenged and sometimes rejected. There is competition and argument about who should fill the roles in the team.

在激荡期,最明显的特征就是团队中存在人际冲突、分化的问题。 尤其当团队成员面对其他成员的观点、见解,更想要展现个人性格特征,矛盾可能会激化。

Step 3: Norming(规范期)

When the routine under which the team will operate become established, the team is now settling down. Consequently, norms and patterns of behavior are established. There will be agreements about work sharing, individual requirements and expectations of output. In this stage, all team members take the responsibility and have the ambition to work for the success of the team's goals.

在规范期,团队成员逐渐明确自己在团队中的角色,产生身份认同感,能够调整自己的行为,以顺应团队发展。 在这个期间,团队的运行会更加自然、流畅,成员们能够有意识地解决问题,促进和谐发展。

Step 4: Performing(执行期)

The team begin to execute its task and to perform effectively. At this stage, the team is complete.

在执行期,团队成员对于任务层面的工作职责有清晰的理解,即便在没有监督的情况下自己也能作出决策。

Step 5: Mourning/adjourning(哀悼期)

The group has fulfilled its purpose, or if it is a temporary group which is due to physically disband. This is a stage of confusion, sadness and anxiety as the group breaks up.

哀悼期是塔克曼在后期的著作中添加的一个阶段。 在这个阶段,团队通常已经完成目标,面临休整与解散。

Example question 5

A team has no shared vision, and everyone has their own opinions about how to lead the team better. Finally, the team members decide to vote for Andy as their leader.

Which stage in the Tuckman team-development model is described by this

statement?

A. Forming   B. Performing   C. Norming   D. Storming

博学多才

布鲁斯·塔克曼（Bruce Tuckman）的团队发展阶段（Stages of Team Development）模型可以被用来辨识团队构建与发展的关键性因素，并对团队的历史发展给以解释。 团队发展的五个阶段是：组建期（Forming）、激荡期（Storming）、规范期（Norming）、执行期（Performing）和休整期（Adjourning）。（休整期是在1977年后加入的）根据Tuckman，所有五个阶段都是必需的、不可逾越的，团队在成长、迎接挑战、处理问题、发现方案、规划、处置结果等一系列过程中必然要经过上述五个阶段。 该模型对后来的组织发展理论产生了深远的影响。

3.4 Building a team

Team building is of significant importance to improve the effectiveness of a team. It is designed to improve abilities of team members working together by：

(a) Better communication. This can be achieved with more frequent meeting；

(b) Building trust with team member to generate synergy；

(c) More social interaction to reduce conflicts and enhance team cohesion.

团队建立并投入运行之后，评价团队的有效性是在之后的工作中承上启下的重要环节，通过这个步骤，我们可以正确认识到团队运行过程的足与不足，并在之后的工作中改进。 那么如何评价团队工作运行的有效性，就是我们接下来要学习的内容。

3.5 How to evaluate team effectiveness?

Many possible methods could be used to measure team effectiveness，including：

(a) Task performance：the degree to which the team has accomplished its tasks.

(b) Team Efficiency：How many input resources is used to achieve objectives.

(c) Team member satisfaction：this could be measured by staff morale or staff turnover.

Answers for example question

1. D
2. B
3. BC
4. B
5. D

Summary

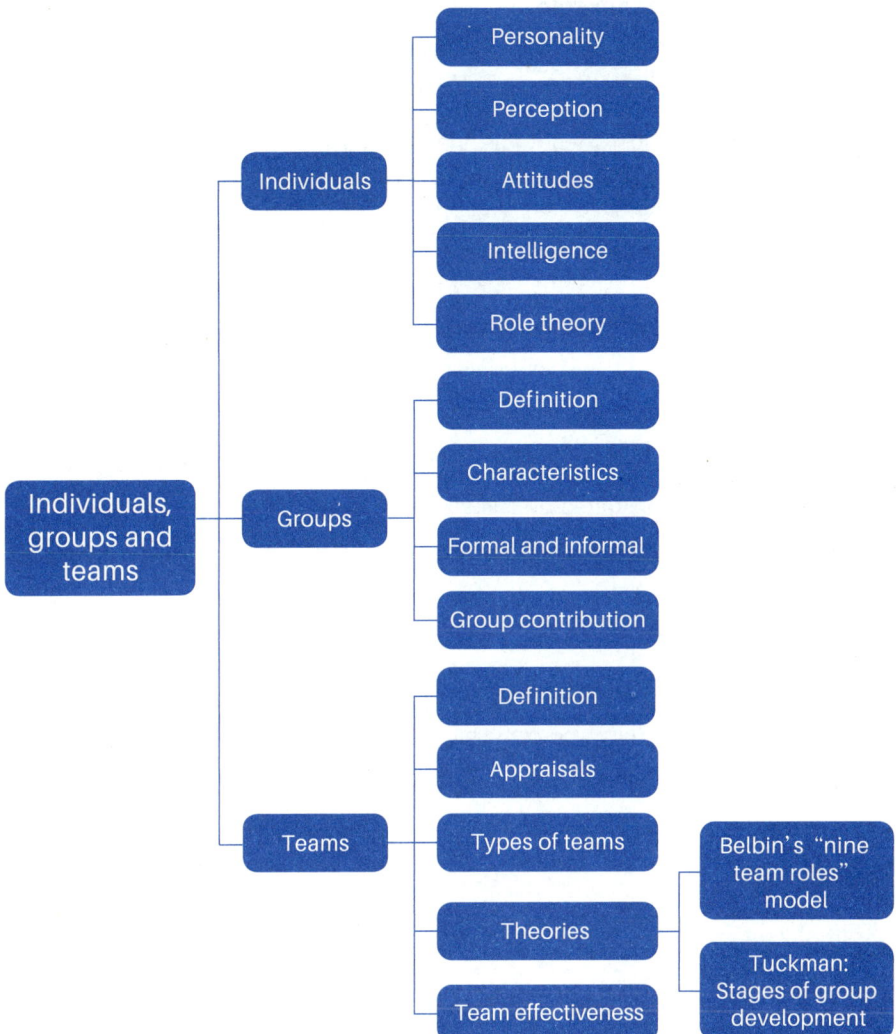

Chapter 12 考试不同问法总结

Section A

1. 针对 Informal organisation

- Which of the following is an example of as an informal organisation?
- Which of the following is a way in which individuals contribute to organisational success?

2. 针对 Group & Team

- What is the term given to a situation when an individual's behaviour changes in order to be consistent with the group norm?
- To determine the composition of the team, A should consider which of the following issues?
- Which of the following BEST describes the relationship between group size and group performance?
- Which of the following is a characteristics of a team as opposed to a group?

- A team distinguishes itself from a group in which of the following ways?

3. 针对 Belbin's 9 team role
- Which TWO of the following are thinking problem solving roles in Belbin's team role theory?
- According to Belbin's team role theory, which of the following statements describes a coordinator?
- In relation to Belbin's team role theory, which team role has the following weakness: "can be seen as manipulative, offloads personal work"?

4. 针对 Tuckman's stages of group development
- In which order will the following stages of Tuckman's team development model occur?
- According to Tuckman's theory which of the following stages of team development is demonstrated by this scenario?
- Which of the following is an appropriate style for the team leader during the storming stage of Tuckman's team development model?

Section B
- Which type of team should A form?
- To which of the following of Belbin's team roles are A and B MOST suited?
- At which of Tuckman's stages of group development is A's current team?

Quick quiz

12.1 Which of the following could be treated as an informal group?

A. Volunteers of a NGO
B. Fan club
C. Management committee
D. Environment protection group

Answer: B

Difficulty level: Easy

Tag: Informal group

Rationale:

Informal group consists of individuals coming together spontaneously for satisfying social or security needs. They are not organised by a formal organisation and not task oriented.

这道题考查的是非正式组织的特征,非正式组织的成员是自发地聚在一起,原因可能是有共同的兴趣爱好或者共同的社交需求。 他们不是被正式组织有意地去组建的,因为没有共同目标或任务要完成,不需要服从正式组织的命令。 题目当中符合这些特征的只有 B 选项粉丝团体,而其他选项都是正式组织,成员有特定的任务要实现,会受到正式组织的管束。 考生要注意区别 A 选项,虽然是 NGO 的志愿者,但是也要服从其所在的 NGO 的管理,要配合实现 NGO 的目标。

12.2 In order to perform a new task, H Co has established a team which is consisted of members from different departments. **Select the order of subsequent stages will the team occur according to Tuckman's team development model.**

A. Forming, Storming, Performing, Adjourning
B. Norming, Storming, Performing, Adjourning
C. Storming, Norming, Performing, Adjourning
D. Forming, Norming, Performing, Adjourning

Answer: C

Difficulty level: Easy

Tag: Tuckman's team development model

Rationale:

The team is experiencing the first stage of forming as members of the team have already been determined, then the right order of stages the team would go through are storming, performing and adjourning.

这道题考查的是 Tuckman 团队建设经历的阶段的正确排序,比较简单。 其中,每个阶段的名称对应的单词比较相像,需要正确记忆。 另外,在这道题中,根据描述,新的团队已经组建完毕,已经确定成员的构成,所以要选后续的发展阶段就可以把 Forming 排除,因此考生做题的时候需认真阅读题目的要求。

12.3 Jack just joined a team, and he was wondering what his role is in the team. When the team was in trouble, he was always positively bubbled with lots of ideas. But it seems that he was not very popular in the team, as he was always criticized for ignoring details. His teammates wished that he could pay attention to important details. **According to Belbin's team roles theory, Jack displays the characteristics of which of the following?**

A. Monitor-evaluator
B. Plant
C. Resource-investigator
D. Company worker

Answer: B

Difficulty level: Easy

Tag: Belbin's "nine team roles" model

Rationale:

The scenario accurately describes the "plant" role. The characteristics of plant are creative, imaginative, and the weakness of it is ignoring details.

案例描述的是"智多星"角色。智多星角色的特点是有创造力和想象力,其缺点是忽略细节。

12.4 Jackie just joined a transnational team, he is quite puzzled about his role. Because he is unsure how his work is evaluated and his scope of responsibilities is determined. He is also afraid to make decisions because he cannot predict how others in his team will respond to decisions he make.

What phenomenon is Jackie experiencing?

A. Role ambiguity   B. Role conflict   C. Role overlap   D. Role duplication

Answer: A

Difficulty level: Normal

Tag: Role ambiguity

Rationale:

This scenario accurately describe the "role ambiguity". Role ambiguity arise where individuals are unsure of what scope of responsibilities is, and how their work is evaluated. Therefore, they are unsure of what role they are to play.

这个案例准确地描述了"角色模糊"。角色模糊发生在人们不清楚他们的职责范围、不清楚他们的工作如何被评估时,因此就不清楚他们扮演着什么样的角色。

Chapter 13
Recruitment and selection

知识导入

上一章我们了解了每个人、每个团队到底有什么不能说的秘密，而去了解他们的目的是为了把合适的人放在合适的位置上。 对于企业用人来说，招聘是至关重要的一环。 谁应该参与招聘？ 怎么去招聘？ 怎么去筛选？ 要秉承什么原则？ 让我们带着这些问题来学习这一章。

单词表

英文	中文
Preliminary interviews	初面
Vacancies	空缺
Recruitment consultants	猎头
Job specifications	工作说明书
Person specification	人员规范
Qualification	资质
Recruit	招聘
School career offices	就业指导中心
Duration	持续的时间，期间
Special aptitude	特殊才能
Disposition	性格，意向
Proficiency	熟练
Psychometric	心理测量的
References	推荐
Stereotyping	刻板成见
Equal opportunity	平等机会
Sexual orientation	性取向
Religious belief	宗教信仰
Direct discrimination	直接歧视
Indirect discrimination	间接歧视
Victimisation	迫害
Harassment	袭扰；骚扰
Diversity	多样性
Ethnicity	种族

学习指南

Learning objectives	Pass level	Distinction level	用时建议
1. Introduction to recruitment and selection(1.1-1.2)	√		10 mins
2. Recruitment and selection process (2.1-2.4)	√		10 mins
3. Selection(3.1-3.5)	√		10 mins
4. Reference checking(4.1-4.2)		√	5mins
5. Evaluating recruitment and selection		√	5mins
6. Equal opportunity(6.1-6.4)	√		15mins
7. Diversity(7.1-7.2)	√		5mins

本章考点

重要考点	难度（1~3）
区分招聘和筛选	1
熟记并理解招聘和筛选的流程	2
着重记忆 Job description，Job specifications 和 Person specification 的区别	2
理解筛选的方法的优缺点	2
熟记并理解各个部门在招聘环节中的责任	2
熟记并理解机会均等，以及不同歧视之间的区别	2
理解多样性原则	1

1 Introduction to recruitment and selection

1.1 Definition

核心考点

Recruitment 是招聘，是一个寻找潜在的应聘者的过程，是企业主动地去市场上寻找人才的过程；Selection 是筛选，企业 recruitment 之后开始有应聘者投简历过来，这时企业就不是主动寻找了，而是在现有应聘者中筛选与淘汰。

Recruitment refers to the company's use of various channels and practices to draw public attention to the vacancies and **attract qualified candidates to apply** for the vacancies. It is a **positive** action.

Selection refers to **choosing between applicants** by eliminating unsuitable ones. It is a **negative** action.

小试牛刀

Example question 1

As regard to recruitment and selection, what is meant by recruitment?

A. Preparing a job advertisement

B. Generating a supply of potentially suitable candidates

C. Choosing the most appropriate candidates from a short list

Example question 2

Jack and Lucy work in the human resources department of a company, where one of the objectives is to ensure that the company has enough people with the right skills.

Jack has a job description for a position in the company which must be filled. He intends to advertise the post externally and prepares advertisements for trade and local press.

Lucy has received a large number of applications for another post. She is examining each application and rejecting those which do not have certain qualifications and experience.

Which activity is each individual undertaking?

A. Both of them are responsible for recruitment

B. Both of them are responsible for selection

C. Jack is responsible for selection and Lucy is responsible for recruitment

D. Jack is responsible for recruitment and Lucy is responsible for selection

1.2 The importance of recruitment and selection

Recruitment and selection are of **strategic importance** to organisations. They help to ensure that a firm has enough high-quality human resources to fulfill objectives of the organisation.

Employees are unlikely satisfied if there is a mismatch between job requirements and their abilities, and they are more likely to leave voluntarily or passively. The following are consequences of poor recruitment and selection:

(a) High staff turnover and expense of advertising/dismissal.

(b) More management time involved in recruitment and selection.

(c) Reduced staff morale and motivation on the organisation.

(d) Reduced quality of organisation's products or service, leading to customer dissatisfaction.

1.3 A systematic process of recruitment and selection

(a) Detailed HR planning.

(b) Identify vacancies.

(c) Job analysis (job description, job specification and person specification).

(d) Recruitment advertising.

(e) Selection (recruitment merges into selection when processing applications and assessing candidates).

(f) Notifying applicants the results.

在学习了系统的招聘选拔流程之后，接下来我们学习招聘和筛选环节的具体细节。

> **知识点解读**
>
> 大部分企业，在成立之初或每年年初都会制定人力资源计划（HR planning），该计划会包括需要多少人、需要具备怎样技能的人、做什么业务等来满足企业目标；在整年发展过程中，由于业务发展，或员工因为种种原因辞职或者被解雇，此时就会形成职位空缺（vacancy）；针对该空缺，企业开始准备招聘，在招聘之前，会对招聘的岗位进行岗位分析（Job analysis），之后再面向劳动力市场发布招聘广告（advertising），吸引求职者。吸引求职者后，企业开始按照自己的要求筛选合适的员工（selection），然后通知筛选结果。

2 Recruitment process

2.1 Detailed HR planning

HR department should continuously audit the situation of current personnel and define future needs of labour resources. In detail, it is plan about recruitment, downsizing, training and development, promotion and retention, etc.

人力资源部门（Human resource）应当对公司的各个职能部门有可持续性的具体管理计划，包括何时招聘、何时裁员、如何培训、员工的晋升等。

2.2 Identification of vacancies

Vacancies occur because of job requisition or occurrence of new job positions. Recruitment begins with this step by reassessing the requirements of the job.

发现职位空缺往往是招聘活动进行的第一步，然而我们应当注意，并不是一发现职位空缺，就立刻开启招聘工作。事实上在这种情况下，人力资源部门需要先评估空缺岗位的要求，力求匹配到合适的人选，这个过程被称作"job analysis"。

2.3 Job analysis

Job analysis produces these outputs：

2.3.1 Job description

A **job description** is a broad statement of the purpose, duties and responsibilities of the job, and the purposes of this statement include：

(a) Forming the basis of job advertisement.

(b) Helping select the right applicant for the job.

(c) Providing the basis for a contract of employment.

(d) Being used as a target to appraise the employees.

职位描述（job description）是针对工作本身的一份"说明书"。它不仅是招聘的参考，也是后续人员管理、规划、考核等流程的依据之一。不同公司不同岗位的"说明书"虽然各有差异，但基本内容一般包括但不限于：职位名称（job title）、职位目标（job purpose）、职位责任（job accountability）和职位任务（job tasks）等。

2.3.2 Job specifications

Job specifications describe the **skills and competences** required for the job. Job specification 描述的胜任某个岗位所必备的技能与能力。

2.3.3 Person specification

Person specifications describe the key **attributes and qualities** the **jobholder** should ideally have, and prospective candidates can then be compared with it in the selection process.

Person specification 描述的是担任某个岗位的职员所需要具备的特质和品性，跟岗位本身无关，跟岗位的职员有关，同时也是选拔合适应聘者的标准。

Alec Rodgers devised a seven-point plan which suggests the content of a person specification.

核心考点

岗位分析总共包含三个部分，即岗位描述（job description）、岗位能力要求（job specification）以及述职人员要求（person specification）。这三者的区别是考试中较频繁的考点，需要考生加以辨析。

知识点解读

Competence 译为胜任能力，指的是能够满足某个岗位需求的特定技能，帮助员工实现特定岗位目标。在工作中，常见的胜任能力包括良好的人际沟通能力以及专业领域的技能，如对于执业会计师需要能熟练运用相应会计准则等。

(a) Physical make-up: Strength, appearance, health.

(b) Attainments: Qualifications, career achievements.

(c) General intelligence: This is usually tested by IQ tests.

(d) Special aptitudes: Skill with words and numbers.

(e) Interests: Mechanical, people-related.

(f) Disposition: Calm, independent.

(g) Circumstances: Location, requirement to work unsociable hours.

在企业对空缺岗位进行分析之后，HR 部门有两种招聘途径可以纳入考虑范围，外部招聘或内部晋升。无论是外部招聘还是内部晋升，都各有千秋。公司到底应该选择哪种方式，往往取决于当下的实际情况。例如，现有的员工是否具备空缺岗位需要的资质，是否可以通过这样的内部晋升对员工起到一定激励作用，鼓舞士气，以及公司是否需要通过外部招聘引进新鲜血液创造新的价值，等等。

2.4 Recruit or promote

As soon as there is a job vacancy, the first thing to consider is whether to recruit externally or use existing staff to fill the gap after job analysis.

Some of the factors to be considered in this decision are as follows.

(a) The comparison between existent staff and external applicants about the expertise and qualities of them.

(b) Uncertainty of the performance of outsiders. Management will be familiar with an internal promote and his or her performance.

(c) The degree of urgency to fill the vacancy should be considered. Usually speaking, existent employees are more familiar with companies' affairs, which can save much time in induction comparing to recruiting external employees.

(d) Internal promotion is kind of motivation through providing employees' career development, which can improve employees' morale spontaneously.

(e) Whether there is the demand of innovation brought by the external fresh blood.

2.5 Advertising

The objective of recruitment advertising is to attract the interest of suitable applicants in the vacancy that the organisation wishes to fill.

广告是招聘的一个主要途径，其主要目标就是以这样的方式有效地吸引合适的应聘者。广告应该包含什么内容，好的广告应当具备什么特质，广告应该通过什么什么样的媒介发布，这些就是我们接下来要了解的内容。

2.5.1 Contents of a job advertisement

招聘广告内容一般包括职位名称（job title）、岗位需求（job demand）、所需资质（qualifications）、薪酬（rewards）、应聘途径（application process）等基本信息。除此之外，公司可以根据自己的不同需求相应地添加其他内容，比如工作地点、外派要求等。

核心考点

在企业中有职位空缺的时候，经常需要考虑是从内部提拔还是从外部招聘。这两种方式各有利弊，如从内部提拔的话，员工能够在新职位上更快地上手工作，工作表现更确定，也能体现企业对于员工培养发展的重视；如从外部招聘的话则需要一段磨合的时间，但能引入新鲜血液，促进企业的创新。所以具体应该怎样做还应该看企业所处的具体情况来判断。

知识点解读

一条合格的招聘广告应当能够有效地吸引到合适的目标应聘者，广告内容应当包括职位名称、岗位需求、所需资质、薪酬、应聘途径等基本信息。除此之外，公司可以根据自己的不同需求相应地添加其他内容，比如工作地点、外派要求等。

但招聘广告所含内容不应过分冗长，好的招聘广告需要在简洁明了的同时，能够最大限度地吸引到目标人群，并且也不应当为了制造噱头而过分美化职位，这种行为可能会造成员工入职后心理落差过大，从而会影响到后续员工维护等工作。

作为一则好的招聘广告，其内容应当完整充分（comprehensive）并且简洁明了（concise），与此同时，应当确保广告内容真实有效（positive and honest），切勿为了制造噱头而过分美化广告内容。保证以上几点的同时，广告的撰写还应当做到最大化地吸引（attractive）目标应聘人群（appropriate and relevant applicants）的要求。

2.5.2 Advertising media

招聘广告投放媒介的选择是一门"对症下药"的学问，例如：

(a) 当公司想要招聘的对象是专业程度高，具备一定技能并且能够迅速上岗的员工时，专业杂志（professional newspaper/magazines）、专业网站/论坛（specialist websites or forums）、公司内刊（in-house magazines）等都是可选项。

(b) 倘若某岗位招聘具有较强的地域性，如某公司招聘特定区域的销售经理，那么这种招聘广告的最佳投放渠道就是一些当地的报刊、杂志（local newspaper and magazines）、广播电视（local radio and TVs）等。

(c) 当公司意图招聘一定数量的基础员工时，最经济的渠道就是那些求职者集中的媒介，如求职中心（job center）、高校就业处（school career offices）、招聘网站（the internet）等。

> **核心考点**
>
> 经常会出现考题要求考生辨析某个职位适合在什么媒体上进行广告宣传。一般比较专业的职位都是用专业杂志，当地的职位就在当地的报纸上，要在理解的基础上去记忆各种不同的媒体适合什么样的职位。

3 Selection

If the recruitment process has been successful, the organisation should now have a large number of potential applicants who have expressed an interest in the vacancy. Then the next step for organisation is to look at how to identify and select the best applicants.

如果说招募是招揽合适候选人的过程，那么筛选就是在这些候选人中择优的过程。在这个过程中，我们会以更为具体和严格的标准去衡量这些应聘者，达到优胜劣汰的目的。

3.1 A systematic process

A systematic process of selection is as below：

Step 1：Response to applicants who demonstrate their interest.

Step 2：Evaluate qualification of applicants against predetermined criteria.

Step 3：Classify applicants into three types（possible，unsuitable，marginal）after assessment.

Step 4：Invite potential candidates to take part in interviews.

Step 5：Require candidates to take selection tests.

Step 6：Reassess other un-interviewed candidates.

Step 7：Send official letter to unsuccessful candidates.

Step 8：Notify successful candidates their results and send provisional offers.

3.2 Selection methods

筛选的方法及事例如表 13－1 所示。

表 13－1　Selection methods

Methods	Examples
Application form	Collecting basic but useful information about applicants
Interviewing (most often used)	Individual or panel interview, selection boards
Selection tests	Test on intelligence, aptitude, personality and proficiency
Reference checking	Job reference, character references
Group selection	Assessment centres

3.2.1 Application form

The primary and easiest way of selecting applicants is through application form. This provides relevant information about applicants and other benefits：

(a) Eliminate unsuitable applicants.

(b) Save interview time.

(c) Form initial personnel records for possible applicants.

3.2.2 Interviews

面试，顾名思义，就是通过面对面的方式使面试官与应聘者直接沟通。 在这个过程中，参与双方可以直接看到对方的言行举止，包括一些细枝末节，这种形式利于双方互相进行评判互相选择。 相较而言，面试是一种更为直观以及公开透明的筛选方式。

(A) Purposes of the selection interview

(a) Selecting persons who are most appropriate for the job.

(b) Communicating the job to the applicants.

(c) Presenting a good image to applicants during the interview.

(d) Providing a fair selection method to applicants.

(B) Types of interview

根据面试官与应聘者的人数进行区分，面试可以分成三种主要形式：

(a) **Individual interview** （单面，一个面试官，一个应聘者）

Advantages：

- Evaluation. During the interview process, the interviewer is able to observe both verbal and non-verbal performance of the candidate though a direct communicating opportunity, which enables a more comprehensive evaluation.
- Relationship. The individual-to-individual interview can relieve the pressure of the candidate to some extent, thus the candidate is more likely to build rapport with the interviewer and present a better performance.
- Flexibility. The interviewer could ask more specific and flexible questions.

Disadvantages：

- Artificial. The candidates may prepare and design their answer in advance and

---

核心考点

不同种类的面试方式是一个高频考点，针对这个知识点，一般会有两种考核方式：
（1）给出一个场景，让考生判断其属于哪一种面试方式，那么这里就需要考生能够理解、熟记并掌握不同的面试种类了。
（2）给出一种面试方式，让考生选择对应的优缺点。 这种考核方式也相对简单，同样需要考生理解、熟记并掌握。

知识点解读

单面这种方式的优缺点比较明显，都集中在一对一这个点上。在一对一的情况下，面试官通能够直接观察应聘者，无论是从谈吐或是穿着等角度，甚至包括一些下意识的小动作。 并且，由于一对一的面试中参与者只有两个人，相对而言，氛围也会比较轻松，更有利于应聘者的发挥。但由于单面中面试官只有一个，因而可能存在由于面试官自身的知识盲区，使得应聘者侥幸逃脱其不熟悉的领域。 除此之外，这种缺乏第三方的面试，也的确更容易出现主观臆断甚至舞弊等现象。

disguise themselves during the interview.
- Subjectivity. The interviewer may be influenced by the rapport built during the interview, and the judgment of the sole interviewer may be subjective.

(b) **Panel interviews**（小组面试，两到三个面试官，一个应聘者）

During a panel interview, an single candidate might face the evaluation of two or three interviewers, and the interviewers commonly come from HR department and other certain departments and they are responsible for assessing different aspects of the candidate.

Compared to individual interview, panel interview could save time and give a more considerate and objective judgement of the candidate.

小组面试跟单面的形式其实大同小异，唯一的区别就在于面试官的人数从一个增加至两三个，这种方式很大程度上规避了单面中可能存在的缺陷，并且大大提升了面试的效率。

(c) **Selection board**（群面，多个面试官以及多个应聘者）

During the selection board, a number of candidates are assessed by several interviewers.

Advantages：
- The performance of different candidates could be assessed and compared in a single interview.
- The interviewers can exchange their opinions and can make a prompt decision without subsequent communication.

Disadvantages：
- The difficulty and pressure that candidates face are increased as the questions raised by different interviewers could be more rule-less and varied.
- The interview may be disturbed if there is a dominating member in the board or in the candidates.

知识点解读

Selection board（群面）这种面试方式的缺陷经常会考到，其实主要问题集中在三个方面：
（1）多个面试官在同一场面试中提出的问题可能各式各样，涉及的方面跨度较大，虽然在很大程度上可以更加全面地考核应聘者的实际水平，但这种模式也非常可能由于提出的问题缺乏主线以及连贯性，使得应聘者的回答受到不良影响。并且，也的确存在着优秀的应聘者不适应这种高强度面试的情况。
（2）如果面试官的小组中出现一个完全掌握决定权的成员，那么这种面试小组的构成也就失去了原本的意义。
（3）即便面试官小组中不存在一手遮天的成员，那么也可能会出现各执己见的状况。简单来说，就是对同样的应聘者持不同意见，那么这种情况要达成共识，可能需要耗费更多的时间和成本。

精益求精

面试过程中，面试官可能会通过以下几种方式进行提问，同学们可以尝试一下作出回答。

（1）开放式问题：你认为公司想要可持续性发展，最需要重视哪一方面？

（2）封闭式问题：你之前是否了解过我们公司？该问题只能回答"是"或者"否"。

（3）探究式问题：你为什么会从上一家公司离职？

（4）解决式问题：倘若你现在跟团队里的其他成员性格不合，工作上出现摩擦，你会如何应对？

（5）引导式问题：难道你不认为以行业地位来说，我们公司的发展并没有达到该有的水准吗？（这类引导式提问，作为HR应该尽量避免，因为可能会使得应聘者说出违心的话）

(C) Appraisals of the interview method

Advantages:

(a) Interviews enable face-to-face interaction between the two parties and allow flexibility of candidates to answer and behave.

(b) Interviews give opportunities to observe more aspects of candidates such as non-verbal behaviour and communication ability thus make more thorough assessments.

(c) Interviews give opportunities for the two parties to build rapport, which may increase the probability of building better working relationships.

Limitations:

(a) **Restraint.** The reasonableness is constrained by the limited time of the interview and qualitative factors of candidates such as moral character are inherently difficult to make assessment.

(b) **Artificial factor.** The candidates may make preparation and hide themselves and the interviewers also cannot be completely immune to subjective factors (as is stated below).

(c) **The halo effect.** Some interviewers tend to make assessment based on the first impression of candidates.

(d) **The horn effect.** On the contrary, some interviewers may magnify the weakness of candidates and reach a negative conclusion ultimately.

(e) **Contagious bias.** Some candidates may observe the preference of the interviewers and then change their behaviours to cater to the interviewers.

(f) **Stereotyping.** Some interviewers may have bias towards certain group of candidates.

(g) **Interviewers'** capability. The capability and experience could influence the process and result of interviews.

(C) Appraisals of the interview method

精益求精

Horns effect，叫作触角效应，该效应跟 halo effect 对面试产生的影响刚好相反，它放大了应聘者的缺点，面试官可能会因为应聘者的某个缺点，作出以偏概全的评价。

3.2.3 Selection testing

Selection testing can be undertaken either before or after the interview has taken place.

Types of selection test

(a) **Proficiency tests**

Proficiency tests require learners take part in a diagnostic test, which identify areas to work on, and a prognostic test, which tries to predict a learner's ability to complete a course or take an exam.

Proficiency tests（熟练度测试），主要考查的是应聘者的专业技能，以及是否

核心考点

Selection test（筛选测试）是一个常见的考点，但考核方式比较简单，基本上是以考核定义的形式出现。考生需要构建这样的概念：筛选测试共两大类——proficiency test 及 psychometric test，在这两种 test 之下，又可以有一些细小的分类。例如 work sampling 是 proficiency test 的一种，personality test 是 psychometric test 的一种。

> **知识点解读**
>
> Work sampling（工作抽样），简单来说，就是通过布置一项实际工作给应聘者作为测试，通过实际操作的结果对其工作能力进行判断。例如，翻译公司的工作抽样，可能会给到应聘者一份文件，在规定的时间内，让其进行翻译。这是最能准确判断应聘者能力的测试方法。

可以胜任当前的工作。

Work sampling is often used in these tests. Selectors may observe the candidate working (trial period) or the candidate may bring a portfolio of past work.

(b) **Psychometric tests**

Psychometric tests（心理测试），考查的是应聘者相对内在且抽象的能力，例如智商、天赋、性格等。

Personality test is often used in these tests to measure a variety of characteristics, such as an applicant's skill in dealing with other people, ambition and motivation, or emotional stability.

小试牛刀

Example question 3

Example question 3

Publish Co produces study material for a professional examination. In order to meet urgent demand for finished texts, it must recruit five copy typists at short notice. The typists must be able to perform the required tasks immediately and the company has to be totally confident that they have the ability to do the job.

Which of the following selection methods is most appropriate for Publish Co?

 A. Proficiency test   B. Panel interview

 C. One-to-one interview   D. Psychometric test

3.2.4 Limitations of selection test

(a) Performance in selection test can be improved by coaching and/or practical efforts；

(b) There is no direct link between high performance in tests and actual performance in the job；

(c) The interpretation of test results (especially personality test) is difficult；

(d) Some tests are highly subjective and cannot fully exclude bias from human-designed tests.

3.2.5 Group assessment（assessment centres）

Assessment centres involved applicants being observed and evaluated by trained interviewers as they are given a selection of pre-programmed tests. **Group role-play** or **case studies** are often used in this process. This selection method provides longer opportunity for interviewers to observe candidates from different aspects. In most cases, interviewers will be looking for evidence that applicants have certain competencies that are important in the job they have applied for, for example, leadership, communication skills, team working and others.

评估中心，首先，考生需要了解这是一种评估应聘者的方式，而非某个具体地点。其次，评估中心的含义是，在一段时间内（通常时间较长，一般为两到三天），通过各种方法的组合（如角色扮演、沙盘模拟、案例分析等），全面考核应聘者，从而进行筛选。例如，四大会计师事务所就非常倾向于采用评估中心这一方式，形式通常为：在两个小时内，分别以单面、群面以及笔试等方式评估应聘者。通过这些方法的组合，可以在短时间内让面试官对应聘者的表现建立起非常立体的印象，作出更好的选择。

3.2.6 Reference checking

The purpose of references is to confirm facts about the applicants and increase the degree of confidence about information they provided during the selection process.

通常情况下，背景调查需要获取和确认候选人简历提供的信息是否属实，如工作岗位与年限的事实性信息；同时，还会获取前任雇主等他人对候选者评语之类评价性信息。为避免因主观信息而导致错误评估，现在背景调查要求获取至少两人以上的信息核实。核实的途径一般分为两种：

（1）书面背景调查：要求候选者前任雇主就候选者相关方面进行确认且对候选者进行客观评价。相较于电话调查，书面背景调查更加正式。如果企业已经有相关的标准格式，还可以帮助企业节约做此调查的时间。

（2）电话背景调查：如果企业没有相关的标准书面格式，那么选择电话背景调查会帮助企业节约时间。此外，选择此类型更可能获取比书面调查更诚实的意见。

> **知识点解读**
>
> 很多考生对这个知识点会产生困惑，主要也是由于推荐（reference）这种方式在国内并非主流渠道。简单来说，推荐就是以个人信誉作为担保，将一个人推荐到某家公司担任某个岗位。
> 推荐可以以推荐信的方式存在，也可以以电话形式存在，主要内容包括推荐人对被推荐人的一些评价和举荐理由。

4 Evaluating recruitment and selection

招聘作为公司人才引进的一个重要步骤，重要性可想而知，那么对于这样的步骤，我们该如何进行评估，这是我们接下来要学习的内容。

How to appraise the efficiency in recruitment and selection?

(a) Performance indicators：是否完成招聘目标；

(b) Cost-effectiveness：招聘活动创造的价值是否大于成本；

(c) Monitoring the workforce：招聘过程对劳动力是否起到了监管作用；

(d) Attitudes survey：通过对应聘者的回访，了解招聘过程是否完善；

(e) Actual individual job performance：入职的应聘者的业绩表现是否达到预期。

During the whole recruitment and selection process, it is vital for organisations to reflect equal opportunity and diversity.

5 Responsibility for recruitment and selection

There are mainly four kinds of people involved in recruitment and selection process. And they each plays a different role in this process.

5.1 The human resource (HR) department

Not all organisations have HR department. This department may be presented in larger organisations to provide professional service. HR function takes the overall responsibility for the recruitment and selection process and their roles may include：

(a) Formulate HR policy and ensure compliance with relevant laws and regulations in recruitment and selection.

(b) Frequent liaison with the labour market.

> **核心考点**
>
> 不同部门和人员在招聘与选拔过程中的职责，是本章较频繁的一个考点，同时也是基本人力资源常识，考生需要熟悉并理解。

(c) Detailed HR planning for each year.
(d) Advertising, including designing application forms and sorting records of new recruitments.
(e) Interacting work with recruitment consultants.
(f) First round selection of applicants.

5.2 Line managers

Line managers are applicant's prospective boss. In smaller businesses, they tend to have sole responsibility for recruitment. In larger organisations, they may be responsible for:
(a) Requesting more human resources.
(b) Advising on attributes required for new vacancies.
(c) Having a final say in selection.

Line management is more involved in recruitment and selection in current trend.

5.3 Senior managers

Senior managers do not participate directly in every recruitment and are usually involved in recruiting vacancies of **senior positions**. In most cases, they are responsible for identifying overall needs of the organisation.

5.4 Recruitment consultants

Recruitment consultants are people whose job is to give expert advice to people for skilled or specialised jobs, or in most cases, to companies looking for skilled or sepcialised workers. In this way, recruitment consultants are often the first step in recruitment and selection.

Their duties include:
(a) Analysing demands of the vacancies.
(b) Offering advice on job analysis and selection criteria.
(c) Searching suitable applicants and designing job advertisements.
(d) Screening applicants by conducting first-round interviews and helping with short-listing.
(e) Offering a list of suitable candidates with notes and recommendations.

> **知识点解读**
>
> Line managers 指的是应聘者未来的直属上级。有很多工作都是专业要求比较高的,这时仅靠 HR 招聘就无法确定候选人的专业技能、经验是否胜任,需要专业人士的参与,提升招聘的效果。

博学多才

Recruitment consultants 即招聘顾问,又称猎头,意为物色人才的人,是帮助优秀的企业找到需要的人才的人,这个词另外的说法叫作高级人才寻访。"头"指智慧、才能集中之所在,猎头也可指猎夺人才,即发现、追踪、评价、甄选和提供高级人才的行为。

猎头原来是指美洲食人部落在作战的时候把对方的头颅砍下来,作为炫耀挂在腰间的行为。真正叫作猎头是"二战"以后,欧美一些战胜国从德国等很多国家寻找自己需要的科学家,他们像丛林狩猎一样,到处派专业公司帮他们物色比较优秀的人。"猎头"这个词后来被借用，意指猎寻人才的人。猎头与一般的企业招聘、人才推荐和职业介绍服务有着很大的不同，猎头追逐的目标始终盯在高学历、高职位、高价位三位一体的人身上，搜寻的是那些受教育程度高、实践经验丰富、业绩表现出色的专业人才和管理人才。简言之，猎头可以理解为高级人才中介，担当的是高级人才和企业的"红娘"的角色。

在公司决定是否外部聘请猎头之前，需要从多个维度进行衡量，包括：

（1）公司内部 HR 招聘能力（The level of recruitment expertise）。如果 HR 已经具备较成熟的能力，则无需外部聘请猎头了。

（2）成本。比较内部招聘和外部聘请猎头成本差异。

（3）新员工入职时间。如果新员工需求特别紧急，则内部招聘会更适合，因为猎头需要大量的时间分析招聘需求，总体耗时更长。

（4）劳动力供给（Supply of labour）。通常只有在劳动力紧缺，公司无法自身招聘合适人选的时候，公司才会使用猎头。

6 Equal opportunity

6.1 Definition of equal opportunity

Equal opportunity refers to the belief that there should be **an equal chance for all workers**. All employment decisions (application and selection for jobs, training and development, promotion, employment termination, working condition and other benefits, etc.) should be **based solely on a person**'s ability, experience and potential.

That is, employers can discriminate only on the basis of ability, experience or potential.

> **知识点解读**
>
> 所谓机会均等，指的是"employers can discriminate only on the basis of ability, experience or potential" other than a person's sex, age, disability or marital status, etc., 即雇主只能因为员工能力、经验和潜能不同而进行区别对待。

6.2 The importance/benefits of equal opportunity

(a) Organisations have a legal responsibility to adopt equal opportunities.

(b) It is not morally to treat some parts of population less favourably and equal opportunity is in line with business ethics.

(c) It is beneficial for organisations to attract and retain the best people for the job, especially widening the recruitment pool in times of skill shortages.

(d) Organisations may also benefit from good reputation for its image as a good employer, which enhances loyalty of customers and retention of staff.

6.3 Types of discrimination

(a) **Direct discrimination**

One group is treated more favourably than another based on gender, race, etc.

In the UK, the legislation outlaws discrimination based on：

- Age.
- Disability.
- Gender reassignment.
- Marriage and civil partnership.

> **知识点解读**
>
> 五种歧视的类型一直都是考试重点，通常是以案例的形式，判断歧视类型，需要同学们掌握各种歧视的关键词，进行区分。其中，前三种类型（direct discrimination/indirect discrimination/victimization）需要掌握，后两种（harassment/positive discrimination）同学们了解即可。

- Pregnancy and maternity.
- Race.
- Religion and belief.
- Sex.
- Sexual orientation.

直接歧视，是指招聘过程中，针对一些特定因素，如性别、种族、国籍、宗教信仰、年龄等，从而对某些应聘者产生歧视。最典型的例子就是，招聘广告上载明："仅限男性"。这就是针对女性的直接歧视。

(b) Indirect discrimination

A policy **is fair in appearance**, **but discriminatory in practice**. This occurs when a rule disadvantageous one group of people more than another. For example, a condition that candidates must be of a particular height.

Indirect discrimination is often illegal, unless it is necessary for the working of the business and there is no way round it.

间接歧视，是指招聘条件中虽然使用了统一的标准或者政策，但是实际操作起来却对某一群人不公平。举个题目中常见的例子：企业不招兼职工。这样表面看上去没什么问题，但是我们要结合一下西方社会的社会背景来考虑。在西方，女性生了孩子之后，家里的长辈不会像大部分中国的爷爷奶奶帮忙照顾孩子，妈妈们要自己照顾孩子。在这种情况下，她们很难兼顾一份全职工作，只能去做兼职，所以在西方，兼职工大部分都是女性。所以，当企业不愿意招兼职，那可能就是暗含着不愿意招女性，这构成了间接的性别歧视。

(c) Victimisation

Victimisation is discrimination against an individual who has brought proceedings or given evidence in another case involving discrimination. This means an employer treating an employee less favourably because they have made, or tried to make, a complaint about discrimination.

当员工认为自己在公司受到歧视的时候，采取相应的措施保障自身权益不受侵害，如向工会进行投诉。然而这种正当行为被公司得知后，对该员工实施报复性行为，这种情况便构成迫害性歧视。

(d) Harassment

The use of threatening, offensive or abusive language or behaviour.

骚扰可以分为身体上的和语言上的骚扰，包括威胁恐吓、冒犯，以及让人觉得不舒服的玩笑/行为/言语。

(e) Positive discrimination

Actions which give preference to a protected people **regardless of genuine suitability** and qualification for the job.

6.4 Formulating an effective equal opportunity policy

(a) The creation of policy needs **support both minority group and top managers.**

(b) Clear **communication** of the policy to all staffs.

(c) Frequent **monitoring** of the application of the policy.

知识点解读

企业可以采取一些积极的行动来充分实施机会均等的政策。比如，在招聘广告中加入少数民族的语言，来传递机会均等的思想。由于企业中的高层岗位女性员工的比例普遍低于男性，企业也可以为女性员工提供一些培训，来提升她们的管理技能。同时，针对性别歧视、种族歧视、宗教歧视及侮辱、骚扰等问题，企业也应该重视，设立相关的惩戒措施，必要时给受到歧视的员工提供心理咨询服务，倡导平等的企业文化。

(d) **Positive action**：the process of taking active steps to encourage people from disadvantaged groups to compete for vacancies.

考生需要学会区别 positive discrimination 和 positive action。

Positive discrimination 是指偏向小众群体、弱势群体，给他们更多的面试机会及晋升机会，使他们有比正常者更好的待遇。 这对其他大部分人来说就构成了歧视。 而 Positive action 指的是为减少歧视而实施的行为。 例如，帮助弱势群体，给他们同等的面试机会以及晋升机会，而不是把他们拒之门外。 这是一种 equal opportunity 的体现，不构成 discrimination。

Remember： **training cannot be regarded as positive discrimination.**

在招聘与选拔过程中，尤其需要体现机会均等，接下来我们来看看需要注意什么：

1. 招聘广告设计

任何显示特定偏好的措辞都需要避免。

2. 猎头

给猎头的中意人选标准中，不应涵盖任何歧视信息。

3. 申请表格/选拔测试

申请表格作为搜集应聘者信息来源，只能搜集工作相关的问题，同时也不能出现某一类群体需要填写等情况。 选拔测试同理。

4. 面试

面试过程中，不能只问某一类群体的特定问题，如只问女性是否有生育打算；也不能只允许某一类群体回答特定问题。 如果条件允许，最好整个过程中有见证人，至少也需要有充分的记录。

7 Diversity

7.1 Definition

Diversity is a more evolving concept than equal opportunity, which It goes **further than equal opportunity**. Diversity involves valuing all individuals for their differences and variety. It refers to the ways in which people meaningfully differ in the workplace include not only race and ethnicity, age and gender, but **personality, preferred working style, individual needs and goals** etc.

7.2 Managing diversity

It implies the need to be **proactive** in managing the needs of a diverse workforce in areas **beyond the requirements equal opportunity and discrimination regulations**. In detail, organisations need to show more tolerance of individual differences in personality, family structure, working styles and career aspiration.

> **知识点解读**
>
> Diversity，用工的多元化，比机会均等的概念更进一步。 如果说机会均等是确保员工都有平等的权利，那么用工多元化就是鼓励组织接纳差异化的员工，构建更为丰富的工作环境。

Answers for example question

1. B
2. D
3. A

Summary

Chapter 13 考试不同问法总结

Section A

1. 针对 Recruitment & Selection

- Within the field of recruitment and selection what is meant by recruitment?
- Which TWO of the following are the primary reasons why effective recruitment and selection processes are important to an organisation?
- Which of the following should NOT be included in a person specification?
- Which of the following limitations of interviewers has the scenario above highlighted?

2. 针对 Equal opportunity & Diversity

- From the following list which statement BEST describes the concept of equal opportunities?
- Which TWO of the following statements about the benefits of an equal opportunity policy are correct?
- Which TWO of the following statements, taken from job advertisements, are examples of Indirect discrimination?
- Which of the following is a benefit to an organisation of operating a diversity policy in recruitment?

Section B

- Which activity is each staff undertaking, recruitment or selection?
- Which TWO of the following will make effective recruitment more difficult?

Quick quiz

13.1 The process of selection and recruitment are distinctive from each other, which of the following would be classed as a 'recruitment' rather than a 'selection' activity?

A. Assessment centre
B. Panel interview
C. Advertising for vacancies
D. Screening application forms

Answer: C

Difficulty level: Easy

Tag: Recruitment and selection

Rationale:

Assessment centre, panel interview and screening application form are all typical means of selection. Assessment centre is a group selection method to thoroughly measure the competence of applicants. Panel interview includes several assessors to simultaneously interview one single applicants. Screening is the primary and easiest way of selecting applicants by sorting applicants into "possible", "unsuitable" and "marginal". They are selection methods because they are negative actions which concerned with finding appropriate applicants by eliminating unsuitable applicants. Recruitment is a positive action concerned with finding applicants, such as by advertising.

评估中心、小组面试和初步筛选都是选拔的方式。评估中心是群组选拔的方式，从而彻底地衡量应聘者的能力。小组面试包含若干个面试官同时面试一个应聘者。初步筛选是最主要也是最简单的选拔应聘者的方法，通常是将应聘者分成可能适合、不适合、介于两者之间。以上三项都是选拔的方式，即通过淘汰不合适的应聘者来找到合适的应聘者，是一个存在着删选和淘汰的消极过程。而招聘是企业主动释放招揽人才的信号的积极过程，例如企业通过刊登招聘广告，引起合适应聘者的兴趣。

13.2 Which of the following statements is/are true?

(1) Regarding to employment decisions, a person can be treated more favourably than another based on his/her ability, experience and potential.

(2) Training for the disabled can be regarded as positive discrimination.

A. They are both true
B. (1) is false and (2) is true
C. (1) is true and (2) is false
D. They are both false

Answer: C

Difficulty level: Easy

Tag: Equal opportunity and diversity

Rationale:

Equal opportunity refers to the belief that there should be an equal chance for all workers. All employment decisions (application and selection for jobs, training and development, promotion, employment termination, working condition and other benefits, etc.) should be based solely on a person's ability, experience and potential. Therefore, statement (1) is true. Training for the disabled can be regarded as positive discrimination. Positive discrimination is an action which give preference to a protected people regardless of genuine suitability and qualification for the job. Therefore, statement (2) is false.

机会均等指对于所有的员工都有一个公平的机会。所有的雇佣决定（有所差异地对待）只能是基于一个人的能力、经验和潜能。因此，第一句话是对的。对残疾人的培训本身不可以被看成积极歧视。积极歧视是给予一个受保护的人以优先权，而不管他能否适合和胜任这个工作岗位。因此，第二句话是错的。

13.3 Last month, Tony's accounting team had significant changes and two of members had resigned. In order to fill those vacancies, Tony is choosing candidates in a recommended list and conducting interviews. The first person who participated interview was well dressed and showed appropriate formalities and ceremonies. Therefore, interviewer was satisfied immediately due to those two attributes and was affected in the following assessment.

Under above scenario, which of the following is drawback in the Tony's interview?

A. Contagious bias   B. Stereotyping   C. The halo effect   D. The horns effect

Answer: C

Difficulty level: Normal

Tag: The limitations of interview

Rationale:

The halo effect means that a tendency for people to make an initial general judgement about a person based on a single obvious attribute, and such attribute normally is good for candidates.

这道题考查的是面试缺点中的光环效应。光环效应，指的是面试官倾向于根据一个明显的特征对一个人/候选者作出初步的总体判断，而这种特征通常对候选人是有好处的、加分的。因此，根据题干给的信息，第一位面试者得体的着装和恰当的礼仪举止都使面试官对他产生了好的第一印象，从而影响了后续的评判，所以答案选 C。

13.4 Which of the following correctly describes the definition of equal opportunities?

A. There should be an equal quota for both women and men in the work

B. The quantities of men employed in the workplace are equal to women

C. All qualified employees have right to apply for promotion

D. All racial employees should have access to potential promotion

Answer: C

Difficulty level: Normal

Tag: The definition of equal opportunities

Rationale:

Equal opportunity refers to the belief that there should be an equal chance for all workers. All employment decisions should be based solely on a person's ability, experience and potential.

机会均等是指所有员工都应该有平等的机会，所有的雇佣决定都应该完全基于一个人的能力、经验和潜力。但这并非指在企业中男女人数和配额人数要一致，因此 A、B 选项排除。此外，机会均等要基于标准之上，也就是有足够的资格，所以答案选 C。

13.5 Which TWO of the following could attribute to an effective recruitment process?

A. Establish an equal opportunity policy with the support from the board

B. Rely on the recruitment agency to select appropriate candidates

C. Design leading question in the selection interview

D. Combine various methods in the selection procedure

Answer: A D

Difficulty level: Normal

Tag: Selection & Equal opportunity

Rationale:

Implementing an equal opportunity policy could enable an entity to possess more valuable human resource and should gain support from the top level.

Not every entity would use recruitment agency to recruit new employees, and the final say would attain within the entity if the recruitment agency were used.

Leading question could mislead the candidates and should be avoided during the interview.

Using different methods during selection can assist the entity reach a more comprehensive assessment thus make more accurate predictions on the performance of new employees.

这道题综合考查一个高效的招聘和选拔的过程应该满足的条件。 贯彻机会均等的招聘政策可以帮助企业得到更优质的人才，因此 A 选项正确。 不是所有的企业都会使用猎头来招聘新人，即便使用猎头，主动权也留存在企业而不会过度依赖猎头，因此 B 选项错误。 引导性的问题会误导应聘者，致使他们在面试中有所伪装，因此在面试中要避免出现引导性问题，C 选项错误。 将各种选拔技巧结合在一起可以使企业对应聘者有更加全面的了解，可以更准确地预估之后的工作表现，因此 D 选项正确。

13.6 Jack is a manager in HR department. He suggests that may be the staff we want to recruit who must be at least 1.80 meters tall and have been in continuous full-time employment for at least three years. **Which of the following is the legal term for this practice?**

  A. Direct discrimination
  B. Indirect discrimination
  C. Victimisation
  D. Implied discrimination

Answer: B

Difficulty level: Normal

Tag: Discrimination

Rationale:

Indirect discrimination defined as: A policy or practice is fair in form, but discriminatory in operation. This occurs when a rule disadvantageous one group of people more than another.

间接歧视的定义是：政策或做法在形式上是公平的，但在操作上是歧视的。 当一条规则对一组人比另一组人不利时，就会发生这种情况。 而 Jack 在招聘的时候建议录取的员工必须身高在 1.8 米以上和连续工作 3年。 在操作上存在歧视。 所以答案选 B。

13.7 Which of the following statements are true?

  (1) Training cannot be regarded as positive discrimination.

  (2) Positive action means taking which give preference to a protected people regardless of genuine suitability and qualification for the job.

  A. They are both true
  B. (1) is false and (2) is true
  C. (1) is true and (2) is false
  D. They are both false

Answer: C

Difficulty level: Easy

Tag: positive action and positive discrimination

Rationale:

This relates to the definition of positive discrimination. It regards the protection of individuals as the most important purpose of actions, although it ignores the genuine suitability and qualification of the job itself. It is pointed out that training cannot be considered as positive discrimination. Statement(1) is true.

Positive action: the process of taking active steps to encourage people from disadvantaged groups to apply for jobs and training, and to compete for vacancies. Statement(2) is false.

这道题意在考查正向歧视和积极行动的区别。 正向歧视认为保护个人是最重要的目的，它忽略了工作本身的是否真正适合。 而积极行动是采取积极步骤鼓励弱势群体的人。 所以这道题选择 C。

Chapter 14
Leading and managing people

知识导入

上一章中，我们了解了如何进行招聘与筛选。经过该过程后，这些优秀的员工已经全部在公司汇聚。试想一下，我们能毫无约束地任由其发展吗？当然不可以。为了组织高效率的运作，作为管理者，理应有一套有效的管理方法去管理不同的员工，让他们更好地为企业创造价值。让我们来学习"领导与管理"这一章。

单词表

英文	中文
Subordinate	下属
Interface	界面
Coercive power	强制力
Incentive	刺激
Harmonise	协调
Micro-designed jobs	工作细分
Psychological needs	心理需求
Economic performance	经济业绩
Figurehead	首脑
Liaison	交流
Disseminator	传播者
Attainment	成就，造诣
Entrepreneurship	企业家能力/职能，企业家
Trait	特点
Foresight	前瞻性
Dimensions	维度
Rapport	友好关系；融洽

学习指南

Learning objectives	Pass level	Distinction level	用时建议
1. Related concepts of management(1.1-1.6)	√		10 mins
2. Management (2.1-2.2)	√		15 mins
3. What is leadership(3.1-3.3)	√		10 mins
4. Schools of leadership theory(4.1-4.3)		√	10 mins

本章考点

重要考点	难度（1~3）
熟记并区分管理和领导的区别	1
熟记并理解 authority，Delegation 和 Power 的区别	2
熟记并理解 responsibility 和 accountability 的区别	1
熟记并区分古典管理学派和现代管理学派的代表人物及他们的观点	3
熟记并理解天资理论	1
熟记并理解风格理论	2
熟记并理解权变理论	3

一般语境下，领导与管理两个词都是同时出现，因此在大众的概念中，领导与管理是一组同义词。但事实上，在学术概念中，领导与管理有着本质的区别。如何正确区分领导与管理，将是我们本章学习的第一步。

1 Related concepts of management

1.1 Management

Management can be defined as "getting things done through other people". It is about the effective use and co-ordination of business resources in order to achieve key objectives with maximum efficiency.

The importance of management（importance of management, n.d.）：

(a) Helps in achieving group goals.

(b) Optimum utilisation of resources.

(c) Reduces costs.

(d) Establishes sound organisation.

(e) Establishes equilibrium.

(f) Essentials for prosperity of society.

> **知识点解读**
>
> 管理，可以被理解为：合理利用人力资源，整合公司其他资源，力求以效率最大化的方式完成目标。简单来说，这就是一个设定并执行公司战略、维持体系稳定运行的过程。

1.2 Authority

Organisational authority is the right to control, judge, or prohibit the actions of others. More general, authority is the right to do something, or ask someone else to do something and expect it to be done.

1.3 Power

Power is not the same thing as authority. Power is referred as the capacity of an individual to influence the will or conduct of others. As against, authority is termed as the right possessed by a person to give the command to others（"Power and Authority", n.d.）.

For example, a manager may have the authority, or the right, to ask his subordinate to undertake a task. However, the subordinate could simply refuse.

> **知识点解读**
>
> 1.2—1.4 中的 Authority, power, delegation 中文解释都接近于权利或者权限，但其英文含义却大有不同，需要同学们辨析。
> 这里表述应该有误，请核。

> **知识点解读**
>
> 在 1.2 中，我们知道了 Authority 的意思为权限，表示有做某事的权限，这个权限往往来自上级授予。
> 这里 Power 的意思为权力，表示有做某事的能力、实力。

Power is what enables the manager to ensure that the subordinate will comply with his request.

The following types of power from different sources have been identified (types of power, n.d.):

(a) Coercive power: It is conveyed through fear of losing one's job, being demoted, receiving a poor performance review, having prime projects taken away, etc. This power is gotten through threatening others

惩罚权力，也可以被称为强制性权力，这种权力基于人们对被惩罚的畏惧。简单来说，人们倘若不服从这种权力，就会产生一些恶性后果。

(b) Reward power: It is conveyed through rewarding individuals for compliance with one's wishes. This may be done through giving bonuses, raises, a promotion, extra time off from work, etc.

奖赏权力，这种权力来自可以对人们的行为作出奖赏的能力。当人们想得到某种奖赏时，他们会屈服于这样的权力。

(c) Legitimate power: It comes from having a position of power in an organisation, such as being the boss or a key member of a leadership team. This power comes when employees in the organisation recognise the authority of the individual. It is very similar to authority.

法定权力，是指一个人因为在组织中所处的职位和承担的职务而拥有的权力，这是组织中最明显也是最重要的一种权力，跟 authority 的来源非常相似。

(d) Expert power: It comes from one's experiences, skills or knowledge. As we gain experience in particular areas, and become thought leaders in those areas, we begin to gather expert power that can be utilised to get others to help us meet our goals.

专家权力，这种权力来自专家拥有的某些技能或专长。值得注意的是，只有当专家拥有的这些技能或专长正是组织所缺乏的时候，这种权力才会产生影响力。

(e) Referent power: It comes from being trusted and respected. We can gain referent power when others trust what we do and respect us for how we handle situations.

参照权力，这种权力往往与个人特质或人格魅力相关，产生的影响力与 leadership 非常相似，是指个人具有的吸引他人并建立起他人对自己的忠诚度的能力。

1.4 Delegation

Delegation is the assignment of any discretion or authority to another person (normally from a manager to a subordinate) to carry out specific activities. It is one of the core concepts of management leadership. Delegation empowers a subordinate to make decisions, i.e. it is a shifting of decision-making authority from one organisational level to a lower one.

授权可以看作是一个从上至下分权（decentralisation，详见 Chapter 5）的过程。上级将某些权力下放给下属，一方面使得自身可以更加集中于核心事务的处理，另一方面也可以通过给予下属适度的自由裁量权，让他们得到亲身实践的机

> **知识点解读**
>
> 这里值得注意的是，Delegation（授予）的只能是 authority。delegation of authority（授权），即给下属做某些事情的权限，让下属在执行任务的过程中不会有阻碍。

会，起到培训与激励的作用。

The benefits of delegation (delegation of authority, n. d.):

(a) Essential for running the organisation: managers will have increased available time for more strategic thinking and development opportunities.

(b) Training: delegation gives the employees an experience of the actual work, thus providing them with practical training of the job. Delegation involves sharing and transfer of knowledge, thus increasing general awareness and know-how of the work.

(c) Motivation: entrusting employees with additional responsibilities works as a great motivator at the workplace. When an employee knows that the higher management trusts him and relies on his capabilities, he works with greater efficiency.

(d) Assessment: assessing how well the delegates are functioning can help a manager rate their performance and take decisions about their promotions.

(e) Decisions: in theory, the quality of decisions made by subordinates is better as they are closer to actual situations and have more knowledge of the problems.

之前我们提到过，授权（delegation）其实可以看成是一个由上至下分权（decentralisation）的过程。那么在这里，通过对比我们不难发现，这两者的优点有异曲同工之妙。考生可以将两者结合起来记忆：

（1）从高管的角度来看，将适当的权力授予基层管理者，可以减轻高层管理者的工作量，让他们能够更加集中地处理核心事务，而不是纠缠在琐碎地日常事务上。这种人尽其才的工作分配方式会使得效率达到新高度。

（2）从基层管理者角度来看，当他们被授权，就相当于他们有了一定程度的自由裁量权，这意味着在实际工作中，他们可以通过自己的判断来作出决策，基层管理者可以通过这种实践出真知的方式获取经验，从而更快地学习、成长，无论是对自己日后的晋升还是公司的继任计划，都是有所裨益的。

（3）从公司绩效角度来看，首先，通过授权，基层管理者有了更多的权限，这本身即是一种激励，会在很大程度上激发基层管理者工作的积极性，从而有益于公司的绩效；其次，处于一线的基层管理者最了解日常经营的员工，他们可以更快速地应对前线的突发状况，避免旁逸斜出的小问题影响整体运营，甚至绩效；最后，通过授权的方式，基层管理者的工作能力可以被更清晰地衡量，表现卓越的被奖赏，表现差强人意的也可以明确不足之处，从而制定后续的培养计划。

1.5 Responsibility and accountability

Responsibility is defined as the "reliability, dependability, and the obligation to accomplish work. Responsibility also includes each person's obligation to perform at an acceptable level, the level that the person has been educated."

Accountability refers to being answerable to a higher authority. Accountability is the ability and willingness to assume responsibility for ones' actions and accepting the consequences of one's behavior. (accountability vs responsibility, n.d.)

知识点解读

Responsibility（责任），指的是对其所处职位的工作范围负责，不同岗位各司其职，即负有不同的责任。

Accountability，也译作责任，指的是对上级授予的任务或工作负责，尤其是当这项任务或工作的执行出现了问题，则应当接受来自上级的问责，并对这个过失承担相应的后果。

小试牛刀

Example question 1

ABC Company values the integrity and ability of its sales mangers highly. And the board has decided to provide them with greater discretion in offering discounts to customers and extending lines of credit in respect of accounts receivable.

The decision of the board of ABC Company reflects a commitment to which of the following organisational values?

  A. Openness

  B. Accountability

  C. Delegation

1.6 Management & Supervisor

  Supervisor is the person in the first-line management who monitors and regulates employees in their performance of assigned or delegated tasks. Supervisors are the **lowest level of management** and are usually authorised to recommend and/or effect hiring, disciplining, promoting, punishing, rewarding, and other associated activities regarding the employees in their departments. The supervisor is a person given authority for planning and controlling the work of their group, but all they can delegate to the group is the work itself.

  总的来说，supervisor 是组织中相对处于基层的 manager，作为管理者，两者的职能大致是相似的。但是，正因为 supervisor 和 manager 所处的层级不一样，所以两者之间也有一些差异，接下来，我们来了解一下 supervisor 的特征。

1.6.1 Key features of a supervisor

（a）Often a first-line manager, the one who solves problems firsthand during the whole work process, and often required to resolve problems quickly.

（b）Needs to spend much time on technical/operational work because of both supervisor tasks and operational work that need to perform. Supervisors should ensure everything is well done.

（c）Plays a role of communication bridge between managers and employees.

（d）Monitors and regulates employees' performance of daily tasks and then gives feedback to managers.

2 Management

2.1 Classical writers on management

  The classical school of management theories were developed during the Industrial Revolution of the mid-to-late 1800s and early 1900s. They are largely concerned with improving **efficiency and productivity**.

知识点解读

Supervisor 也是 manager 的一种，但级别相对较低。当员工在本职岗位上的专业能力越来越纯熟，不仅能完成自己的本职工作，还能够承担其他责任，如处理同事之间的沟通等。那么，此时他的角色就从一名普通员工转变成了一名 supervisor。由此可见，supervisor 不仅是一个单纯的领导者，他本身也要承担一部分专业工作。

知识点解读

古典管理理论：
（1）管理的五大职能——法约尔（Fayol）；
（2）科学管理理论——泰勒（Taylor）；
（3）人际关系学说——梅奥（Mayo）。

核心考点

这部分内容在考试中出现的频率非常高，是需要同学们务必理解记忆的知识点。一般考核形式会有以下几种：
（1）给出某个核心思想，让考生判断其属于哪种理论，提出者是谁；
（2）直接给出理论名称，让考生选择与之匹配的内容表述；
（3）区分古典理论与现代理论的种类。

鉴于这些考核方式，考生在学习过程中，务必要能够将理论名称与提出者的名称相对应。此外，虽然没有必要将理论内容一字一句地背下来，但一定要抓住每个理论的核心思想，这样在考试中才能有效率地进行判断和选择。

2.1.1 Henri Fayol: Five functions of management

Fayol classified five functions of management which apply to any organisation. These five functions focus on the relationship between personnel and its management and they provide a creative manner to solve problems.

> **核心考点**
>
> 对于法约尔的五大管理职能，首先，考生需要记忆五大职能是哪些，我们可以采用缩写进行记忆，如 POCCC。其次，考生需要理解这五大职能的含义，以及每个职能需要涉及哪些方面的工作。

博学多才

亨利·法约尔（Henry Fayol，1841—1925），是古典管理理论的主要代表人之一，其管理学著作的基础可以说主要来自他一生成功的实际管理经验。1841年，法约尔出生在法国一个富裕的资产阶级家庭，这位大师的成长、学习以及工作之路都相当顺遂。但非常有意思的是，法约尔并非管理学专业科班出身，他最初崭露头角是在矿业工程师领域。法约尔17岁就读于圣艾蒂安国立矿业学院，是同级中最年轻的学生，19岁毕业时他随即取得了矿业工程师资格，1860年就被任命为科芒特里—富香博公司的科芒特里矿井组工程师。转折点发生在1872年，法约尔被任命为某批矿井组的主管，从这个时间节点起，这个年轻人才算是误打误撞进了管理的领域。

The five functions he classified include Planning, Organising, Commanding, Co-ordinating and Controlling.

(a) **Planning**

It is incumbent on managers to set out plans, objectives and strategies for the future of their businesses.

(b) **Organising**

Managers need to find and ensure an efficient pattern of organising the work and workforce of the business. Specifically, they should rationalize tasks and activities, and then, allocate sufficient resources and assign appropriate employees to complete.

(c) **Commanding**

Managers should inform the company's goals and policies to subordinates and give guidance to ensure their behaviours and outcomes are in line with the company's prospects and goals.

(d) **Co-ordinating**

Managers should ensure the harmony between employees and tasks, ensure they are mutually supportive for each other.

(e) **Controlling**

Managers should supervise and rectify deviations of the employees' work in order to achieve the company's objectives.

2.1.2 F·W·Taylor: Scientific theory

Frederick Winslow Taylor was an American mechanical engineer and **sought the most efficient methods of management**. He summed up his efficiency techniques in his 1911 book *The Principles of Scientific Management*. It was one of the earliest attempts to apply science to the engineering of processes and to manage-

> **核心考点**
>
> 泰勒的科学管理理论也是考试中的"熟面孔"，这个考点一般集中在科学管理的原则上，因此考生需要把握本节对于科学管理原则的总结，不用逐字背诵，但务必理解然后记忆关键词。

ment.

Scientific management is **about improving economic efficiency, especially labor productivity**.

> **博学多才**
>
> 与法约尔一样，泰勒也是出生于一个富有的律师家庭，并且从小也是聪慧过人，高中毕业后就考入哈佛大学，就读其王牌专业——法律系，光明的前途唾手可得。但命运却跟他开了个大玩笑，大学期间，泰勒染上了眼疾，不得不含恨辍学。1875年，这个年轻人进入一家小机械厂当学徒，埋头3年，1878年才转入了一家规模较大的钢铁厂当机械工人，这份工作一做就是将近10年，泰勒在该厂一直工作到1897年。这期间，生活的不如意并没有磨灭泰勒的意志，他保持着极大热忱，努力工作学习，后因表现优异，不断升迁，从普通的机械工被提拔为了车间管理员、小组长、技师，直至最后的总工程师。也正因为泰勒的这些一线经历，泰勒注意到工作环境缺乏工作标准，培养出了效率低下的工人，工作分配给了与技能和能力不匹配的人。除此之外，工人与经理之间还存在许多冲突。这些经历使他看到提高管理水平的极大的可能性，因此，泰勒一生大部分的时间所关注的，就是如何提高**生产效率**，至今为止依然被使用的计件工资制度就是出自这位大师之手。

Taylor finally reached a conclusion that the management could be improved under the guidance of the following principles (scientific management, n.d.):

(a) Developing a true science of management, which means find a best way of work and discard the old rules.

(b) Selecting, training and developing workers in a scientific manner.

(c) Using techniques when designing (e.g. micro-design) and assigning works (e.g. allocate compatible works to employees).

(d) Reducing the confrontation between managers and staffs and improving their co-operation (e.g. use money as an incentive).

2.1.3 Elton Mayo: human relations

事实上，随着社会与时代的飞速发展，人们的自我意识逐渐觉醒，主观能动力逐步增强，在生产过程中，人们不再满足于仅仅是充当与机器一样的角色了。泰勒提出的，单是靠报酬已经不能完全激励员工，言下之意也就是，提高生产效率的议题进入了瓶颈。在这种情况下，管理学家们开始意识到，尽管科学是第一生产力，但人的因素也的确是不可或缺的，我们应当给予同样的重视。

Elton Mayo underlined the importance of relationships among people who work for such organisations. This work helped to lay the foundation for the human relations movement.

Mayo's experience shows that the attitude and group relationship between workers are more evident for impacting the working efficiency, and the implication for management is that managers could motivate subordinates by meeting their psychological, social and belonging needs.

> **知识点解读**
>
> Mayo（梅奥）的人际关系学说通过霍桑实验，得出了以下两个重要结论：
> （1）人是"社会人"而不是"经济人"。所谓社会人，意味着金钱并非是唯一引发人们某些行为的动机，人是存在社会需求的，包括追求友情、安全感、归属感和外界尊敬等。
> （2）企业中存在着非正式组织。企业中除了存在着为了实现企业目标而明确规定各成员相互关系和职责范围的正式组织之外，还存在着非正式组织。非正式群体就是企业成员在共同工作的过程中，由于怀有共同的社会感情而形成的非正式团体。这在之前的Chapter 5中，可以在此回顾一下。

Note: Mayo also emphasized that alongside the formal organisation there exists an informal organisational structure as well. His ideas on group relations was based partly on his **Hawthorne research** (Chapter 5).

2.1.4 Neo-human relations

Based on previous research of relationship between employees' psychological needs and motivation, Maslow and Herzberg established Neo Human Relations School in 1950s.

Their work widen the scope of research into employees' psychological needs and put up theories in terms of motivation.

Limitations:

(a) The approach ignores economic issues;
(b) There is no proven link between job satisfaction and motivation.

2.2 Modern writers on management

2.2.1 Peter Drucker: the management process

Peter Drucker, the founder of modern management, invented the concept known as management by objectives and self-control. He argued that all managers perform five basic functions, including setting objectives, organising, **motivating and communicating**, establish job measurements and developing people. However, he emphasises that the manager of a business has one basic function—**economic performance**.

(A) Management tasks

Drucker categorised the basic management jobs into three types:

(a) Managing a business.
(b) Managing managers.
(c) Managing employees and work.

(B) Management processes

Drucker grouped the work of the manager into five categories.

(a) Determining or modifying objectives of the organisation.
(b) Organising and assigning the tasks to employees.
(c) Motivating and communicating with employees regularly.
(d) Monitoring employees' work and progress.
(e) Developing employees such as mentoring and rewarding them.

2.2.2 Mintzberg: the manager's role

Management expert Henry Mintzberg has argued that a manager's work can be divided into ten common roles. According to Mintzberg, these roles, or expectations for a manager's behaviour, fall into three categories: interpersonal (managing through people), informational (managing by information), and decisional (managing through action) (managerial roles, n.d.).

(a) Interpersonal

Figurehead (Representing in all formal occasions).

Leader (Dealing with personnel affairs such as evaluating and training).

Liaison (Acting as a networker between his organisation and the outside).

(b) **Informational**

Monitor (Gathering all relevant information from both inside and outside).

Spokesperson (Communicating the company to the outside).

Disseminator (Transmitting information inside).

(c) **Decisional**

Entrepreneur (Looking continually for problems and opportunities to help departments react to a changed environment).

Disturbance handler (Establishing solutions to respond accidents).

Resource allocator (Allocating resources to support the implementation of activities).

Negotiator (Participating in negotiations and protecting organisation's interests).

表 14-1 管理层角色

人际类角色:	
代表人	对于组织而言，代表人有着象征意义，通常需要代表公司出席一些对外的场合，履行社会职责
领导者	领导者通常负责雇佣和培训职员，负责对员工进行激励或者引导，以使他们的个人需求与组织目的达到和谐
联络者	联络者指的是经理同他所领导的组织以外的无数个人或团体维持关系所形成的重要网络
信息类角色:	
监督者	监督者通过询问联系人和下属，收集关于各种内部事务、外部事情和分析报告等信息
发言人	发言人这个角色是面向组织的外部的，简言之，就是把相关信息发送给组织之外的人。例如，CEO 可能要花大量时间与重要的利益相关者沟通信息，以及就财务状况向董事会和股东报告
传播者	组织内部可能会需要将获取的信息在企业内部进行传达，传播者角色承担的就是这样一种在企业内部，尤其是向下属传达信息的角色
决策类角色:	
企业家	企业家角色指的是经理在其职权范围之内充当本组织变革的发起者和设计者。管理者必须努力组织资源去适应周围环境的变化，要善于寻找和发现新的机会
干扰处理者	干扰处理者指的是，当组织面临着重大的动乱或者突发状况时，经理需要负责制定战略，采取补救行动
资源分配者	资源分配者需要负责组织结构的设计，包括分工和协调工种之间的关系，值得注意的是，这里说的资源分配，也包括经理自身的时间分配
谈判者	组织的运营过程中，会出现多种多样的谈判，不管是与内部（如员工、工会等）的谈判，还是与外部（如供应商、社会团体等）的谈判。谈判者的角色就是负责带领成员们进行诸如此类的谈判

The challenges on the classical view:

(a) In addition to managing employees and their works, managers also have their own routine tasks especially ceremonial work.

(b) Managers could also use informal communication channels and prefer informal communication.

(c) Management is complex and flexible which cannot be summed up by a simple profession or a science.

3 What is leadership

3.1 Definition

A basic definition of a leader is someone who exercises influence over other **people**.

事实上,到目前为止,业内并没有一个明确的概念能够定义"领导",但我们可以这么理解:领导并非一定来自授权,领导往往是通过自身的某种特质(如人格魅力、专业能力等)能够对他人产生影响,并使得他人心甘情愿地为组织目标工作的一种能力。

3.2 Management and leadership

Kotter distinguish management and leadership from two aspects:

Management deals with **complex and repeating matters** while leadership is about coping with **dynamic ones**.

From another aspect, management can be reflected through exerting power over non-personal **things** (**e.g. resources**) while leadership can only be exercised over **people**.

Being a leader can be an important part of being a management. More specifically, **a manager is not necessarily a leader**. A manager will only be a leader if he or she is able to influence people to achieve the goals of the organisation without relying on the use of formal authority.

领导与管理者这两个角色并非是独立存在,领导者通常是管理者,但管理者并不一定能够是一个领导者。 最理想的状态是,管理者同时又是领导者。

之所以会有上述说法,是因为要成为一名领导者,会有更高的要求,例如:

(1)具备发现商机的敏锐嗅觉,并能迅速作出反应,调配资源,抓住机会;

(2)具备优秀的沟通技能,能够维护和谐的工作环境,有冲突时能够解决冲突,并且能够倾听员工的意见,对员工进行有效开导;

(3)具备严格的管理时间的能力;

(4)具备自我不断学习的能力。

4 Schools of leadership theory

4.1 Trait or "qualities" theories

Trait theories identify the specific personality traits that distinguish leaders from non-leaders. Trait theories are based on the premise that **leaders are** "born, not made". In other words, leadership is largely innate, rather than being developed through learning.

知识点解读

领导理论可以分为三大类:
(1)特质理论:物质理论认为领导力源自天赋异禀;
(2)风格理论:风格理论又可以分为阿什里奇提出的管理学院理论以及布莱克提出的管理方格理论;
(3)权变理论:权变理论中具有代表性的有费德勒的权变模型和阿代尔的模型。

The qualities of a good leader consist of: Judgement, Initiative, Integrity, Foresight, Human relations skills, Fairness, Energy etc.

特质理论认为，领导力是先天的能力，不能通过后天的培养而形成。 领导者往往都具备同样的特质，如坚韧、果决、公平、公正等。 然而这样的理论，由于缺乏实证分析，并没有数据支持。 除此之外，该理论所列举的一些特质彼此之间也的确存在矛盾，很难同时出现在一名领导者身上，所以在业界，特质理论也受到相当一部分学者的批评。

There are several obvious flaws on the theory, however, for example:

(a) The so-called "traits" include too many qualities, which may be contradictory with each other;

(b) In addition, due to lack of empirical research, it is also difficult to substantiate these traits, and to prove the relations between these traits and success.

4.2 Style theories of leadership

In response to the early criticisms of the trait approach, theorists began to research leadership as a set of behaviors, evaluating the behavior of successful leaders and identifying broad leadership styles. Style theories of leadership argues that certain leadership approaches or style can be learnt and used by a leader depending on the situation.

In Paper AB, we should be aware of these two main style theories.

4.2.1 The Ashridge Management College Model

The research unit at Ashridge Management College distinguished four different leadership styles.

(a) **Tells (autocratic).** The leaders handle the power of decision making totally and their orders must be obeyed. This style of leadership maximise the speed of decision-making, while sacrificing the possibility of initiative and commitment form subordinates.

专制型（autocratic）——权力完全掌握在领导者个人手中，领导者极其注重工作效率以及目标的达成。 在这种团队中，除领导以外的其他成员均无权参与决策的制定。 他们只负责执行领导者的指令，服从具体的工作安排和人员调配。

(b) **Sells (persuasive).** Compare with the autocratic style, sells style prefers **to motivate subordinates to accept and obey decisions**, while **the power of decision making is still under control of superiors.** However, it is quite a problem needs to be considered that communications are still largely one-way, and employees are not necessarily motivated to accept the decision.

劝说型（persuasive）——权力虽然依然牢牢掌握在领导者手中，但是，领导者会采用相对循循善诱的方式劝说团队成员接受他所制定的决策。 值得注意的是，虽然领导者会就决策的实施与团队成员沟通，但很大程度上，这种沟通是单向的，也就说，还是带有强制性的。

(c) **Consults (consultative).** Leaders take the subordinates' views into consid-

---

知识点解读

风格理论认为：
领导力在特定的情况下，是可以后天培养的。

核心考点

四种领导方法由上到下的民主程度依次增加，同时，做决策所花时间也依次增加。 注意辨别区分四种领导方式下，员工参与决策的程度以及最终决定权的归属。 本考点属于高频考点，请熟练掌握。

eration, although they **still hold the final say**. Under this style, employees can contribute their knowledge and the leader may make a better decision. However, it maybe time consuming.

咨询型（consultative）——权力有所下放，然后最终决定权（final say）依然掌握在领导者手中。团队成员可以参与决策制定过程，对决策作出建议，但并不能最终拍板。在这种情况下，团队制定决策可能需要花费较长时间。

(d) **Joins** (**democratic**). Under Joins style, decisions are made on the consensus basis, which can effectively boost employees' motivation and commitment. However, it has the same problem as consults style, time consuming.

民主型（democratic）——权力掌握在团队全员手中，这种情况下的领导者只起到一个指导者或委员会主持人的作用，其主要任务就是在成员之间进行调解和仲裁。团队的目标和工作方针要尽量公之于众，征求大家的意见并尽量获得大家的赞同。具体的工作安排和人员调配等问题，均要经共同协商决定。

知识点解读

管理方格图（见图 14-1）是一张纵轴和横轴各 9 等分的方格图，纵轴表示企业领导者对人的关心程度，横轴表示企业领导者对业绩的关心程度。其中，第 1 格表示关心程度最小，第 9 格表示关心程度最大。

4.2.2 Blake and Mouton's managerial grid

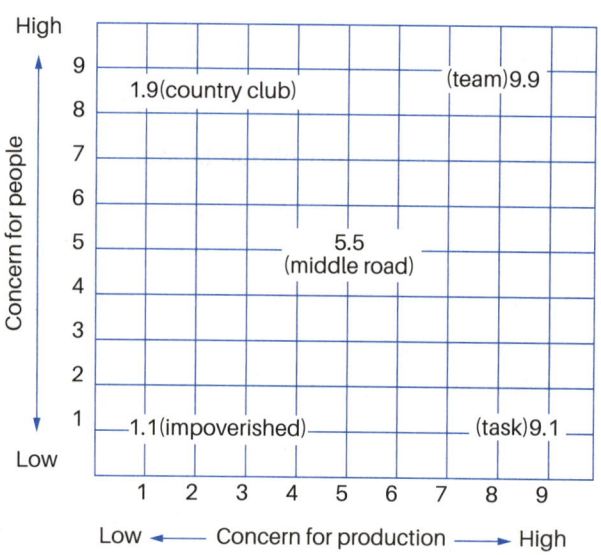

图 14-1　Black and Mouton's managerial grid

Robert Blake and Jane Mouton carried out research about leadership style and observed through two aspects of leadership: **concern for production** (or task performance) and **concern for people**. There are five key points here:

(a) **1.1 Impoverished** (**Low production/Low people**): such leaders neither care about staff nor production, who are quite lazy.

贫乏的领导者既不关心业绩也不关心员工，这种领导者几乎已放弃自己的职责，只想保住自己的地位。

(b) **1.9 Country club** (**Low production/High people**): such leaders put more attention on employees' requirements, aiming to build satisfying relationships. However, little attention is paid on results.

俱乐部式领导者对人的关心多过对业绩的关心,这种领导者致力于营造出一派和谐的轻松氛围,但很严重地忽略了业绩的重要性。

(c) **9.1 Task management/Authoritarian**(**High production/Low people**):Such leaders are converse with those of country club. All their concentration is put on achieving results, while ignoring people's needs.

专制式领导者对业绩关心多,对人关心少,员工在这种领导者眼中与生产使用的机器并无不同,他们只关注业绩,丝毫不在乎员工的需求。

(d) **5.5 Middle of the road**(**Medium production/medium people**):this leader is able to balance the task in hand and motivate the people to achieve these tasks.

小市民式领导者这种领导者秉持着中庸之道的理念,既不偏重于关心生产,也不偏重于关心人,不会设置过高的目标,影响团队氛围和士气,也不会过分忽略业绩,但这种领导方式很难作出卓越的成效。

(e) **9.9 Team**(**High production/High people**):It is a rather ideal style that leaders can balance the emphasis of production and people simultaneously.

理想式领导者这种领导者对生产和对人都很关心,在管理过程中把企业的生产需要同个人的需要紧密结合起来,既能带来生产力和利润的提高,又能使员工得到事业的成就与满足。

This model is used to help leaders analyse their own leadership styles. This is done by administering a questionnaire that helps leaders identify how they stand with respect to their concern for production and people. The training is aimed at basically helping leaders reach to the ideal state of 9.9.

The limitations of the theory:

(a) People sometimes are not free to move to "team".

(b) Over-simplification. In fact, many other factors will also affect the leadership style except those two concerns.

(c) Resulting in inconsistency in operation.

4.2.3 Limitations of style approaches

The style theory of leadership had been an advanced research in this field, however, there is a problem which cannot be ignored, that is, there is no one style which can be suitable for all conditions. The demand of task, difference of culture, utilisation of technology etc., may require different types of leadership to achieve effectiveness and final goals.

Simply speaking, the demands are dynamic, while the leadership according to style theory is relatively stable, which may not be matched perfectly.

4.3 Contingency approaches to leadership

In essence, contingency theory suggests that there is no constant leadership style or approach. A number of variable or contingent factors should be taken into consideration to achieve effective leadership.

知识点解读

相较于特质理论来说,风格理论的出现已然是一个很大的进步,然而,它依然存在着一些问题:
(1)根据风格理论来看,领导是可以后天培养的,然而,这并不意味着每一个管理者都可以被培养出理想的领导风格;
(2)事实上,并不存在一种万能的领导风格可以应对所有情况;
(3)鉴于领导风格的一致性对于员工来说极为重要,那不断变化的领导风格又该如何保持这种一致性,这是一个问题。

知识点解读

权变理论:
领导力不是一成不变的,应该随着情况的变化而变化。

> **知识点解读**
>
> 图 14-2 的意思是，在下属非常喜欢和非常不喜欢领导的情况下，领导应该和下属保持距离，因为如果下属非常喜欢领导，领导就不需要刻意和下属搞好关系，而如果下属非常不喜欢领导，领导在人际关系上花再多精力也没用。只有在下属比较喜欢领导的情况下，领导才需要主动和下属打成一片。这样的处理方式有利于团队效率的提高。

4.3.1 F·E·Fiedler

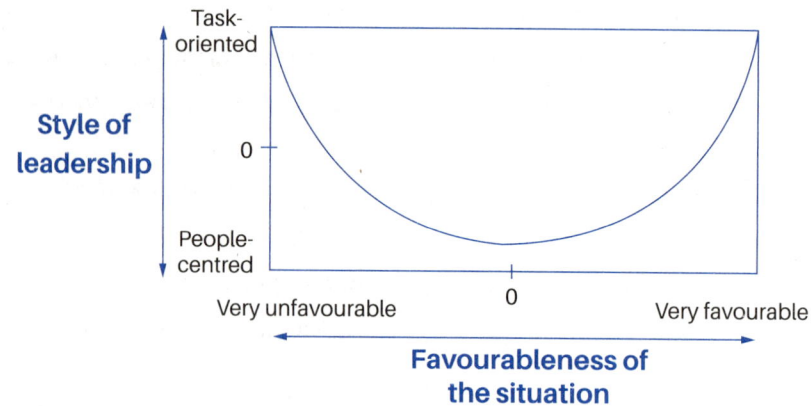

图 14-2　Fiedler-two types of leader

费德勒权变模型又被称为情境模型，该模型提出的观点是：领导风格应当与不同情境相匹配。首先，我们可以解决第一个问题——情境该如何区分。

(a) **The favorableness of a work group depended on three key variables.**

Fielder argued that leaders should adopt different styles to suit different circumstances. And three key variables should be considered first:

● The relationship between the leader and the group.

● The extent to which the task is defined and structured.

● The power of the leader in relation to the group.

In Fielder's research, the situation is most favourable for leaders when they have a strong relationship with their group while group tasks are well defined and when their power is high.

费德勒认为会有三个方面影响情境：

（1）**上下级关系**。例如，下属对其领导者的信任、喜爱、忠诚、愿意追随的程度。

（2）**任务结构**。例如，团队所执行的工作是枯燥乏味的例行公事，还是需要具备一定创造性的。

（3）**职位权力**。这是指与领导者职位相关联的正式职权以及领导者从上级和整个组织各个方面所取得的支持程度。简言之，就是领导者的权限大小。

其次，我们需要了解不同的领导风格。

(b) **Two types of leader**

Feidler distinguishes between two types of leader-those who are psychologically close and those who are psychologically distant.

● Psychologically distant managers prefer formal relationships. They tend to be reserved in their personal relationships even though they often have good interpersonal skills. This approach is sometimes called "task oriented".

任务导向型领导，这种领导风格非常偏重生产效率，领导会为了保证团队目标的顺利达成而与下属保持一定距离，这种风格会使得会议之类的正式途径成为上下级之间的主要沟通渠道。

● On the contrary, psychologically close managers prefer informal relationships, are sometimes over concerned with human relations, and favour informal rather than formal contacts. This is sometimes called 'relationship oriented

与之相反的，是人文导向型领导，这种领导风格以人为本，注重员工价值，领导会倾向于跟员工打成一片，形成亲密关系，这种风格之下，非正式渠道会成为上下级之间的主要沟通途径。

最后，我们可以得出结论，即在不同情景下，适用不同的领导风格。

(c) **The conclusions**

PDMs perform well when the situation is either very favourable or very unfavorable to the leader.

PCMs perform well when the situation is moderately favourable to the leader.

4.3.2 John Adair: action-centred leadership

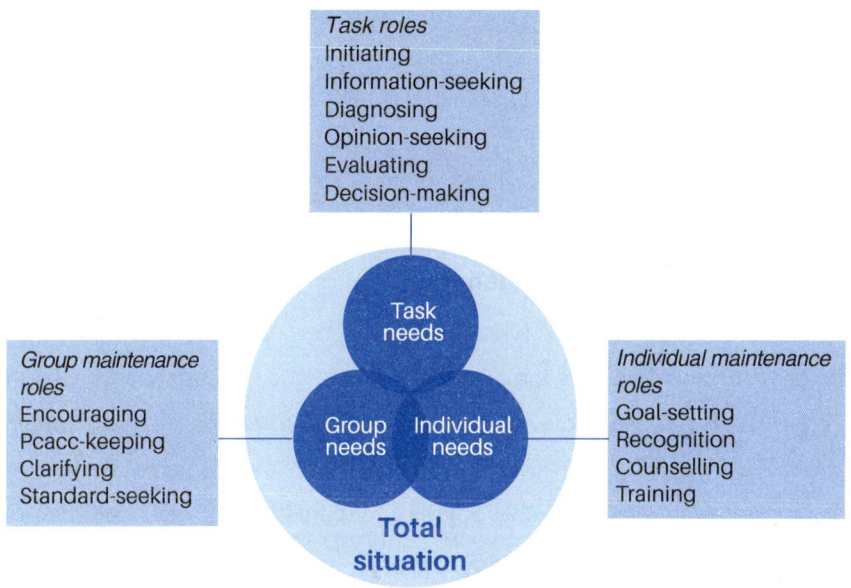

图 14-3　John Adair: action-centred leadership

> **知识点解读**
>
> John Adair 的以行动为中心的领导模式（如图 14-3 所示），三个环具有重叠的部分，因为：
> （1）任务只能由小组执行，不能由一个人执行；
> （2）只有在所有个人都得到充分发展的情况下，团队才能取得出色的任务绩效；
> （3）个人需要具有挑战和激励的任务。

It sees the leadership process in a context made up of three interrelated variables as a whole:

(a) **Task needs** (achieving the task).

(b) **Individual needs** (motivating and developing the individuals).

(c) **Group needs** (building and maintaining the group).

Good leaders should be able to consider each of the elements according to the situation to identify the priority of each task and keep the right balance between get results, build morale, improve quality, develop teams and productivity.

4.3.3 Theories of Bennis

(A) Distinction between management and leadership

Bennis hold the view that:

Managers administer and maintain, by focusing on **systems and controls** and holds a short-term view. That is, manager is someone who **does things right.**

Leaders innovate, focus on people and inspire trust, and hold a long-term view. That is, leader is someone who **does the right thing**.

(B) Two types of leaders

(a) Transactional leaders: leaders promote service, loyalty and compliance by followers through rewards.

(b) Transformational leaders: leaders are able to inspire followers to change expectations, perceptions, and motivations to work towards common goals. Only transformational leadership is able to change organisational cultures and move the organisation to a new stage.

(C) Six leadership qualities

(a) **Integrity.**

(b) **Dedication.**

(c) Magnanimity.

(d) Humility.

(e) Openness.

(f) Creativity.

4.3.4 Heifetz: dispersed leadership

Heifetz states that no one will be an ideal leader in every circumstance. Each member in organisations has the area that they are good at so that anyone within an organisation may have provide some degree of leadership in certain circumstances. This means that leaders may sometimes simply emerge, rather than being formally appointed. This is known as 'dispersed leadership'.

4.3.5 Appraisals of contingency theory

Contingency theories are often seen as the most practical, as they encourage leaders to understand the current circumstances and adapt their approach accordingly.

However:

(a) It is difficult to identify exact variables to measure conditions to match appropriate leadership;

(b) The theory ignores the technical competence required by leaders' jobs and positions;

(c) It is also difficult for leaders to vary their leadership approach on a regular basis.

Answers for example question

1. C

Summary

Chapter 14 考试不同问法总结

1. 针对 Basic concepts

- Which of the following describes the power of an individual to instruct another person to undertake a task?
- Are the following key tasks of operational supervisors?

- Which statement correctly defines leadership?

2. 针对 Management theory
- Which TWO of the following are included in Fayol's five functions of management?
- According to Mintzberg, which management role is A performing?
- Which TWO of the following are relevant to the informational role category?
- Herry Mintzberg suggests that in their working lives, managers perform three types of managerial role. The roles are interpersonal, informational and _____.

3. 针对 Leadership theory
- According to Kotter, leadership is primarily about which of the following?
- Which of the following is used by Blake and Mouton in their leadership grid?
- What status is A's new leadership style moving towards on the Blake and Mouton Managerial Grid?
- According to Blake and Mouton's Managerial Grid, which managerial style is exhibited by each directors?
- Which of the following describes the "country club" style of management identified by Blake and Mouton's managerial grid?
- Which TWO of the following are leadership qualities according to Warren Bennis?
- Which of the following statements is consistent with the leadership theory of Warren Bennis?
- Would psychologically distant managers display the following characteristics?

Quick quiz

14.1 Which of the following describes the PDM style identified by Fiedler?

    A. PDM only performs well in very unfavourable circumstances

    B. PDM are liked by the group as they are highly skilled

    C. PDM have a high distance of hierarchy from subordinates

    D. PDM prefer formal channel of contacting with the group

Answer: **D**

Difficulty level: **Normal**

Tag: **Contingency theory- F·E·Fiedler**

Rationale:

    PDM means the manager has a higher psychological distance than power distance with employees. They prefer formal relationship and communicating methods with employees. This style performs well in both very favourable and unfavourable situations.

    PDM 的领导风格指的是领导与其下属的心理距离比较遥远，而非权利距离或者权利分配上比较遥远。 具有这种风格的领导喜欢将自己与员工的关系和沟通正式化。 并且，由于他们往往是以任务为导向的，会以工作或任务的实现为目标，因而这种领导风格在情况非常有利和非常不利的情况都更加适用。 另外，PDM 与 PCM 是对领导管理员工、与员工沟通的风格和方式的分类，与领导自身的技能不相关。

14.2 Yi has a leadership style that emphasis too much on task completion. After experiencing complaints by its subordinates, he is now considering better treatment for them.

    According to Blake and Mouton's Managerial Grid, what status is Yi's new leadership style moving towards?

    A. Authoritarian   B. Country club   C. Middle of the road   D. Team

Answer: **D**

Difficulty level: **Normal**

Tag: **Blake and Mouton's Managerial Grid**

Rationale:

    According to Blake and Mouton's Managerial Grid, the leaderships of different person could be categorised via two dimensions: the degree of concern for people and task. Based on the descriptions in this scenario, the leader Yi concerned more on outcome but cares little on subordinates' feeling, which means its leadership style ranks high in the dimension of task and low in the dimension of people. However he is now thinking improve the treatment for employees, which will lead to an increase of the degree of concern for people. Thus the desirable outcome for him is to arrive at the status of Team.

    管理方格理论从两个维度对领导风格进行了分类，这两个维度分别是关心任务的程度和关心员工的程度。 根据题目的描述，Yi 之前的领导风格更偏向于任务导向，而忽略了员工的感受，因此他的风格很可能是 9.1Authoritarian 类型。 在收到大量的员工的抱怨之后，他想要提高对员工的待遇和态度，所以他想要最终实现的结果是 9.9Team 类型，即 "双高型"——既关心结果又关心员工。

14.3 Which of the following writers is not a member of the classical writers on management thought to which the others belong?

    A. F·W·Taylor   B. Elton Mayo   C. Henri Fayol   D. Peter Drucker

Answer: D

Difficulty level: Normal

Tag: writers on management

Rationale:

The classical school of management theories were developed during the Industrial Revolution of the mid-to-late 1800s and early 1900s. They are largely concerned with improving efficiency and productivity. They include Henri Fayol, F·W·Taylor, Elton Mayo, but Peter Drucker belongs to Modern writers.

这道题考查的是考生能否清晰地区分各个著名的学者所属流派。在这道题里，Peter Drucker 是属于现代管理学派的典型代表，他也被称为现代管理学之父。而其他的 3 位作者属于古典管理学派的代表。所以答案选 D。

14.4 Which of the following is an 'Decisional' role of management, according to Mintzberg's nine managerial roles?

    A. Spokesperson   B. Figurehead   C. Liaison   D. Resource allocator

Answer: D

Difficulty level: Easy

Tag: Mintzberg's nine managerial roles

Rationale:

Management expert Henry Mintzberg has argued that a manager's work can be divided into ten common roles. According to Mintzberg, these roles, or expectations for a manager's behaviour, fall into three categories: interpersonal (Figurehead, Leader, Liaison), informational (Monitor, Spokesperson, Disseminator), and decisional (Entrepreneur, Disturbance handler, Resource allocator).

这道题意在让考生区分 Mintzberg's nine managerial roles 的 3 大类 10 小种，而题目问属于决策角色的是哪一项，这一大类应该是"资源分配者"，所以答案选 D。

14.5 There are all leadership qualities according to Warren Bennis except one. **Which is the exception?**

    A. Magnanimity   B. Superiority   C. Dedication   D. Humility

Answer: B

Difficulty level: Easy

Tag: Warren Bennis-six leadership qualities

Rationale:

Bennis stated that leader should have six qualities: Integrity, Dedication, Magnanimity, Humility, Openness and Creativity. Therefore, option B is answer.

Bennis 认为一个优秀的领导应该包含六个品质：正直、无私奉献、宽宏大量、谦卑、公开以及有创造力。因此，只有 B 选项没有包含在内，故选 B。

14.6 Which of the following description correctly matches the 'authoritarian' style of management according to Blake and Mouton's managerial grid?

    A. Highly care for subordinates and for tasks

    B. Pay less attention on tasks and people

    C. Emphasize on production but not concentrate on people

    D. Prefer to "sell" style of management

Answer: C

Difficulty level: Easy

Tag: Blake and Mouton's managerial grid

Rationale:

According to Blake and Mouton's managerial gird, "authoritarian" style means that leaders concern for production but not for people. Thus, option C is correct.

布莱克和莫顿的管理网格理论中的"authoritarian"风格,指的是那些只关注生产但是不关注人的领导风格,所以答案选 C。

Chapter 15
Performance appraisal

知识导入

上一章中，我们跟随着管理学界的大咖们学习了领导与管理的精髓。 大道至简，我们研究领导和管理，都是为了我们整个组织的高效运营。 如何衡量管理与领导的有效性？ 这就是本章我们要学的绩效评估。 事实上，绩效评估从属于一个更大的体系，即绩效管理。 绩效评估是绩效管理的一个环节，所以我们会先补充绩效管理的知识，但是本章的重点仍然是绩效评估。

单词表

英文	中文
Continuous	连续的
Appraise	评价
Reprisal	报复
Confrontation	对抗
Bureaucracy	官僚主义
Objective	客观的

学习指南

Learning objectives	Pass level	Distinction level	用时建议
1.Performance management（精益求精）		√	3 mins
2.Performance appraisal（1）	√		5 mins
3.The process of formal performance appraisal（2）	√		15 mins
4.Benefits and barriers of performance appraisal（3）		√	8 mins

本章考点

重要考点	难度（1~3）
熟记绩效评估的目的是什么	1
熟记并理解一个正式的绩效评估流程的运作方式	1
着重记忆几种绩效评估的方式和各自的优缺点	2
着重记忆绩效评估使用技巧的不同	1
熟记并理解 Maier's three approaches	2
理解绩效评估的优点和绩效评估的一些阻碍	2

> **精益求精**
>
> 绩效管理，是指各级管理者和员工为了达到组织目标共同参与的绩效计划制定、绩效辅导沟通、绩效考核评价、绩效结果应用、绩效目标提升的持续循环过程。绩效管理的目的是持续提升个人、部门和组织的绩效。
>
> 业绩管理一般有如下五个步骤。
>
> （1）在业务计划初期，确定执行该计划所需的要求和能力。
>
> （2）起草绩效协议，拟定个人或团队的期望标准，包括绩效标准、考核指标以及岗位所需的技能。
>
> （3）与个人或团队共同制定绩效和发展计划。
>
> （4）全年持续管理绩效，而不仅仅是在人事部门要求的评估过程中进行。管理者可以在一年中的不同时间通过更非正式的临时审查来评估实际绩效。
>
> （5）绩效考核。每年在一个确定的时间段内，对年初计划的实施进行审查，审查不应局限在过去发生的事项，还应当评估未来的影响。

1 Performance appraisal

Performance appraisal, also referred to as performance review or performance evaluation, is part of performance management and is a method by which the key results an individual needs to achieve within a time period are established and also individual's performance can be compared against it.

绩效考核是业绩管理中非常重要的一项。通过绩效考核，员工以及团队的表现可以得到合理的评估，从而得到相应的奖惩。值得注意的是，绩效考核的意义并非局限于奖惩，其对员工或团队后续的发展有着同样深远的意义。

Appraisal exists to improve organisational efficiency by ensuring that individuals perform to the best of their ability, develop their potential and earn appropriate reward, which in turn leads to improved organisational performance.

1.1 The three main purposes of performance appraisal

(a) The first is to measure the extent to which an individual may be **awarded** a salary increase compared with his or her peers. This is the **reward review** component.
(b) The second purpose of an appraisal is to identify any **training needs** and, if appropriate, to provide training and development to enable an individual to help the organisation to achieve its objectives. This is the **performance review** component.
(c) Finally, appraisals are also important to aid an individual's career development by attempting to predict work that the individual may be capable of in the future. This is the **potential review** component.

> **知识点解读**
>
> 绩效考核的目的：
> （1）奖惩；
> （2）通过考核发现员工的实际能力与岗位需求之间差距，从而给予员工合适的培训以提高技能；
> （3）通过考核发现员工的潜力，在日后的工作中可以更好地实现人尽其才物尽其用。

2 The process of formal performance appraisal

A formal appraisal system can be depicted as follows.

典型的绩效评估应该包含以下的几个环节，接下来我们就分别来学习每个环节具体做什么，其中，report 以及 interview 的环节是 FAB 学习的重点，其他环节了解即可（见图 15 – 1）。

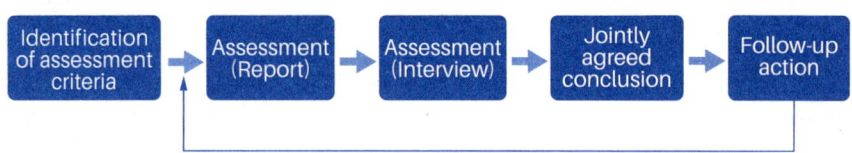

Feedback

图 15 – 1　Process of performance appraisal

> **知识点解读**
>
> 绩效评估是同学们需要理解的一个知识点。首先，评估活动并不是单项活动，它是需要 feedback 的，也就是评估者与被评估者之间的沟通。其次，评估不是一项独立的活动，它是一个在日常经营中循环往复的过程，即通过评估，员工应当有更好的业绩表现体现在后续的生产经营中。

2.1 Identification of assessment criteria

The formulation of desired traits and standards against which individuals can be consistently and objectively assessed. The process requires constant and thorough discussions among managers and subordinates.

第一步：确立评估的标准。这个步骤需要上下级共同参与讨论确立，而不应该是单方向的，这样才能保证评估标准的客观性与合理性。

2.2 Assessment（report）

第二步，制作公允的绩效评估报告。在这个过程中，我们需要绩效数据作为依据，接下来我们来学习获取数据的方法（appraisal methods）和技巧（appraisal technique）。

2.2.1 Appraisal methods

（a）**Downward-appraisal**

This is quite common in all organisations.

这是企业中最常见的一种评估方式，从上至下，即上级对下级作评估的方式。

（b）**Upward-appraisal**

表 15 – 1　Appraisal of upward-appraisal

Advantages	Disadvantages
More reliable (Subordinates know their superior better)	Fear of reprisals
A useful way to collect information from lower levels	Some bosses refuse to act

与 downward-appraisal 刚好相反，upward-appraisal 指的是下级对上级进行评估的方式。

（c）**Self-appraisal**

Many schemes combine managerial appraisal and self-appraisal.

表 15 – 2　Appraisal of self-appraisal

Advantages	Disadvantages
Save management time, as the employee identifies the areas of competence which are relevant to the job and his/her relative strengths	Not the best judges of own performance, as employees tend to **overestimate** to gain approval

> **知识点解读**
>
> 实施自下而上评估的企业，员工在对上级进行评估时，会因为害怕被上级打击报复而不敢对上级作出真实的评价（见表 15 – 1、表 15 – 2）。

续表

Advantages	Disadvantages
Increase responsibility to individuals, which may improve motivation and lead to better performance.	—

自我评估是一种非常能发挥员工主观能动性的评估方式，从某种程度上可以调动员工的积极性。当然非常显而易见的是，在这种评估方式之下，是否能保持客观性是最大的关注点。

(d) **Customer appraisal**

In some companies, especially those in service sector, part of employee's appraisal result are taken from customers (whether internal or external).

客户评估是指从客户角度来评估员工，这种评估方式在服务行业特别常见。这里的 internal 和 external 指的是 customers 是来自公司内部还是外部。公司外部的顾客是公司最为重要的利益相关者之一，搜集来自外部 customer 的评价对提升公司产品和服务质量至关重要。而内部的顾客指的是一些特殊情况下产生的来自公司内部的 customer，比如公司拥有 IT 共享中心，为公司其他部门提供服务，则其服务质量的高低，完全可以由公司其他部门员工来评判。

(e) **360-degree/multi-source appraisal**

It means taking downwards, upwards and customer and self-appraisals together. The feedback can be collected from managers, subordinates, peers and co-workers, customers and the individual himself. It is the **most objective** appraisal approach among all.

360-degree appraisal，顾名思义，指 360°无死角的评估方式。简单来说，就是融合了以上考核方式的信息来源，将该员工在工作中所接触的所有角色（如上司、下属、同级、客户等）都纳入考核的范围，通过这种方式，可以建立一个更加立体的评估对象，很大程度上规避了评估的片面性。

2.2.2 Appraisal techniques

A variety of appraisal techniques may be used to measure critical criteria from different perspectives. The most appropriate method will depend upon the circumstances and people involved.

(a) **Overall assessment**

Managers write in **narrative form in judgement** about the appraisees. There will be **no guaranteed consistency of the criteria and areas of assessment**, however, some managers may not be able to convey clear, effective judgements in writing.

总体评估，也叫定性评估，指的是上级用一段描述性的文字对下属评价。

(b) **Guided assessment**

Managers are required to comment on a number of **specified performance elements**, with guidelines as to how terms are used.

引导性评估，评估者被要求根据从几个特定方面对员工进行评估。比如，个人品性、业务能力、沟通能力等。

> **核心考点**
>
> 关于绩效评估的技巧，考试中很容易以案例题的形式考查考生的理解能力，考生需要掌握每种评估技巧的特征，做题时请留意关键词，如 overall assessment 的关键特征在于 narrative judgment，上级写一段描述性的文字，则每个上级的文风和评估标准均有不同。

(c) Grading

Managers are asked to select the **levels or degrees** to which employees display under a given appraisal criteria. Grading facilitates managers to **compare** performance among employees and to decide follow-up rewards or training more quickly.

等级评估法，给出不同等级的定义和描述（如优秀、良好、中等、及格、不及格），然后针对每一个评价要素或绩效指标按照给定的等级进行评估，最后再给出总的评价。

(d) Behavioural incident method

This method concentrates on **employee's behaviour**, which is **measured against typical behaviour** of each job, as defined by common critical incidents of successful and unsuccessful job behaviour reported by managers.

关键事件法，要求将最有利和最不利的工作行为进行书面记录保存。当一种行为对部门产生重大影响（无论消极还是积极）时，管理者都把它记录下来，这样的事件便称为关键事件。在考绩后期，评价者运用这些记录和其他资料对员工的业绩进行评价。

(e) Results-orientated schemes

This reviews **performance against specific targets and standards** of performance agreed in advance by manager and subordinate together.

目标考评法，考评人和被考评人事先对需要完成的工作内容、时间期限、考评的标准达成一致，在时间期限结束时，考评人根据被考评人的工作状况及原先制定的考评标准来进行考评，这种考核方式在跟业绩挂钩的部门中十分常见。

小试牛刀

Example question 1

Which of the following is likely to be the most accurate approach to appraisal?

A. Self-appraisal   B. Customer appraisal

C. Upward appraisal   D. 360-degree appraisal

2.3 Assessment (interview)

The basis of successful appraisal system is the appraisal interview. The interview must be organised properly and carefully. Prior to the interview, the appraiser, who should be the immediate supervisor, must prepare the correct and relevant documentation. This comprises the job description, a statement of performance or appraisal form, and a record highlighting the employee's performance. Other relevant documentation used at an appraisal can include peer assessments, if appropriate, comments from clients and customers, and any self-assessment forms issued to the employee prior to the interview.

2.3.1 Maier's three approaches: The appraisal interview

(a) The tell and sell style

The appraiser **explains** how the assessment is to be undertaken, **trying to gain acceptance** for the evaluation and improvement plan. Interpersonal skills are important with this approach to motivate the appraisee.

经理完全主导，告知员工绩效评估的结果，同时告知改进计划以及争取员工的同意，基本不与员工进行商讨。

(b) The tell and listen style

The appraiser **explains** how the assessment is to be undertaken and the appraisee is **invited to respond** to the way that the interview is to be conducted. This requires counselling skills and careful encouragement to allow the appraisee to participate fully.

经理部分主导，告知员工绩效评估的结果，同时给员工对自身表现进行解释的机会，共同商讨改进意见。

(c) The problem-solving style

This is a more helpful approach which **concentrates on the work problems** of the appraisee, who in turn is encouraged to think through any problems. After the interview, both parties should agree on any actions to be taken, an agreed action plan on improvement, and methods of monitoring progress and appropriate feedback.

员工从自身出发，对自己的绩效进行评估和提出改进计划，经理仅仅给予咨询和指导。

> **核心考点**
> 这个知识点是本章最核心也最高频的考点，考核方式很直接，基本都是针对不同评估方式的定义出题，往往会给出一个背景或者案例，让考生进行判断。因此，考生需要对这个知识点进行理解并运用。

2.4 Jointly agreed conclusion

It involves getting the appraiser and appraisee together for feedback and planning.

2.5 Follow-up action

This involves improvement on behaviour. The actions involve:

(a) Inform appraisee of the results.

(b) Take action as agreed.

(c) Continually monitor progress.

(d) Help the appraisee to ascertain improvement objectives.

小试牛刀

Example question 2

Jack is the director of the finance department. He tells Mary, his subordinate, her annual performance and then gives her a chance to explain about the results of performance and the suggestions on improvement.

Which approach of appraisal interviewing does Jack use according to Maier's classification?

A. Tell and listen   B. Sell and listen   C. Problem solving   D. Tell and sell

Example question 3

Example question 3

Mary is carrying out a performance appraisal interview with Katezim, her assistant. Katezim has described her views on the job and the responsibilities it entails and has given opinions on how she would like to progress in the future. Mary has acknowledged Katezim's views and has prompted further input by asking open questions and noting the responses given. Mary has invited Katezim to ask questions and has given short, focused responses to her concerns.

The approach to performance appraisal adopted by Mary is which of the following?

A. 360-degree appraisal   B. Joint problem solving

C. Tell and sell   D. Tell and listen

3 Benefits and barriers of performance appraisal

3.1 Benefits of appraisal

For organisation, it benefits from identifying employees for promotion, noting areas for individual improvement, and using the system as a basis for long term human resource planning.

For employees, they often question the value and usefulness of the time and effort taken up by an appraisal. However, as we have learned above, appraisal establishes key results that an individual needs to achieve within a time period while also comparing the individual's performance against a set and established standard. Through this process, employees can have a clearer view of their performance and managers' expectation.

在之前,我们已经罗列了很多绩效评估的益处。 但倘若绩效评估本身出现一些障碍,会直接影响评估的结果。 因此,我们还需了解的最后一个相关问题就是:影响有效绩效评估的障碍有哪些?

3.2 Barriers to effective performance appraisal

There is often misunderstanding as to how an appraisal should be conducted:

(A) **Appraisal as confrontation**

This is often due to a lack of agreement on performance or poor explanation by management.

评估进行之前,如果管理层缺乏沟通解释或者与下属没有对评估内容达成一致,员工很容易对评估这项活动非常抵触。

(B) **Appraisal as judgement**

The appraisal is seen as a one-sided process based entirely on the manager's perspective.

好的评估应当是双向沟通,而并非是由评估者一家独断。

(C) **Appraisal as chat**

At the other extreme to judgment, some managers treat appraisal as relaxed chat, and do not hit the right note after appraisal.

评估应当是一项严肃客观的活动,不能因为日常经营活动中形成的密切关系,影响到评估活动的进行和结果。

(D) Appraisal as bureaucracy

Appraisal is a form-filling process designed to satisfy the requirement of management and HR department. Consequently, the main purpose of an appraisal that of identifying individual and organisational performance shortage and improvement is forgotten.

(E) Appraisal as annual event

Appraisal is carried out only once a year. Thus, the results become irrelevant or out-of-date. Feedback, goal adjustment and improvement planning should be a continuous process.

正如之前我们提到过的，管理者可以在一年中的不同时间通过一些非正式的临时审查来评估实际绩效，通过这种方式管理层可以获得更及时有效的信息，自然也能对日常中的问题形成更快的应对。

(F) Appraisal and pay

Another problem is the extent to which the appraisal system is related to the pay and reward system. Many employees consider that positive appraisals should be rewarded, but there are major drawbacks to this approach.

(a) Pay rises rarely depend on individual performance only.

(b) Continuous improvement should not be rewarded as extra.

(c) Performance management should also be forward looking.

Answers for example question:

1. D
2. A
3. B

Summary

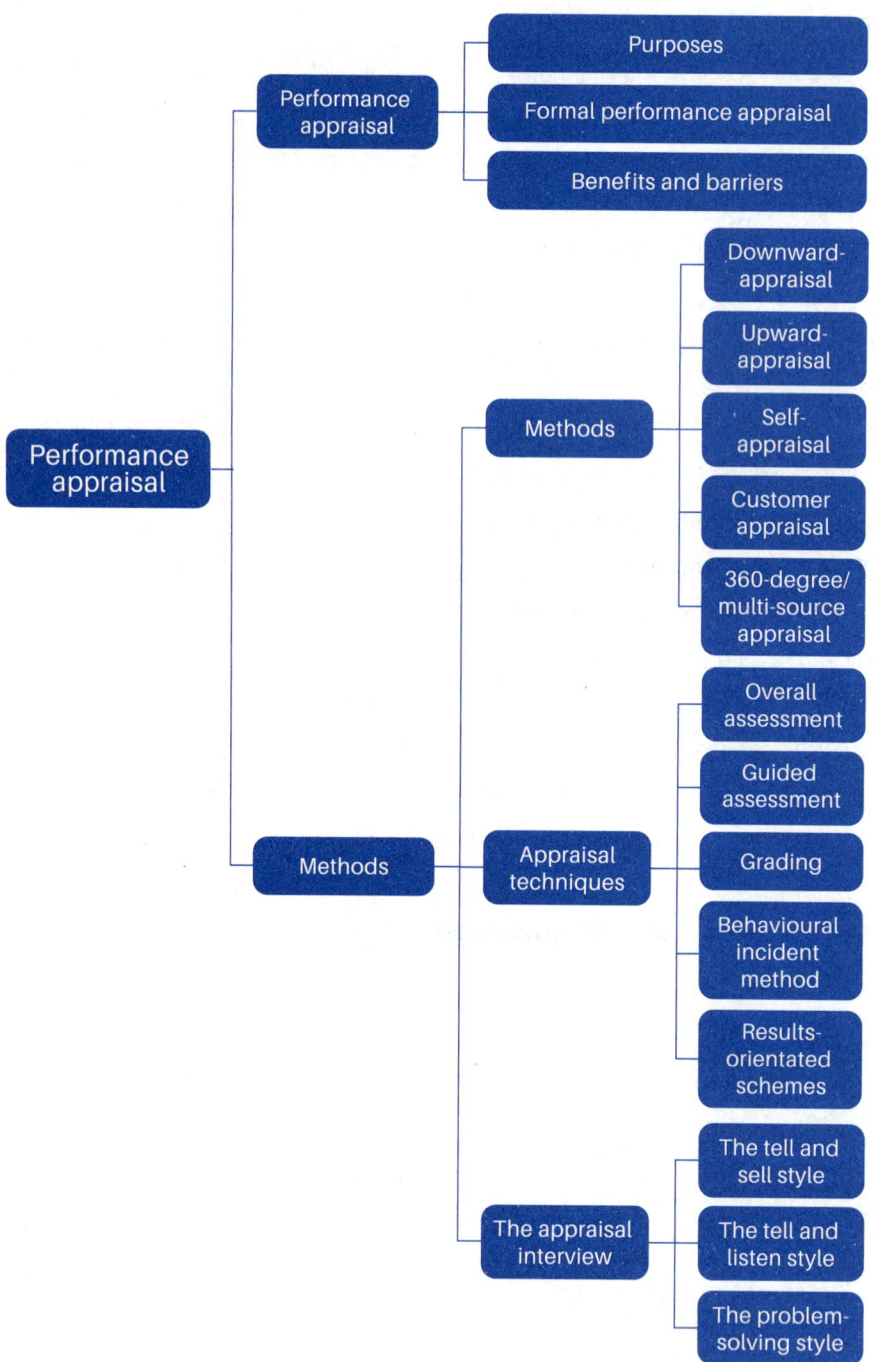

Chapter 15 考试不同问法总结

Section A

- Which TWO of the following are fair criteria to assess A's performance?
- Which purpose of the appraisal process does each statement demonstrate?
- What is the correct order for the following elements of the appraisal process?
- Which of the following are essential characteristics of a good appraisal?
- Which of the following would be involved as part of an effective appraisal system?

- Which of the following is the key benefit of 360° appraisal?

Section B

- Is each of the following a benefit of an effective appraisal system?
- Which barriers to effective appraisal have been described by each of the employees?

Quick quiz

15.1 Which of the following attributes should be included in a good appraisal?

(1) Continuous follow-up.

(2) Individual desire.

(3) Forward looking.

(4) Pay reward.

A. (1) and (2) only
B. (2) and (3) only
C. (1) and (3) only
D. (1) (3) and (4)

Answer: C

Difficulty level: Normal

Tag: Performance appraisal

Rationale:

Appraisal should be part of a continuing future-focused process of performance management, so continuous follow-up and forward looking should be contained. In addition, rewards should not relate to appraisal due to some drawbacks. Therefore, option C is correct.

一个好的绩效评估应该着眼于未来而非过去,它需要包含持续的后续动作和前瞻性。 而同时,一个好的绩效评估中,不能将报酬和绩效挂钩,因为薪酬的上涨会受很多因素影响,因此答案为 C 选项。

15.2 Which of the following is a target of performance appraisal?

A. Ensure all appraisees' performance is enhanced

B. Ensure individual objectives are known and met

C. Ensure all involved employees' disadvantages will be eliminated

D. Ensure right financial rewards were paid to current employees

Answer: D

Difficulty level: Easy

Tag: The purpose of performance appraisal

Rationale:

Performance appraisals have three main purposes: reward review, performance review and potential review. Therefore, reward review means that appraisers should measure the extent to which an individual may be awarded a salary increase compared with peers. Then option D is correct.

绩效评估有三个主要的目标:奖励复核、业绩复核、潜力复核。 奖励复核,强调的是去检查员工所获得的的报酬或加薪是应得的,因此选 D 选项。

15.3 Which one of the following is NOT a purpose of performance appraisal?

A. To link between appraisal and reward

B. To measure the extent to which an individual may be awarded a salary increase compared with his or her peers

C. To identify any training needs

D. To aid an individual's career development by attempting to predict work that the individual may be capable of in the future

Answer: A

Difficulty level: Easy

Tag: Purpose of performance appraisal

Rationale:

Appraisals have three main purposes: reward review, performance review, potential review. Option B is reward review, option C is performance review, and option D is potential review.

Option A is incorrect, because this will discourage some people who do not like appraisal.

绩效评估有三个主要目的：奖励复核、业绩复核、潜力复核。

B 选项是奖励复核，C 选项是业绩复核，D 选项是潜力复核。

A 选项不正确，因为有些员工并不愿意做绩效评估，这样做反而会让他们丧失动力。

15.4 Performance appraisal, also referred to as performance review or performance management, **is this statement true or false?**

                                                                                                      True False
                                                                                                                ○   ○

Answer: False

Difficulty level: Easy

Tag: Performance management

Rationale:

This question examines the differences between performance appraisal and performance management. Performance appraisal, also referred to as performance review or performance evaluation, is part of performance management and is a method by which the job performance of an employee is documented and evaluated. However, performance management is a process to establish a shared understanding about what is to be achieved, and an approach to managing and developing people in order to achieve it.

这道题考查的是绩效评估和绩效管理的不同之处。 绩效评估，也被称为绩效复核或者绩效评价，绩效评估是绩效管理的一部分，它是一名员工的绩效被存档和评估的方法。 然而，绩效管理是一个流程，用来建立一个共识，即应该达到一个什么样的目标，然后发展一个方法以管理和培训人们去实现它。

15.5 Choose the correct answer regarding the merit of having a formal assessment system for the organisation.

    A. It can help to identify those employees who are suitable for promotion

    B. It can help employees have a clearer view of their performance and manager's expectation

    C. It can help to make employees' goal congruent with organisation's goal

    D. It can help to identify job vacancies

Answer: A

Difficulty level: Normal

Tag: Benefits of formal appraisal system

Rationale:

This question is set to ask the benefits of having a formal assessment system for the organisation. Candidates should be able to distinguish the difference between organisation's view and employees' view. For organisation, it benefits from identifying employees for promotion, noting areas for individual improvement, and by using the system as a basis for long term human resource planning. For employees, employees can have a clearer view of their performance and managers' expectation.

这道题考查的是从组织的角度评价正式评估系统的好处。考生应该能够区分从组织的角度与从员工的角度的不同。从组织的角度，它能够有助于识别那些需要晋升的员工，指出员工可以提升的领域，以及作为长期人力资源计划的基础。从员工的角度，员工对于他们的绩效以及管理层的期望能有一个清晰的认识。

Chapter 16
Training and development

知识导入

上一章中我们学习了绩效评估，而绩效评估有一个非常重要的作用在于，通过它可以判断员工是否需要培训。我们每个人都有自己的学习方法，相应地，如果想要培训有效就要具体问题具体分析。接下来让我们通过这章来了解，我们到底可以怎么样进行培训？培训就是我们的人力资源管理的终点吗？

单词表

英文	中文
Cognitive	认知的
Impose	强加、施以影响
Rationalise	使合理化
Intellectual	理智的
Succession	继承
Retention	留住、保留
Portfolio	组合
Absenteeism	缺席
Ultimate	最终的
Career path	职业道路
Tailored	定制的
Demonstration	演示
Rotation	轮岗
Distraction	干扰
Hamper	阻碍
Confer	授予
Induction	就职
Premise	场所

学习指南

Learning objectives	Pass level	Distinction level	用时建议
1. Learning(1.1-1.4)	√		10 mins
2. Training and development (2.1-2.4)	√		10 mins
3. Training methods(3.1-3.3)	√		10 mins

本章考点

重要考点	难度（1~3）
熟记学习型组织的特征	1
熟记并理解 Kolb 的学习周期理论	2
熟记并理解 Honey and Mumford 的学习风格理论	2
区分培训、发展、教育的区别	1
熟记并理解培训的步骤	2
熟记并理解各种发展的区别	1
熟记并理解各类人对培训的责任	1
熟记并理解培训的方法	2

1 Learning

常言道，学习是终身制的。之所以这么说，是因为不管对于组织来说，还是对于组织中的个人而言，只有通过不断的学习与反思，自身才能得到不断强化与提高。接下来，我们就来了解一下，职场学习的那些事。

1.1 The importance of learning in the workplace

（a）It can lead to improved productivity by increasing **competence** of employees.

（b）The employees who enjoy learning are more likely to be flexible under constant **change** of environment.

（c）Lack of learning opportunities may result in demotivation of employees as they may feel they are undervalued, thus learning is of great significance for staff **morale**.

（d）It can give a significant **advantage** of organisations **over competitors**.

1.2 The learning organisation

A learning organisation is a term given to an organisation that facilitates **learning** among **all** its members and continuously transforms itself to absorb new information.

1.2.1 Key characteristic of a learning organisation

（a）Encouragement of the generation and share of knowledge.

（b）A tolerance for risk and failure by considering them as precious learning opportunities.

（c）A systematic, on-going and scientific approach to problem-solving.

学习型组织（learning organisation），顾名思义，即鼓励全员参与学习的组织。在这种氛围之下，除却鼓励学习之外，组织还会有一些明显的特征：

（1）鼓励全员共享知识。

（2）学习的过程中，出现差错是在所难免的，在学习型组织中，对于这样的差错会持有较高的容忍度。

（3）组织会更偏向采用系统性的、一致性的科学解决办法。简言之，就是根据过往的学习经验，针对某个问题组织内部会形成一套解决办法，在以后遇到同样

知识点解读

在职场中的学习极为重要，我们可以从两个方面来看：

对于个人来说，技多不压身，不断的学习可以帮助个人提高自身技能，灵活地应对外界环境发生的变化；并且组织提供给员工的学习机会，很大程度上会让员工感到被重视，形成激励。

那么自然而然，**对于由人构成的组织来说**，员工的不断学习带来的是丰富的知识积累、良好的工作氛围、稳步提升的生产效率。在这几个优势的驱动下，组织会逐步形成竞争优势，从而在同类竞争者中拔得头筹。

的问题时，会采用同样的办法解决，以确保高效。

1.3 The learning cycle: Kolb

Kolb, the famous professor of organisational behaviour in the world, proposed the theory of learning cycle, which is the cornerstone of many theories of learning.

In Kolb (1984,41), he stated that:

"Learning is the process whereby knowledge is created through the transformation of experience. Knowledge results from the combination of grasping experience and transforming it."

Therefore, in Kolb's learning cycle（见图 16 – 1）, there are four stages during learning, which starts from concrete experience.

> **核心考点**
>
> Kolb 的学习圈理论（learning cycle）是考试中经常出现的考点。考核点集中在针对循环中的四个步骤的具体含义。因此，同学们需要对一块内容进行理解记忆。

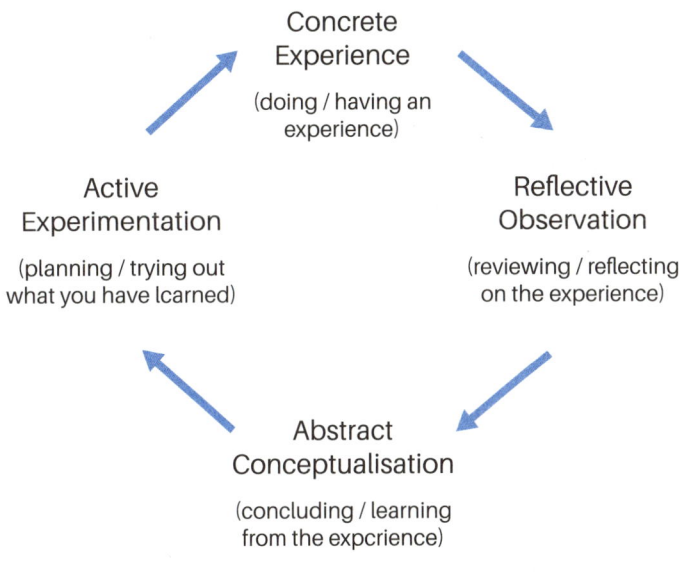

图 16 – 1 Kolb-learning cycle

(A) Concrete experience

It is considered as the first step of learning, which means people learn from what they do every day, e.g. routine activities or specific task in workplace. In this phase, the experience people got is directly related to their feelings. Therefore, sometimes we can call this step as "**feeling**".

在这个阶段，人们初步接触了到了某项事物，获得了相关的经验，但此时这种经验并不成形，它更多的是一种直接经历与直观感受，也是人们在后期需要加工的"原材料"。

(B) Reflective observation

After having the experience, people will "reflect" what they have done. Reflection is quite similar to "watch" the process of experience again, which includes recollection, reorganisation and integration of information that they got from previous experience. Therefore, this part can also be called as "**watching**".

在这个阶段，人们会在脑中回忆发生的经历，这个过程与我们所说的"每日三省吾身"非常类似。通过回忆，人们会像一个旁观者去仔细观看整个过程，在这个观看的过程中，更多当时被忽略的细枝末节会被发现。

(C) Abstract conceptualization

After "watching" the whole process of experience, just like after watching a film, people will comment and conclude what they have seen. In the learning cycle, people begin logical analysis, aiming to have a systematic thinking about it, and forming collective conclusion to the past experience or finding out a scientific resolution to the past problems. Consequently, this stage can be called as "**thinking**".

这是一个加工梳理的过程。在"脑补"完之前的经历后,我们会做一个"有则改之,无则加勉"的动作,即再对本次做的好的方面,总结出具体经验,形成一套自己的理论,或者对本次做的不好的地方,思考出改进方法,以供下次使用。

(D) Active experimentation

After all the steps, people will put what they have conceptualized to the reality, and test if it really works. If not, then, it is another beginning of learning cycle. So, this part can be called as "**doing**".

这是一个将自己总结出的理论运用到实际的过程。当然这并不是最后一步,整个学习圈是不断循环的,每一次实践的过程,都会是一个新的开端,人们会在这个不断循环的过程中不断完善,没有最好,只有更好。

As we referred, Kolb's learning cycle is the milestone of many consequent theories, for example, Honey and Mumford's learning style theory.

1.4 Learning styles: Honey and Mumford

Different people have different preferences for learning and people tend to learn more effectively if they are aware of their learning preferences.

Honey and Mumford 的 learning style 理论(见图 16-2)是基于 Kolb 的 learning theory 发展起来的。不过值得注意的是,在 Kolb 的理论中,concrete experience 是起点,即人们都是先通过具体的实践才有了后续的分析思考等活动,但 learning style 理论颠覆了这样的想法。Honey and Mumford 认为,人的不同学习风格源自不同的偏好,如有人偏爱理论,那么他的学习风格就会是从理论着手,从理论到实践。学习风格没有优劣之分,完全是因人而异的选择。

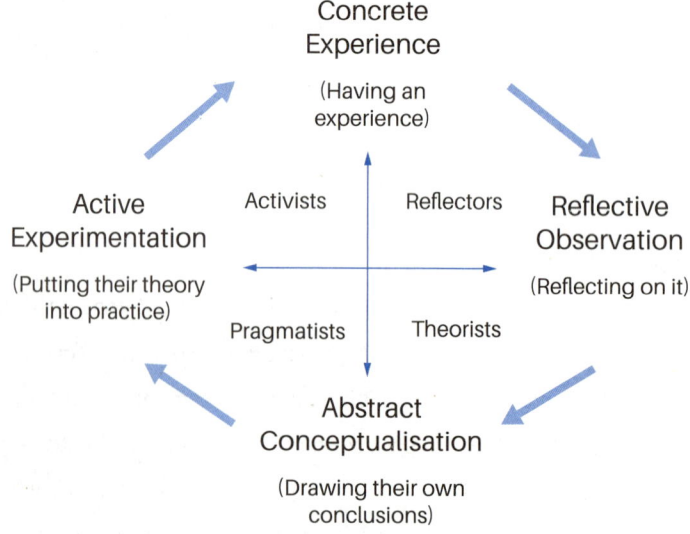

图 16-2 Honey and Mumford-leaning style

(A) Theorists

(a) They prefer to build the basic understanding of things and figure out principles through analysis step-by-step.

(b) They are more suitable to the hands-off learning methods.

(c) They are keen on logic and clarity.

理论家：理论家偏好从书本、原则、理论等着手。例如，当我们学习做菜的时候，理论家会选择先下载食谱，从食谱着手获取相关信息，随后才会进行实践。

(B) Reflectors

(a) They prefer to think, observe and review；

(b) They should be allowed to work with their own pace；

(c) They are also more suitable to the hands-off learning method.

反思家：反思家信奉眼见为实，他们喜欢通过观察来分析和总结某件事情的做法，然后选择最适合自己的方法并运用到实践中去。同样以做菜为例，反思家就会选择站在厨房近距离观察，从起锅到收汁，所有工序尽收眼底，然后通过所见所学，自己慢慢尝试。

(C) Activists

(a) They like to be involved in activities, that is, learning through practice；

(b) They will be excited with challenges and new problems；

(c) They are tired with theories, therefore, prefer practices and **hands-on** learning method.

行动主义者：行动主义者崇尚"实践出真知"。属于这种类型的学习风格的人，热衷于通过实际操作发现问题所在，从而再去寻找解决办法。还是做菜这个例子，行动主义者既不会看菜谱也不会观察别人，而是凭着自己的感知直接操作，然后根据结果，进行调整。

(D) Pragmatists

(a) They are fond of planning and putting ideas into practice；

(b) They will only be interested with those theories, techniques and discussions which are obviously and directly related to practice；

(c) They pursue the "right-now" result.

实用主义者：只有当实用主义者觉得所要学习的内容与所要做的事情有直接联系时，也就是觉得有用时，才会去学习。也就是说，实用主义者并不会毫无目的地学习做菜，而是当存在这样的需求时，才会学习。

精益求精

非常有意思的一件事情是，其实人们的 learning style 并非一成不变，换句话说，学习风格不仅会跟着人们的偏好变化，它也会随着外界环境以及需求的变化而变化。

例如，你在初次学习 AB 这门功课时，首先，你会预习、看书，这就是 **theorist**；其次，学习过程中你可能会发现有些学长、学姐或者是一些班级里的"大神"，学得又快又好又轻松，那么此时你就会观察他们的学习方式，试图选择适合你的可以达到事半功倍的途径，这个时候，你就是 **reflector**；再次，你可能觉得书本上的知识点实在繁多，着实让人眼花缭乱，于是你想想那就不看书了，干脆直接做高顿题库吧，那么在这个时候，你就转变成了 **activist**；最后，临近考试，你机智地缩减复习范围，根据考纲给出的知识点，一一复习，此时，你就是一名 **pragmatist**。

但遗憾的是，当考生想在 AB 这门功课中成为一名 pragmatist 而去看考纲，试图缩减复习范围的时候，会发现考点依然多如牛毛。因此，从平时就开始好好学习、好好复习吧！

小试牛刀

Example question 1

Which of the following describes the learning style entitled "pragmatists" by Honey and Mumford?

  A. Those who adapt and integrate information in a step way

  B. Those who prefer to step back and observe others before acting

  C. Those who involve themselves fully without bias to new experiences

  D. Those who are interested in new ideas only if they can see a direct link to reality

Example question 2

Topi's preferred learning style is to form opinions based on what should work in practical situations. He dislikes management theories, finding it difficult to relate them to real life experiences and his personal situation.

Which of Honey and Mumford's learning styles does George demonstrate?

  A. Reflector B. Analyst C. Pragmatist D. Theorist

2 Training and development

既然我们已经明确学习的重要性，知道了学习的不同风格等内容，那么我们接下来就会产生一个问题，职场肯定是不同于学校这样的象牙塔的，那身处职场的人们到底是通过怎样的途径学习的呢，这就是我们接下来要探讨的内容。

(a) **Training** is the **planned** and **systematic** modification of behaviour through learning events, programs and instruction which enable individuals to **achieve the level of knowledge**, **skills** and **competence**.

(b) **Development** is the **growth** or **realisation** of a person's ability and potential through the provision of **learning** and **educational experiences**.

(c) **Education** is **acquiring general knowledge and skills gradually** by **learning** and basic instruction.

2.1 Benefits of training and development

我们需要从两个角度来看培训与发展的意义，一是员工，他们是直接受益者；二是组织，总的来说，组织是通过员工的成长与进步来获得培训与发展的益处的。

对于员工而言，培训和发展可以带来的好处可以从三个方面考虑。

知识点解读

Training，培训，往往是提供给员工的一种短期的、有针对性的学习过程。其目标非常明确，即根据岗位需求查漏补缺，缺乏会计知识，就培训会计知识；英语能力欠缺，就培训英文水平。

Development，发展，这个概念要比培训更宽阔。它不局限于现有工作的需求，主要在于发掘员工的潜力。组织会通过提供给员工一些发展的学习机会来最大限度地帮助他们成长，从而为组织作出更有价值的贡献。

Education，教育，这是一个最为基础的概念，它指的是获取最普遍的知识与技能的学习过程，这个过程往往是循序渐进的，如考生都经历过的九年制义务教育。

(a) **提高技能(Enhance their skill portfolio)**

培训与发展的第一要务就是学习更多知识或技能,这些知识技能或与目前的工作岗位直接相关,或与未来的职业发展相关,但无论是从哪个角度来说,员工都是受益匪浅的。通过这些培训,他们可以在工作上取得事半功倍的效果(Employees can provide better performance, which brings job satisfaction and achievement);

(b) **提升士气 (Increase their morale)**

从员工的角度考虑,公司之所以愿意提供培训与发展的机会给某一部分人,很大程度上是因为想要在以后重用这部分员工(employees may feel being valued)。因此,基于这样的想法,得到培训与发展机会的员工会受到无形的激励,继而会产生更高的士气以及从工作中获得更大的满足感(It is kind of psychological benefits, which can increase the morale of employees)。

(c) **拓宽社交(Extend their social networks)**

在培训与发展过程中,员工可以结识更多相同圈子的人,从而建立更广阔的社交圈,满足其社交需求(employees can extend their social circles, through which they may enjoy some social benefit, e.g. wide and useful social network)。

Additionally, it is known to us that most organisations in the market are profit-seeking ones. Therefore, it is rational that organisations will not provide the chance of training and development to employees totally for charity, that is, organisations themselves can benefit from providing training and development to employees.

正如我们之前所说,公司可以通过员工的培训与发展间接获益,那么这些对公司的益处同样可以从以下几个方面来看。

(a) **生产效率的提高(Increase productivity of organisations)**

It can minimise the costs of keeping up with the newest skills and technologies through providing training and development to employees, thus increasing productivity of organisations and also enhancing the operation and performance of organisations.

员工通过培训可以不断更新行业内先进的生产技术和知识,进而提高其工作效率,保质保量地完成任务。

(b) **组织结构的变化(Optimisation of the structure of organisations)**

It can improve the structure of organisations, that is, less supervisory levels will be needed because employees are trained well, and they will understand their positions and functions in the whole system of organisations.

通过培训,员工不仅能够提高相关的工作水平,并且会对自己的工作有更深入的认识与了解。例如,自己的岗位在整个组织体系或任务中处于如何承上启下的环节,通过员工自身对这种认知的加深,可以在一定程度上减少公司中上传下达的层级以及一些监督监管的层级,简化组织结构。

(c) **组织文化的提升 (Improvement of organisation culture)**

When employees feel motivated, their loyalty to organisations will be increased. As a consequence, employee retention rate can be maintained, which reduces the cost of recruitment and selection to certain extent. Furthermore, it is also beneficial to the building of learning organisation and positive organisation culture.

组织给予员工培训与发展的机会,有利于营造浓厚的学习氛围,打造积极的组织文化,构建学习组织。

通过上面的学习,我们了解了学习的重要性,并且知道了职场中可以通过培训与发展进行学习。 接下来的问题就是:培训与发展应该从何开始,如何进行,如何结束。 那么,我们接下来就来看与此相关的内容。

2.2 Training and development process (a systematic approach)

Step 1: Identify and define **training needs.**

Step 2: Define **training objectives** (what must be learned and what the level of skills should be achieved after the training exercise).

Step 3: Design training programs.

(a) Who provides the training.

(b) Where the training takes place.

(c) Division of responsibilities among trainers, managers and individuals.

(d) What training approaches, techniques, styles and technologies are used.

Step 4: Delivery of training programs.

Step 5: Evaluation.

2.2.1 Step 1: Identification of training needs and objectives

Training needs can be determined through a number of methods.

(A) Formal training needs analysis

This involves identification of the skills, knowledge and experience needed for a particular job and comparing this to a current jobholder. If the current jobholder is lacking any of these required competences, there is a learning gap and thus a training need.

Formal training analysis may also be triggered by external changes to an organisation.

Indicators of the need for training:

(a) **New laws or regulations.**

For example, HR staff need to be trained as various EU Directives have been enacted in UK law.

(b) **The introduction of new technology.**

For relevant employees to learn how to apply.

(c) **High absenteeism, labour turnover, crises, conflict, poor motivation and performance.**

Such factors will need to be investigated to see what the root causes are, and whether training will solve the problems.

(d) **Critical incidents such as customer complaints.**

For example, receiving bad press coverage because of a number of complaints

---

知识点解读

什么情况下需要进行培训?
(1)颁布新的法律、法规,如 2019 年 1 月 2 日 lease 准则实行全面改革,涉及的企业需要进行相关培训;
(2)出现新的技术,如企业引入新的会计记账系统;
(3)员工士气低下,流动较大时;
(4)出现重大的意外状况时,如客户投诉,可能反映一些环节的员工素质欠缺。

about the rudeness of its customer service staff on the telephone.

(B) Performance appraisal

Most organisations appraise their staff (carry out a performance review) at least annually. During this process, managers could use employee's past performance to identify possible training and development opportunities in the future.

(C) Organisation strategy

Training and development should be closely linked to the overall strategy and there should be senior support for the training program.

2.2.2 Step 2: Setting training objectives

Compared to training needs, training objectives are more **specific**, **observable** and **measurable**.

培训需求与培训目的的区别，举例如下（见表16-1）。

表16-1 Differences between training needs and training objectives

Training needs	Training objectives
To know about the new accounting standards	Can answer 4 relevant questions after training
To pack boxes more quickly	Can pack each box in thirty seconds

2.2.3 Step 3: Program design

Training and development of individuals can include formal training courses (in-house and external, offline and computer-based), mentoring and coaching (learn in chapter 19). The organisation needs to consider which training methods to use. If in-house training is chosen, infrastructure and staffing must be carefully considered.

2.2.4 Step 4 & 5: Delivery and evaluation of training program

The five-level evaluation model:

Step1: Reactions of trainees to the training.

Step2: What new skills and knowledge have been acquired.

Step3: Changes in the job behaviour following training.

Step4: Impact on organisational goals.

Step5: Ultimate value: The impact of training on the wider 'good' of the organisation in terms of stakeholder benefits, greater corporate social responsibility, corporate growth/survival.

2.3 Development

It is a **wider** approach to fulfilling an individual's potential than **training** and **education**.

知识点解读

Performance appraisal，业绩评估。通过业绩评估，可以最直观地发现员工与目标之间的差距。这种差距就是"training needs"，即"培训需求"。

知识点解读

员工培训与发展的目的与方向必须要与组织目标和战略相符，当组织的战略出现调整，人员的技能配备同样需要调整，这种情况下，就需要对员工进行培训。

知识点解读

为了确保培训的有效性，每一次培训的过程与结果都需要被评估，我们可以从以下五个方面进行考虑：
（1）作为被培训的主体，员工对此次培训有何看法，对培训的内容、方式、提供培训的老师等方面是否满意。
（2）从培训中，员工是否获得了具体的知识技能。
（3）在后续的工作中，员工是否能够将培训中获得的知识技能学以致用，是否对实际工作产生正面的效应。
（4）是否对组织目标的实现有正面影响。
（5）是否对更深远的目标产生影响，为组织增加最终价值。例如，是否能够优化组织的声誉，是否能为组织带来竞争优势等。

> **专有名词**
>
> Career development 是指在职业上发展，如晋升、调任等。
> Professional development 是指专业水平、专业知识方面的发展。

Approaches to development are as follows（见表16-2）：

表16-2　Four approaches of development

Approach	Comment
Management development	This may include the development of management/leadership skills, and planned experience of different functions, positions and work settings, in preparation for increasing managerial responsibility and improving managerial effectiveness
Career development	This is associated with employee's **career paths**. Opportunities may be planned for **horizontal transfers** to offer new opportunities
Professional development	**Maintain and enhance professional standards through** learning opportunities such as a CPD (continuing professional development)
Personal development	It is related to **wider aspect** of development rather than the skills needed in the current job. The development of skill may be beneficial for the future needs of organisations and also helps to foster employee job satisfaction, commitment

2.4 Responsibility for training and development

2.4.1 The trainee

The **ultimate** responsibility for training lies with the trainee.

Technological change means that new skills are always needed, and people who can learn new skills will be more employable. Multi-skilling is often preferred in modern corporations.

> **知识点解读**
>
> 考生应当注意这个知识点：在培训中，最终的责任承担者是受训者本人。

2.4.2 HR department

The HR department has overall, high-level responsibility for training and development. This will often mean that they will need to：

(a) Create frameworks for job appraisals and the analysis of learning gaps.

(b) Identify when and if training is needed within the organisation.

(c) Design career pathways for employees.

2.4.3 Line manager

Line managers bear some of the responsibility for training and development within the organisation by：

(a) Identifying the training needs of the department or section.

(b) Assessing the current competences of the individuals within the department.

(c) Identifying opportunities for learning and development on the job.

(d) Coaching staff.

(e) Offering performance feedback for on-the-job learning.

(f) Organising training programs where required.

2.4.4 The training manager

The training manager is a member of staff appointed to arrange and sometimes run training.

培训经理的责任如表16-3所示。

表 16-3 Responsibility of training manager

Responsibility	Comment
Liaison	With HR department and operating departments
Scheduling	Arranging training programs at convenient times and location
Needs identification	Assessing existing and future skills shortages
Program design	Developing tailored training programs
Feedback	To the trainee, operating department and the HR department
Evaluation	Measuring the effectiveness of training programs

3 Training methods

3.1 Off-the-job training

It is formal training conducted **outside the context of the job itself** in special training rooms or off-site facilities.

One important thing to note is that off the job training does **not** always support transfer of learning to the job.

3.1.1 The methods of off-the-job training

最常见的脱产培训方式就是参加培训课程，可能是周末上课[包括了面授（Day release）与在线网课（E-learning）的方式]，或者是停止工作再返回学校深造（full-time course at a university for one or two years）。

3.1.2 The appraisal of off-the-job training

表 16-4 Appraisal of off-the-job training

Advantages	Disadvantages
Low risk	Irrelevant to jobs
Focus on learning	Waste of working time
Standardisation of training	Slower feedback
Confer status	Not suit hands on jobs

3.2 On-the-job training

It maximises transfer of learning by incorporating it into real work.

3.2.1 The methods of on-the-job training

常见的在职培训方式包括了轮岗（job rotation）、临时调配与提拔（temporary promotion）、担任高层助理（"assistant to" positions）、辅助完成项目（project work）、工作中受到他人教导（coaching）等。以上都是难得的工作中的学习机会，能够快速帮助员工熟悉相关事务。

3.2.2 The appraisal of on-the-job training

表 16-5 Appraisal of on-the-job training

Advantages	Disadvantages
High relevance and transfer	Undesirable aspects of job context
Suit hands on jobs	Risk of error

知识点解读

Off-the-job training，脱产培训，顾名思义，是指脱离了职场、脱离了工作的培训。进修就是一种典型的脱产培训，指的是员工暂时地从工作岗位上离开（如停薪留职），通过几个月到两年不等的时间，完全投入学习，以获取知识技能。

知识点解读

Low risk，这里的风险低，意思是：脱产培训与工作并不挂钩，即便在培训过程中出现了错误，也不会影响工作。例如，护士接受培训学习扎针，如果是在病人身上直接进行，那么一旦出现失误，后果就会非常严重。但如果是 off-the-job training，那这种风险就会大大降低。

知识点解读

On-the-job training，在职培训，从名称中我们不难看出，这种培训是在不脱离职场、不脱离工作的前提下进行的。这种培训可能是以公司组织经验交流讲座或课程的方式进行，也可能是直接将员工投放到需要学习的岗位工作中去，跟着前辈边做边学。

知识点解读

Risk of error，出现错误的风险加大，比如财务方面的 on-the-job training，培训一个新员工做账，就要把账务处理的工作交给新手，一边工作一边培训，就会出现新人把工作做错的风险。

Advantages	Disadvantages
No adjustment barriers	Not suit hands off jobs
Develop working relationships and skills	Distractions hamper learning focus

在职培训和脱产培训，两者各有优劣（如表 16-4、表 16-5 所示），因此在选择具体培训方法的时候，应当根据各人的不同情况来决定。例如，根据 learning style 的几种类型来区分，倘若 A 是一个典型的 theorist，那么更适合他的方式就会是 off-the-job training；如果 B 是一个信奉实践出真知的 activist，那么就应当选择 on-the-job training。这也就是所谓的因材施教。

小试牛刀

Example question 3

Which of the following is an advantage of on-the-job training?

    A. It has less risk

    B. It allows focus on learning

    C. It suits hands-on learning styles

3.3 Induction training

It is the process whereby a person is formally introduced and integrated into an organisation or system.

（A）The purpose of induction

（a）Helping new recruits to find their relationships within the company.

（b）Socialising new recruits into the culture and value.

（c）Supporting recruits in beginning performance by avoiding initial problems at the 'induction crisis' stage of new recruits' employment lifecycle. They may have frustration, disorientation and disappointment that otherwise cause new recruits to leave the organisation prematurely.

（d）Identify on-going training and development needs.

（B）The process of induction（On-going process）

    Step 1：Introduce the main areas to be learned.

    Step 2：Introduce work premises and facilities to recruits.

    Step 3：Briefing the HR policies and procedures.

    Step 4：Introduce the key people.

    Step 5：Introduce work procedures, including：

（a）Explain the nature of the job, and the goals of each task.

（b）Explain hours of work.

（c）Explain the structure of the department：to whom the recruit will report, to whom he/she can go with complaints or queries and so on.

    Step 6：Plan and implement training program.

    Step 7：Monitor initial progress.

知识点解读

Induction training，入职培训，顾名思义就是在员工进入公司后、正式投入工作前，进行的培训。这种培训的目的很明显，即快速让新员工熟悉环境，更好地投入工作。

Answers of example question

1. D
2. C
3. C

Summary

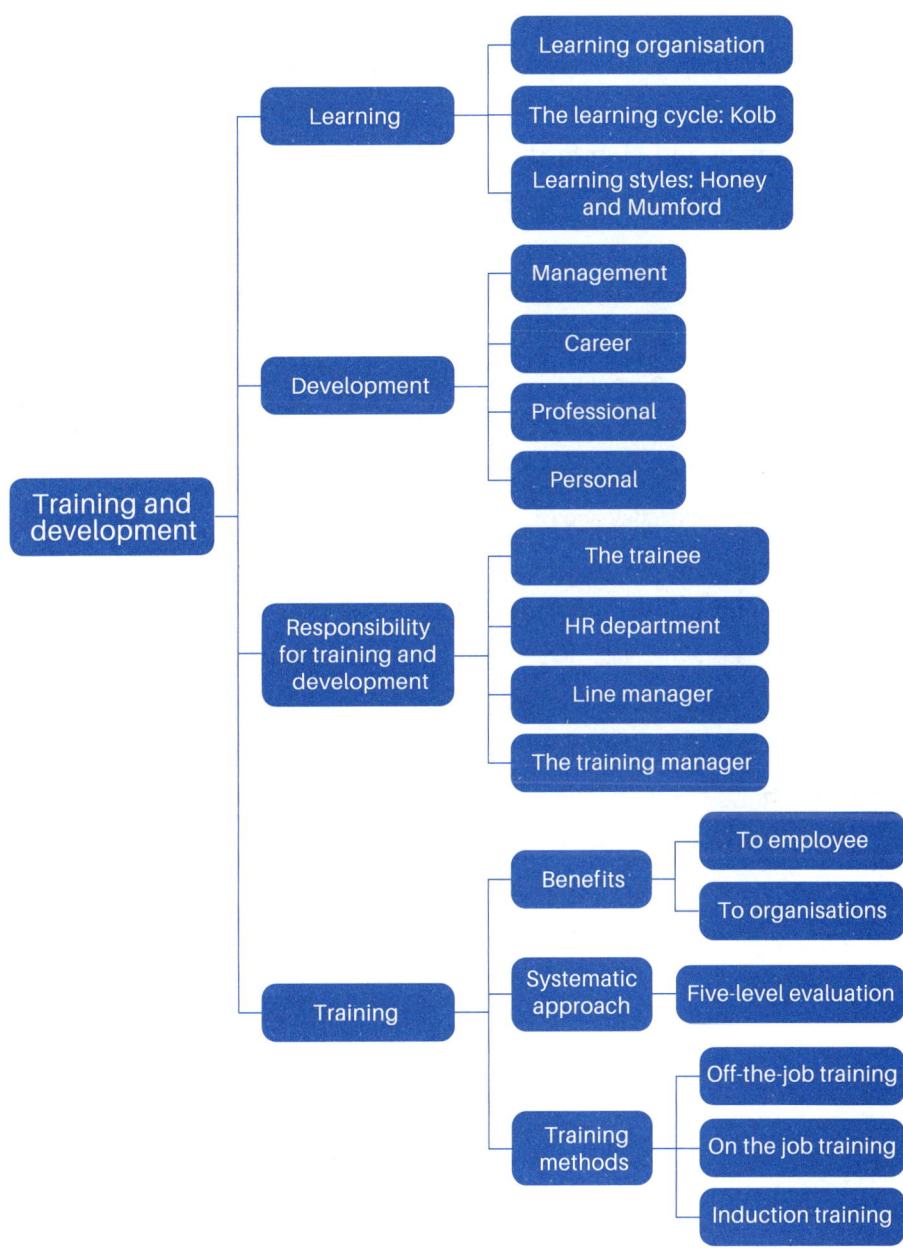

Chapter 16 考试不同问法总结

Section A

1. 针对 learning organisation

- Which TWO of the following are characteristics of a 'learning organisation'?

2. 针对 Kolb's learning cycle

- Which of the following are stages of learning as suggested by Honey and Mumford?
- Which of the following is a characteristic of the second stage of Kolb's learning cycle?
- In Kolb's learning cycle, which stage immediately precedes the active experimentation stage?
- Kolb's learning cycle emphasised the cyclical nature of learning. Which stage of Kolb's learning cycle is described as the 'begging of internalisation'?

3. 针对 Honey and Mumford's learning style

- Which of the following is an example of Honey and Mumford's learning types?
- Which of the following describes the learning style entitled 'reflector' by Honey and Mumford?
- What learning cycle would Honey and Mumford describe A as having?
- Are the following statements regarding Honey and Mumford's activist learning style true or false?
- Which of the Honey and Mumford's learning style is represented by this employee?

4. 针对 Training and Development

- There are a number of stages in the training and development process. Which of the following is the final stage in this process?
- Is each of the following statements about development true or false?

Section B

- With reference to the theory of Honey and Mumford, indicate the preferred learning style of four individuals.
- For each factors below, identify whether it is a recognised benefit for the organisation, for the employee or for both.

Quick quiz

16.1 Which of the following is NOT a stage of a learning cycle developed by Kolb?

　　A. Programmed
　　B. Active experimentation
　　C. Concrete experience
　　D. Reflective observation

Answer: **A**

Difficulty level: **Normal**

Tag: **Learning cycle**

Rationale:

Kolb's model identifies four learning stages, they form a learning cycle from experience to observation to conceptualization to experimentation and back to experience.

这道题考查的是 Kolb 的学习周期，有 4 个步骤：获得经验，反思，理论化，应用。 因此答案选 A。

16.2 Which one of the following is true?

　　A. Kolb identifies that learning is a four-stage cycle which starts from observation

　　B. Honey and Mumford argue that while people all follow the same learning cycle, different people have different learning style

　　C. Pragmatist prefers the hand-off leaning style

　　D. Reflector enjoys leaning basic principles and logic analysis

Answer: **B**

Difficulty level: **Normal**

Tag: **Learning cycle**

Rationale:

Kolb's model identifies four learning stages, they form a learning cycle from experience to observation to conceptualization to experimentation and back to experience.

这道题考查的是 Kolb 的学习周期，有 4 个步骤：获得经验、反思、理论化、应用。 在 Kolb 的基础上，Honey and Mumford 对该理论进行了优化，提出了不同人的学习风格不同，学习圈可以从任何地方开始，故 B 选项正确。 Kolb 认为学习开始于实践，即"having an experience"，故 A 选项错误；Pragmatist 是不喜欢纯理论不动手操作的学习方式的，因为纯理论的学习方式没法直接和实际工作结合，故 C 选项错误。 D 选项描述的是 theorist，故 D 选项错误。

16.3 Which of the following is NOT a characteristic of a learning organisation?

　　A. The learning organisation usually react proactively to the environment change

　　B. Members in the learning organisation shares systematic approach of problem solving

　　C. Learning organisations emphasis on new theories developed by itself

Answer: **C**

Difficulty level: **Normal**

Tag: **Learning organisation**

Rationale:

Learning organisation encourages all its members to obtain and share new knowledge in order to transform itself in the changing environment. A systematic and continuous approach is formed during the accumulation of learning and experiencing. The efforts of learning organisation are focused on growth and development of it but not what knowledge it has gained.

学习型组织的目的和好处在于，它通过培养良好的学习氛围、鼓励成员学习及共享新知识的方式使其自身能够积极主动地应对外部环境的快速变化。 学习型组织往往期望并不断通过过往的积累形成科学系统的解决问题的途径。 但是，学习型组织强调的是培养自身的成长和发展而不是自身研发了什么新的理论，因此答案选 C。

16.4 Amy enjoys the training provided by her company now. During the on-the-job training, she does not need to recite the bothering text which has no direct link with real work. Instead, she finds it is easier to handle works after the hand on training carried out by the coach.

Which of the Honey and Mumford's learning style is represented by her?

A. Theorist　　　　B. Activist　　　　C. Reflector　　　　D. Pragmatist

Answer：D

Difficulty level：Normal

Tag：Learning style

Rationale：

Pragmatists are down-to-earth, they have a keen eye of watching ideas and theories applied into practical work. Theories that have no relationship with real work would be seen as useless and unnecessary. The scenario describes that Amy dislike reading text however her company training is satisfying because the training makes her work easier. Besides, on-the-job training is always the option of pragmatists as it directly facilitate current work.

实用主义者是非常务实的，他们热衷于将理论或想法应用于实践，指导实践。 与实际工作没有直接关联的理论在他们看来是不值得去学习的。 题中的 Amy 不喜欢学习枯燥的课本内容，而公司提供给她的在职培训使得她工作起来更容易，因而她很满意。 根据这些描述很容易判断出 Amy 是实用主义者，喜欢学习能对她的工作起到帮助作用的内容，并且在职培训往往也是实用主义者更青睐的学习方式。

16.5 Which TWO of the following describe the effects that training could bring to an organisation?

A. The potential for employees are identified and realised

B. Retention rate and morale are improved

C. Obtain higher quality human resource compared to other employers

D. Own more senior position employees in the organisation

Answer：B,C

Difficulty level：Normal

Tag：Training and Developing

Rationale：

Training could bring lots of benefits to an organisation, including reduced costs and incidents, increased productivity, employee retention and morale etc. As a result, the overall employee competence could be stronger which means the organisation would possess better human resource. Training facilitates an organisation's succession plan but would not increase the arrangement of senior positions in it. Training could also help the identification of employees' potential but the realisation of the potential can only be work out by development. Training is the modification of employee skill in a short time, but development could achieve a longer time improvement of employee in many areas.

培训可以给企业带来多种好处，如减少成本及出现事故的概率，提高员工生产效率、技能和士气等，这些最终都会使企业员工整体素质提高，使企业拥有更优质的人力资源。但是需要注意的是：首先，培训有助于企业的继承规划，但不会影响企业对于高层管理者职位的设置安排；其次，培训可以帮企业识别不同员工身上的潜质，但是这些潜质的挖掘只能通过长期的发展才能实现，因为培训只能在短期提高员工的工作表现和改进他们的技能。

Chapter 17
Motivating individuals and group

知识导入

上一章我们已经了解了如何培训员工，让员工提升自我的同时又能更有效地为公司作出贡献。事实上，鉴于通过培训可以使得员工自我提升，我们不难发现，培训也是一种有效的激励手段。所谓激励，就是让员工自发地努力工作。而之前所学的培训只是激励的手段之一，针对不同的人有不同的方法，在这一章中，我们将深入地了解激励的相关内容。

单词表

英文	中文
Motivation	激励
Esteem	地位、荣誉
Self-actualisation	自我实现
Deferred gratification	递延满足感
Altruistic	无私的
Hygiene	保健
Preference	偏好
Coerce	强制、迫使
Carrot and stick	胡萝卜加大棒
Token	标记
Vertical	垂直的
Horizontal	水平的

学习指南

Learning objectives	Pass level	Distinction level	用时建议
1. Overview of motivation (1.1-1.2)		√	3 mins
2. Content theories (2.1.1-2.1.3)	√		10 mins
3. Process theories (2.2.1-2.2.2)	√		10 mins
4. McGregor：Theory X and Theory Y(2.3)		√	5 mins
5. Reward system(3.1-3.2)		√	5 mins

本章考点

重要考点	难度（1~3）
熟记并理解马斯洛的需求金字塔理论	2
熟记并理解赫茨伯格的双因素理论	2
重点区分 job enrichment, job enlargement, job rotation	1
熟记并理解弗鲁姆的期望理论	2
熟记并理解不同的奖励方式	1

1 Overview of motivation

1.1 Definition

Motivation is a process that stimulates desire and energy of people. As a result, they could be continually encouraged to make efforts towards their role, job, career and so on.

Motivation results from both internal and external factors, such as:

- Intensity of desire.
- Reward of achieving goals.
- Expectation from important individuals.

1.2 Importance of motivation

It is beneficial for organisations to be possessed of motivated employees. (如表 17－1 所示) In addition, the feeling of being motived is also meaningful for teams and employees themselves.

表 17－1　Benefits of motivation

For organisations	For individuals	For teams
Best utilisation of human resources and thus higher productivity	Improvement of skills and efficiency	Increased willingness and commitment
Better achievement of organisational goals	Improved career prospects	More friendly relationship and cooperation
Stability of workforce and a good image	Higher job satisfaction	Better generation of ideas

知识点解读

激励的定义在考试中不会直接考到，不需要记忆。但是考生需要理解其精髓：所谓公司中的激励，指的就是让员工自发有动力并调动自己的行为去取得对公司和员工都有益的结果，以此达到双赢的效果。

知识点解读

激励因素包括 reward、expectation、desire 这些内、外部因素。例如，学生自发愿意花更多时间准备考试，因为父母答应考到 90 分就能买想要的礼物，这是 reward；又或是能够满足父母老师对其的期待，这是 expectation；或者是自己想要学到更多知识，想成为更优秀的人，这是 desire。

激励对于公司来说是存在着飞轮效应的。飞轮效应是指当我们想要使静止的飞轮转动起来，一开始需要耗费很大气力，循环往复地去不停转动齿轮，虽然一开始很辛苦，但随后飞轮会转动得越来越快。在商业中，这意味着，只要我们坚持不懈地推动某件事情的发展，待到步入正轨之后，公司就可以收获其带来的利益。激励同样如此，在刚开始面临巨大挑战的时候，公司需要投入大量人力物力财力，通过不断激励员工，以实际业绩来证明选择的正确性，强化员工信心，形成良好的合作文化，从而保证公司之后的高效运作。

核心考点

关于激励的两大类（三个理论）是本章核心考点，概念题以及案例题均会出现，需要同学们能理解并应用。

知识点解读

Content theory，内容理论，关注的是什么东西和事情能够激励；process theory，过程理论，关注的是如何激励。

2 Theories of motivation

Motivation theory falls in two categories：

(a) Content theories：These theories primarily put emphasis on identifying "the thing" which could motivate people. Simply speaking, **what** motivates people.

(b) Process theories：These theories hold more dynamic views which focus on identifying the mechanism **how** people are motivated.

2.1 Content theories

2.1.1 Maslow's hierarchy of needs

> 博学多才

亚伯拉罕·哈罗德·马斯洛（1908—1970年），美国社会心理学家、比较心理学家，心理学第三势力的领导人。他的主要成就是提出了人本心理学方法论、人性本质观和需求层次论三大理论。

除了激励相关的理论之外，马斯洛需求金字塔理论（如图17-1所示）对于教育的发展，以及优化学校的教学工作作出了巨大的贡献。马斯洛认为，人的行为会受到多种因素的影响，如外部环境、情感、社会、人的智力水平，种种复杂的因素都会影响学习过程（刘烨，2008）。

Maslow's Hierarchy of Needs

图 17-1　Maslow hierarchy

This theory can be summarised as everyone has a hierarchy of needs throughout life, and these can be placed in five ascending categories as above.

刘烨（2008）认为马斯洛需求金字塔理论可以从以下几个方面理解：

（1）生理需求（physiological needs），如食物、水、空气、睡眠等。

　　对应激励措施：改善劳动条件、给予更多的业余时间和休假等。

（2）安全需求（safety needs），其中包括对人身安全以及免遭痛苦、威胁或疾病等。

对应激励措施：强调规章制度、福利待遇（医疗保险和退休福利）等。

（3）社交需求（love and belonging needs），如对友谊、爱情的需求以及归属感。

对应激励措施：提供同事间社交往来机会，开展有组织的体育比赛和集体聚会。

（4）尊重需求（esteem needs），如成就、名声、地位和晋升机会等。尊重需求既包括对成就或自我价值的个人感觉，也包括他人对自己的认可与尊重。

对应激励措施：公开奖励和表扬，强调工作任务的艰巨性以及成功所需要的高超技巧，颁发荣誉奖章、在公司刊物发表文章表扬、优秀员工光荣榜。

（5）自我实现需求（self-actualisation），是最高层次的需求。只有前面四项需求都能满足，最高层次的需求方能相继产生，它是一种衍生性需求，如自我实现，发挥潜能等。

对应激励措施：设计工作时运用复杂情况的适应策略，给有特长的人委派特别任务。

(A) Main conclusions

(a) People have five ascending categories of needs. Each of them is essential and important until it is satisfied and then the next need will replace it.

(b) Every person has the desire to move towards self-actualisation, but such desire can hardly be satisfied.

需求层次理论有两个基本出发点，一是人人都有需求，但是需求存在着层次，低层次需求获得满足后，更高一层需求才会出现；二是在多种需要未获满足前，首先满足迫切需求，该需要满足后，后面的需求才显示出其激励作用。一般来说，某一层次的需求相对满足了，就会向高一层次发展，追求更高一层次的需求就成为驱使行为的动力。相应的，获得基本满足的需求就不再是一股激励力量。

(B) Appraisals of the theory

(a) People are greedy, that is they may have different claims at the same time.

(b) Different people have different standards about fulfilling the same hierarchy of needs.

(c) Maslow's theory focuses on the culture of the UK and US, ignoring deferred gratification and altruistic behaviour.

(d) People's needs may not occur sequentially as Maslow referred.

知识点解读

Deferred gratification：递延满足感，指人们会为了将来的美好愿景，忍受现在所受的痛苦。即为了未来获得更高层次的满足牺牲此刻的低层次的需求。与马斯洛的结论刚好相反。

Altruistic behaviour：无私的行为，指人们可能会为了满足别人的需求，而放弃自己的需求。例如，父母对孩子的关心。

小试牛刀

Example question 1

XYZ Co is a computer manufacturer who is concerned that levels of motivation in the workforce are declining. The work environment is comfortable and secured with a guarantee of future employment. The company has been advised that to improve motivation the staff need to improve social conditions.

According to Maslow's hierarchy of needs theory, which level of need is XYZ Co going to satisfy?

A. Physiological B. Social C. Safety D. Esteem

2.1.2 Herzberg's two-factor theory

The theory was developed by psychologist Herzberg, who theorised that job satisfaction and job dissatisfaction act independently from each other.

The two-factor theory states that there are certain factors in the workplace that create job satisfaction, meanwhile another set of factors cause dissatisfaction.

博学多才

弗雷德里克·赫茨伯格（Frederick Herzberg, 1923—2000 年），美国心理学家、管理理论家、行为科学家，双因素理论的创始人，双因素激励理论又叫激励因素-保健因素理论。

20 世纪 50 年代末期，赫茨伯格和他的助手们在美国匹兹堡地区 11 家工商企业机构中对 200 名工程师、会计师进行了调查访问，调查中他设计了许多问题，例如，"什么时候你对工作特别满意？""什么时候你对工作特别不满意？""原因是什么？"等等，请受访者一一回答。 目的是验证下列假设：人类在工作中有两类不同性质的需要，即作为动物要求避开和免除痛苦的需要和作为人类要求在精神上不断发展和成长的需要。

这次访问主要围绕两个问题：在工作中，哪些事项是让他们感到满意的，并估计这种积极情绪持续多长时间；又有哪些事项是让他们感到不满意的，并估计这种消极情绪持续多长时间。 赫茨伯格以对这些问题的回答为材料，着手去研究哪些事情使人们在工作中快乐和满足，哪些事情造成不愉快和不满足。

研究结果表明，政策与行政管理、监督、薪金、人际关系和工作条件都属于保健因素，正如缺少保健就会导致疾病，但保健条件的具备并不能保证健康那样，当我们无法获得良好的工作环境，有效的公司政策、安全和薪金时，不满意就会产生，但这些因素本身又不能产生满意。 而与工作内容、成就、认可、责任感、发展相关的都是激励因素或成长因素，它们的出现带来工作满意，它们的缺少并不导致不满意，这就是赫茨伯格的双因素理论。

（A）Hygiene factors: maintenance factors called "dissatisfier".

Hygiene factors are those maintaining factors, simply speaking, if these factors are fulfilled, employees will not be motivated because these are the most basic requirements which should be satisfied. Furthermore, one thing to be noted is that dissatisfaction and unpleasantness may be resulted from absence of these hygiene factors.

Examples of hygiene factors:

(a) Working environment;

(b) Holiday, etc.

（B）Motivator factors: creating job satisfaction called "satisfier"

Motivator factors are those factors which can really stimulate employees to provide better performance. Compared with the hygiene ones, these motivator factors represent the higher requirements of employees which they can only be exchanged from harder working.

Examples of motivator factors:

(a) Career progression and status increases;

(b) Challenging work;

(c) A sense of achievement;

(d) Recognition by colleagues and management;

(e) Increasing level of responsibility.

(C) Appraisals of the theory

(a) The sample size of the theory is not sufficient, which means the result may not be representative.

(b) There is the same problem as Maslow theory, which is mostly focused on the western culture.

你可能已经发现了，大部分的激励因素都来自做一份工作本身带来的价值和满意度，而且往往都是非财务的。之所以如此，是因为赫茨伯格认为，通过工资上涨（即经济方面）对员工带来的激励是非常有限的，除了工资，他还提出了三种岗位设计的方法，能够用来有效地激励员工。

2.1.3 Job design

It is the fact that management level can motivate employees through non-financial motivators. Here we will introduce such method through job designing.

(a) Job enrichment

It is a vertical extension of jobs, and the extension often means the delegation of authority from upper management level to a lower level. Such design is planned to build greater responsibility and challenge of work into a job.

(b) Job enlargement

It is the concept of widening jobs by increasing the number of operations in which the employees are involved. It is a "horizontal" extension of contents of jobs. Simply speaking, it means increasing the workload of employees' existing jobs.

In real workplace, both of job enrichment and job enlargement are signs of promotion for employees. This is known as more power, more responsibility. As a consequence, employees will be motivated.

(c) Job rotation

Job rotation is a good choice to avoid repeatability of work that may restrain employees' working enthusiasm. It is done by transferring employees from one role to another, through which they can experience the variety of work, and understand the importance of their position in the whole organisation structure and system. In addition, they may find out the role that they are most suitable for.

知识点解读

Job enrichment 是工作的垂直变化，工作内容向上一个层次的提升，侧重深度；
Job enlargement，仅仅是工作量的增加，内容上没有质的变化，处于同一水平，侧重宽度。

知识点解读

Job rotation 指的是轮岗，能够很好地规避员工工作的重复性和单一性，也能帮助员工快速熟悉公司内的多项职能与流程，找到自己最擅长的工作内容。此举在大公司管培生计划当中特别常见。

2.2 Process theories

2.2.1 Vroom's expectancy theory

> **博学多才**

期望理论又称作"效价-手段-期望理论",是管理心理学与行为科学的一种理论。这个理论可以公式表示为:激动力量=期望值×效价。是由美国著名心理学家和行为科学家维克托·弗鲁姆(Victor H. Vroom)于1964年在《工作与激励》中提出来的激励理论。

Expectancy theory is a typical process theory, and it puts forward that the extent of motivation depends on two factors, one is people's preference for the reward provided, and the other is the probability of achieving the requirement to gain the reward.

$$F = V \times E$$

F = force: the extent of motivation for individuals to behave in line with employers' requirements

V = valence: the degree of the individual's **preference** for the given outcome or reward

E = expectancy: the **probability of success** from individual's perception

在这个公式中,激动力量(F)指调动个人积极性,激发人内部潜力的强度;期望值(E)是根据个人的经验判断达到目标的把握程度;效价(V)则是对达到的目标的渴望程度。这个理论的公式说明,人的积极性被调动的大小取决于期望值与效价的乘积。也就是说,一个人对目标实现的渴望度越高,估计达到目标的概率越高,激发起的动力越强烈,积极性也就越大,在领导与管理工作中,运用期望理论对于调动下属的积极性是有一定意义的。

2.2.2 The implications of the theory

(a) **Clearly intended tasks and reward**: By doing this, individuals can know the possibility of successfully accomplishing tasks and whether the reward is attractive, thus the extent of both "V" and "E".

(b) **Set specific goals to satisfy individuals' needs**: Different staffs are committed to specific goals. Some individuals are motivated by increase of salaries while others by promotion of status, therefore goals should be set by taking their specific needs and expectations into account. Therefore, "V" can be enhanced.

(c) **Immediate and ongoing feedback**: Feedback could be used as an indication and check of the level of achievement of tasks, thus "E" could be known.

> **小试牛刀**

Example question 2

Alina is working in the finance department of a retail company. She is performing well during this year and her director wants to promote her to a senior position. Alina hesitates whether to accept the chance because she wants more spare time with her boyfriend. According to the Vroom's expectancy theory, which of the following statement is true?

A. Low V, High E, High F
B. High V, High E, High F
C. High V, Low E, Low F
D. Low V, High E, Low F

2.3 McGregor: Theory X and Theory Y

XY 理论（见表 17-2）是由道格拉斯·麦克里戈（Douglas McGregor, 1906—1964 年）于1957 年在他著的《企业的人性面》一书中首次提出来的，实质上是XY 假设。

表 17-2　Theory X and theory Y

Theory X: Under theory X, employees are assumed to:	Theory Y: Under theory Y, employees are assumed to:
Dislike work	Enjoy work
Have to be coerced, threatened or forced to work adequately	Be able to be motivated to take responsibility
Dislike taking responsibility, and prefer to be directed and told what to do	Are able to exercise self-control and self-direction in order to achieve their goals
Managers who believe in theory X, may adopt strict supervision above employees, and prefer to exert the policy of 'carrot and stick'	Managers with the assumption of theory Y, prefer to play as leaders. It means that they will set the framework of tasks, and delegate some authority to subordinates, which can motivate staff to some extent

Y 理论是与 X 理论根本对立的。从现代管理发展的趋势来看，似乎 Y 理论更容易被大多数人接受，但这并不代表说 Y 理论就十分正确，任何情况都适用；也不等于说 X 理论就完全错误，毫无用处。在实际管理工作中，还是要将两者结合起来，根据不同情况灵活运用。

小试牛刀

Example question 3

Jack is CEO of ABC Co, and he considers his subordinates to be lazy, passive, and avoiding taking on responsibility.

In this case, which theory of McGregor are the above assumptions based on?

A. Theory X　　B. Theory Y　　C. Theory Z

3 Reward system

Reward is a **token** given in recognition of some **contribution** or **success**.

3.1 Types of reward

This classification is closely linked to Herzberg's two-factor theory.

(a) **Extrinsic rewards**

Extrinsic rewards are isolated from the job itself, which are externally related

> **核心考点**
>
> 考试多为判断题，让考生选择以下哪个为 extrinsic reward。
> 考生在这里可以类比双因素理论，判断标准是一样的。
> Extrinsic rewards 是独立于这份工作本身的外部因素，对应 hygiene factors；Intrinsic rewards 来自做一份工作本身，如成就感、别人的认可，对应 motivator factor。

to the jobs, for example, salaries, bonus, office environment etc.

(b) Intrinsic rewards

Intrinsic rewards arise from the performance and work themselves. Mostly, these rewards are psychological, for example, the degree of satisfaction, the feeling of achievement and so on.

小试牛刀

Example question 4

Example question 4

John is a sale manager. He loves the excitement of getting a challenging work. He is paid a good salary and has job security. He likes to deal with difficult issues.

Which of the following are John's intrinsic reward?

(1) Getting a challenging work.

(2) Good salary.

(3) Job security.

(4) Deal with difficult issues.

  A. (1)(3) and (4)   B. (1)(2) and (3)

  C. (1) and (4) only   D. (2)(3) and (4)

3.2 Design of reward system

  为表现优异的员工提供正向的奖励是最主要的激励方式，同学们需要掌握如何设计以及履行激励的措施。 好的激励体系需要详细设计，以确保其有效性。

When designing reward system, companies should ensure that they:

(a) Comply with relevant legislation and regulation.

(b) Are attractive enough to retain best employees (at least not below market rates).

(c) Are fair for all employees and help to improve their performance.

(d) Designed after thorough job evaluation (job evaluation is a systematic process for establishing the **relative worth** of jobs within an organisation to provide a rational basis for the design and maintenance of an equitable pay structure).

3.2.1 Types of incentive scheme

(A) Performance-related pay

It links employee's salary and wages to corporate performance. However, it focuses on short-term performance rather than the longer-term.

(B) Executive share options plans

Share options allow directors to purchase shares at a specified price on a specified future date, encouraging them to make decisions which exert an upward pressure on share prices.

(a) Advantages

● Goal congruence: align the objectives of managers and shareholders in the long-term;

- Improve staff motivation and retention and thus lower staff turnover costs.

(b) **Disadvantages**
- There is little evidence of a positive correlation between share option schemes and the creation of extra share value;
- Share prices frequently move for reasons which have nothing to do with directors' effort.

Answers for example question

1. B
2. D
3. A
4. C

Summary

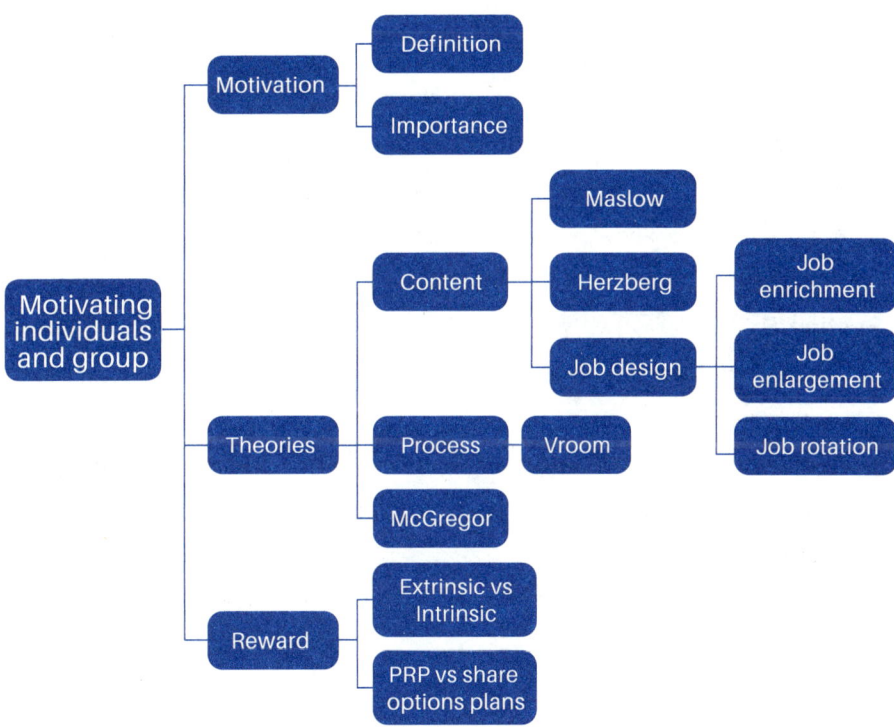

Chapter 17 考试不同问法总结

Section A

1. 针对 Maslow's hierarchy of needs
- According to Maslow's hierarchy of needs theory, which level of need is A Co. going to satisfy?

2. 针对 Hertzberg's two-factor theory
- Which of the following classifications of motivational theory reflects the work of Hertzberg?

- According to Hertzberg's two-factor analysis in which of the following categories does salary fall?
- Which TWO of the following would Hertzberg identify as motivation factors?
- Which TWO of the following types of reward are considered by Hertzberg to be effective long-term motivators?

3. 针对 Vroom's expectancy theory

- What does the V in Vroom's motivational equation stand for?

4. 针对 Theory X and Theory Y

- A and B both follow one of McGregor's motivational approaches. Indicate which approach each manager is taking?
- Which TWO of the following would you believe if you agree with McGregor's Theory X?
- Which of the following characteristics describes McGregor's Theory X?
- "Because of their dislike for work, most people prefer to be directed, and tend to avoid taking on responsibility and desire security above anything else".
- Which theory of McGregor are the above assumptions based on?

5. 针对 Motivators

- Which of the following reflects the nature of job enrichment?
- Which of the above statements are relevant to the intrinsic rewards of A's job?

Section B

- According to Maslow's theory, which TWO of the following are examples of lower order needs?
- With reference to McGregor's theory, for each statement made at the meeting, indicate whether it suggests a Theory X or Theory Y attitude to people at work.
- Which FOUR of the following types of reward are extrinsic or intrinsic?

Quick quiz

17.1 Which of the following belongs to McGregor's Theory X management style?

   A. Consultative   B. Authoritative   C. Sells   D. Joins

Answer: **B**

Difficulty level: **Easy**

Tag: **McGregor's Theory X and Theory Y**

Rationale:

   In Theory X, employees are assumed to dislike work, dislike taking responsibility and have to be coerced, threatened or forced to get them to work adequately, while managers who operate according to these assumptions will tend to supervise closely, apply detailed rules and controls, and use "carrot and stick" motivators. Therefore, option B is correct.

   这道题考查的是 McGregor 的 X 理论和 Y 理论中的 X 理论，作为 X 理论，它的核心观点是人性本恶，人本质上是不喜欢工作的，同时也不喜欢承担责任，因而只能通过威胁或者强迫使员工努力工作。而管理者要采取严格的监管来管理员工，必要时，软硬兼施是一种有效的措施。

17.2 Which of the following correctly describes the meaning of 'V' in Vroom's expectancy theory?

   A. Valence   B. Value   C. Variety   D. Venture

Answer: **A**

Difficulty level: **Easy**

Tag: **Vroom's expectancy theory**

Rationale:

   In expectancy theory, V stands for valence and its meaning is the strength of the individual preference for a given outcome or reward. Therefore, option A is correct.

   根据 Vroom 提出的期望理论，V 全称叫 Valence，指的是对于所期望的结果的偏好程度，如果越渴望，V 就越高；反之，亦然。

17.3 Tim is an employee in sales department. The sales team has a sales competition at the year end and the winner will be the sales team leader for the next year. Tim has confidence that he will be the winner, but if so, he would have to work much longer hours. Thus, he is quite reluctant to do this for family reasons. If the expectancy equation was used to assess Jim's motivation to work hard at the end of the year, based on the information given, which of the following results would you expect to see?

   A. Valence would be high, expectancy high, motivation high

   B. Valence would be high, expectancy low, motivation low

   C. Valence would be around 0, expectancy high, motivation low

   D. Valence would be around 0, expectancy high, motivation high

Answer: **C**

Difficulty level: **Easy**

Tag: **Process theory**

Rationale:

   Jim believes that he will win the competition, which shows the Expectancy is high. However, he also considers the time apportion between work and family. Reluctant clearly illustrates that the willingness is low, in other words, Valence is around 0. According to the formula: F = V x E, Motivation will be low.

Pitfalls: Well understanding of the two variances are crucial for this examination point.

Ways in: Equation is the exam point, evaluating V and E separately.

Jim 相信他能够赢得比赛，这说明期望值 E 很高，然后他在担心时间在工作和家庭之间分配的问题，不愿意（加班）很显然表明他的意愿是低的，也就是 V 是接近 0 的。根据公式，激励力量的大小（F）= V×E，所以激励力量的大小也很低。

17.4 Sarah works as a software engineer in DEF CO. The company offers its employees a pay package including basic salary and paid vocation. The workplace is also safe. Sarah is satisfied with her salary and workplace, but she expects more challenges in her work. She said her work in DEF was boring because she had to do bulk duplicated work.

Which of the followings is a motivator according to Herzberg's two factor theory?

A. Basic salary   B. Paid vocation   C. Duplicated work   D. Challenged work

Answer: D

Difficulty level: Easy

Tag: Herzberg's two factor theory

Rationale:

Candidates should clearly tell the difference between hygiene factors and motivator factors. Motivation factors give positive satisfaction, arising from intrinsic conditions of the job itself, which stimulates improved performance.

Hygiene factors do not give positive satisfaction. What can hygiene factor do is to avoid dissatisfaction and unpleasantness. Thus, the first three are hygiene factors.

考生需要清楚地区分保健因素与激励因素的不同之处。激励因素能够带来工作满意度，通常是由工作内容本身引起的，进而刺激员工的业绩表现。保健因素不会带来工作满意，它能做到的就是避免不满意和不开心。因此，前三个选项是保健因素。

17.5 Which of the following is not an advantage of job enrichment under job design for the organisation?

A. It facilitates quality of output   B. It reduces the risk of error

C. It contributes to career paths   D. It reduces management expenditures

Answer: C

Difficulty level: Easy

Tag: Motivators-Job design

Rationale:

Job enrichment is planned, deliberate action to build greater responsibility, breadth and challenge of work into a job. It is similar to empowerment and represents a "vertical" extension of jobs. Thus, above options are all good results. However, option C is good for individuals other rather the organisation and option C is answer.

C 选项的确是 Job enrichment 的优点，但却是对于个人而言的优点，而并非是针对组织的优点。

Chapter 18
Personal effectiveness and communication

知识导入

本章我们要学习个人有效性以及沟通的相关问题，通过这章的学习，我们会了解如何通过个人自身的行为和努力进行自我提升，以及如何沟通，才是最有效的。从实务上来讲，这章内容非常实用，非常具有阅读价值，切勿掉以轻心。

单词表

英文	中文
Bin	丢弃
Urgent	紧急的
Transferable	转移的
Puzzle	疑惑
Incompatible	不兼容
Denial	否决
Trivial	微小的
Suppression	镇压
Compromise	妥协
Exaggerate	扩大
Authoritative	有权威性的
Diagonal	斜对角线的
Reinforce	增强
Yawn	打哈欠

学习指南

Learning objectives	Pass level	Distinction level	用时建议
1. Importance of time management (1-2)	√		10 mins
2. Competence framework (3.1-3.3)	√		20 mins
3. Conflict (4)	√		15 mins
4. Communication in the workplace (5)	√		20 mins

本章考点

重要考点	难度（1~3）
理解如何进行时间管理，以及有哪些因素影响时间管理	1
理解 competence framework 的定义	1

重要考点	难度（1~3）
理解熟记并区分 coaching，mentoring 和 counselling	2
理解并熟记处理冲突的手段	2
理解并熟记沟通网络	3
理解并能够区分如何选择合适的沟通媒介	3
熟记信息质量的要求	1

1 Time management

Time management is a set of principles, practices, skills, tools, and systems working together to help you get more value out of your time with the aim of improving the quality of your life ("Time management", n.d.).

1.1 Principles of time management

(A) Set "SMART" goals

(a) **S**pecific.

(b) **M**easurable.

(c) **A**ttainable.

(d) **R**elevant.

(e) **T**ime-based.

博学多才

以 SMART 为导向的"华为"目标原则（葛梅，张晋光，2005）：

"华为"的时间管理培训指出，目标原则不单单是有目标，而且是要让目标达到 SMART 标准，这里 SMART 标准是指：

（1）具体性（Specific）。这是指目标必须是清晰的，可产生行为导向的。比如，"我要成为一个优秀的'华为人'"不是一个具体的目标，但"我要获得今年的华为最佳员工奖"就算得上是一个具体的目标了。

（2）可衡量性（Measurable）。这是指目标必须用指标量化表达。比如，上面这个"我要获得今年的华为最佳员工奖"目标，它就对应着许多量化的指标——出勤、业务量等。

（3）可行性（Attainable）。这里可行性有两层意思：一是目标应该有能力范围内；二是目标应该有一定难度。一般人在这点上往往只注意前者，其实后者也相当重要。如果目标经常达不到，的确会让人沮丧，但同时也应注意：太容易达到的目标会让人失去激情。

（4）相关性（Relevant）。这是指与现实生活相关，而不是简单的"白日梦"。

（5）及时性（Time-based）。及时性比较容易理解，是指目标必须确定完成的日期。在这一点上，华为的时间管理培训指出，不但要确定最终目标的完成时间,还要设立多个小时间段上的"时间里程碑",以便进行工作进度的监控。

成功地界定问题就已经解决了问题的一半,但如果没有切实可行的计划和解决方案,困境还是不会改变。接下来我们来学习如何制定有效的计划。

(B) Action plans

(1) 制定具体工作目标及重点;

(2) 选择有效利用时间的方法与策略;

(3) 列出时间安排表。

(C) Priorities

著名管理学家科维提出了一个时间管理的理论,把工作按照重要和紧急两个不同的程度进行了划分,基本上可以分为四个象限:既紧急又重要(如人事危机、客户投诉、即将到期的任务、财务危机等),重要但不紧急(如建立人际关系),紧急但不重要(如电话铃声、不速之客、行政检查等),既不紧急也不重要(如客套的闲谈、无聊的信件等)。

时间管理理论的一个重要观念是应有重点地把主要的精力和时间集中地放在处理那些重要但不紧急的工作上。在人们的日常工作中,很多时候往往有机会去很好地计划和完成一件事。但常常却又没有及时地去做,随着时间的推移,造成工作质量的下降。因此,应把主要的精力有重点地放在重要但不紧急这个象限的事务上是必要的。要把精力主要放在重要但不紧急的事务处理上,需要很好地安排时间。一个好的方法是建立预约制度。建立了预约制度,自己的时间才不会被别人所占据,从而有效地开展工作。

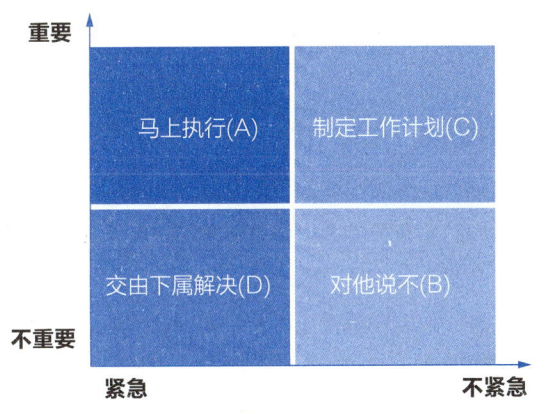

图 18-1 ABCD 时间管理法

这种时间管理方法,我们也可以记为 **ABCD** method(如图 18-1 所示),即针对不同情况的任务,分情况处理:

(a) **A**ct immediately.

(b) **B**in it, if you are sure it is worthless.

(c) **C**reate a definite plan and put it into 'to-do list'.

(d) **D**elegate it to someone else to handle.

(D) Focus—one time one thing

1.2 Tips for effective time management

(A) Write things down

Do not try to use memory to keep track of too many details of the work, as this may probably lead to information overload. Using a memo or **to-do list** to write things down is a great way to handle heavy task needs and keep yourself organised.

(B) **Plan your week**

At the beginning of each week, you could spend fifteen or twenty minutes to plan your in-coming schedule. This will help increase your productivity and balance the long-term projects with more urgent tasks.

(C) **Stay in control of the telephone**

For example, only take calls during certain urgent hours.

(D) **Learn to say no**

Many people become overloaded and frustrated with too much work because they overcommit and feel embarrassed to say no. Once the task needs are above your limit, you just need reject and you will free up time to spend on things that are more important.

(E) **Don't do other people's work**

Some people have the habit of doing others' work because of a "hero" mentality. However, doing this takes up much of your time. Instead, you should focus on your own projects and goals, learn to delegate well and teach others how to do their own work.

(F) **Don't be a perfectionist**

Some tasks don't require your best effort. Learn to distinguish between tasks that deserve to be done excellently and tasks that just need to be done.

2 Ineffectiveness at work

工作中的低效可能体现在方方面面，例如：

（1）对于员工来说，最常见的是，没有与同事进行准确沟通，导致没有明确任务需求，最终造成生产的产品有误，错过截止日期。

（2）对于公司来说，如果在运营过程中，出现了危机却没能及时解决，导致了与供应商和顾客之间的误会，可能最终会对名誉造成损失。

在日常运营中，公司可以通过很多渠道，提升其运作效率，接下来我们通过2.1来进行学习。

2.1 The effect of information technology on improving efficiency

(A) **Office automation**

Office automation refers to the collective hardware, software and processes that enable automation of the information processing and communication tasks, integration of office functions usually related to managing information in an organisation. It involves using software to digitise, store and process business data like invoices and basic accounting information. Also communicate most routine tasks and processes in office.

(B) **EDI—electronic data interchange**

EDI makes it possible to share information between computers. For instance, a customer may electronically place an order with their suppliers. This order will automatically be placed on the supplier's system without the need for physical forms to be printed, posted and then processed. This saves time and increases efficiency.

(C) **Intranets**

These are internal networks where employees can access a central store of information which speeds up communication by the company with its employees.

(D) **Homeworking or remote working**

Many employees now work at home. While this may make it harder for the organisation to control their activities, it offers increased motivation for workers, as well as lower overheads (i.e. smaller offices are needed) for employers.

3 Competence frameworks

Competences are the critical skills, knowledge and attitudes that a jobholder must have to perform effectively. **Competence frameworks attempt to identify all competences that are required by anyone taking on a particular role within the organisation**.

Most competences frameworks cover the following categories:

- Communication skills.
- Team skills.
- Problem-solving skills.

Employees should regularly review competency frameworks to assess whether they are competent for the skills required. The framework also provides a basis for employees to plan their personal development.

3.1 Coaching

3.1.1 Definition

It means helping another person to improve awareness, to set and achieve goals in order to improve a particular behavioural performance.

3.1.2 Characteristics

(a) Shorter-term relationship.

(b) Specific, realistic targets.

(c) Relevant to the current job.

(d) The coach often has direct experience of their client's formal occupational role.

3.2 Mentoring

3.2.1 Definition

It means help to shape an individual's beliefs and values in a positive way.

3.2.2 Characteristics

(a) Longer-term relationship.

(b) Takes a broader view of the person.

核心考点

Competence frameworks 本身的概念理解，以及提升 competence 的三种方式。Coaching/mentoring/counselling 各自的特征以及区别，是考试中的核心考点，需要考生掌握。

知识点解读

Coaching：指导，进行手把手的教学，内容与现在的本职工作直接相关，如足球教练、驾驶证的教练。

Mentoring：教导，内容范围远大于本职工作，大部分情况是不直接相关的，如人生规划方面的指导。

Counselling：咨询，这里更多指的是心理咨询，典型特征是这种咨询类型是非指导性的，通过沟通交流帮助被咨询者渡过难关。

(c) Mentor is usually more experienced and qualified than the 'mentee'. They are often a senior person in the organisation who can pass on knowledge, experience and open doors to otherwise out-of-reach opportunities.

(d) Focus is on career and personal development.

3.3 Counselling

3.3.1 Definition

It means helping an individual to improve performance by resolving situations from the past.

3.3.2 Characteristics

(a) Do not give directive advices or suggestions.

(b) To solve problems or puzzles.

(c) Counselling can be used to address psycho-social as well as performance issues.

(d) The goal of counselling is to help people understand the root causes of long-standing performance problems/issues at work.

4 Conflicts

人与人之间总有方面存在差异，如个性、利益、思维模式、信仰等。 在一个团队中，差异的存在很容易导致成员之间出现摩擦和冲突。 在大众的概念中，冲突意味着不和谐的团队氛围与合作，从而对团队目标的达成产生负面影响。 然而事实上，冲突并不一定是坏事，有时团队成员之间的冲突也的确能产生"头脑风暴"的效应。 因此，对于管理者来说，针对冲突这个议题，第一件需要做的事情应当是确认冲突来自何处，其次才是如何解决冲突。

4.1 How does conflict arise?

冲突的来源大致可以分为一种争夺、三种不协调，以及一种拒绝。

（1）一种争夺（compete for the limited power and resources）：

资源有限是争夺的诱因。 团队中，资源的限制是司空见惯的现象，不管是管理权，还是其他可以给个人带来利益的资源。 在这种僧多粥少的情况下，团队成员可能就会出现互相竞争，从而引发冲突的现象。

（2）三种不协调：

- 目标与利益的不协调（incompatible goals and interests）：当团队目标的设置与个人利益并非完全挂钩甚至背道而驰的时候，冲突是必然会发生的结果。

- 团队成员性格的不协调（incompatible personalities）：世界上没有两片完全相同的树叶，人的性格千差万别，在团队中，协调得好，就是百花齐放；协调得不好，团员之间就会因性格摩擦产生冲突。

- 工作方式与风格的不协调（incompatible work methods, styles）：其实这种不协调很大程度上也是由于团队成员性格的差异导致的，每个人都有自己的工作节奏和步调，在团队协作过程中，这种不协调非常容易导致出现

"杂音"。

（3）一种拒绝（poor communication and co-ordination）：

还有一种非常直接的冲突，简单来说就是来自团队成员的拒绝沟通与合作。

4.2 Managing your own interpersonal conflicts

(a) Denial/withdrawal

This method tries to solve conflicts by evading the real problem. This is a common method for problems that are not very urgent.

回避：是指试图通过逃避问题情境的方式来平息冲突。这种比较消极的冲突管理方式在应对不太紧要的问题时比较有效。此外，当问题需要冷处理时亦可采用回避作为权宜之计，以防止冲突进一步激化。但是，回避无法从根本上解决问题，且容易导致自己和对方产生挫败感。

(b) Suppression

This method tends to preserve working relationships despite of conflicts.

镇压：是指以他人的利益为代价，试图在冲突上占上风。这种极端不合作的冲突管理方式通常并不是最佳解决方案。但是，当确信自己是正确的，且分歧需要在较短时间内解决时，镇压是必要的。

(c) Dominance

It means that managers will make final decisions by using their power and/or authorities. However, this measure may result in 'win-lose' situations.

控制：是指通过自身权力或者影响力解决冲突，但是这种相对比较强硬的解决方式的处理结果中总有一方会作出让步，很难达到双赢。

(d) Compromise

Decisions are made after the process of bargaining, negotiating and conciliating. In order to balance interests of different related parties, final results may be compromised.

折中：是指试图寻求一个中间位置，使自身的利益得失相当。折中方法比较适合难以共赢的情境。当双方势均力敌时，且解决分歧的时间期限比较紧迫时，折中比较有效。但由于忽略双方共同利益，因此折中往往难以产生非常令人满意的问题解决办法。

(e) Integration/collaboration

Members in the team should always focus on the task and groups' sake even though they need to modify their views and behaviours.

协同：是指双方通过积极地解决问题来寻求互惠和共赢。其特征是双方乐于分享信息，并善于在此基础上发现共同点，找到最佳解决方法。通常，协同是首选的冲突管理方式。但只有在双方没有完全对立的利益，且彼此有足够的信任和开放程度来分享信息时，协同才能有效地发挥作用。

不同处理冲突的方式会有三种后果，包括：

（1）Win-win，双赢，解决方案满足冲突双方（个体或者团队之间）自身的诉求；

（2）Lose-lose，双输；

（3）Win-lose，单方面获利，这是最常见的解决方案。

5 Communication in the workplace

Communication is a two-way process involving the transmission or exchange of information and the provision of feedback. It is necessary to direct and coordinate activities.

在组织中，沟通是一个无时无刻不在发生的过程，无论是上下级之间传达指令汇报工作，平级之间协调工作，抑或是与外部利益相关者就相关事宜进行磋商，沟通可以说是无处不在，这也侧面说明了沟通的绝对重要性。因此，我们接下来需要了解以下内容：

（1）选择适当的沟通工具；
（2）沟通信息的质量需求；
（3）沟通渠道；
（4）沟通网络；
（5）正式沟通流程图；
（6）非正式沟通以及影响沟通有效性的障碍。

5.1 Deciding a communication tool

> **核心考点**
> 本段重点是对比各种沟通工具的优劣势，结合理解进行记忆。这个知识点也比较贴近生活，但需要考生熟悉英文表达，确保能够解题。

The **channel of communication** will impact on the effectiveness of the communication process. The characteristics of the message will determine what communication tool is best for a given situation. In addition to those common communication tools, for example, telephones, e-mails, meetings, reports and so on, two other tools will be illustrated as follows：

(a) **Team-briefing**(简布会)

　　For：Increase commitment and understanding of workforce.

　　Against：Has a limit of participants.

(b) **Noticeboard**(公告板)

　　For：Transmit information cheaply to a large number of people.

　　Against：Cannot provide information if having no access to noticeboard.

小试牛刀

Example question 1

The directors of ABC Co are considering restructuring the company and wish to inform the company's 30 employees of their proposals. The restructuring will require the commitment and understanding of the employees if they are to succeed.

Which medium of communication will be MOST suitable for this purpose?

　A. Noticeboard　　B. Team-briefing　　C. Report　　D. E-mail

5.2 The qualities of good information (ACCURATE)

> **知识点解读**
> 好的信息需要具备怎么样的质量，这里有一个记忆的小诀窍，这8个质量的首字母刚好组成一个单词：ACCURATE。考生可以根据这个方式去记忆。

It should be admitted that in the modern society, with the development of IT and medium, information become quite overload. Therefore, we should select and use good information. As good information, there are eight common qualities for reference:

- **A**ccurate：准确性；
- **C**omplete：完整性；
- **C**ost beneficial：效益性；
- **U**ser-targeted：针对性；
- **R**elevant：相关性；
- **A**uthoritative：权威性/可靠性；
- **T**imely：及时性；
- **E**asy to use：易用性。

5.3 Direction of communication

(a) Vertical communication

Vertical communication operates in line with scalar chain, that information passes upward and downward between superiors and subordinates.

(b) Horizontal or lateral communication

Horizontal or lateral communication is communication between people on the same level of authority.

(c) Diagonal communication

Diagonal communication facilitates people from different levels and different departments to transfer information.

> **知识点解读**
>
> Vertical 强调是同部门的上级和下级沟通，是垂直的沟通；
> Horizontal 强调跨部门，同级别同事之间的沟通；
> Diagonal 是跨部门，跨级别的沟通。

5.4 Communication patterns

In Leavitt's experiment, each member of a group of five people had to solve a problem and each had an essential piece of information. The findings of the experiment are illustrated below.

H.J.里维特(1951)研究了 5 人群体的几种典型的沟通网络，分别表示为星型、环型、链型、Y 型和轮型，各型的集中化程度不同，信息交流的自由度以及参与者满意度也不一样。接下来我们来逐一了解这 5 种沟通网络。

> **核心考点**
>
> 考生需了解这 4 类沟通方式解决问题的快慢程度和工作满意度的排名。

(A) All channel or star network

All the members in this network communicate with each other freely and regularly.

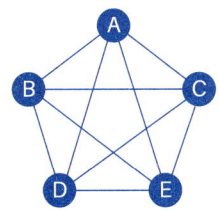

图 18-2　All channel/star network communication

全通道式沟通是指所有沟通参与者之间穷尽所有沟通渠道的全方位沟通(如图 18-2 所示)。这是一个开放式的网络系统，其中每个成员之间都有一定的联系，彼此了解。此网络中组织的集中化程度及主管人的预测程度均很低。由于沟通渠道很多，组织成员的平均满意程度高且差异小，所以士气高昂，合作气氛浓厚。

这对于解决复杂问题，增强组织合作精神，提高士气均有很大作用。但是，由于这种网络沟通渠道太多，易造成混乱，且又费时，影响工作效率。

（B）The circle

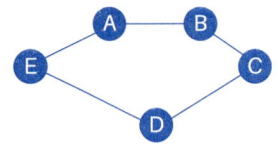

图 18-3　The circle communication

Circle indicates that such pattern is a closed loop. As we can see from the graph, for example, A can communicate with either B or E, after receiving information, B and E can then pass what they get from A to the next members. It can be seen that each member in the circle can only communicate with two other members directly, as a result, the message will be received in sequence.

环式沟通中的成员处于相互平等的沟通地位，这个形状可以看成是链式形态的一个封闭式控制结构，如图 18-3 所示的 5 人（ABCDE）之间依次沟通。其中，每个人都可同时与两侧的人沟通信息。

（C）The chain

图 18-4　The chain communication

This pattern is quite similar to the circle, the main difference is that the chain is an open communication method, which results two points distinguish the chain from the circle：

(a) In the chain, the first member and the last one cannot communicate with each other, which may not frustrate these two members during the communication to some extent；

(b) Due to the lack of communication between A and E, distortion of information may occur in such pattern.

链式沟通又称为直线型沟通（如图 18-4 所示），在这种结构中，A 和 E 处于沟通的两个端点，我们可以把 A 当作信息传递的最初发送者，E 看作最终的接收者，也正因为 A 与 E 之间并不能直接沟通，需要通过 BCD 传递信息，很可能会出现信息的失真。

（D）The 'Y'

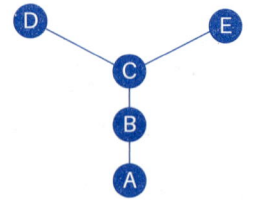

图 18-5　The "Y" communication

The pattern of Y is a typical vertical communication channel. In the Y, C occupies the central position, there are two ways how such pattern works：

(a) A passes information to B, and then B passes to C, at last, C disseminates what he/she receives to both D and E;
(b) D or E transmits message to C, and the C delivers message to B, and at last, B to A.

This "Y" pattern often occurs alongside the scalar chain, which is a formal channel adopted to give instruction downwards and to report upwards.

Y 式沟通是一个纵向沟通网络，C 处于沟通的中心地带，他负责的是上传下达或者下情上报的工作，是一个典型的信息传播媒介。但从图 18－5 中我们不难发现，D 与 E，A 与 B 能收到信息的质量和数量，都取决于 C。因此，C 的位置是至关重要的。

(E) The wheel

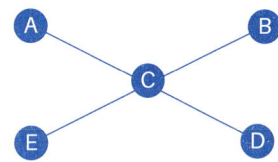

图 18－6　The wheel communication

As the same as the "Y", C occupies the core part in the wheel, which means only C can communicate with all other members in the pattern directly. It is indicated that C should be in charge of receiving, processing and transmitting messages, which also means the importance of C in such pattern.

轮式沟通网络（如图 18－6 所示）的沟通核心同样是 C，只有 C 能够与其他任何人交流，所有其他人也只能与中间人进行交流，C 是各种信息的汇集点与传递中心，他起着一种领导、支配与协调的作用。

这 5 种沟通模式，由上至下，沟通速度逐一增加，同时，参与者满意度也在逐一下降。

A direct trade-off between speed and job-satisfaction is evident.

5.5 Formal communication process

The formal communication process is as follows（见图 18－7）。

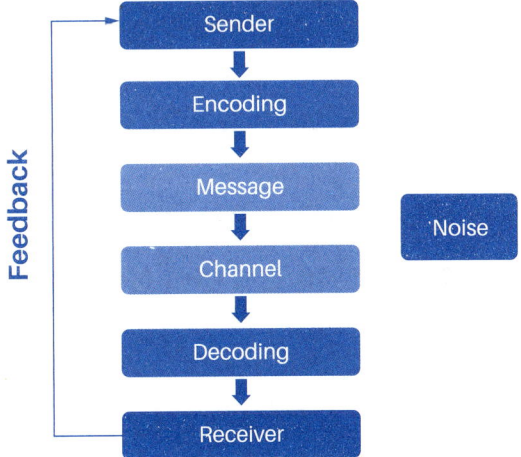

图 18－7　Formal communication process

(a) **Sender**: the message creator.

(b) **Encoding**: the process of putting thoughts into messages through the creation of content and symbols.

(c) **Message**: the transmitted information.

(d) **Medium/Channel**: the medium through which the message passes.

(e) **Decoding**: the process of interpreting and assigning meaning to a message.

(f) **Receiver**: the target of the sender and collector of the message.

(g) **Feedback**: The sender of a message needs feedback on the receiver's reaction. This is partly to test the receiver's understanding of it and partly to assess the receiver's reaction.

(h) **Noise**: those distractions which interfere with the transmission of the message, e.g. a bad telephone line.

精益求精

Distortion: the meaning of a message can be lost at both the coding and decoding stages, e.g. the different culture may distort the understanding of information.

小试牛刀

Example question 2

What are the six basic elements of communication?

A. Sender, receiver, information, message, direction and code

B. Information, message, decode, sender, receiver and channel

C. Sender, message, channel, receiver, noise and feedback

D. Direction, information, sender, code, noise and feedback

5.5.1 Desirable qualities of the communication system

Clarity. Communication information need to be clear and easy to be understood.

Recipient. The recipient should be clearly identified to minimise distortion and noise.

Medium. The appropriate channel or medium should be chosen to ensure information reaches the target audience.

Timing. Information has to be timely to be useful.

5.6 Informal communication and barriers to communication

5.6.1 Grapevine

(a) The grapevine spread rapidly;

(b) The recipients of the grapevine are selective;

(c) The grapevine does not spread outside the working place;

(d) The grapevine cannot cover the shortage of ineffective formal communica-

---

知识点解读

沟通系统作为传播信息的载体很重要，那么一个好的沟通系统需要具备什么特征，其实很简单：

（1）信息尽量要简洁，避免传播过程中的失真；

（2）接收者要明确，避免将信息传达给错误的人，造成不必要的损失；

（3）应当根据信息的性质和重要性选择合适的传播媒介；

（4）及时传递。

tions, it only flourishes when there is much information and news from official sources;

(e) Senior level staffs possess and spread more grapevines than their subordinates as they have widened span of control and access to information. Also, technostructure executives know more about events than line managers.

5.6.2 The importance of informal communication

Managers might prefer to use grapevine rather than formal channels for communicating as informal communication process has its own strengths:

(a) Transmitting more instant messages in a more convenient way;

(b) Revealing information about the informal organisation.

> **知识点解读**
>
> 小道消息，也叫"葡萄藤式"沟通。美国心理学家戴维斯曾在一家皮革制品公司专门对67名管理人员进行调查研究，发现了集束式的非正式沟通形式——把小道消息有选择地告诉自己的朋友或有关人。集束式又称葡萄藤式。

> **知识点解读**
>
> 非正式沟通渠道的重要性与我们之前学习过的非正式组织的优势有相似之处，同学们可以结合复习。

小试牛刀

Example question 3

Which **TWO** of the following describe the MOST usual impact of the informal organisation on the business and the people working within it?

A. Informal information can be inaccurate and negative, causing stress

B. Informal leaders may undermine managerial authority

C. Informal communication methods tend to be slower than formal channels

D. Informal networks discourage horizontal communication

Example question 4

Which **TWO** of the following statements regarding the "grapevine" (the informal system of communication) are correct?

A. It is more current than the formal system

B. Information tends to be divulged randomly

C. It is more active when the formal network is active

D. It usually operates outside the place of work

5.6.3 Non-verbal communication

The Non-verbal Communication is the process of conveying meaning without the use of words either written or spoken. In other words, any communication made between two or more persons through the use of facial expressions, hand movements, body language, postures, and gestures could be called as non-verbal communication. Non-verbal communication also has its importance and could assist formal communication.

(a) In certain situations, non-verbal communication such as yawn and applause gives the sender proper feedback relevant to the receiver.

(b) Non-verbal communications such as a smile and/or handshake enable the sender to demonstrate a favourable impression and form a desired atmosphere.

(c) Non-verbal communications such as gestures and frown could heighten the

> **知识点解读**
>
> 语言沟通的重要性无需赘述，值得我们关注的还有非语言沟通，包括交谈时的眼神、语气、姿势以及动作等，这些"小动作"对于我们而言是重要的信号，我们可以从中发现沟通背后更深的含义。例如：
> （1）一场演讲中，观众报以热烈的掌声，这就是一种积极的沟通，传达着对演讲者的赞赏；
> （2）一场约会中，对方的穿着，也可以传达出其对这次约会的态度和想法；
> （3）一段讲话中，重要的词用强调的语气读出，或是适当的停顿，都传达着需要人们注意的信号。

words and the effects.

5.7 Barriers to communication

大家可以自行回顾一下，在日常的沟通过程当中，有哪些妨碍有效沟通的因素。 有一些词汇大家肯定不陌生，如"忠言逆耳""不明觉厉"或是"选择性失聪"等。 这些说法其实都是暗示着在交谈或者是接收信息的过程中，我们总会受到各种各样的干扰，从而产生沟通障碍。 这些障碍总的来说可以分为两类（5.7.1）。

5.7.1 General faults

(a) **The personal barriers** relate to the factors that are personal to the sender and receiver and act as a hindrance in the communication process. These factors include the life experiences, emotions, attitudes, behaviour that hinders the ability of a person to communicate.

- Lack of listening skill.
- Lack of knowledge.
- Lack of vocabulary.

> 知识点解读
>
> 个人障碍，简言之就是由于沟通双方自身能力的缺乏导致的沟通不畅。

(b) The **psychological or emotional Barriers** refers to the psychological state (i.e. opinions, attitudes, status consciousness, emotions, etc.) of a person that deeply affects the ability to communicate.

- Lack of attention.
- Premature evaluation.
- Distrust.
- Emotion.

> 心理障碍，最典型的就是情绪。同样一句话，在人们心情好与不好的情况下，产生的效果可能会是两个极端。

5.7.2 Improving the communication

(a) Writing down important instructions and make sure records update immediately and could be easily accessed.

(b) Using proper language and make sure the messages and any terminology could be understood.

(c) Using informal channels and non-verbal communicating tools to cover the shortages of formal communication system.

(d) Using exception reports to avoid information overload of recipients.

(e) Selecting proper communicating tools and issue confirmation letters in certain situations

(f) Conducting staff meetings and in-house journals at regular intervals to improve internal communications.

(g) Holding appraisal interviews to facilitate the communication and understanding between staffs and superiors in regard to the jobs and performance.

Answers for example question

1. B
2. C

3. AB

4. AC

Summary

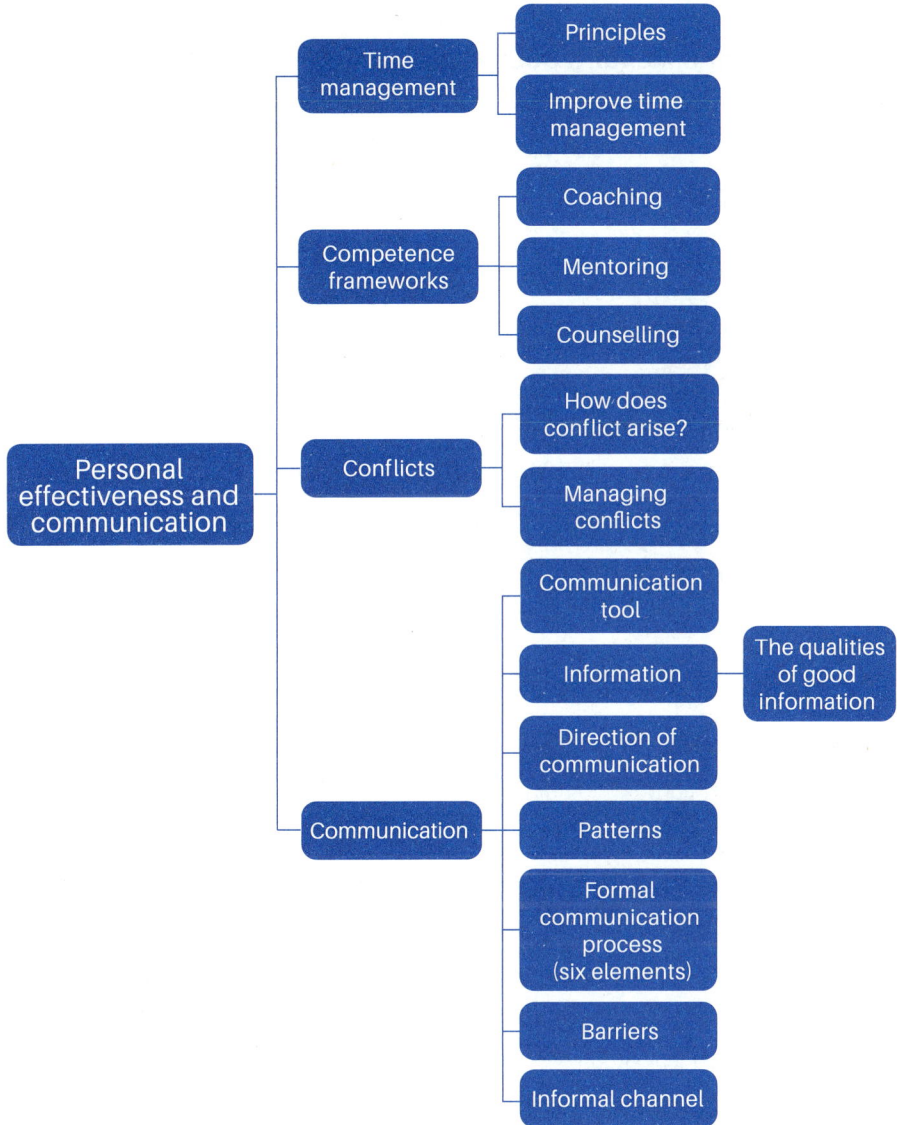

Chapter 18 考试不同问法总结

Section A

1. 针对 Time Management

- Which TWO of the following are examples of EXTERNAL barriers to effective time management?
- A's time management problems can be attributable to which of the following?

2. 针对 Ineffectiveness

- Which TWO of the following are direct benefits of using information technology as a mean of improving personal effectiveness?

3. 针对 Competence framework
- Which of the following definitions is BEST mapped with a competence framework?
- Which TWO of the following should be included in a competence framework?

4. 针对 Coach & Mentor & Counsellor
- Which of the following are accepted qualities of a counsellor?
- Which TWO of the following activities should be carried out by a mentor?

5. 针对 Conflict
- Are each of the following statements regarding conflict true or false?
- Which of the following is the MOST appropriate type of behaviour a person should adopt when attempting to reduce conflict with another person in the workplace?

6. 针对 Communication
- Which of the following statements about good quality information is true?
- Which TWO of the following factors are considered to be DISADVANTAGES of communicating using a formal report?
- For which of the following is horizontal communication used?
- An instruction given simultaneously to several subordinates reflects which pattern of communication?
- Which method of communication will be most appropriate for A to use when communicating to the board?
- Which of the following are typical of team briefing meeting?
- What is the correct order in the communication process for the following elements?
- What are the six basic elements of communication?
- Which general fault in the communication process is caused by excessive use of technical jargon?
- Which TWO will increase the efficiency of A's communication?
- Which TWO of the following statements regarding the 'grapevine' are correct?

Section B
- For each of the service provided by the staffs in the above scenario, indicate whether they are coaching, counselling or mentoring?
- Complete the following to show whether the direction of each memorandum is vertical, horizontal or diagonal.

Quick quiz

18.1 Which TWO of the following would cause barrier to effective time management?

  A. Excessive workload of superior   B. Conflicts among group members

  C. A culture of extreme centralisation   D. Focus on one task at a time

Answer: A, C

Difficulty level: Normal

Tag: Time Management

Rationale:

  Time management is concerned about reasonable allocation of time, with the aim to improve efficiency. Principles for managers generally include setting proper goals, making arrangements based on prioritisation, organising works appropriately and concentrating on current task. As a manager, adopting a centralised management style would lead to overload of work which definitely reduces the efficiency.

  时间管理很大程度上取决于时间分配与提高效率。对管理者来说，设定合适的目标、进行适当的工作分配、优先级考量等都是很有必要的。所以，倘若一个管理者采用集权的方式进行管理，那么也就意味着他的工作量不会少，这可能会导致他为了达到面面俱到而丧失效率。

18.2 Which of the following is the correct order of communication process?

  A. Sender, decode, channel, encode, receiver, feedback

  B. Sender, encode, channel, decode, receiver, feedback

  C. Sender, encode, decode, receiver, feedback, channel

  D. Sender, channel, encode, feedback, receiver, decode

Answer: B

Difficulty level: Easy

Tag: The communication process

Rationale:

  In a formal communication process, the correct order is sender, encode message, channel, decode message, receiver, feedback. Therefore, option B is answer.

  正式沟通流程的顺序是一个重要考点，考生应当记住。

18.3 Jack is a manager in Sales department. Lucy is a Finance Director. **Which of the following describes the direction of the communication flow when Jack asks for help from Luck?**

  A. Vertical   B. Horizontal   C. Diagonal

Answer: C

Difficulty level: Easy

Tag: Communication flow

Rationale:

  As Jack and Lucy are from different level of the organisation and departments. Communication here is both upwards and sideways.

  杰克和露西分属于组织中的不同层级和部门，所以这种沟通方式是对角线状的。

18.4 Nica works in a team that all members in this team can communicate with each other freely and regularly. There is no leader in their team, and all members are satisfied with their work style. However, Nica often complains that their processing speed is too slow.

Which of the following describes the communication pattern in Nicas team?

A. The circle   B. The Y   C. The wheel   D. The all-channel

Answer: D

Difficulty level: Easy

Tag: Communication pattern

Rationale:

The circle means messages are disseminated from one to another in the circle pattern.

The Y involves a message going from person to person up a chain, until it reaches someone who is in contact with more than one person.

The wheel involves a person occupies the central position, responsible for all messages between members.

All channel describes a pattern where everyone sends messages to everyone.

题目中所阐述的沟通方式，速度慢，参与者满意程度高，每个人都可以自由与他人沟通，这是典型的 all-channel。

18.5 Which of the following definitions is BEST mapped with a competency framework?

A. Personality traits an organisation requires of its employees

B. Physical resources required by an organisation

C. Abilities which the organisation will value

D. Levels of motivation an organisation requires

Answer: C

Difficulty level: Normal

Tag: The competence framework

Rationale:

Competence frameworks attempt to identify all competences that are required by anyone taking on particular role within the organisation. Employees should regularly review competency frameworks to assess whether they are competent for the skills required and need further continuing professional development. Thus, option C is the best answer.

能力框架是用来明确组织中某个岗位所需要的能力的。员工应当经常通过能力框架的要求来判断自身能力是否足够或者是否需要进一步的提升。

Chapter 19
Ethics

知识导入

我们终于来到了这一章，这是本书最后一章，也是最重要的一章，叫作道德。我们说过这本书主要的学习脉络就是构成商业世界的两个重要组成部分：组织和人。无论是组织也好，人也罢，都要遵守一定规章制度，门槛是法律，制高点就是道德。那什么是道德？为什么道德对于一个专业人士来说会更加重要？让我们来学习这非常重要的最后一章。

单词表

英文	中文
Corporate Social Responsibility	企业社会责任感
Utilitarianism	功利主义
Egoism	利己主义
Pluralism	利他（多元）主义
Ethical relativism	相对主义
Ethical absolutism	绝对主义
Extortion	敲诈勒索
Grease money	润滑金
International Federation of Accountants	国际会计师联合会
Conflicts of interest	利益冲突
Ethical dilemmas	道德困境

学习指南

Learning objectives	Pass level	Distinction level	用时建议
1. Framework of rules（1.1–1.2）		√	5 mins
2. Corporate social responsibility（2.1–2.2）	√		10 mins
3. Ethics（3.1–3.4）	√		20 mins

本章考点

重要考点	难度（1~3）
熟记并理解道德困境产生的原因	1
理解 CSR	2
掌握职业道德五个准则要求	1
理解职业产生利益冲突的原因	2
掌握如何解决职业利益冲突	2

1 Framework of rules

Level 1: The law

Level 2: Non-legal rules and regulations

Level 3: Ethics

表 19-1 Framework of rules

Law	Corporate governance	Social responsibility	Ethics
It is the **minimum level** requirement of behaviour that everyone **must** follow	Only **publicly listed** companies are regulated to follow	There are no formal regulationsin this area but failure to do so may cause some social pressure	They are the values and principles that are **expected to follow**
More regulations, less freedom of choice		Less regulations, more freedom of choice	

组织需遵守的规则层次有三层（见表19-1）。

第一是最低层次的要求，也是企业必须遵守的，即法律；第二是一些规章制度及准则；第三是道德，即组织并非必须遵守，而是社会期望组织能遵守。

我们在第2章讲大环境分析的时候，已经讲到了PESTEL中的legal environment，即法律环境的部分。同时，在第9章我们学过了公司治理（corporate governance），知道了法律规定上市公司必须要执行公司治理，以及广义的公司治理与企业社会责任（CSR）的关系。在这一章，我们就来学习道德（ethics）的部分。

2 Ethics

The ethic is mainly about what society considers to be right or wrong. It is therefore certain standard of behaviour.

In most cases, ethical problems involve difficult judgments and many factors should be considered: the duties, consequences, exceptions etc. This is a situation called as ethical dilemma.

2.1 Ethical dilemma

Ethical dilemmas arise when a person has to consider two or more incompatible ethical obligations.

道德困境产生于会计师需要同时承担两个或两个以上不兼容的道德义务。例如，会计师被上级要求对于财报中存在的问题保持沉默，于是，他需要在对上级忠诚的价值观与履行专业会计师责任这两者之间进行抉择。通常情况下，以下4种价值观任意一种不兼容，都会造成道德困境的产生：

- Societal values- the law.
- Corporate values- the values and principles of the employer.
- Professional values- the values and principles of the professional body.
- Personal values-values and principles held by the individual.

通过上面的学习同学们会发现，在日常工作与生活中，道德困境屡见不鲜，因此接下来我们就需要了解如何应对道德困境。

总的来说，处理道德困境的方法可以分为两大类，即基于道德标准与基于结果，分别在 2.2.1 与 2.2.2 学习。

2.2 Approaches to ethics

There are several possible approaches to make decisions under ethical dilemmas.

2.2.1 Ethics based on duty

(a) **Absolutists** (**deontological approach**)

Under this approach, it is argued that certain core duties are imperative, and are always needed to apply, regardless of circumstances. That is, they admit no exceptions.

(b) **Relativist** (**pragmatists**)

Under this approach, it is argued that there is no universal unchanging rules and the criteria of judgment may vary with different. Simply speaking, they admit exceptions.

绝对主义认为存在绝对的道德标准，在任何情况下都适用；而相对主义认为不存在绝对的道德标准，情况变化，道德标准也随之变化。

> **知识点解读**
>
> 这部分知识点在考试中出现频率很低，所以了解基本概念与特征即可。

精益求精

相对主义绝对主义各有优劣，对于相对主义来说，在处理道德问题过程中考虑到了不同群体的认知差异和文化差异，从而也更灵活；但相对主义本身也存在一些明显的缺点，即如果认为万物皆为相对，其实本身这个理念就是绝对的，即在支持绝对主义；同时，如果认为任何事情在不同情况下都可以合理化，其实也同时允许了很多负面的可能性存在。

对于绝对主义来说，最大的优点就是明确了孰对孰错，能够有一个清晰统一的标准。但同时，绝对主义也存在着局限性，例如，没有考虑到事态的发展与演变，当两个绝对主义价值观不兼容的时候，会再次造成道德困境。

2.2.2 Ethics based on consequences

Under this approach, the right course of action is which will result in the most acceptable outcome.

(a) **Utilitarianism**: It regards the right course of action as which will benefit the majority or serve the "**greater good**". In doing so, the ethical decision may disregard the impact on the minority, believing that they should defer to the greater needs and the majority.

(b) **Egoism**: It decides to pursue decision makers' **own** interests.

(c) **Pluralism**: It pursues **consensus** in order to accommodate the needs of both the majority and the minority.

2.3 Business ethics

在整个社会中，商业运作是社会组成的一部分。社会的道德建设肯定离不开组织的参与。所以，社会不仅期望个人具有道德，同时也会期望组织能够有道德

> **知识点解读**
>
> 对于这里的"most acceptable outcome"的理解，强调的是对"谁"来说是最能接受的（most acceptable to whom？）：
> Utilitarianism（功利主义），是指判断是否做某事取决于事情的结果是否使得大多数人受益。
> Egoism（利己主义），是指判断是否做某事取决于能够最大化决策者自身的利益。
> Pluralism（多元主义），是指追求多数与少数群体需求的共识。

地运营，这便引出了我们下面需要学习的 business ethics。

Business ethics can be seen as the application of ethical values to business behaviour.

To put business ethics into practice, organisations must adopt values that will promote adherence to the principles（如表 19 – 2 所示），thereby maintaining the confidence of stakeholders.

表 19 – 2　**Principles of business ethics**

Value	Meaning
Openness	Full and complete during provision and disclosure of information
Trust	Reliance on the judgments and information provided by other professionals, and also been trusted by others
Honesty	Not only telling the truth, but being prepared to give complete information
Respect	Treat others with dignity and adopting professional manners
Empowerment	Ensure proper authority to carry out tasks
Accountability	Taking full responsibility for outcomes

2.4 Corporate codes of ethics

Corporate codes of ethics are published by private sector organisations in order to illustrate their values and beliefs to stakeholders.

2.4.1 Contents of corporate code of ethics

> **核 心 考 点**
>
> Corporate code ethics 的内容是考试中常考的知识点，需要同学们理解并记忆。

The contents of typical code of ethics are set out below：

(a) Core principles：These should refer not only to its commercial objectives but the manner in which they will be pursued. For example, they may state social and environmental commitments as well as best practices that will be adopted.

(b) To customers：Customers may refer to the statement in order to confirm the minimum standards that can be expected from their purchases, especially in terms of benefits to be derived from the products and services. They may also be interested in matters such as customer service and distribution channels, supply chain policies and animal testing.

(c) To finance providers：how the organisation will deal with providers of share and loan capital.

(d) To suppliers：The code may refer to how suppliers will be chosen and the standards to which they must adhere.

(e) To employees：The code should confirm employment practices in relation to engagement of workers, including equal opportunities and diversity, working conditions and how employees will be developed.

(f) To community：Organisations bring value to the community by providing employment and generating income, but may also have adverse effects through traffic congestion, emissions and even unemployment if the company decides to downsize or relocate. The code may provide assurances in respect of such factors.

Example question 1

The management team at ABC Co is preparing the corporate code of ethics. The following statements are commitments of ABC Co's directors and employees. Which TWO of these are legitimate entries into the code?

A. Avoid engaging in any activity where their personal interests interfere or appear to be interfered with those of the company

B. Obey the law and conduct themselves with honesty and integrity

C. Ensure we maintain the same standards as other companies operating in our business sector

D. Ensure that any dealings with customers and suppliers maximise ABC's profits at all times

2.4.2 Ethical problems facing by managers

(a) **Extortion**

The practice of obtaining something, especially money, through force or threats.

敲诈勒索，是指使用威胁或要挟的方式，向他人强行索要财物的行为。例如，以散播他人秘密为要挟。

(b) **Bribery**

This refers to payments for services to which a company is **illegally** entitled to.

贿赂，是指通过财物买通他人，以谋取不当利益。

(c) **Grease money**

Some local officials will deliberately not issue the entitlement of certain service to companies. Cash payments to the right people may then be used to speed up the process of permission.

润滑金，是指通过给予他人财物，疏通由于种种原因而被人为停滞的项目。

(d) **Gifts**

This is quite common under certain countries' culture but strictly forbidden in others.

礼物，在商业道德中，这是一个相当模棱两可的概念。在很多欧美国家的观念中，礼物被认为是商业关系中贿赂的一种形式，是试图拉近关系以便不当得利的表现；然而在一些亚洲国家，如中国、日本、韩国等，礼物的馈赠是一种文化礼仪的表达，初次见面或会谈，尤其是有一方远道而来的时候，人们都会通过礼物来表示礼貌。

知识点解读

注意 bribery 和 grease money 的区别。虽然两者同为通过给予他人钱财来谋利，都不道德，但还是有明显的区别的。
Bribery（贿赂）的目的在于使得**非法的事项**能够被批准；
Grease money（润滑金）的目的在于推动或者加快**合法事项**的进程。

小试牛刀

Example question 2

Jim is an ACCA member worked in ABC Co as an executive director. He has been asked to pay a bribe to secure a project in this country where bribery is quite common.

Which of the following statement is correct?

    A. The bribe is unacceptable because a professional accountant should not behave in an unethical way

    B. The bribe should be paid because it is in the interests of the company

    C. The bribe is acceptable because it is normal business practice in the country

Example question 3

ABC Co has the right of building a factory in BCD area. But the government approval will take a longer time as the office is busy. The company made payments to some key officials in order to obtain the approval quickly.

Which type of ethical problem does this company have?

    A. Extortion   B. Bribery   C. Grease money   D. Gifts

2.5 Professional ethics

2.5.1 What is a profession?

Profession, as opposed to other types of occupation, has the following characteristics:

(a) Act in public interest.

(b) Governance by a professional organisation.

(c) Compliance with ethical code.

(d) A process of certification before being allowed to practice.

2.5.2 Accountants and ethics

International Federation of Accountants(**IFAC**): IFAC is the global organisation for the accountancy profession, which is dedicated to serving the public interest by strengthening the profession and the development of strong international economies. The members of IFAC are **the major accountancy bodies** in more than 130 countries and jurisdictions across the world.

To enable the development of high standards, IFAC's ethics committee established the **code of ethics** which represents **the minimum level of conduct for all accountants**.

知识点解读

执业与工作有很大区别，总的来说，执业的水准要高于工作，要求也会更高：
（1）与公众利益直接挂钩；
（2）执业资质一般是由专门的专业组织授予的，如国际会计师的从业资质就是由 ACCA 协会授予的；
（3）执业会有特定的道德要求；
（4）在从业之前，需要获得执业资质的认可。

知识点解读

IFAC，国际会计师联合会是一个会计师组织联合会，也就是说 IFAC 的成员是各个国家的会计师团体，而并非是会计师个人。例如，ACCA 就是 IFAC 的成员之一。

博学多才

IFAC，国际会计师联合会（简称联合会），于 1977 年 10 月 14 日在德国慕尼黑成立，联合会的宗旨是以统一的标准发展和提高世界范围的会计专业，促进国际范围内的会计协调。 其任务是决定国际会计师大会的主办国，保持与参加国际会计师大会的各国的联系，促进国际/地区机构的发展和信息的交流，参考和吸收各国提出的意见，扩大国际会计职业协调委员会的业务，并为改进业务提供咨询。

As a member of IFAC, ACCA released its own code of ethics which is **aligned** to the IFAC code. **Members** are required to comply with the following **fundamental principles**:

(a) Integrity: Fair dealings and truthfulness; accountants should not be associated with any false, misleading statements.

(b) Objectivity: Accountants must ensure that their professional judgement is not compromised because of bias or conflict of interest.

(c) Professional competence and due care: Accountants should keep up with the development of accounting rules and principles and maintain skepticism during work.

(d) Confidentiality: Accountants should not disclose customers' information to the third party, unless it is required by the court or law.

(e) Professional behaviour: Accountants must comply with relevant laws and regulations and avoid any action that discredits the profession.

> **知识点解读**
>
> 作为ACCAer，我们需要遵循以下道德准则：
> （1）正直：诚实守信，杜绝作假；
> （2）客观：避免带有色眼光看待事物，不能持有偏见；
> （3）专业能力与谨慎：能够及时了解并掌握最新的知识技能，提供服务时能持有谨慎态度，如在提供审计服务的过程中保有适当的怀疑；
> （4）保密性：不得向第三方透露工作过程中因职务之便而获取的信息，除非是受法律要求或法庭传唤；
> （5）专业行为：时刻牢记自身的专业身份，如不能因为自身利益而违反道德。

小试牛刀

Example question 4

Ethical standards of behaviour within accountancy are mainly promoted by which of the following?

A. Laws implemented by central governments

B. Rules established by education committees

C. Regulations issued by government departments and agencies

D. Codes of conduct implemented by professional bodies

Example question 5

Jack is an accountant. He has not yet read information received yesterday, which is about recent changes of tax legislations, however he is about to visit a client to give him some tax advice.

Which fundamental principle appears to be compromised in this situation?

A. Professional competence

B. Integrity

C. Objectivity

Example question 6

Which fundamental principle would be affected if a professional accountant in public practice performs services for clients whose interests are in conflict.

A. Confidentiality   B. Objectivity   C. Integrity

博学多才

除了以上道德准则以外，执业会计师还需要具备一定的专业特质，如独立、合理的怀疑态度(skepticism-you should question information given to you so that you form your own opinion regarding its quality and reliability)、承担对其工作内容的问责(accountability)以及社会责任(public duty- either audit work, accountancy work or investment decision may affect the public interest. Thus, besides of the due care to employer or client, accountants should also be responsible to the public)。

2.5.3 Conflicts of interest

Conflicts of interest may arise between ACCA members and their clients. Members should evaluate the threats and unless they are insignificant, they should apply safeguards.

(a) **Self-interest threat**

This could occur where a **financial or other interest** influences an accountant's judgement and causes the conflict of interest.

自我利益威胁：指的是审计师和被审计单位或者会计师和所在单位存在利益关联，特别是存在经济利益的关联。例如，审计师持有客户公司的股票，这种情况下，审计师的利益是与公司股价绑定在一起的，他可能会因为担心不利的审计报告会波及股价，而难以保持客观的态度。

(b) **Self-review threat**

This may occur when an accountant is required to **re-evaluate** their own previous judgement, for example, by providing **multiple services** in an assurance firm.

自我检查威胁：当审计师检查自己之前的工作成果，倘若发现其中有错误，那么很可能为了自我包庇而选择不披露，这种有失公允的情况就是自我检查威胁。例如，有些企业会选择把会计处理工作直接外包给外部的专业人士来做，如果一家客户同时将会计处理和审计的业务交给同一家会计师事务所来做，那么对于审计师而言就是自己在查自己做的账了，这就会极大地削弱会计师的独立性。

(c) **Advocacy threat**

An advocacy threat arises in certain situations where the assurance firm is in a position of **taking the client**'s part in a **dispute** or somehow **acting as their advocate**.

For example, a firm offered **legal services** to a client and, say, defended them in a legal case or provided evidence **on their behalf** as an expert witness.

过度推介威胁：这是指当一家会计师事务所成为客户的某种代表时容易产生的威胁，然而对于审计师来说，保持独立形象是提供客观意见的根本，这种代表行为相当于将自身与客户捆绑，此时其独立性就很容易受到影响。这种代表行为包括为客户辩护，或者作为客户的代表出庭作证。

(d) **Familiarity threat**

If the audit firm **has a long association** with the client, there is a substantial risk of loss of professional skepticism, thus losing independence and compromise professional judgement.

熟悉性威胁：指的是审计师对于被审计单位的情况非常熟悉，就很可能失去一些应有的职业怀疑；同时，被审计单位对于审计师审计流程的熟悉，也一定程度上给舞弊提供了条件。 一家事务所的审计师与客户公司的某高层领导是多年的好友关系，在审计过程中，就很难保持公允态度。

(e) **Intimidation threat**

An intimidation threat arises when members of the assurance team have certain reasons to be intimidated by client staff. It occurs when an accountant is deterred from acting objectively by actual or perceived threats, for example, an accountant is threatened with dismissal over a disagreement about application of an accounting principle.

恐吓性威胁：是由恐吓产生的威胁，包括形式上（光说不练型）和实质上（说了，也确实以实际行动对审计师进行了恐吓）。 例如，某会计师事务所80%的收入都来源于同一个客户，那么这种情况下，该客户的讨价还价能力就非常强，很可能出现以换事务所为要挟，要求该事务所对财报发表一些不公允的意见。

2.5.4 Safeguards against ethical conflicts

(a) Ethics **training** for all professional accountants on an ongoing basis.
(b) Creation of **code of ethics.**
(c) **Professional or regulatory monitoring.**

具体的举措可能包括：签订保密协议（**confidentiality letter**），及时将利益冲突告知相关上级（**notifying relevant senior managers**），如果利益冲突过于严重，也可以直接不参与任务（**remove from the project**）。

2.5.5 Resolution of ethical conflicts

在面临道德冲突的情况下，作为ACCAer，我们可以从以下三个角度考虑如何解决：

（1）透明性（Transparency）：通俗地说，如果我们选择采用某种方法解决，那么这种方法是否能见得光，是否能经得起大众的审视；

（2）影响程度（Effect）：倘若选择某种解决方法，我们是否将跟此相关的方方面面都考虑周全；

（3）公平性（Fairness）：这种方法的选择对第三方是否公平，是否忽略甚至侵害了少数群体的利益。

Possible options：

Step 1：Select an action consistent with principles.

Step 2：Consult with whoever is responsible for governance such as compliance officers，audit committee or board of directors.

Step 3：Obtain advice from professional bodies（e.g. ACCA）.

Step 4：Report to relevant authorities and change roles or resignation.

> **知识点解读**
>
> 在考虑解决方案的时候，有以下一些步骤可以采用：
> （1）在道德准则中选择最为适用的一条运用；
> （2）倘若没有合适的准则以供使用，那么可以咨询一些相关人士，值得注意的是，选择的相关人士应当是那些可以提供专业并且独立意见的人；
> （3）可以咨询一些相关的专业团体，如ACCA；
> （4）当以上方法均不可行时，可以选择换岗或者辞职，以避免卷入道德问题。

小试牛刀

Example question 7

When a professional accountant has encountered an ethical dilemma at work，who could the accountant consult?

(1) A legal adviser.

(2) His professional body.

(3) The board of directors or the audit committee in his own organisation.

A. (1)(2) and (3)   B. (1) and (2) only

C. (2) only   D. (1) and (3) only

Answers for example question

1. AB
2. A
3. C
4. D
5. A
6. A
7. A

Summary

Chapter 19 考试不同问法总结：

Section A

1. 针对 ethics 的基础知识及 common sense
- Which term describes the study of moral principles used to determine right from wrong in the dealings of organisations with others?
- Which of the following circumstances, if they occurred, would represent potential ethical issues for A to deal with?
- Does each of the following actions that the company take represent ethical behaviour?
- The decision the board made would promote which TWO of the following organisational values?
- Which TWO of the following are indicates that an organisation's actions are consistent with acting in the public interest?
- Which of the following will present an ethical dilemma to A at work?
- Indicate whether the following statements are applicable to the principle-based or rule-based approach?
- Which TWO of the following are true in the context of law, governance, social responsibility and ethics in business?

2. 针对 Corporate code of ethics
- What is the MAIN purpose of an organisational code of ethics?
- Which of the following actions may be taken by a professional body against a member who is found to have breached its code of conduct?
- Which TWO of the following are typically included in a corporate code of ethics?
- Will each of the following benefits result from the introduction of a corporate code of ethics?
- Do the following are typical matters included in a corporate code of ethics?
- Which TWO of the following are benefits of a corporate code of ethics to an employee?

3. 针对 professional ethics
- Which of the following is the overriding consideration in the work of a professional accountant?
- Which TWO of the following are purposes of the IFAC code of ethics?
- Which of the following is a fundamental principle in the IFAC code of ethics?
- If an ACCA member fails to comply with the fundamental principle of the IFAC code of Ethics. Which of the following should take action against him?
- Which TWO threats to ethical behaviour does this indicate?
- Which of the following safeguards would counter the threat identified above?

Section B
- Which of the employees has a profession, and which has an occupation?
- Which FOUR of the following are typical features of a profession?
- Which threat to ethical behaviour is inherent in each of the situations faced by accountants?

Quick quiz

19.1 Which TWO of the following about corporate code of ethics are CORRECT?

A. Corporate code of ethics include employee training programme

B. Professional ethics can be part of corporate code of ethics

C. Corporate code of ethics offers the employees job description

D. Corporate code of ethics must align with company law

Answer: **BD**

Difficulty level: **Normal**

Tag: **corporate code of ethics**

Rationale:

This question is set to examine corporate code of ethics. Corporate code of ethics is a principle that promote corporate value. Corporate code of ethics can refer to professional ethics but must align with law. Therefore, B and D are correct.

Employee training programme has no connection with corporate code of ethics. It is part of human resource planning, therefore A is incorrect.

Job description is a part of job analysis that should not be included in corporate code of ethics, therefore option C is incorrect.

这道题考的是公司道德条例。公司的道德条例提升了公司的价值观，是用具体的条例体现的。公司道德条例能够参考职业道德进行制定，但是它的制定必须遵守法律。因此，B 选项和 D 选项是对的。

员工培训计划与企业道德准则没有直接联系，它是人力资源计划的一部分，所以 A 选项不对。

岗位描述是岗位分析的一部分，这个并不包含在公司道德条例中，因此 C 选项也是错的。

19.2 Murakami is a Nordic offshoring company that provides software service for many companies over the world. Recently, to secure a contract in a new country, Jack who is the CEO of Murakami, attempts to pay a bribe to secure the contract in this country where bribery is quite common. Which of the following statements is true of this action?

A. It is not unethical, because bribery is common in this new country

B. It constitutes extortion

C. It constitutes bribery

D. It constitutes grease money

Answer: **C**

Difficulty level: **Easy**

Tag: **Ethical problems facing managers**

Rationale:

This question is set to examine the difference between extortion, bribery, grease money.

Extortion refers to the practice of obtaining something, especially money, through force or threats.

Bribery refers to payments for benefits to which a company is not legally entitled.

Grease money refers to payments for speeding up the process of permission.

这道题考查的是勒索、受贿、润滑金的区别。

勒索是指用暴力的手段获取某些东西，尤其钱财。

行贿是指花钱请他人帮助自己做不合法的事情。而润滑金是花钱请他人帮助自己做本来就合法的事情，只不过为了加快办事的效率。

19.3 _____ is a set of moral principles used to determine what is right or what is wrong.

A. Corporate governance
B. Business ethics
C. Corporate codes of ethics
D. Professional ethics

Answer: B

Difficulty level: Easy

Tag: The definition of business ethics

Rationale:

Business ethics is a set of principles that examine the concept of right and wrong.

本题考查的是定义，道德定义的关键词为"right and wrong"，因此选 B。

19.4 Which of the following correctly describes the concept of corporate social responsibility?

A. The system in which an organisation is directed and controlled by senior managers

B. Lists of acceptable and unacceptable conduct

C. A set of principles that examine the concept of right and wrong

D. Acting in the public interest, over and above the legal obligations

Answer: D

Difficulty level: Normal

Tag: The definition of corporate social responsibility

Rationale:

Corporate social responsibility (CSR) refers to the idea that a company should be sensitive to the needs and wants of all its stakeholders, rather than just the shareholders. The aim of CSR is to encourage a positive impact on the stakeholders. Therefore, option D is correct.

这道题考查的是企业社会责任的定义，企业社会责任指的就是企业不仅需要对股东负责，帮助他们实现目标，还应该关注所有其他的利益相关者，因此公众的利益也是企业需要关注的。并且，道德是高于法律这个最低行为水平要求的，所以答案选 D。

19.5 Joanna is a professional accountant who works in a multinational corporation. Which of the following situations will lead to ethical dilemmas at work for Joanna?

(1) Joanna argues with her immediate superior's decision at the meeting regarding procurement of equipment.

(2) Joanna receives her annual performance-related bonus.

(3) Joanna identifies some omissions in the financial statements and then reports to her managers, but her financial directors insist on current reports.

(4) Joanna's subordinate gives her a valuable gift before his annual performance appraisal.

A. (1) and (2)
B. (2) and (3)
C. (3) and (4)
D. (1)(2)(3) and (4)

Answer: C

Difficulty level: Normal

Tag: The ethical dilemma

Rationale:

An ethical dilemma arises when a person has to consider two or more incompatible ethical obligations. It usually occurs where two ethical values seem to be incompatible or where two conflicting demands or obligations are placed on an individual.

道德困境指的是一个人在某种情况下很难做决策，因为两种价值观或者责任以及需求相互之间有所冲突。这道题中，只有（3）和（4）构成冲突。

结束寄语

恭喜你们完成了 Business and Technology（BT）的学习。

在前面的十九个章节中，同学们通过对环境、组织和人员三个篇章的学习，掌握了 BT 的必备专业技能，接下来需要自主地巩固与强化。

BT 科目内容多而杂，同学们可能会觉得略有难度，请不要慌张，合理规划时间，制定一份复习计划并勤加练习（建议翻阅前面的"教材使用指南"，使用三个学习阶段中"备考复习阶段"的工具）。希望同学们能做好充足的准备，勇敢地迎接挑战。

最后，祝大家在"A 考"路上踏实前行，坚持走到终点，成为真正的 ACCAers！

高顿财经研究院

Reference list

1. Accountability Versus Responsibility. (n.d.). Retrieved June 17, 2019, from https://www.termpaperwarehouse.com/essay-on/Accountability-Versus-Responsibility/292625
2. Administrator. (2018). Porter's value chain[Image].Value Chain Analysis: An Internal
3. Assessment of Competitive Advantage. Retrieved from https://www.business-to-you.com/value-chain/
4. Authority. (n.d.). In freedictionary. Retrieved fromhttps://www.thefreedictionary.com/authority
5. Banton, C. (2019). Complementary Goods. Retrieved April 19, 2019, from https://www.investopedia.com/terms/c/complement.asp
6. Bloomenthal, A. (2019). Above the Margin: Understanding Marginal Utility. Retrieved April 16, 2019, fromhttp://www.investopedia.com/terms/m/marginalutility.asp
7. Boundaryless organisation. (n.d.). In Business Dictionary. Retrieved from http://www.businessdictionary.com/definition/boundaryless-organisation.html
8. Bruce, J. B. (1979). Role Theory. doi: 10.106/C2009-0-03121-3
9. Cadbury, A. (1992). The Financial Aspects of Governance. London: Burgess Science Press.
10. Coffield, F., Moseley, D., Hall, E., & Ecclestone, K. (2004). Learning styles and pedagogy in post-16 learning: A systematic and critical review. www.LSRC.ac.uk: Learning and Skills Research Centre. Retrieved January 15, 2008:http://www.lsda.org.uk/files/PDF/1543.pdf
11. Consumer rationality. (n.d.). Retrieved April 17, 2019, from https://financial-dictionary.thefreedictionary.com/consumer+rationality
12. Data Protection Act 2018 (UK). Retrieved from https://www.gov.uk/data-protection
13. Difference Between Power and Authority. (n.d.). Retrieved June 17, 2019, from https://www.quickbase.com/blog/the-5-types-of-power-in-leadership
14. Family life cycle. (n.d.). In BusinessDictionary. Retrieved from http://www.businessdictionary.com/definition/family-life-cycle.html
15. Group norms. (n.d.). In Business Dictionary. Retrieved from http://www.businessdictionary.com/definition/group-norms.html
16. Higgs, D. (2003). Review of the Role and Effectiveness of Non-Executive directors. London: The stationary Office.
17. Hofstede, G. (n.d.). The 6-D model of national culture. Retrieved June 21, 2019, from http://geerthofstede.com/culture-geert-hofstede-gert-jan-hofstede/6d-model-of-national-culture/
18. Honey, P. & Mumford, A. (2000). The learning styles helper's guide. Maidenhead: Peter Honey Publications Ltd.
19. Importance of Management. (n.d.). Retrieved June 17, 2019, from https://www.managementstudyguide.com/management_importance.htm
20. Informal organisation. (n.d.). In Encyclopaedia Britannica. Retrived from https://www.britannica.com/topic/informal-organization
21. Kenton, W. (2019). Substitute. Retrieved April 18, 2019, from www.investopedia.com/terms/s/substitute.asp

22. London Stock Exchange. (2014). Corporate Governance Guide 2014. Retrieved 9 May 2019, from http://www2.londonstockexchangegroup.com/l/6522/2012-09-19/clykk

23. Mintzberg Managerial Roles. (n.d.). Retrieved June 17, 2019, from https://www.toolshero.com/management/mintzberg-managerial-roles/

24. Porter, M. E. (1980). Forces Driving Industry Competition [Graph]. COMPETIEIVE STRATEGY (p. 4). New York, NY: THE FREE PRESS.

25. Schein, E.H. (2004).Organizational Culture and Leadership (5th ed.). San Franciso, CA: Jossey-Bass.

26. Scientific Management. (n.d.). Retrieved June 17, 2019, from http://www.learnmanagement2.com/scientificmanagement.htm

27. Span of Control. (n.d.). In Encyclopedia. Retrieved from https://www.inc.com/encyclopedia/span-of-control.html

28. Supervior. (n.d.). In BusinessDictionary. Retrieved from http://www.businessdictionary.com/definition/supervisor.html

29. The 5 Types of Power in Leadership. (n.d.). Retrieved June 17, 2019, from https://www.quickbase.com/blog/the-5-types-of-power-in-leadership

30. The Key Advantages and Disadvantages of Delegation of Authority. (n.d.). Retrieved June 17, 2019, from https://workspirited.com/delegation-of-authority-advantages-disadvantages

31. The Nine Belbin Team Roles. (n.d.). Retrieved July 16, 2019, from http://www.belbin.com/about/Belbin-team-roles/

32. The Organisation for Economic Co-operation and Development. (2004). Principles of Corporate Governance 2004, Retrieved 2 May 2019, from https://www.oecd-ilibrary.org/docserver/9789264015999-en.pdf?expires=1561355381&id=id&accname=guest&checksum=952D4A977FE21BE523AF8CC70EC32E10

33. The Organisation for Economic Co-operation and Development. (2004).Principles of Corporate Governance 2004, Retrieved 2 May 2019, from https://www.oecd-ilibrary.org/docserver/9789264015999-en.pdf?expires=1561355381&id=id&accname=guest&checksum=952D4A977FE21BE523AF8CC70EC32E10

34. The role of the secretary. (n.d.). Retrieved June 17, 2019, from https://info.lse.ac.uk/staff/divisions/Secretarys-Division/Assets/Documents/Committee-Guidance-Notes/The-Role-of-Committee-Secretary.pdf

35. Time Management. (n.d.).Retrieved July 17, 2019, from http://www.timethoughts.com/time-management.htm

36. Types of Committees In a Business Organization. (n.d.). Retrieved June 17, 2019, from https://hosbeg.com/types-of-committees-in-a-business-organization/

37. What Is Market Orientation? Definition And Meaning. (n.d.). Retrieved June 17, 2019, from https://marketbusinessnews.com/financial-glossary/market-orientation-definition-meaning/

38. 丁家云, 谭艳华. 管理学 [M]. 合肥: 中国科学技术大学出版社, 2010: 11.

39. 于玉林.会计大百科辞典[M].上海: 上海财经大学出版社, 2010: 235-236.

40. 刘烨.马斯洛的人本哲学[M]. 呼伦贝尔: 内蒙古文化出版社, 2008.

41. 周三多. 管理学［M］. 北京：高等教育出版社，2012：6-7.
42. 财务欺诈之安然事件.（2016）. Retrieved 9 May 2019, from http://news.cpd.com.cn/n19016/n47141/c32775578/content.html.
43. 我们在可持续咖啡方面的未来.（2016）. Retrieved 9 May 2019, from https://www.starbucks.com.cn/about/responsibility/our-future-in-sustainable-coffee/
44. 杨圣雄.内部控制理论研究新视野[J]. 会计研究，2005（7）：49-55.
45. 段锦云.管理心理学[M].杭州：浙江大学出版社，2010.
46. 王玉蓉.安然公司破产的根源：内部控制分析[J].南方农村，2003(6)：20-23.
47. 范月光.浅析内部控制环境在内部控制中的重要性[J].中国乡镇企业会计，2010（10）；190-191.
48. 葛梅，张晋光. 时间管理:"华为"成功之法宝[J].商业研究，2005(4)：66-68.
49. 谢志华.内部控制、公司治理、风险管理：关系与整合[J].会计研究，2007（10）：37-45.
50. 邹瑜.法学大辞典[Z].北京：中国政法大学出版社，1991：23-24.